Much More on Yma Sumac Exclusively on CD-ROM

See page vii (the Foreword in this volume) for information on a very substantial supplementary volume available on CD-ROM only.

Contains 125 pages of *additional* text and 140 illustrations, many in color, many never before published, including family snapshots. Among them are all the illustrations in this volume, more generously sized and many of them in color!

Order on line at:
http://yourbookpublisher.com/sumac_cd.htm

Yma Sumac
The Art Behind the Legend

Nicholas E. Limansky

YBK Publishers, Inc.
New York

For examples of Yma Sumac's astonishing vocal range we recommend that you visit the music section of Amazon.com on your computer. In the search box insert "Yma Sumac" (quote marks optional). At each of her recordings advertised there you have the opportunity to listen to a free sampling of each track of a recording. You will be amazed.

Copyright © 2008
by Nicholas E. Limansky

All rights reserved
Including the right of reproduction
in whole or in part in any form.

YBK Publishers, Inc.
39 Crosby St.
New York, NY 10013
www.ybkpublishers.com

Yma Sumac: The Art Behind the Legend

ISBN 978-0-9790972-9-4

Library of Congress Control Number: 2008921651

Manufactured in the United States of America, or in the United Kingdom when distributed elsewhere.

Ver 08-05

The painting reproduced on the cover:
Through the Looking Glass, oil on canvas by Tyler Alpern, 1991.

Contents

Foreword		vii
Acknowledgments		ix

Part I: The Life

Introduction	Legend of the Sun Virgin	1
Chapter One	The Beginning: Emperatriz Chavarri (1922–1942)	7
Chapter Two	Waiting: Imma Sumack (1942–1949)	15
Chapter Three	The Arrival: Yma Sumac—"Intypa Wawan" (Daughter of the Sun) (1949–1952)	25
Chapter Four	"Accla K'Ory" (Chosen One of Gold) (1952–1954)	67
Chapter Five	"Taita Inty" (Virgin of the Sun God) (1954)	91
Chapter Six	"Lament" (1955–1957)	121
Chapter Seven	"Kuyaway" (Inca Love Song) (1958–1970)	141
Chapter Eight	"Miracles" (1970–1974)	155
Chapter Nine	"Remember" (Miracles) (1975–1985)	175
Chapter Ten	"Tumpa!" (Earthquake!) (1987)	191
Chapter Eleven	"La Molina" (The Mill Song) (The Ballroom, New York City 1989)	211
Chapter Twelve	"La Pampa Y La Puna" (The Plains and the Mountains) (1989–1993)	217
Chapter Thirteen	"Especially for You" (1996–2007)	223

Part II: The Voice

Yma Sumac: The Voice	249
The Effects	256
The Repertoire	262
Yma and Opera	263
Incan Chants	267
Peruvian Music and Flute Singers of Peru	269

Epilogue	277
Index	281

This book is dedicated to:

My parents, **Igor and Virginia Limansky**,
who, when I was young,
suffered through countless hours of Yma Sumac
blaring from my bedroom.

My wife, **Gale**,
who always had faith in me
and belief in this book.

and to:

Hernán Braña,
without whose help it
could not have been written.

Foreword

This book's subtitle, "The Art Behind the Legend," is meant to refer not only to the vocal artistry of Yma Sumac, which prompted the legends, but also the artfulness—artistry is surely too grand a term for it—of those who created the Sumacian mythology. Regrettably, the two are inseparable.

Among other stories told here is one of the corruption of musical and ethnic innocence; of artistic ideals. Yma Sumac's story is her own but the often bitter ironies wrought from her artistic compromises are to be found throughout the history of music. If the compromise had not been made, most of us would not have known Yma Sumac at all. At the same time, her surrender to her managers and handlers and their cynical commercial exploitation of her gifts had dire consequences for her ability to establish and sustain a meaningful career as an artist.

Although it contains considerable biographical material based on personal interviews, this book is not a biography in the fullest sense—nor was it ever meant to be. It is a book about a woman and her voice—a career overview.

This book was a long time in the making. I began work on it in 1980. One of my earliest contacts, in 1980—he was generous with time—was Les Baxter. Les suggested that I contact Bob Covais and Jim Branciforti, two of the producers of Yma's last album *Miracles*. They lived at that time in my home city of New York. Bob Covais, in turn, made sure I met Hernán Braña, who had worked with Yma before and after she broke into international fame. It is thanks to those three men—whom I interviewed in great depth over the course of more than a year—that this book was able to take form. (Numbers of others who might have had interesting things to impart, however, declined to be interviewed, for reasons that never became entirely clear.)

Although this book was begun in 1980 I did not work on it every year. For 25 years I was working as a freelance classical singer in New York City, so there were entire years where not much work was done on the book at all. Still, over time it took form and the final result is in your hands.

Or perhaps I should say that *most* of the final result is in your hands—for in fact a good deal of rich material simply burst the seams of any practical book-making capacity, and had to be held in reserve, to be made available as a supplementary volume on CD-ROM, available from

http://yourbookpublisher.com/sumac_cd.htm

The CD contains a PDF file viewable on any computer using Adobe Acrobat Reader, usually found preloaded on all computers, or easily available via free download at http://www.adobe.com.

The most substantial of the chapters on the CD is a detailed critical discussion of every track of Yma Sumac's recorded performances. On the CD also are many more photographs, many in color, many of them never before published, including family snapshots. All the photographs in this book appear on the CD, and all of those that came from color originals appear in color on the CD. Appendixes on the CD are:

- a specific discussion with musical notation of the actual range of Yma's voice as displayed on her recordings
- a precisely detailed international discography
- a brief introduction to the Peruvian folk music tradition from which Yma arose, including some discussion of the Incan influence
- an expansion of discussions to be found in this book of the "exotica" movement in American popular music, under which Yma Sumac's music became subsumed
- a brief history of *acuto sfogato* (extended vocal range) singers including short critical considerations of many such individual singers

A truly satisfying biography of Yma Sumac can never be written, for the simple reason that Yma herself will not cooperate with any biographer, and will not write an autobiography. She is simply not interested in revealing herself in that way—or, perhaps, in any way at all. Also, unfortunately, many of the key players in her career and development are no longer with us.

As to all the myths and legends? Sometimes I was successful in penetrating them; often I was not. When all's said and done, no matter what is written about the unusual Peruvian diva, there will always be a certain air of inscrutability surrounding her. That should please her. Yma Sumac has always preferred being a mystery.

Nicholas E. Limansky
New York, March 2008

Acknowledgments

This book could not have been written without the help of many people. I would especially like to thank:

In Memoriam:
Les Baxter, who showed great interest in the book during its early stages and who contributed invaluable observations.
Robert Covais and *James Branciforti,* who gave uncomplainingly of their time and experiences with Sumac and the producing of the *Miracles* recording, and who also put at my disposal their extensive collections of Sumac memorabilia and recordings from Peru, Argentina, Cuba, etc. Without their help and belief in the book during its early stages it would never have been completed.

I would also like to thank:
Dr. Cecil Riggs of Baltimore, Maryland
Hall Daniels of BAX Music, who supplied me with the existing lead-sheets for the *Miracles* recording.
John Groomers of the Library Department, Capitol Records
Anne Karle of EMI Music Publishing, who labored mightily researching original Vivanco manuscripts and sent me lead-sheets for many of the Capitol songs of the 1950s.
Andrew Gordon for his invaluable help in the transcribing of Yma's improvisations. A wonderful musician, he did it for the love of it and I will always be grateful.
Steven Gelber of Capitol Records.
Kenneth Shire.
Dawn Downey-Smith for early editorial help.
Robert Barrows.
John Lehman, who first introduced me to the 1943 Yma Sumac recordings.
Phil Mealy, who provided me with a tape of the 1953 Lewisohn Stadium concert.
Anna Schumate for help with translations.
Manar Zaher and *Giancarlo Cifuentes* for their help with translations.
Larry Espiritu for his help in the translation of Peruvian official documents.
Don Pierson of the Sunvirgin.com Web site for his support, suggestions, and corrections of the manuscript.
Günter Czernetsky for allowing me to use material and interviews that he gathered for his 1992 German documentary, *Yma Sumac, Hollywood's Inkaprinzessin.*
Betsy Rae Watson for her early help in typing and organizing my very first attempts at a Sumac book back in the days when a writer still used a typewriter.
Sue Herner for her advice during the final stages of the book.
John Carroll for his invaluable assistance in the putting together of the *acuto sfogato* Appendix. I could not have done it without him.
Chris Creaghan for his help with the construction of the range sheets.
Dennis Weiscopf for his help with final proofing of this manuscript.

Part 1

The Life

Introduction

Legend of the Sun Virgin

Yma Sumac was a unique performer in popular music. In the 1950s she offered international audiences atmospheric songs of exotica and vocal impressions based on nature which were delivered with an impeccable if unorthodox technique, staggering virtuosity and a vocal range of four octaves. Yma Sumac used her voice like an odd, hybrid orchestral instrument, or like a painter's palette, creating utterly unparalleled works of aural art. An improvisationalist, she was able to ornament her music with subtle grace and elegance. Les Baxter, the popular composer and conductor who worked with Sumac on her first (1950) and last (1971) solo North American albums, said to me that Yma was "enormously talented and one of a kind. Her ability to do what she did was absolutely remarkable."

Because of her distinct musical individuality, but also because of her absurdly bombastic initial American publicity and promotion—which billed the singer as an Incan priestess and/or princess and relentlessly emphasized and even overstated her vocal extensions—Yma Sumac was almost never taken seriously as an artist. Instead, she was relegated to the ranks of curiosity entertainers, a freak performer. Critics shied away from analyzing her strange voice, technique and odd repertoire. Baffled, they did not attempt to unravel the mystery of the origin of such singing or of the mind behind it. An isolated figure in the annals of performing, Sumac has always had mystery surrounding her. She was as exotic to American culture as she was glamorous.

There are drawbacks to being so unique. One, it does not stand up to repetition. Also, although extraordinarily gifted, Yma Sumac did not fit into the categorized vocal ranges sedulously created in the classical music field throughout the centuries. Artistically, she also straddled the borders of the classical and popular musical fields, which only increased her general isolation.

Yma remained a vocal enigma, a singular phenomenon. Because her talent was not of the type acquired through study but based on instinct and emotion, she was unable to articulate its working secrets to others. These factors, combined with the type of publicity she received, made her the brunt of ridicule.

During the 1940s she was successful as a professional folk artist in South America (as Imma Sumack), but it was not until the decade of the 1950s that she achieved world renown. A number of things contributed to her gaining preeminence at that time and not before. One was the introduction of outré effects into her singing. Another was the finding of a suitable presentation/promotion to frame her singular gifts—though, as much as it contributed to her stardom, the presentation of this singer caused both her and the managerial powers governing her many problems.

The course of Yma's career tells much about the difficulties with her "presentation." Simplistically, her career can be divided into four sections of differing presentations to the public. Each phase was an outgrowth of the one before and had its own merits and weaknesses, and all four merge at certain points.

In her initial phase, from 1942–1947, Yma specialized in authentic performances of the folk music of the Andes.

The second phase, which began in 1949, found her specializing in impressions of nature and the (purported) resuscitation of ancient Incan melodic or rhythmic fragments, presented in a modern, commercialized, popular music idiom. This was the height of her popularity in America; despite the controversy surrounding her "Incan" material, after it was discarded Yma was never able to fully regain her initial popularity.

The third phase, which began around 1964, found Yma returning to folk material, though broadened to encompass folk music of other countries as well.

The fourth phase, begun in 1984, found the singer concentrating on cabaret work; promoting popular music of South America and her own compositions, with an occasional nod to her "Incan" days.

During her career, Yma Sumac went full cycle in both popularity and repertoire—a rare occurrence. In her particular case, however, it was done out of necessity because her career was in a constant state of compromise.

As a musician, during the 1940s, Yma Sumac was a study in contrasts. The incongruity of a singer offering simple ethnic, or popular Peruvian folk music, with a voice that had the finesse, range, and quality of an operatic singer, alienated or simply baffled producers, who were afraid that her eccentric singing would alienate both popular and classical audiences. By the onset of 1950, however, Yma's artistic development emphasized these contrasts, exploited the capabilities of her imitative talent and, surprisingly, audiences now proved ready for this type of exotic diversion. It must have been a factor that Peru, Yma's homeland and once in truth the home of the ancient Incas, was still a mysterious country to most Americans. Even though the ruins of Machu Picchu had been discovered in 1911 by the American explorer Hiram Bingham, modern source books on the country did not begin to appear until the 1930s.

Finally, with the emerging tropism of the American pop music scene for the unusual and exotic, everything seemed to click into place. In 1950, Imma Sumack became Yma Sumac, the queen of vocal exotica, and the new packaging was perfected. Gone were the humble, authentic peasant outfits, replaced by costly gowns and exotic jewelry. Simple, traditional folk arrangements of Andean music were replaced by quasi-operatic compositions of intricate vocal filigree often enhanced by bizarre impressions of nature. Simple staging was replaced by colossal extravaganzas.

Ignoring her previous success as a serious folk artist in South America, North American publicity heralded Yma as a figure shrouded in mystery: a priestess/princess of ancient royal blood, a descendant of the fabled Incan kings of Peru. Scores of photographs were taken of the singer in various exotic costumes and moods—dramatic poses with even more dramatic facial expressions—all of which Yma quickly learned to work. One expression became representative, an effectively seductive "come and get me" look: eyes half closed, mouth half open. So described it sounds comic, but because of Yma's superb facial structure, almond-shaped eyes and full mouth, there was a definite visual impact.

And indeed the "package" was so effective precisely because it exploited Yma's very real natural assets. She was exotic, very feminine, subtly mysterious and alluring. Her natural beauty, skin tone, glossy dark hair, superb figure and proud bearing added up to the perfect framing for her enormously dramatic and eccentric vocalism. Costumed, bejeweled, regal, captivating and yet oddly distant in her demeanor—again, a version of her very real combination of shyness and pride—Yma's presentation to audiences was absolutely crucial to her success.

Because of World War II, America's political alliance with South America was very strong while cultural connections to Europe had been frayed by the terrible destruction of the war. As a natural outgrowth of this situation, North Americans became fascinated by the countries and culture of its hemisphere. As a matter of course, music from the Latin countries began to enter the sensibilities of North America. It was an influence that is still felt today. In 1950, the horrors of war were still fresh in the minds of the world's people, having only ended five years earlier. Audiences were ready for diversion. Indeed, they craved distraction. This led to the growth of an unusual movement in American popular entertainment called "exotica" (discussed in greater depth in the supplemental materials CD available from the publisher).

Kevin Crossman, in his article "Evolution of Exotica" (www.kevdo.com, February 2000) noted: "Narrowly defined, Exotica is a form of mostly instrumental pop music featuring orchestral or lounge instrumentation, augmented by Latin, African, or Polynesian rhythms or tribal-sounding chanting or singing. This music had its roots in the early Fifties, reaching its apex in late 1959." (Many believe that the exotica movement can actually be traced as far back as to the classical composer, Maurice Ravel whose "Bolero" caused a frenzy with the Parisian public in 1928.)

There were primarily two branches of exotica, "Jungle" and "Tiki." Les Baxter (1922–1996) was considered the king of the Jungle branch while Martin Denny (1911–2005) ruled the Tiki branch. One of the contrasts between them was that Les Baxter was primarily a studio musician, creating his imaginary tonal canvases for the recording microphone while Martin Denny was an active performer, who recorded his albums to document what he and his quartet had accomplished in front of audiences.

The genesis of American exotica can be traced back to the end of World War II when soldiers returning home had gotten a taste for the South Pacific. Around this time, Les Baxter released his first Capitol album (78 rpm discs) *Music from the Moon*, which featured the music of Harry Revel and the sound of a theremin. (Soon following, *Perfume Set to Music*, released by RCA Victor, also used the theremin.) *Music from the Moon* was the first example of what is now termed "Space Age Pop" and was enormously successful. Coinciding with this was the publication of James Michener's *Tales of the South Pacific* in 1948. Closely following on the heels of that was the mounting of the Broadway musical based on it, Rogers and Hammerstein's great hit, *South Pacific,* which began its long run the next year. Yma's first North American recording, *Voice of the Xtabay,* appeared the next year, in 1950, and was followed by Les Baxter's *Le Sacre du Sauvage* album in 1951. By that time it was obvious that a certain niche was slowly being carved into the American popular music scene. But it would not be until 1957, when Martin Denny released his first recording, called *Exotica*, for Liberty Records, that the movement got an actual name.

"A journeyman piano player named Martin Denny was performing with his group in Waikiki at the Hawaiian Village's Shell Bar. Denny and his group were quickly becoming local favorites by mixing up both pop music standards and more exotic pieces with the Latin rhythms and percussion supplied by band member Augie Colon. Denny's group also featured Arthur Lyman on vibraphone and marimba and bassist John

Kramer. Instead of the complex, sweeping arrangements favored by studio musicians such as Baxter, Denny rearranged the songs so they could be played by a four piece band live in Waikiki and beyond." (Crossman, ibid)

Hawaii's entrance as the 50th State in America in 1959 gave a surge of popularity to the exotica genre—especially the Tiki branch. This was the period when Tiki bars and lounges suddenly popped up throughout the United States. Tying in with all this was the emergence of the LP as the main listening medium and the new recording techniques that were beginning to be explored. The length of the LP allowed for greater variation in the length of popular pieces, and encouraged the creation of what would later come to be called "concept" albums—rather than simple collections of single songs. The recording technology that was termed "high fidelity" (and "hi-fi") created an urge to exploit the wider range of sound possibilities that were becoming available. Some of these recordings have stood up remarkably well. The digital re-mastering by Scamp CD of Denny's original Liberty LP recording (Exotica) has brilliant, clean sound that could have been created yesterday.

Exotica became the music that middle class "grown-ups" relaxed with during cocktails after a hard day's work. It was pure escapism music that allowed listeners to experience far away lands from a safe distance. It was not important that these visions be authentic. Composers offered these creations as musical representations of vaguely, generically mysterious countries and customs.

There were distinct differences between the approaches of Baxter and Denny, outlined neatly by J. Scott McClintock in a recent review for the online All Music Guide while discussing a re-release of one of Martin Denny's CDs.

> Denny's predilection for whimsy was also what set him apart from exotica's other major figure, Les Baxter. For the most part, Baxter was deadly serious in his arrangements. In his hands, exotica was all about the fantasy—atmospherics and theatricality were the primary focal points. Denny was more concerned with fun and there's no better example of their differing approaches than the title track "Quiet Village." Penned by Baxter, "Quiet Village" became the poster-song of the exotica scene—forming the template for a thousand copycat lounge excursions. In Baxter's hands, "Quiet Village" was a mysterious and slightly ominous piece of aural cinema, with distant percussion echoing through misty and eerie strings. Denny's take was decidedly more stripped, laid-back, unfussy and congenial. His was backwater exotica (rather than Baxter's uptown exotica) and, ultimately, it was Denny's version that found the most success with the public. (www.allmusic.com/cg/amg.dll?p=amg&sql=10:y8ue4j679wal)

Martin Denny's contributions to the Tiki branch had the novelty of the additional use of bird calls, jungle sounds, frogs, various chimes and percussion. These external noises enhanced the listener's ability to evoke remote regions. Denny's success in that branch was continued by many others. Probably the most famous is his former vibraphone player, Arthur Lyman (1932–2002). Arthur also made a number of fine albums for that branch of exotica including two classics, *Taboo* and *Taboo 2*. Although Lyman branched out on his own, settling with Hi Fi Records and making a number of albums that rivaled Denny's in popularity, the two remained good friends throughout their lives.

"Lyman's style was softer than Denny's, but he went much further in his use of exotic environmental sounds. The combination of macaw shrieks and gentle vibes was a vein Lyman mined consistently for over 30 albums. Unlike Denny, whose heavy touring schedule often forced his label to use a stand-in pianist on his albums, Lyman recorded almost exclusively in Hawaii. His Hi-Fi albums were usually recorded in Kaiser's Aluminum Dome auditorium in Honolulu, and still stand out for their superb audio qualities." http://www.spaceagepop.com/lyman.htm)

But our interest in Exotica centers mainly on the Jungle branch. Baxter was not the only one to produce Jungle exotica albums at that time but he was the first and his remain, by far, the finest and the most enduring—lush, inventive and colorful. Yma Sumac's albums belong within this subgenre. With Capitol, Baxter released such exotica cornerstones as *Tamboo! Caribbean Moonlight, Skins, Ports of Pleasure, African Jazz, Jungle Jazz, Sacred Idol,* and *Jewels of the Sea.* For the Liberty Label he collaborated with Martin Denny and Si Zentner and released *Exotica Suite* (1960), while in the 1960s, with the label Reprise, he continued with *The Primitive and the Passionate, Soul of the Drum,* and *African Blue.*

As David Toop commented in his book *Exotica*: "Baxter offered package tours in sound, selling tickets to sedentary tourists who wanted to stroll around some taboo emotions before lunch, view a pagan ceremony, go wild in the sun or conjure a demon, all without leaving home hi-fi comforts in the white suburbs." (*Serpent's Tail*, London 1999)

These recordings, whether they stem from the jungle or the tiki branch of exotica, all share one thing in common. They need to be listened to without distraction. They are mood compositions, not music to accompany chores. Yma's entries demand the same. In creating atmosphere through countless vocal effects, she prompts her listeners to use their imagination to form their personal mental scenario of what she was portraying. Much of Yma Sumac's repertoire was program music—that is, music where the only effect sought is the creation of a mood or atmosphere, the listener guided by titles or program notes, a popular-music version of classical composers' tone poems and much symphonic literature. Its premise is similar to many of the best effects of classic era radio, when listeners would crowd around the radio for such programs as "The Shadow" and "Inner Sanctum," creating their own private scenarios guided by the words and the voices of the actors. Succeeding generations have grown up with television, which quickly superseded radio in importance. It was no longer necessary to create a scenario—television provided that. Yma Sumac's music, however, requires mental participation; with it, the listener's mind may wander to a new land via her singing.

It was at the very beginning of this new musical movement that Yma suddenly appeared as an Incan Princess. In truth, the 1950s American popular music scene was surprisingly arid and badly in need of a jolt. Yma Sumac provided that jolt—and more. With a physical beauty and personal charisma that matched her vocal sheen, she presented an elegance previously not encountered in popular music performance. Fortunately, for her first album, she was paired with Les Baxter since they suited one another musically. The suave, classical elegance of Baxter's arrangements perfectly matched the striking elegance of Yma's voice. Through her voice and music listeners were transported far from everyday worries and taken to distant lands. These were places of ancient legends, odd pagan rituals, misty mountain peaks and lush steamy jungles that hid fabled, crumbling temple ruins of forgotten civilizations.

This was of course, before anyone had landed on the moon. By the mid 1960s, and the new preoccupation with the then burgeoning space exploration program and the coincidental arrival in America, in 1964, of the English music group, the Beatles, exotica slowly began to fade a way as minds and tastes shifted.

What had previously been considered exotic and wonderfully mysterious had become quaint, passé, and on the borders of good taste. Audiences slowly turned their interests from fantasy. America had entered the space age full force and its curiosity centered on the mysteries of the heavens not the earth.

In that respect, Yma Sumac was both a product and a victim of her era. She was purposefully shrouded in mystery and in that veil of ambiguity she was boldly presented to a hungry world that, for a while, stuffed itself. For millions of people in the 1950s her name was synonymous with "magic." Yma Sumac was the dream incarnate—exotic and beautiful, mystifying and sexy. While it lasted, it was a most magnificent dream.

Author's Note:
Contacted numerous times, Yma Sumac declined to be interviewed or to participate in any aspect of the creation of this book.

CHAPTER 1

The Beginning: Emperatriz Chavarri 1922–1942

Yma Sumac was born Zoila Augusta Emperatriz Chavarri del Castillo, in Peru. Her date of birth has always been problematic. Most sources accept September 10, 1927, as the correct date. Family members in Peru, however, contend that the correct year is 1922. In an interview with Richard Lamparski for his book *Whatever Happened to*, Yma stated that she was fourteen years old when she was "discovered" in 1950, but then said that she was sixteen when she and her husband, Moisés Vivanco, first came to the United States in 1946. Another time she stated that she was 17 in 1950, when she recorded the famous *Voice of the Xtabay* album. Such discrepancies are not unusual. It is a common practice, as much in the field of classical music as in pop entertainment, for female performers (especially) to move their date of birth continually forward.

In a 1950 article (August 28), *TIME* magazine stated that Yma was 28 years old at the time of her famous Hollywood Bowl concert. This places her date of birth in 1922. *TIME* was the only publication to state Yma's age at the onset of her North American career and was the only one to contradict the birth date given by the Sumac publicists of the time. With all the voluminous publicity pouring into the media at the time, one suspects that the date given to *TIME* may have been an unintentional slip that was allowed to pass by the Sumac management. Not helping matters were the contrary comments and terrible arithmetic that Yma often displayed during interviews.

Don Pierson, the webmaster of the Sunvirgin.com Web page, notes on his site: "[The date 1922] is based on many things. For one thing, her first radio broadcast was in 1942 and people who were there indicate that she was a woman in her early 20s at the time rather than a young teenager as she would have been had she been born in 1927 or 1928 (or 1929). Her family says that the date was the 12th but Yma has always celebrated it on the 10th which we believe to be the correct day." Finally: a document issued by the Peruvian ministry of culture on the occasion of a celebration of her career in 2006 states her date of birth: September 12, 1922.

From her birth until 1943, facts are few and confusing. Contributing to this is their entanglement with half-truths and legends that were concocted by over-zealous press agents and public relations doyens of the 1950s.

According to most sources, Yma was born in the small village of Ichocán (population then about 400) in the department of Cajamarca, in Peru. This village rests on the side of a mountain range called Cumbe-Maita. In Sumacian press material, this mountain's elevation has been given as:

16,000 feet (Liner notes from the 1950 original release of *Voice of the Xtabay*)
15,000 feet (Program notes from a 1955 Concert at Carnegie Hall)
12,000 feet (*Collier's* Magazine article, 1951)

Even Yma's place of birth is in dispute. According to Angel Humberto Velasquez Alcori, who was born in Ichocán himself, Yma was born in the city of Callao, Lima's seaport, where Yma's father met her mother, Emilia (*Yma Sumac: Hollywood's Inkaprinzessin*, Rubicon Film GbR, 1992). David Espena, a friend of one of Yma's uncles and a friend of the family, also asserts that she was born in El Callao and not Ichocán. But then, contradicting what she and her publicist had circulated for decades, Yma herself said in 1990, during an interview for *DISCoveries* magazine with Gino Falzarano:

"I have a very happy childhood!...I was born in North Lima. In North Lima the climate is usually beautiful. Is high, but not too high like in the south. I lived on the farm with my parents, and then I continued my studies in Lima." (*DISCoveries*, 2/90)

Augustus Leguana Valazquez, who was born in Ichocán in 1927, remembers seeing Yma only once in Ichocán—in 1933, when he was six years old and she was approximately eleven. "I knew her very well then, because they lived in front of my house and Yma and I played together all the time. By then she was singing in the church. Although my uncles have said that Yma was here three times, that is not true. She sang only once in the church when she was in El Callao." (*Yma Sumac: Hollywood's Inkaprinzessin*, Rubicon Film GbR, 1992) (translation, Manar Zaher)

Most probably Yma Sumac (that is, Zoila Augusta Emperatriz Chavarri del Castillo) was born in El Callao, and then immediately taken to the family *estancia* or ranch in Ichocán, where her mother, Emilia, could recuperate. Yma would have been predominantly raised at their city home in Cajamarca.

The reasons for all this conflicting information are not hard to understand. According to William P. Mitchell, professor of anthropology, and Freed Chair in the Social Sciences at Monmouth University, West Long Branch, New Jersey, and author of *Peasants on the Edge: Crop, Cult, and Crisis in the Andes* (University of Texas Press, 1991) there are clear reasons why Yma would insist she was born in or near Lima.

> All parents, if they possibly can, try to get birth certificates for their children in Lima, which carries more social prestige than being born in the mountains. To be from the highlands, or from the Sierra, is to be a Serrano, and that means to be Indian. In Peru to be an Indian is to be at the bottom of the social scale—there is a lot of racism against Indians. So what parents do, and I know lots of parents who have done this, is to try and get a birth certificate for their child on the coast to show that he or she is not a Serrano but from the coast. At the same time medical care is far better in Lima and Callao—Callao is the port city of Peru, really almost part of Lima—so anyone who has the possibility, wants to have their medical attention in Lima or Callao.

The biography that originated from Capitol Records stated that Yma was born in Ichocán; according to Professor Mitchell, again, there are reasons:

> One of the things I have discovered from working with Peruvians both in Peru and here in the United States is that in Peru they try to hide their Indian ancestry, but in the United States they try to claim it. In the United States, Indian ancestry provides prestige ("I am a descendant of the Inca....") but in Peru it stains people as Serranos. There are, of course, exceptions. Many Peruvian intellectuals and activists glorify their Indian roots, but in general people know that to be considered an Indian will impair economic and social success in Peru.

Although not surrounded by luxury in her youth, by Peruvian standards of the day Yma's family was apparently well off—they owned a large amount of land and several houses. These included the estancia in Ichocán, an estate in Ancash and various farms in the highlands of Peru. Supposedly there were occasional servants present since Yma has referred to domestic help during her youth. This included a nanny and a personal tutor who was responsible for Yma's education until the age of twelve.

From both her mother, Ima Sumack Emilia Atahualpa Chavarri del Castillo, who (according to publicity releases) was pure Quechuan, and from her father, Sixto Chavarri del Castillo, who was part Spanish, Yma seems to have inherited her brooding volatility. According to a 1987 interview, Yma's grandparents originated from Vasco, Spain.

As she coyly explained: "[M]y mother is half Indian and half Spanish. On that side I am descended from a real Incan princess. But I don't like to mention that." (*New York Native*, 3/9/87)

The roots of this account of her ancestry go back to original (1950) publicity statements: For example: "Yma Sumac's mother is full-blooded Inca Indian, directly descended from Inca kings and known to her people in the mountains as 'Mama Cuna' (Great Lady of Music)." This last was boasted despite the fact that there was never any mention of Yma's mother being musically gifted. In the Inca temples, the chosen women were known to the Spaniards as "Mama Cune."

In addition to temperament, Yma must have likewise fallen heir to at least some of the fruits of social respectability and responsibility. Not only was Yma's father an acknowledged authority on the civic affairs of Cajamarca, but her two paternal uncles were similarly distinguished. One was the head of the Peruvian Supreme Court, while the other was an established physician. In addition to this, her mother was a highly respected schoolteacher.

One can only marvel at the thought processes that would later lightly dismiss these impressive, at least haute-bourgeois, social credentials in favor of the phantasmagoria of poverty, somehow mixed as it became with Incan Princess gold and feathers. In an article from the Parisian *Samedi Soir*, one can see how far the truth had already been stretched in 1951 (5/12/51): "From poor people, Yma never imagined, in spite of her beauty, that one day she could abandon her mountain and the miserable hut of dried earth of her parents." (Translation: Anna Schumate)

Reputedly, Yma was the youngest of six children (3 sisters and 2 brothers). To this happenstance of fate was appended a convenient myth which became central to the evolution of her image as an Incan Priestess-Princess. According to Incan mythology and legend, the royal line is passed on through the youngest child "on the principal that the youngest child benefits from the experience and wisdom of the other children of the family." Since Yma's mother's maiden name was supposedly Atahualpa, the same as that of the last ruler of the Incan civilization, Yma could be regarded as "a princess royal and spiritual leader of the mountain people of Peru ... (occupying) a unique position in the Inca religion." (Publicity notes supplied by Sumac's agents to the New York Public Library.)

Professor Mitchell explained the probable origin of this. "Peruvian highlanders practice a form of ultimogeniture, in which the family home is often inherited by the youngest child, because it is the youngest child who remains at home to care for aging parents. There was no clear line of royal succession for the Inca, however, and the death of the emperor often resulted in wars over the succession."

Into this portentous fabric was now embroidered a fantastic prophecy. Some 600 years before the fall of the Incan empire in 1553, a prophet foretold the defeat of king Atahualpa at the hands of Francisco Pizarro. The prophet warned that the empire would be lost to the world for many years. "He further predicted that one of great beauty and true blood would appear and travel to the far ends of the earth bringing fame and glory to the lost empire." (From 1955 Yma Sumac Carnegie Hall concert booklet.)

Interestingly, although those notes were written in the middle of the 1950s they themselves made a prediction of sorts. During the 1960s, after Yma had validated her talents during an international career, recordings of authentic Peruvian music performed by various peoples of the highland regions began to appear. World appreciation for this nation's exotic musical forms had been vigorously stimulated through Sumac's notoriety. The tenth century prophecy had, in some respects, come true. Whether the prediction originated from the vision of an ancient soothsayer or from the meditations of a Madison Avenue votive, the result was the same: Peruvian folk music was enjoying a vast new audience, and a beautiful, uniquely gifted woman was partly responsible. It should be remembered, in any case, that the 1960s was the time of burgeoning popularity of folk music in general, and, with the famous Folkways LP recordings of ethnic music from around the globe, the genesis of what has become a great upsurge in popularity in what is now called "world music."

The Andes abound in numerous colorful religious ceremonies, many of which are quite ancient. These festivals are now basically Christian in nature—although mixed with varying influences from earlier, ancient Sun-worship practices. According to Dr. Bernard Mishkin (*The Contemporary Quechua*; 1946; Smithsonian Institution for the Bureau of American Ethnology), "[M]any Quechuans believe that God and Christ are one. This divinity often is equated with the Sun, Inty Huayna Capac."

A typical religious ceremony consists of a Mass and Procession accompanied by the playing of music, singing, dancing and drinking, as people march through the streets and visit homes, a bacchanal that can last as long as a week. Obviously during all that time, various musical entertainments were provided by local folk singers. Whether on a local or national level, every village and city participates.

Reared in the strict religious traditions of her family, Yma evidently participated in many of these ceremonials at an early age. The turning point in her life came when she was chosen to sing as soloist for the great Inty Raymi Festival (Feast of the Sun). The most famous of the Peruvian religious ceremonials, it is still held every June at the time of the Winter Solstice, in honor of San Juan (Saint John), the patron saint of the Indians.

Most probably, Yma was chosen to be one of the local folk performers during the entertainment after the ceremony and that it was the quality of her solo singing that drew attention. Local legends began to spring up concerning Yma's vocal prowess. One boasts that her unusual vocal abilities came from the powerful lungs she developed while chasing her father's goats about the mountains.

Whether it was during a religious service or a folk entertainment afterward, this particular event took place on June 24, 1941, before no fewer that 25,000 spectators in the Pompe de Amancaes, a beautiful natural amphitheater on the outskirts of Lima. (Professor Mitchell, however, questioned this attendance figure. "That seems very high for 1941. Lima only had about 500,000 inhabitants then.")

A government employee (in publicity releases he is referred to simply as an "official") who was present was impressed enough with Yma's singing that he mentioned it to the Ministry of Education. Based on what he had heard, he recommended that she be given a scholarship to study in Lima. (Some sources state Yma was taken to Lima in 1939.)

In his book, *Peru, Bolivia, Ecuador, The Indian Andes*, (Thomas Nelson, Inc. 1969), Charles Paul May stated that Carlos Valderamma, "one of Peru's most famous musicians of recent times, discovered (Yma) and provided much of her training." Whether or not this is quite true, Valderamma certainly played an important part in Yma's career, since his vocal arrangement of "Virgenes del Sol" (Virgins of the Sun) was one of her most famous songs during the formative years of her career.

Among those responsible for inviting Yma to Lima was Dr. Moisés Saens, Mexican Ambassador to Peru. A concert/audition was arranged to assess Yma's capabilities. At its conclusion, she was awarded a full scholarship and enrolled in the Institute de Santa Teresa, an extension of the University of Lima, well known as a teacher's college (Yma's mother had wanted Yma to become a teacher). After enrollment, Yma's major interest of study was psychology.

Moisés Vivanco (1918–1998), later Yma's husband, manager, and artistic mentor, remembers it differently. "I discovered Yma Sumac when she was 14 years old. At this age she was singing in the City of Cajamarca (Peru), almost 2000 km. from Lima, near the Amazones [the tropical rain forests of the Amazon]. At that age, she used to sing, imitating the birds and nature" (private correspondence).

From her earliest years, Yma always expressed herself through song. She was fascinated by music and by its many forms and sang not only for the pleasure it gave her, but also in the hope that one day she would sing professionally. Although she had never had any voice training, Yma's youthful voice was unusually full and strong, and had a distinctive polish to it that was uncommon in the voices of Peruvian singers usually heard at such festivals. Without verbalization, her instincts told her she was born to sing.

Consider how these facts are subsumed within the legends fed to audiences during the 1950's. The following is taken from liner notes for the original release of her first North American recordings, *Voice of the Xtabay:*

> No one in her native village of Ichocan, 16,000 feet high in the Andes of Peru had ever heard such a voice in human form when this "chosen maiden" sang at their annual festivals to the sun.
>
> No one in the big cities below had heard such a voice either. So when exciting rumors of her rare talent and beauty reached officials of the Peruvian government, they arranged to bring Yma Sumac down to the coastland . . . a decision that almost caused an uprising among some thirty thousand Indians over the loss of their revered ritual singer.

Even more inventive are these notes from the 1956 re-release of these recordings on LP:

> Born high in the Peruvian Andes, a descendant of the last of the Incan kings, Yma Sumac spent her childhood literally "talking" with the birds, the beasts, the winds, the sound of life and nature surrounding the little village of Ichocan.
>
> While still a small girl she began taking part in the religious services of the sun-worshipping Indians and became almost deified by them.
>
> Word of her phenomenal vocal powers reached Lima, the Peruvian capital, and an official government delegation traveled into this remote mountain region to see and hear what they secretly believed to be a myth.

These legends continue to be used as liner notes for any Capitol or EMI re-pressings of this singer's recordings.

During the 1950s, these fabrications harmonized with Yma's natural, exotic beauty, her shyness when meeting people and her proud, elegant bearing when on stage. Unfortunately, her strange displays of aloofness, coupled with these legends, increased the isolation between not only herself and her audiences but also other performers. She soon became an enigmatic sort of vocal machine, beyond human dimension—an oddity.

About a year before Yma began her studies at the Institute in Lima, a young musician, Moisés Vivanco, had formed a folk music group called the "Compañia Peruana de Arte." Moisés was born Moisés Vivanco De Allende in 1918, in Ayacucho, Peru, about 700 km from Lima. Ayacucho is a beautiful colonial city where the Spanish army was defeated and the independence of South America was proclaimed on December 9, 1824.

Moisés had been reared in an artistic family and showed evidence of musical talent at an early age. Music, especially the guitar and the harp, is integral to the culture of Ayacucho. Indeed Ayacucho is known as a center for guitar playing, and most boys learn to play the instrument and sing at an early age. "I think I must have started strumming instruments already as a baby. I first actually studied music in the second grade of primary school with professor Romani, when I was very young. My mother played the guitar, and she said that as a baby, I started strumming the strings while sitting on her lap. When I finished high school, I went to Lima and there continued to study by myself. I was decorated as a prodigious child at the age of eight by the President of Peru at that time, Don Augusto B. Leguia, as since my very early childhood, I played and dominated [sic] almost 40 different Inca instruments for melodies and all kinds of music making." (Moisés Vivanco, private correspondence)

The folk ensemble that Moisés formed the year before Yma arrived in the capital comprised some forty-six musicians and dancers including his sister Rosa (Rosita), who was the group's leading vocalist. Rosita was very beautiful. She "sang pure Andean folk music and (was) also a sensation reciting poetry." (ibid.) The Compañia was one of the first Peruvian art groups of its kind and quickly became regarded as preeminent in the authentic performance of the music and dances of Peru and Latin America. Like Peruvian groups that were to follow, the primary musical emphasis of Moisés' group was on ensemble, not solo display. The Compañia boasted solid ensemble work and an admirable authenticity of presentation.

When Yma came to audition for the institute in Lima, Moisés was an executive with the Peruvian Broadcasting Company. Because of his musical credentials he was in attendance at the audition as a matter of course. After hearing her voice he immediately decided that Yma should become a member of his Compañia. Although her skills were as yet unfinished, Moisés recognized the inherent potential in her voice and the unusually authoritative quality of Yma's singing. It was not just a matter of Moisés recognizing that it would be advantageous for him to secure Yma for his group; however, he also sensed that with correct guidance Yma's possibilities were limitless. According to his brother, Dr. Alejandro Vivanco, Moisés had always envisioned a female voice representing his ensemble. Dr. Vivanco was himself a folklore musician of Ayacucho and with his brother, Moisés, spearheaded the first movement of that vein of Peruvian music in 1935. (According to Dr. Vivanco, Yma was 14 when she met Moisés.)

After the concert/audition, Moisés sought out the young singer and her chaperoning mother to suggest that she join his ensemble. With the exuberance of youth, Moisés approached Yma's mother. "I insisted with her parents to let her go to Lima, to study with me a revolutionary way of singing, which was my idea, after hearing her voice."

Yma's mother was dubious at best. She was not impressed by Moisés' credentials, to begin with; but then, singing for religious festivals (or church) was one thing. A career on the stage was an entirely different matter. Yma was to become a teacher, like herself.

Yma, whose dream it was to sing professionally, was flattered by Moisés' invitation and delighted with the prospect it offered her of pursuing her dream. It did not hurt Moisés' cause that he was exceptionally good looking, with sensitive dark eyes and an intensity, an excitement about music, that Yma found perfectly simpatico.

Unfortunately, Mother was adamant and advised Yma to forget such frivolous notions about performing in public. She was to concentrate on her upcoming studies at the institute. For Yma's mother, the fact that her daughter had been awarded a full scholarship on the merit of her singing was honor enough. It was time to get on with the serious things in life.

Yma's mother returned to Cajamarca, satisfied that she had quelled her youngest daughter's notions about a music career. Yma remained in Lima to begin her studies.

Headstrong and impetuous, Yma quietly made her own decision concerning Moisés' offer. Despite her mother's admonitions Yma was determined to join Moisés' group. Not only did she find his offer appealing, she found him appealing as well. The main problem would be how to join the ensemble and yet keep the fact from her parents. Yma devised an outrageously clever plan. To put it into action she would need to enlist the help of her older, married sister who was living in Lima, and who had been charged by Mother to keep a watchful eye on the young, headstrong Yma.

Yma knew that her sister had always been supportive of her singing, Yma also thought that she might be convinced to help her accomplish a certain deception. It was a deception that was not only audacious but might even be dangerous for Yma if discovered.

After fully developing her plan, discussing it with her sister and obtaining her agreement to fully cooperate, Yma asked to hold a family conference. During the course of their conversation, she happened to casually mention that there were a few extra courses at the Institute that she desperately wanted to take. Unfortunately, they only met in the evening. Because of her age, Yma understood that her parents would, naturally, insist upon a chaperone for her safety while she was out in the evenings. Yma came up with the brilliant suggestion that, since her older sister already lived in Lima, perhaps "she could be persuaded" by the parents to act as an escort for Yma's travel to and from classes. Pleased with Yma's academic enthusiasm and her surprisingly adult suggestion for a solution, they readily agreed to her taking the extra courses. Mother and Father contacted sister—who was expecting their call and who graciously agreed to be Yma's evening chaperone.

So Yma went to "night school"—actually, of course, rehearsals of Moisés' Compañia—accompanied by her sister, who would sit quietly and watch Yma rehearse.

At this point, a number of people became involved with Yma's musical and artistic education. Gamaiel Concha Vargas, from Cuzco, remembers working with an inexperienced Yma during this early period. According to him, she was coached in music and ballet by him for two years. He proudly told Günther Czernetsky for the German television documentary, *Yma Sumac: Hollywood's Inkaprinzessin*: "Every time Yma came back to Peru to perform, the first thing she did was to call us, because we used to be good friends. She would always say to me, 'thanks to you I am what I am.' Not many musicians remember, when they are famous, where they came from." (translation by Giancarlo Cifuentes)

According to Moisés, everyone seemed to have their own ideas about the course Yma's singing should take—including himself. "In Lima, everybody was dedicated to the opera singing, and they insisted that she should be sent to Italy to study bel canto, but she ... refused, preferring to join my company the 'Compañia Folklorica Peruana De Moisés Vivanco.'" (ibid)

Early in 1942, after many secret rehearsals, Yma made her radio debut with the Compañia Peruana de Arte at the age of 20 (or 15). This created a problem that she handled with what will come to seem characteristic efficiency. Realizing that she could not use her real name in so public a performance and risk her deception being detected by her parents (or their informing friends) the girl chose a stage name: Imma Sumack, as it was spelled at that point. In one spelling or another, this was to remain her stage name throughout her career.

Why she adopted this particular name is not documented. Its origin, however, may be relatively easily traced. According to accepted Capitol Records biographical information, Yma's mother's full name was Imma Sumack Emilia Atahualpa, so presumably she could have borrowed from there—an almost tongue-in-cheek defiance. But the name appears much earlier in Peruvian history. A character of this name, with a variant spelling, appears in a classical Peruvian drama called "Ollantay," attributed to the Incan period but which may actually date to the early colonial period. The career of Yma Sumac—translated from the original Quechua to mean "how beautiful"—had begun.

CHAPTER 2

Waiting: Imma Sumack
1942–1949

During the months that Yma rehearsed with Moisés and his ensemble, she and her sister successfully kept her secret safe from her parents. Yma made tremendous musical progress in that period. In an instance of perfect timing, Rosita Vivanco, Moisés' sister, announced plans to leave the Compañia to marry a wealthy businessman, thereby vacating the position of ensemble soloist. This was fine with Moisés since, with his special tutoring and Yma's intense dedication, he felt she was ready to fill Rosita's position. Out of recognition of Yma's thrilling vocal potential, Moisés began to institute changes to the ensemble's music to accentuate her talent. Already beginning to demonstrate his managerial gifts, Moisés began to reform the ensemble and its artistic priorities. Yma was now the fulcrum.

> We used to study seven to eight hours every day, including holidays, again against the opinion of all the—at that time—professional maestros, who criticized me, telling me that I would destroy her and that she should go to Italy and study opera. In which case she would have merely become—and only after many years of study of technique—a simple common opera singer, forced to remain within the actual European musical structure, competing with other opera singers.
>
> I taught Yma to vocalize the normal musical scale, and then I discovered that she could reach more octaves, so I created special lessons for her until we reached five octaves with her voice, which no singer in the world has managed to date. (Several singers have approached me, asking for lessons from me, during the past years, claiming they had a similar voice, but when listening to them, their voices were never even close to the voice of Yma and never ever five octaves.)
>
> I was right to work with Yma, creating music written exclusively for her unique range of voice, making a worldwide revolution in music, both in written music, as I use at times half notes and when I play the guitar for her, for her unique voice, as well as to have developed her voice range to the fullest, which due to the special music written only for her, she can offer this exceptional voice to our audiences. (private correspondence)

Although young and inexperienced, Yma's instincts for improvisation were showing themselves to be unusually advanced. Indeed, Yma also proved to be extremely proficient at imitation and Moisés, recognizing her potential, encouraged and guided Yma to more fully explore this innate ability. Her radio debut in 1942 is a vivid example of how sophisticated Yma's instincts were. Her youthful singing generated both audience interest and, subsequently, parental shock.

When Moisés proudly informed the ensemble that he had secured them an important radio broadcast appearance, both he and Yma were reasonably confident of her continued anonymity since no one at her home listened to the radio with any regularity. The fact that she was also using the name Imma Sumack probably added to her false sense of security. After all, how could anyone deduce that the Imma Sumack singing on the radio was in actuality Emperatriz Chavarri? Although it was clearly an important event in the ensemble's career to that point, Yma (and Moisés) failed to anticipate the tremendous attention the broadcast would attract to the group. No one in the Compañia foresaw the sensation that would be caused by this broadcast and, in particular, Yma's singing. They all knew she was good but they were accustomed to her singing and her odd ability to imitate instruments.

Well-rehearsed and eager, the Compañia Peruana de Arte was a tremendous success, not only with the radio audience but also the press. Newspaper coverage of the ensemble and its gifted young soprano soloist spread rapidly, complete with photographs. It spread right into the Chavarri home where Mother was all too easily able to piece together the names Vivanco, Compañia, and Imma Sumack—especially with the help of some damning photographs. (One especially charming one was of Yma in traditional peasant costume, accessorized with white bobby socks.) Furious with the deception, Mother called Yma home to explain herself and to receive proper recompense for her actions. To quote Yma, when she was asked what happened: "Big, big spank!"

Numerous and very lengthy family discussions and arguments followed. Yma apologized for her deception but pleaded her cause. Her father, Sixto, readily forgave. Mother, however, was not so easily won over to Yma's side. Thanks to the efforts of the rest of the family, the supportive comments made by relatives and friends and the good reviews that had appeared in newspapers, Yma's mother was eventually persuaded to allow Yma to continue pursuing a career in music. Although completely foreign to her thinking when it came to a career choice for her daughter, she relented.

The many offers of appearances throughout South America that began to pour in certainly did not hurt Yma's cause. With the family's blessing secured, Yma began to put all her concentration into the furtherance of her career. For the time being, scholastic priorities were put on hold as she concentrated on rehearsals.

Before long the group had secured another radio broadcast—one of the most important to date. In April of 1942, the Compañia Peruana de Arte, starring Imma Sumack, performed over Radio Belgrano in Buenos Aires, Argentina. A certain inconsistency should be mentioned now. Although slight, it can be confusing. In Peru, Yma's mother's name was spelled Ima. As was Yma's when she appeared in that country. In Argentina, however, where Yma reaped her first success and where she made her first recordings, the spelling of her name was Imma.

Yma in 1939
(Courtesy of Yma-Sumac.com)

While in the first flush of their success, Yma and Moisés decided to act upon the extreme attraction they felt for one another and married. The civil ceremony took place on June 6, 1942, in the city of Arequipa, at the foot of a famous Andean mountain, El Misti. Yma was twenty (or 15); Moisés was twenty-four.

Shortly after the wedding, Moisés began to make arrangements for the Compañia's first tour. This was an important step for the ensemble; to this stage, all their performances had been single engagements. The prospect of a tour provided the group not only with an opportunity to expand their musical horizons, but would also serve to introduce them to a host of new audiences. Moisés realized, however, that for the tour to work efficiently and economically, some reorganization would be necessary, beginning with reducing the ensemble to a more manageable number. Moisés dismissed thirty-two members to create a new ensemble of fourteen. The new group, now called Imma Sumack and the Conjunto Folklorico Peruana, set off on an extended concert tour that included much of Peru, Brazil, Argentina, Chile, and north into Mexico. Over the next months they gave numerous radio broadcasts, appeared in theaters, casinos and nightclubs. Their reputation for both authenticity and solid entertainment value quickly spread outside their native Peru.

Reviews throughout the tour were extremely positive and forecast a great professional future for the group. The following quote from *Variety* (6/16/43) is a good example; it is also one of the most realistic ever written about the Peruvian singer. It dates from an engagement at the Ta-Ra-Bis, at the time the number-one nightclub in Buenos Aires. The troupe's program was called "Peruvian Folklore" and lasted twenty-five minutes.

Ray Joseph wrote: "Group is really complete show in itself and can vary its bill anywhere from the 25-minute floor show caught to a two-and-a-half hour concert, and that's just starting. Formed a couple of years ago when government of Peru stopped being ashamed of its Indian background and decided to go in for native arts, outfit has been developed by Moisés Vivanco. . . . Señorita Sumack is topliner and it's her voice (which can imitate any of the Inca instruments played) that provides high spot. [Yma's voice has] an unusually high, piercingly sweet quality which helps much to lend unusual quality. [The group] needs a little more finish for the U.S., but looks as if it has the stuff."

Other reviews of the time applaud the ensemble's careful attention to production values. Above all, the ensemble's emphasis was on the presentation of authentic folkloric material in accurate, ethnic costuming. During the ensuing years, however, such attention and artistic integrity would slowly disintegrate, as Moisés became more enamored with surrounding Yma with exotic spectacle.

Moisés commented on this particular time in Yma's career: "Once we became an overnight sensation on the radio in Lima, we then toured all Latin America, especially Argentina. You must remember that at that time Latin America had a period of glory, wealth and prosperity and was not in crisis like it unfortunately is today. In all these Latin American countries, including Mexico, where we were invited by President Miguel Alemán, we had an overwhelming and breathtaking success." (private correspondence)

In the meantime, according to Moisés, he also continued his studies. "Our first stop of the tours was La Paz, Bolivia, where I met the best specialist of folkloric music, with whom I studied. From Bolivia, we left by train, for four days and three nights to Buenos Aires, Argentina. We were received there by the Peruvian Ambassador and hundreds of people as my company had become famous. In Argentina, I studied (harmony and composition) under D. Manuel de Falla. However, after eight months, Maestro de Falla, to

Publicity shot c. 1948

whom I was recommended by the Great Duchess, Maria of Russia, told me not to study anymore, because I would stifle my own talent and become the same as any other European musician. He told me to create and use my own musical inspiration, which is then what I did." (ibid)

Even at this early stage in her career Yma showed a preference for diverse performance practices. Although intrigued with nightclub work and its intimate atmosphere, she also enjoyed the huge space and elegance of the concert hall where the accent was more formal and she could more easily play the part of diva. Reviews of her appearances in contemporary newspapers and periodicals were similarly diverse and indeed perplexing, reflecting the wide audience appeal Yma would enjoy for many years and also the general confusion as to exactly what kind of performer she was. Not knowing whether to categorize her as a popular singer, folk artist, semi-classical artist, or ethnic performer with eccentric musical tastes, most reviewers simply left out any comment on that very important aspect of her persona.

It was also during these early years that Yma's rehearsing habits became firmly established. They were habits that she would maintain until at least the late 1960s. As Moisés relates, "Rehearsals were every day, even when on tour, 3 to 6 hours per day." (ibid)

It was at this time, flush with the success of her tour, that Yma made her first recordings for the Odeon company in Buenos Aires, Argentina. Originally released as 78 rpm disks, the songs selected were taken from the group's performing repertoire at the time. Most of the selections featured Yma as soloist, showing the change of artistic priorities of the ensemble from their inception. About twenty recordings were released in South America and sold extremely well all over that continent. (In 1952, the American recording firm *Coral* re-issued eight of these 78 rpm sides on 45 rpm disks and a 10" LP disk called *Presenting Yma Sumac*. This was the first time these early recordings were released in America. This album is now a valued collector's item.)

After the making of the recordings the next stop on the tour was a series of appearances in Brazil, booked by George Boronski. During the next few years the group continued to tour throughout South America, increasing their renown and carefully building their popularity with audiences.

In 1945, after performances in Argentina, Yma was personally invited by President Comacho of Mexico to perform at Mexico City's famous cultural center, Palacio de Bellas Artes. (Five years later, this theater was to become Maria Callas' proving ground for new opera roles.) Moisés remembers this as being an exciting time for them both. "We went to Mexico, I think in the year 1945, and worked for more than one year with a full house every night, at the Palacio De Bellas Artes." (ibid)

Both Yma and Moisés were thrilled with such important attention and their confidence grew to the point that they felt that it was now time to travel to North America and conquer those audiences. It was presumed that they would reap an identical harvest of success there. Also, they wanted to take advantage of an important offer of help that had come from the famous American opera and film star, Grace Moore. Grace had heard Yma perform during one of her own tours of South America and had offered to help Yma once she came to America. Unfortunately, it was shortly after their arrival in New York City in 1946, and before they could take advantage of that important backing and mentorship, that Ms. Moore was tragically killed in an airplane crash in Copenhagen, Denmark (January 26, 1947).

Yma and Moisés were to find that a career in America was not as easy as they had supposed. Before their departure for North America, Moisés realized that another reformatting of the ensemble was necessary. After much thought and discussion with Yma, he decided to completely disband the Compañia. In its stead he formed a simple trio: Yma, himself, and a cousin of Yma's, Cholita Rivero.

(Here, as often in this story, there is some confusion as to the exact details. Don Pierson of Sunvirgin.com wrote to me in an email on November 21, 1998: "It is sometimes indicated that she was Moisés' cousin; other times she was Yma's. Robert [Covais], who had met her, said her name was actually Yolanda Rivera ... and she wasn't related to either one.")

Cholita was, in any case, a beautiful young woman and an excellent interpreter of traditional Peruvian dances, and the perfect complement to Yma. In addition to being an excellent dancer and back-up singer for Yma, Cholita was also a very capable tango singer in her own right. Although the revision of the group was primarily done for financial reasons, Moisés knew that it was also his chance to provide Yma with the solo spotlight he felt she merited. Each member of the trio would contribute their own particular gifts but Yma would remain the primary focus. With Moisés playing the guitar and Cholita dancing, Yma's singing would be supported but never in danger of being overshadowed by others' contributions. Despite various frustrations with this arrangement, and the various changes forced upon the trio, it was one that was retained for many years. In fact, during the international phase of Yma's career (1950–1956) remnants of this simple trio set were to be found integrated into all concert performances. Rather sweetly, these sets were a nostalgic nod, or tribute, to earlier, less complicated times. Because of the natural intuitiveness that grows between a small group of musicians over a long period of time, by the time of the famous world tours these sets had acquired a near-magical quality.

Moisés decided to call the new trio the Inca Taqui Trio. (The spelling of the word "Taqui" can be confusing. Sometimes it is spelled "Taki"—the accepted Peruvian spelling—sometimes "Taky," and on Yma's third Capitol album it is spelled "Taqui." For simplicity I have decided to use this last spelling). In their native tongue of Quechua "taqui" means *dance*. In Peru, it means not only *dance* but *song* as well. In the religious customs of that country the two are inseparably linked. Appropriately, most of the trio's repertoire at this time was chosen from the various indigenous dance forms prevalent in Peru: huaynos, marineras, tonderos, pasacalles, laments and danzas. Moisés played guitar, Cholita danced, and Yma sang in her inimitable fashion.

Early in 1946, the trio arrived in North America, excited with the prospect of work and settled with great expectation in New York City. Accustomed as they were to a high standard of living and expecting similar prosperity in America, they took an apartment in the famous Waldorf-Astoria Hotel on Park Avenue in Manhattan. When they began to seek work, however, they discovered that America was quite different from South America, since no one knew of their work. Jobs were few and far between at first, and were of nowhere near the quality that they were used to in South America.

Inca Taqui Trio
Performing c. 1949

To preserve their financial independence the trio was forced to relinquish their suites at the Waldorf and take a cheaper apartment on Park Avenue, and soon enough this also proved to be too much of a strain on finances and so they left Park Avenue for Greenwich Village, and a small, three-room, third-floor-front apartment at 16 Perry Street. Moisés viewed the move to Perry Street philosophically. "Yma goes from Park Avenue to laundry machine, and to market with little bag. She learns many important things." (James Poling, "The Most Exciting Voice in the World," *Collier's* Magazine 4/14/51)

Frances Treacy, an elderly widow who lived across the hall from Yma and Moisés on Perry Street remembered them quite well. In an interview with James Poling (Collier's Magazine), she recalled often sitting on the stoop of their building during the sweltering summer days listening as the trio rehearsed inside. From time to time neighbors would stop by to chat and would join in eavesdropping. "There was always someone who'd say, 'That's no human voice.' And I'd tell them—quite sharply—that it was too!" (ibid) (James Poling's article was unusually comprehensive and to this day remains one of the best-researched and most informative articles ever written about the Peruvian singer.)

Like all freelance musicians living in New York City, the trio grabbed work wherever and whenever they could. They quickly lost their artistic pretensions and realized that any job was a good job as long as they were performing and were getting paid. They would perform anywhere. One night stands predominated and their quality was as eccentric as the trio's music was for most listeners. They ranged from a real estate convention at the Commodore Hotel to the back room of a Greenwich Village Jewish delicatessen.

Important engagements were rare—although they did manage to snag a few. In 1947, for instance, they made their debut in Washington, D.C. at a Pan American Union Con-

Performing c. 1949

cert sponsored by the Peruvian Ambassador. A social event, it was reviewed in the newspapers. The critic for the *Washington Times Herald* was most impressed with what he heard from the trio, especially Yma, and commented in his review, "There is no voice like it in the world of music today." He also asked "What's the matter with the Met?" (The management of the Metropolitan Opera remained silent for the duration of Yma's career.)

Then in 1948, as a favor, Yola Miller, a production assistant to the prominent Broadway and Hollywood songwriter E. Y. "Yip" Harburg (*The Wizard of Oz,* among many others) took Yma to one of New York's leading theatrical agents. The agent took a look at Yma's exotic beauty and launched into a speech that, according to Yola, went something like: "Look, kid, you want to get yourself a red satin dress, see, cut down to here. You're the Spanish senorette type. Do your hair up in spit curls and stick one of them big combs in it, see? Then learn some numbers like 'Begin the Beguine,' and I think I can place you." (James Poling, "The Most Exciting Voice in the World" *Collier's* 4/14/51))

When he was finished, Yma broke into a torrent of virulent Quechua and left his office livid with fury. Yma was a proud, authoritative woman with a successful career in South America behind her. The idea that she should be typecast into some kind of "novelty" ethnic stereotype infuriated her. Yola, embarrassed, was also angry. Amusingly, later "[W]hen M-G-M asked to test her for a role in a Clark Gable picture and then rejected her because she didn't 'look like an Indian,' [Yma] laughingly asked them if she could have the part if she wrapped herself in a blanket, braided her hair, and hopped about grunting 'How' and 'Ugh.'" (Ibid.)

Despite occasional night club and concert engagements, the problems of securing steady work remained unresolved. One engagement, a South American Folk Song Festival, was considered prestigious because it took place at the great New York concert venue, Carnegie Hall. Although only one of a number of groups and not prominently billed, the *Inca Taqui Trio* performed well and did not go unnoticed. Nevertheless, Leonard Jacobson, who was responsible for the trio's bookings during those lean years, continued to find that club owners and concert organizers were hesitant to commit to this unique trio and its odd music. The uncertainty of their reception by bookers was only matched by the confused reception by audiences.

By mid-1948, the trio was at a professional low point. It was at this time that Yma discovered she was pregnant. She and Moisés welcomed an addition to their family, but in terms of the trio and the progress of Yma's musical career, it was scarcely a fortunate development. Still, since her career in the United States did not seem to be moving in the way they had anticipated, Yma decided it was time to stop singing and concentrate on something more practical—having and caring for her baby. Moisés, also disillusioned with the musical situation, felt called on to become involved in a more lucrative business. His new endeavor was a business venture with a friend who was importing Peruvian tuna to the United States. Much preparation went into bringing some 26,000 cases of tuna to the States. Unfortunately, the result was a miserable failure. Although the tuna was edible, it was not profitable. Feeling the pressure of their situation and unable to come up with a suitable solution, Moisés fell into black moods. With all of this surrounding her, Yma grew despondent and wanted only to return to Peru and her family to have her baby. They didn't make it to Peru that year. Their son Carlos, (Papuchka) or Charlie, was born in America on February 7, 1949.

Ironically, after Charlie's birth, musical offers began to trickle in for the trio. Because of these renewed prospects of work Yma and Moisés decided to give the music business one more try. With the birth of their son, however, a small problem had arisen. Moisés had believed that the trio would stand a better chance for success with the American public if Yma were presented as an alluring single woman. With this in mind, he had camouflaged his relationship with her, pretending to be just another musician in the group whenever they performed. When baby made three, an adjustment of image had to be made, and was in fact easily enough accomplished.

The new resurgence of employment, which included a two-week stint at a theater in Montreal and a two-month engagement at the Cine-America Theater and Montmartre Cabaret in Havana, turned out to be short-lived. By mid-1949, their financial situation was again bleak. An offer popped up to participate in a vaudeville revival at a Bayonne, New Jersey theater, paying just $60.00 for four nights—but the trio unanimously felt this was simply too far a fall to accept. Instead, they tightened their belts and hoped for better. Nonetheless, December 20th found them performing for an office party given by a dress manufacturer in a loft in Manhattan's garment district.

Looking back, it is doubtful that Moisés would have considered altering the trio's presentation at this time, despite the serious problems they were experiencing obtaining quality work. In his book, *What Ever Became Of...?* (Crown Publishers, 1974) Richard Lamparski commented that he felt that part of their problems lay in Moisés' stubbornness. "Furthermore, Vivanco's very definite ideas about her repertory, arrangements, and publicity turned off several promoters."

To look at this another way, however, the music that the trio performed was based on the musical traditions of their home country, Peru. This was the area of their expertise as performers, and it was also precisely the product that had won them rich success in South America. Small wonder that they found it hard to consider a desperate change to what some American advisor or another was urging on them.

Hernán Braña, Cholita, Yma, baby Charlie (crawling toward us, face in shadow), 1949

In time however, persistent failures exerted enough pressure so that a reevaluation of the trio's presentation and material became unavoidable. Once done, this new attitude and artistic emphasis drew toward itself fresh job opportunities and creativity. It would take a legendary myth to finally corral America's curiosity and secure for Yma, at long last, financial independence and success.

A publicity shot, c. 1950, captioned "M. Vivanco, Imma Sumack with Inka Trio"

CHAPTER 3

The Arrival: Yma Sumac "Intypa Wawan" (Daughter of the Sun)
1949–1952

To pursue a public career, whether in entertainment, government, or sports, is to court the important variable of chance. There are no guarantees of success. The vapors of New York City have incorporated numberless ghosts of fallen dreams and unfulfilled desires of aspiring artists, actors, and musicians. There is the classic show-biz saying: "For each bright light on Broadway there are a hundred broken hearts."

Some artists who arrive in the city with dreams of conquering its audiences are driven out by the tremendous amount of rejection they must endure and ignore (at whatever inner cost) in the process of seeking to work at their art and craft. Adding in the high cost of living in the city, the pressures are monumental, and to some, crushing. Others stick with the city but modify their career goals to fit the new reality they face. Some give up their dreams as artists and explore new avenues of making a living, to survive in New York City. (Just being able to live and survive in the city of New York is a measure of success in itself.) Some artists manage to hold down a regular job and still actively pursue a professional career. It's a very rare performer in New York City who has not, at one time or another, fallen back on a "civilian" job, a job that gives them a certain amount of financial security and yet allows them the freedom to pursue their art.

The musical life of New York has many subdivisions. For instance, to simplify just a little, take the subdivision of opera. At the top you have institutions like the Metropolitan Opera and the New York City Opera. Directly below that you have smaller independent companies like the former Bel Canto Opera. Underneath this you find small groups where, more often than not, singers pay for the privilege of singing rather than being paid as a professional. These latter companies tend to spring up in the city and last for a while then disappear, to be replaced by others. If a singer cannot be hired by such companies as the Met or City Opera, they learn to compromise and fit themselves into one of the other levels so that their creative instincts can be satisfied. Often work in these companies can be productive for the singer's art—a new role can be learned or polished, for instance—but as to the career, in regard to one's professional artistic resume, work with such companies is worthless.

In any event, luck and fate play an indispensable part in any professional singer's life.

In the case of Yma and the Trio, jobs were becoming a little more frequent and, fortunately, of better quality. A year earlier they had to content themselves with tiny audiences at Prudencio Comacho's La Parisienne delicatessen in Greenwich Village. There the petite Peruvian soprano could be found "in a back room richly blanketed with the aroma of pickled herring, salami and liverwurst. At that time, about the only audience she could reliably count on were those friends who gathered in Prudencio's for an evening of music, cake and coffee" (James Poling, "The Most Exciting Voice in the

Clockwise: Yma, Cholita, Moisés and Hernán rehearsing, New York City 1949

World," *Collier's,* 4/14/51). But by 1949, things were beginning to look better; gradually their fees began to rise as did the quality of their jobs. And, correspondingly, the emotional moods within the trio began to lighten and better music was made by each member. This time period was crucial for Yma, who began to regain her confidence and discover more of her performing potentials—always under the ever watchful and critical eye of Moisés.

In early 1949, the trio had a return engagement at the Blue Angel, a now defunct supper club in Manhattan that was then (and well into the 1960s) one of the finest nightclub spots in New York City for promising new acts and fashionable artists. By chance as well as by virtue of Yma's and the group's talent, this ended up being the most important job of their career. By one account: That particular night Walter Rivers of Capitol Records was in the audience, sent by the recording firm to hear another singer they were interested in signing to a recording contract and who was performing on the same bill as the Inca Taqui Trio. The Peruvian group performed first, however, and that was enough for Rivers, who immediately went backstage to discuss a recording contract with them. He never heard the other singer.

That is the accepted version of what happened that night. Here is another (Hernán Braña, 1910–1997, who joined the trio shortly after this, was told this story by Yma and Moisés): The other singer (Bill Lawrence was his name) became ill and had to cancel his appearance at the Blue Angel that evening. Desperate to fill the blank spot, the management of the Blue Angel called in the Inca Taqui Trio at the eleventh hour. Understandably, the trio welcomed the impromptu return to the supper club, no matter what the circumstances. Walter Rivers arrived at the club that night unaware that Lawrence had cancelled.

Whatever the exact facts about that evening, by all accounts Walter Rivers was impressed with what he heard from the group, especially the unique singing of Yma. Although not exactly sure what could be done with them, he approached Moisés and Yma backstage about the possibility of making a few demo recordings that would then be sent to the main office of Capitol Records to see if a recording contract could be negotiated. Moisés, Yma and Cholita were thrilled with the prospect. Rivers explained that although there were no guarantees, together they would select some of the trio's most impressive numbers to record. Once the recordings were completed, Rivers would send them to Alan Livingston, then vice president of Capitol Records in Los Angeles, to see what his thoughts were.

After much discussion about the course the demo sessions should take, Walter Rivers put in a call to Ramon Littlè to ask for advice and assistance in the presentation of the trio. Neither Rivers nor Littlè wanted necessarily to change the "sound" of the trio but it occurred to them that perhaps the addition of a flute would enhance their quality without altering the ensemble—and that led them to the next piece of what was soon to be a completed puzzle picture.

Littlè suggested to Rivers that he send Hernán Braña to the sessions. Braña, born in Cuba in 1910, was a flutist, percussionist and composer-arranger. He had been in New York City collaborating with Ramon Littlè and was also the chief musical arranger for Carlos Molina and his orchestra. Braña agreed to go to the first rehearsal at Nola Studios, on the third floor of the Steinway Building on West 57th Street. Hernán had never seen or heard the trio perform but rumors of their startling lead singer had reached him through the musical grapevine of the city, and he was very curious to hear their work.

When Walter Rivers called Moisés to introduce Hernán Braña and to inform him that he would be joining them at the rehearsal, Moisés suggested that the rehearsal also be an audition. Moisés had begun to re-think the trio's situation and was formulating new plans of his own. It was becoming apparent to him that they needed new arrangements of their music. Having experienced the hot-cold reception of North American audiences for these years, Moisés had come to understand that he and the trio needed the help of someone—indeed, someone like Hernán Braña—to broaden its potential audience. Moisés felt that American audiences were much more sophisticated than those in South America. He also felt that it was entirely feasible to add another member to the group if he and Yma liked Hernán and his work and if an agreement could be reached that would satisfy everyone.

It seems that what happened when Hernán arrived at the rehearsal was something like love at first sight: Hernán, Yma and Moisés all liked each other at once. At Moisés's request, Hernán sight-read some pieces and played the flute and some accompanying percussion during the songs. At his own instigation, Hernán also did some on-the-spot arranging of pieces that had been chosen for the demos.

Hernán was thrilled by the trio, its concept and its potential. He was especially impressed by Yma's voice. "It was exquisite," he told me later when he recalled first hearing Yma, "It was so free and natural and beautiful. I fell in love with her voice." So the audition was a success—so much so that Hernán felt comfortable making a few crucial musical suggestions to Moisés concerning the trio's demo recordings. It was at his suggestion that three more musicians were hired for the recording sessions in order to fill out the sound.

Moisés was impressed with Hernán's credentials, his tremendous musical versatility and knowledge. He appreciated and also, importantly, respected Hernán's advice concerning the recordings since it came from an obviously sincere concern for the trio's success. Within a short time he began to rely on Hernán's advice. The next rehearsal saw the addition of bass, bongo, and mandolin players, all of whom Hernán had contacted and hired for the sessions.

Both Moisés and Yma respected Hernán's suggestions and it quickly became apparent to Moisés that Hernán must be added to the trio. Not only did Moisés value the older man's musical experience, he also was excited by some of Hernán's novel musical concepts, which he freely shared with them. He also liked Hernán's no-nonsense way of cooperating and contributing to the ensemble. Although he showed enormous potential in managerial and production concepts (at least when it came to Yma), Moisés' musical abilities were limited and provincial. He lacked the capability to propel the group forward into more musically sophisticated spheres. He realized that if the trio was to grow in the way he had originally envisioned, it would be necessary to surround it with seasoned professionals.

Musically speaking, Hernán Braña was a goldmine for them. And, although Yma's attitude toward her music and her performing was always of the utmost seriousness, she too was not a professional—at least not in the sense that she had thoroughly studied her craft or had mastered college-level courses in music. Throughout her career there were always times when her lack of grounding in legitimate musical training was apparent. It was her razor-sharp instinct that managed to carry her through many such awkward moments, rather than professional knowledge or training.

During the rehearsals for the demo recordings it was decided that the addition of a flute to the group would be permanent. Moisés had always liked the sound of that instrument with Yma's voice—he had used it on occasion years before—but he also liked the idea of Yma having a "dueling" instrument to highlight her high register and agility. After only a few sessions, Yma and Hernán found they had an artistic rapport, both enjoying these musical battles, which became more and more intricate as time went on.

The demo recordings were made in June of 1949 at the WHN Studios on Fifth Avenue. They included "Zana" (Hernán's arrangement), "Taita Inty" (Hymn to the Sun), "Babalu" (Hernán's arrangement), and "Repica Timpal." After discussion with Moisés and Yma, and a solid contractual offer, Hernán agreed to join the trio after their return from an engagement in Havana. Originally the contract specified that Hernán would be the group's principal musical arranger. All parties agreed, however, that he would also join as a musician, playing flute and percussion in concerts. From that time until late in 1955, Hernán performed and recorded with the Sumac Troupe whenever his schedule would allow. (Like most touring groups, the Sumac Troupe hired freelance artists as needed—whoever was available was hired when, for instance, other contracts prevented Hernán from leaving New York.) Most importantly, in his musical arrangements for the group, Hernán introduced the traditions of Afro-Cuban music. This was an influence that would be of the utmost importance during the next decades. It was during such segments that Yma would take off on coloratura extravaganzas to the rhythmical accompaniment of ritualistic timpani and drive audiences into frenzy.

Moisés Vivanco remembers that history a little differently: "Mr. Hernán Braña looked for work with us as a drummer. However, he has no participation in the creation of any of my musical compositions. I always compose alone. . . . Mr. Braña is a good musician and a good person. He used to have a solo number of flute and drums during our tours, and played the drums under my supervision. I repeat he did not intervene in the composing of my music." (private correspondence)

Immediately following the Capitol demo sessions the trio traveled to Havana, Cuba, to fulfill a very successful month's engagement at the Theatro American. As per his contract, Hernán joined them upon their return to New York City. One of the first things on the agenda was an important audition for the television show, "We the People." The audition went well and they were hired to appear on the show, which aired in New York City on Channel 4.

Moisés always chose Yma's repertoire for appearances. His decisions as to their placement within a program bordered on genius, always showing an innate understanding and sensitivity to Yma's peculiar programming needs. Because of the great importance of their first television appearance, Moisés put much thought into which piece should be performed for "We the People." It should be representative of the group but must also highlight Yma's vocal gifts. He chose "Taita Inty" (Hymn to the Sun). There was another small issue, which Moisés solved quickly. Because the addition of Hernán to the group made the trio a quartet, Moisés decided to change its name to "Imma Sumack and the Inca Taqui Trio." Moisés had finally created the perfect showcase for Yma's talent.

The appearance on "We the People" was a great success and led to other exposure. Arthur Godfrey saw the show, was intrigued by Yma and the trio and invited them to appear on his own television show, "Arthur Godfrey and His Friends" which aired nationally on Wednesday nights at 8:00. Thrilled with the prospect of yet another television appearance within such a short time, Moisés decided to again use "Taita Inty" (Hymn to the Sun) as their selection. Arthur Godfrey was so pleased with their performance he invited them to return the next week and repeat the piece.

Hernán told me an amusing anecdote about one of these performances. Because of the very hot lights in the television studio, the glue on one of the pads of his flute melted and the pad fell off. Finding it impossible to play all the notes he was supposed to, Hernán mimicked playing the flute and whistled his part instead. The charade worked well. Arthur Godfrey thought it was part of the act.

Because of the television exposure they were now receiving and the quality of their performances, by the fall of 1949, offers for at least eight weeks worth of engagements for the "Borscht Circuit" began to pour in from hotels in the Catskills region in upstate New York. These jobs, though strenuous—they were mostly very short engagements— were nevertheless lucrative and prestigious (comparable nowadays to the resort hotels of Las Vegas, for instance). Moisés and Yma decided to accept the offers. Moisés wisely realized that it would give them the opportunity (and a certain amount of leisure) to perfect their act while also expanding and experimenting with new repertoire.

Moisés, Yma, Hernán in the Catskills 1949

Private snapshots of the group at this time show them to be enjoying themselves despite the strain of one-night engagements. One contributor to Yma's cheerful mood was the fact that the diet she had recently begun was showing signs of success. Her figure now began to display the curves and shape for which she would soon become famous.

Reports of Yma's singing and her unique stage presence spread quickly. It is obvious that during this time she was consciously beginning to develop a mystique with which to surround herself. Mel Leonard, a night-club comedian active at the time, was master of ceremonies for the acts at the Premiere Hotel in South Fallsburg, where the group appeared. He vividly remembers Yma: "The show goes on that night. I introduce all the acts and I got a spot for myself where I'm very funny for the people. But I made a big mistake. I bring Yma on just before my spot. Believe me, the audience was stunned.

"And I gotta follow that. I almost gave up being a comedian. I'm depressed for weeks. She's the one who should've been depressed—I know what she gets paid for stunning the people. I tell you I never saw a dame with such impact, she's not only a tough act to follow the same night, she's tough to follow a week later. And still, she makes absolutely no concessions to her audiences. She's a regal, haughty-type dame and she stays haughty the whole distance. But then, maybe that's just superior showmanship. She needs showmanship with that figure?" (James Poling, "The Most Exciting Voice in the World" *Collier's Magazine* 4/14/51)

It is apparent that by 1949, Yma had decided upon and established an extraordinary relationship with audiences. Her stage demeanor rarely altered and did much to enhance her personal and professional charisma. This was because of a complex combination of personality traits: strict, conventional South American upbringing, tremendous personal pride in her work, an inherent shyness and insecurity in having to deal with large groups of people—contrasted by a real enjoyment of performing in public. Singing was a serious vocation to Yma and because of this she approached it with little humor but rather with a sense of momentous responsibility to her art and her audiences.

So, her stage manner served her unease in dealing with the public on a personal level. A shy woman, the haughty manner set her apart from audiences, creating a type of protective shield from them while simultaneously creating an aura of mystery. Although most popular artists of that era took great pains to endear themselves to audiences while performing, Yma did not. She remained uninvolved with her surroundings to the point of formality. Combined with her eccentric singing and balletic stage movements, this gave her concert performances an unearthly quality. In the intimate atmosphere of a nightclub the powerful combination of Yma's voice, physical beauty, unusual musical material, and aloof stage demeanor was mesmerizing.

Yma's emotional personality is also a study in contrasts. Although her personal life was never what one might call placid, it remained her own business—she was little gossiped about. As fierce as was her hunger for recognition and fame, she remained equally fiercely private and resentful of intrusion. Though some might interpret this as egotism, the reasons and causes for this odd dichotomy go much deeper than mere *amour propre*. It is true that she was self-involved. But intertwined with this self-involvement were countless vulnerabilities and always a profound pride in her work. Yma felt a great need to be successful, to be respected (and most importantly, accepted) by her peers and to be acknowledged for her sincere dedication to her art. Later, she would want to be seriously recognized for her unique contributions to vocal stylization.

As her career progressed and grew into international stature, there surfaced the odd and interesting tendency to refer to herself in the third-person-singular, suggesting she had trouble identifying with the famous artist she had become and that millions of people clamored to hear. *Yma Sumac—singer* became a separate identity. This is not uncommon with famous performers; many artists have difficulty adjusting to the split-personality aspect of having and maintaining a public, professional, career persona. Dreaming of fame and actually achieving it are two entirely different things. In Yma's particular case, there was also a certain residual bitterness because of the tremendous resistance she and Moisés had endured early in her North American career, and the many changes they had to make to themselves and their art before their dream of fame could become a reality.

The immature aspects of her character provided both the fire and the trauma in her life. These included willfulness, self-preoccupation and a certain almost cold disregard for others. These traits were all enveloped within her extensive moodiness. This fiery temperament and vacillating moods were products of Yma's heritage and family upbringing, as well as an expression of the sense of responsibility she felt toward her talent. As mentioned before, Yma took her singing very seriously. Her self-involvement is understandable when one examines her concert tours during her international phase. Performances were frequent, and because of advance publicity, audiences had definite expectations. It was a great deal of pressure for Yma to cope with; it hardly needs saying that her peculiar repertoire and its vocal demands did not make the situation any easier.

It is unfortunate that Yma was never to come to full terms with certain problematic facets of her emotional make-up. During her career, many unnecessary events took place that were entirely due to clashes of will and temper. Yma's character traits, as listed by those who have worked with her, are fascinating for their diversity: generous, selfish, child-like, haughty, humorless, coquettish, egotistical, insecure, demanding and defensive, sweet and sincere, shy, vicious, charming. (Actually, this complex batch of traits could be used to describe any number of "personalities" now appearing before the public.)

In his article, "Most Exciting Voice in the World" (*Collier's Magazine* 4/14/51), James Poling reported:

> (Yma's) reactions are never predictable. She can give the butcher and the baker a bad time if she feels that she is being imposed upon, but she didn't see anything unreasonable in paying $65 for a taxicab ride from Harrisburg, Pennsylvania to New York.
>
> Yma is herself a study in contradiction. Professionally, she conducts herself with such hauteur that Charles Baker, of the William Morris Agency which handles her says, "She acts the way a duchess should but never does. I've seen Broadwayites who haven't called a woman anything but 'Baby', 'Honey' or 'Darling' in 20 years suddenly pull out their moth-eaten party manners and start calling her 'Madame Sumac'. But Yma still says a humble 'thank you' to anyone who asks for her autograph. And in private life she can be so child-like that she will hide under a dining-table at a house party until the guests are assembled, so she can tickle their ankles."
>
> You can question her about her early successes in South America and get only bored monosyllables in reply. And then, suddenly, she is on her feet exclaiming, "When I was a girl in school . . . what you call in English? . . . You know, plenty of earth, then I run very fast like this and . . . boom! I land'. You discover she was some sort of broad-jump champion, and proud of it too."
>
> Although Yma's agents tried to impress upon her that she needed to associate herself with important people, Yma's reaction was one of amusement. "VIP's . . . I know what you mean. All VIP's have more money, or else they can do very important things for you. But no one asks are they good or bad."

When Yma sang at a soiree given by Mrs. Charles Blackwell, a New York socialite, she found herself surrounded by such VIP's. They ranged from Ethel Merman to the Duke and Duchess of Windsor. When asked how the evening went, Yma succinctly replied "Very nice people. The Duchess say she like my music, I say t'ank you." (ibid)

The child-like quality stressed by so many of the people who have worked with Yma stems from an inherent innocence. It was an innocence that, after later disillusionment, turned to bitterness. Her naiveté, also inherent in her personality, was responsible for many of the mistakes made later in the international phase of her career (1952–1962). Yma had no business acumen, consequently it was necessary for her to rely on her husband, Moisés, or her agents for career decisions. Unfortunately, this reliance extracted a very embarrassing price. Never did the cost seem higher than when she was obliged to give lip-service to early publicity releases concerning the story of her youth and her early career.

During 1949, Yma and the trio were busy performing for typically diverse functions. By far the most important job for the group was an eight-week engagement on the New York television show, "Tropic Holiday." Not only because of the unusual amount of exposure they received during the eight-week run, but also because they were performing traditional folk music of Peru and South America, rather than their usual "Taita Inty" (Hymn to the Sun) repertoire.

Because of the publicity the group had been receiving, the television studio was often visited by musical agents and other representatives curious to see and hear the unusual act. One evening John Rose, a representative of the William Morris Talent Agency, happened to be in the studio. He was very impressed with the sound of the group and their performing credentials. John Rose had originally heard Yma years earlier while he was on a survey tour in South America for Walt Disney in connection with the State Department.

Immediately after the television show he went backstage to talk with Yma and Moisés. During the course of the conversation Rose was proudly told of the demo recordings that had been made the past June for Capitol Records. When asked of their status Yma and Moisés confessed they had no idea; they had not yet heard from Capitol. Rose (soon to become their personal representative) decided it was time to find out and offered to approach Alan Livingston on their behalf and find out what was transpiring.

Alan Livingston, however, had not been idle. As a young man, Livingston had begun at Capitol Records as a writer and a producer. Later he became Vice President in charge of repertoire—responsible for the creative operations such as signing artists and recording them. With Yma and her trio, however, he had come across a stumbling block. After he had received and listened to the demo disks he thought about what could be done with such an unusual group. Although the music and performances on the disks were well executed, the group was too ethnic for Capitol's marketing tastes at the time. But he liked them and Yma's voice. The problem was to find a way that Yma could be marketed to the public while still retaining her individual style of performing. He drew a blank, however, and as other pressing matters arose and took precedence, the project was put on a back burner. When John Rose contacted Livingston and told him of the definite career upswing of the group, however, Livingston decided it was time to face the "Sumack problem" head-on.

As Livingston remembers: "[Yma] had been signed by M.C.A., which at the time was a major talent agent in Los Angeles. They took her to my New York office (I was in Hollywood at the time) and nobody seemed to know what to do." (film interview from *Yma Sumac, Hollywood's Inkaprinzessin* by Günter Czernetzky)

He decided to set up a formal meeting with the Vivancos to discuss the feasibility of their recording with Capitol Records. But when he met with them he was in for a surprise.

"She spoke no English at all. She had an associate who was her musical director at the time, Moisés Vivanco, and he spoke enough that we could communicate." (ibid)

It was decided that Livingston should hear first-hand what Yma and the trio could do and a time was set for them to give him a generous sampling of their current work. Alan was still concerned with what could be done with such an unusual act but was determined to come up with an answer.

"I listened to what she sang. She sang what I suppose you would have to call folk music . . . Her music was absolutely unique. She could not read music, she could not write music, she did not sing songs, she sang only what she had learned as she grew up in this very high altitude. In trying to decide how to harness this talent, I felt that it had to be done using her music rather than trying to get her to record or to do anything which would be particularly American or Western or European in its sound." (ibid)

Livingston decided to enlist the aid of Les Baxter, (1922–1996) a composer/arranger who was currently on the Capitol roster. Baxter had recently released a futuristic album called *Music Out of the Moon,* which was inventively scored for drums, bass, guitar, piano, choir, electric organ, and theremin. Against all odds, the album had been wildly successful and Livingston felt that perhaps, after hearing the group, Baxter might have a few suggestions as to a suitable artistic and musical presentation.

Les Baxter studied at the Detroit Conservatory of Music and attended Pepperdine College in Los Angeles. By 1935 he was doing dance band jobs, working his way up through the ranks of free-lance musical arrangers, writing for such bandleaders as Tommy Dorsey. By the late 1940s he was also doing radio work and this led into his being hired at Capitol Records. While primarily employed as a music arranger, he had the opportunity at Capitol to record some of his own arrangements and compositions. Baxter gloried in creating unusually lush sounds on recordings. Going against the norm at the time, which emphasized the use of brass and woodwinds, Baxter preferred to frame singers with lush string choirs. Soon he was in great demand—even major vocalists from other recording companies asked for Les Baxter, because they preferred his attractive settings for the voice. Baxter's first album for Capitol, *Music Out of the Moon,* used not only a vocal choir—an unusual touch at the time—but also the theremin, an unusual classical electronic instrument popular in the 1930s. Much to Capitol's surprise the album was a tremendous success. Les soon became known as an arranger of innovative and fresh musical concepts.

Les Baxter and Alan Livingston agreed that the best course of action was to build on Yma's exotic appeal. "We sat with Yma Sumac and listened to her natural incantation, or music, or whatever you might call it, which was totally foreign to anything that we know as Western music or European music or anything else. I give Les Baxter credit. He sat with her and managed to isolate certain portions of what she was doing to write and create a background to go with it."

Baxter's solution was to compose a type of musical suite of eight movements based on the "Incan chant" melodies given to him by Moisés. This became the now famous *Voice of the Xtabay* album. (Orchestral suites were obviously a form that intrigued Baxter. He wrote a number of others including his very successful next LP album, *Le Sacre du Sauvage,* as well as *The Passions* with the singer Bas Sheva, and *The Exotica Suite.*) As Baxter recalled in an interview with Gino Falzarano, (*DISCoveries Magazine,* 2/90):

"These were Incan folk melodies and I arranged them in a concert style. The studio musicians I used were concert masters from all the studios; Fox, MGM, everywhere, from all over the world. Those orchestras don't exist anymore because they don't carry them at the studios."

Actually, with their collaboration on *Voice of the Xtabay,* Yma Sumac and Les Baxter spearheaded the exotica movement. Although Les' first album with Capitol, *Music Out of the Moon,* might arguably be called the first album in the exotica genre, it is generally held that Yma's 1950 *Voice of the Xtabay* is the cornerstone. The next year, 1951, Baxter produced *Le Sacre du Sauvage* (Rituals of the Savage), which contained the song "Quiet Village." In 1956, Martin Denny added "Quiet Village" to his Honolulu lounge band's repertoire—complete with frog noises. By creating an arrangement suitable

Yma and Moisés, 1950 publicity shot

for any bar combo, Denny made the piece accessible to local bands that could add it to their repertoire for color. By about 1958 that song had become a sort of theme for the whole exotica genre, which had become a distinct musical category; but again, *Sacre du Sauvage* was recorded more than a year after Yma's *Voice of the Xtabay* had struck the sensibilities of the American public like a thunderbolt.)

In any case the one connecting thread in the swift development of this genre was certainly Les Baxter's gift for understanding current trends and exploiting the recording techniques of the day to produce albums full of exotic and, very importantly, entertaining sounds. (Les was extremely successful as a recording artist in his own right, with more than 30 albums during the course of his career, and in addition to recordings he was known for his over 250 scores for television, radio and film. This included such films of horror and the supernatural as *The Pit and the Pendulum* (his first atonal score), *The Raven, The Fall of the House of Usher, Frogs,* and *Black Sunday*—but one of his most famous compositions was the whistling theme on the TV series "Lassie."

Voice of the Xtabay also had the distinction of being the first long-playing record with a cover printed in full color. Even the titles for some of the songs on Baxter's albums pale in comparison to titles used for Yma's songs or albums: "Virgin of the Sun God," "Xtabay—Lure of the Unknown Love," "Kuyaway," "Legend of the Sun Virgin" and "Chuncho!" These descriptive titles, and the program notes that accompanied them, were of utmost importance for Yma's success with audiences during her international career. They were the gateway into Yma's musical realm.

By January of 1950, the Sumac ensemble was in Hollywood and staying at the Knickerbocker Hotel, compliments of the Capitol recording firm, preparing for their first sessions in North America. Simultaneous with the decision to record Yma with Baxter's assistance, decisions were also made concerning the promotion of the "newly discovered" singer and her recordings.

There were numerous meetings with the publicity people of Capitol Records to formulate plans for Yma's new image. Although in hindsight it is easy to say that serious mistakes were made at this time by the Capitol firm, it remains a fact that for many years, their publicity ploys worked exceedingly well with the American public. Eventually, however, all the clever fabrications and deceptions wore thin on American sensibilities. Times change and what had once been considered quaint was now considered tacky. (Along those lines, the web master of *Space Age Pop* muses with humor, "I've always wondered if 'Xtabay' was pig Latin for 'Baxter'.")

Yma now became suddenly altered. First, it was decided to slightly alter the spelling of her name from Imma Sumack to the somehow more American yet still exotic "Yma Sumac." The new name signaled the beginning of the Sumacian legends which were quickly fed to the world.

Years later, when Walter Rivers was shown a review of Yma's first Capitol disks, *Voice of the Xtabay,* a review which stressed that Capitol had taken "something which (was) essentially good and crummed it up, he grinned self consciously and said, 'We just used what we were given. Maybe we sweetened it up a bit. But we've learned our lesson.'" (James Poling, "The Most Exciting Voice in the World," *Collier's Magazine* 4/14/51)

What were some of the changes? First and of major consequence were those made to Yma's music and its presentation. Gone were the simple folk music and their authentic presentation in native costumes. Instead, glamour became the operating word. Similarly, Yma's singing lost its innocent simplicity and became almost conniving; complex in nature and execution. Exploitative emphasis was now placed on her unusual vocal range and "exotic" heritage. Yma's voice, originally put to the service of Peruvian folk melodies, was now promoted as a gimmick in itself.

From all private accounts, it seems that initially, Yma was very unhappy and resentful of the changes she was required to make in herself, her singing and music. Being fiercely independent by temperament, she disliked being told what to do by managers, agents and recording companies. She listened to Moisés, but he was her husband, and she trusted him.

Still—out of necessity, desperation, and a very real fear of not succeeding, she quickly learned to adapt and accept the "new" Sumac direction. One must remember that those few months of early 1950 were crucial for Yma and Moisés. For the first time in her career Yma had the opportunity to make recordings with a first-class, international recording firm and the future of her career depended upon the success of this venture. If she truly wanted to succeed she could not afford to create problems with the firm. Both she and Moisés doubted that another such opportunity would come along. This was their only chance.

Actually, the alterations made to Yma's singing were only the culmination of an evolution that had begun before her pairing with Capitol Records. By the time Hernán Braña first met the group, Yma's voice had settled into a homogenous column of rich beauty and uncommon vocal poise. It was just after Hernán joined the trio in 1949 that various changes began to manifest themselves in the structure and arrangements of the ensemble's music and, consequently, Yma's singing. Through his arrangements Hernán introduced certain aspects of his own musical heritage into the ensemble's music.

It is interesting, however, that when confronted with this fact, Hernán was absolutely adamant that Moisés was responsible for Yma's outré vocal effects. Moisés readily accepts the honor. When directly asked, Yma was evasive except to state that she taught herself to sing and that she is responsible for her improvisations.

But listening tells a different story.

One has only to compare Yma's 1943 Odeon recordings, before Hernán was part of the group, with her more famous Capitol recordings of the 1950s, after Hernán's influence had been completely integrated into the ensemble, to understand the tremendous influence he exerted over the group and their music. For, although the early recordings boast an ethnic innocence and musical naiveté that had its own merits, nowhere is there the professional, complicated and imaginative arrangements that became the Sumac trademark during her heyday. Many of Yma's most intriguing vocal effects derive from the Afro-Cuban musical tradition. It was not until Hernán's influence that one finds the distinctive use of intricate operatic coloratura flights highlighted and contrasted by coloristic and bizarre vocalism. Hernán, as did Moisés, recognized Yma's enormous potential for imitative singing. But he pushed this much harder. He guided and encouraged Yma to play with her resonances, find new sounds, colors and expressionistic devices and explore the complete capabilities of her instrument. Under the guidance of both Moisés and Hernán, Yma found she relished this type of eccentric and exhibitionistic singing. Soon she surpassed even Moisés' expectations. Yma quickly developed into a masterful colorist capable of changing the timbre and vibrato of her voice at will, and a technician capable of ricocheting from one register to another within seconds. By the time Capitol Records became seriously involved in the Sumac project, Yma had finished her exotica studies and was ready to startle the world. Whereas before, bizarre vocal effects were reserved for rare special moments, now they were freely incorporated. The only problem was that the vocal effects were disorganized.

Capitol decided that since Yma was such an obviously enigmatic and exotic singer, both in manner and in her repertoire, they would build on this to create an equally unusual and exotic product for the American people. The recording firm was taking a chance with the strange, unknown singer but decided to use all their imagination and creativity in solving the problem of making her accessible to the American public. New clothes, make-up techniques, and jewelry were deliberated on and then carefully selected for Yma, and her diet was intensified. Yma soon carried only 110 pounds on her 5 foot, 1-inch frame.

This was the fulcrum of the fantastic Incan Priestess/Princess theme concocted with the use of glamorous costuming, exotic biographical "information" and a clever but gimmicky emphasis on Yma's now huge vocal range and unique style of singing. Capitol's publicity writers worked overtime and Yma metamorphosed into a mysterious figure shrouded in legends, a woman sacred to the Peruvian Indians. In what amounted to a brazen defiance of history, Capitol publicists and writers ignored the fact that Yma had been performing as a successful folk artist in South America for a number of years (and was, incidentally, a wife and mother) and re-created her as an entirely new entity. Colorfully descriptive Peruvian-English titles became synonymous with the name Yma Sumac:

"Intypa Wawan" (Daughter of the Sun)
"Accla Sumac" (Chosen Sumac)
"Accla K'ory" (Chosen One of Gold)
"The Bird That Became Woman"
"Princess In Service to the Sun"
"Golden Virgin"

"Virgin of the Sun"
"Voice of the Earthquake, Voice of the Birds"

Taking Yma's Peruvian heritage in hand, press agents built upon the Incan theme with a vengeance. She soon began to resemble a mythical character from an H. Rider Haggard romance novel. Bejeweled, mysterious, deified, she was recreated into a Peruvian relic.

The problems with this publicity did not arise immediately but there were always certain problems apparent. As James Poling noted in his article "The Most Exciting Voice in the World" (*Collier's Magazine* 4/14/51): "The 'Chosen Maiden' tale is an excellent example of what happens when a press agent's mind is overstimulated. Of the 30,000 Indians said to have risen in protest against Yma's journey into the lowlands, only one has been uncovered. Dona Emilia Atahualpa Chavarri [Yma's mother] at first protested very vigorously against the plan to have her daughter 'sing for profanos.' Yma, with one of her rare smiles, says, 'Mama seem like 30,000.'"

It was at this time, too that a fantastic Yma Sumac biographical machine was invented that would spew out to newspapers and magazines all over the world "facts" concerning the mysterious singer's early life and vocal abilities. It was the beginning of a fascinating international career—but it was also the beginning of the end. The Capitol-created Yma Sumac persona was doomed from the beginning. Her unusual voice and its capabilities automatically set her apart from other performers—a situation reinforced by her musical material. For the entirety of her career Yma was confined to a special niche. Her very uniqueness eventually phased her into relative obscurity and precluded any possibility for artistic expansion or musical growth. Alan Livingston observed during an interview for the 1991 German documentary film, "*Yma Sumac, Hollywood's Inkaprinzessin*" by Günter Czernetzky:

> When an artist has a hit record or a hit album, as (Yma) had, even if they never have a hit record again or a successful album again, that record can last them for almost a lifetime. They can play Las Vegas and they can play Miami, and they can play Chicago and New York; and they can play clubs, because it just has become a standard. Yma Sumac, unfortunately, could not follow that up because she did only her own native thing. She could not sing songs as such. She could not go into a nightclub and do a whole repertoire. So it was very difficult for her to take full advantage of her success. She had to do what she did and was confined to that. And therefore, it was not possible for her to have the kind of career that somebody can who has a tremendous hit record . . . which they can then follow up with additional records, additional songs and hopefully have another hit, or if not, at least have the kind of identity which makes them a box office draw in a nightclub. Yma Sumac had it for a while, but she was working under the handicap of the limitations of the kind of music that she did. So her career had to fade. She was in too narrow a channel to take advantage of what might have been great opportunities."

In 1950, however, all this was far from anyone's minds. All concentration was on propelling Yma into the world's sensibilities with as much imaginative force and fanfare as possible. Considering the problems that Yma and Moisés faced when first pursuing their career in America, the question arises: Why were they successful in 1950 and not earlier? What factors were responsible for her breakthrough and international popularity? In an article for *Records and Recording*, "The Legendary Sumac," (11/79), Maurice Leonard provides some insight:

> [S]he was absolutely right for her time. Many artists have suffered from being ahead of their time, and others have paid because they could not keep up with the

An iconic shot, for *Voice of the Xtabay* used by permission of Tom Kelley Studios, Ventura, CA

times. When Yma Sumac made her debut (and by debut I refer to the by now historic 1950 Hollywood Bowl recital, not the times she sang in near obscurity, preceding that date) the popular music scene was arid. Safely competent singers sang ballads which had not changed in basic format since Roses of Picardy. And in the area of serious music there were few good singers about, as Grove's Dictionary of Music and Musicians puts it, referring to the 1950s "there are few who will deny the present inferiority in the art of singing."

She burst upon this sterility by offering a voice of great loveliness and range, and implementing a technique superior to most of her operatic peers, specializing in the unlikely, but to the public, quite new field of sacred Incan chants and Peruvian folk music. An uncompromising field, and one fraught with danger, for apart from the recondite nature of the material—which most impresarios felt would leave the general public cold, hence her pre-1950 period of neglect—the way she sang could well have alienated both the serious and popular arena. But instead, the unlikely reverse happened, and everyone was intrigued.

One has to remember that rock and roll had yet to take over the popular music scene in America. The first rock and roll song to make number one on the charts would be Bill Haley's "Rock around the Clock" and that was not until June 29, 1955.

There was also a peculiar situation in the area of classical music during the 1940s and 1950s that contributed to Yma's allure. This was the public's fascination with artists who had what must be termed "freak voices." The careers of such European singers as the German soprano Erna Sack and the French soprano Mado Robin, both of whom could ascend to rarified regions of the voice, were avidly followed by audiences and record collectors. Yma fit in nicely with such vocal phenomena.

Another factor was that Yma Sumac was immediately controversial. This practically guaranteed her success, at least for a time (it might, of course, also have ensured that her success would be short-lived). Public responses included everything from skepticism to hysteria. Audiences adored her, hated her, or found her highly suspect, but no one heard her recordings or left her concerts without feeling strongly one way or another. Audiences loved the mystery that surrounded Yma. As an article in the weekly magazine of that time *Quick* (1/28/52) notes: "No one has yet been able to prove anything about Yma. No one has really tried. The U.S. loves a mystery, and Yma Sumac is one of the best."

This love of a mystery that American audiences preferred at that time stemmed from a reactionary romanticism prompted by the atrocities that occurred during the Second World War. uring the 1950s, this situation was catered to by the voluminous number of "tiki" and "jungle music" exotica recordings that were so popular at the time. These lush orchestral impressions of jungle life and obscure African tribal rituals were manna to cosmopolitan listeners who craved an escape from the left-over horrors that surrounded them. Mysteries and secrets were exciting, safe contemplations for listeners. Composers such as Les Baxter provided audiences with atmospheric, colorful and inventive compositions that lured them away from the day's problems and took them on exotic excursions to unknown, and safe, fantasy regions.

Those (most of us, now) who have grown up after the advent of television may find it hard to imagine, but at the time of Yma's tremendous surge into celebrity, television was still barely a factor in it—much of the public did not own television sets. They relied mainly on the radio and recordings for their entertainment. As if building on the premise of Baxter's popular recordings, Capitol neatly edged Yma into a new, profitable, corner of their enterprise. If listeners found Baxter's *Music Out of the Moon* (Capitol T390) 10" recording (1947) full of mysterious power and surprises, Yma's album of three years later had a jolt equal to the electrical charge of a flash of lightning.

It is also important to remember that Yma's homeland, Peru, was still very exotic to most audiences and listeners. Distance lent the Peruvian empire a certain enchantment for Americans. Even now, to see a picture of the mysterious ruins of Machu-Picchu on the heights overlooking the Urubamba River, the viewer cannot help but be struck by the awesome beauty of the landscape. The complex of terraces and temple ruins with mountains rising in the distance covered with mists and carpeted with luxurious greenery—the romantic impulse of something mysterious and unexplained is undeniable. All of this having much the same allure as the temple of Angkor Wat in Cambodia, the Mayan sacred sacrificial well (cenote) of Chichen Itza, or the pyramids of Egypt. Taking all this into consideration, one begins to understand the public's fascination with the exotic in the 1950s.

Why did Yma willingly promote the Incan romance? I believe the reason is simple. It was done out of necessity. It was intimated to her by those in charge that if she wanted success in America, she had no choice. Stimulating her willingness to obey her management would have been the still fresh memories of failures with U.S. audiences. It is also important to realize that Yma feared being categorized as an ethnic performer. Ironically, despite her caution, she was typed as such during her early years in America when "[She stuck to Peruvian folk-music—and was promptly 'typed' as a purveyor of ethnic musical oddities.]" (*Pathfinder Magazine*, 11/11/50)

Also, the royalty aspect of the Incan concept obviously appealed to Yma's vivid imagination. It was as grand a concept as she was a theatrical personality. It was a wonderful game of fantasy which appealed to the ingenuous side of her nature and it was a part that she could play with aplomb.

There was, of course, a price to be paid. For the time being, however, she and the Sumac publicity machine were on a roll. Articles such as the *Pathfinder*, did not hurt either. After claiming that she had lived down the tendency to be considered an ethnic performer, they noted that: "nightclubs, radio and concert managers are on her trail. So is Hollywood, where sharp-eyed scouts noticed that Yma has assets which have nothing to do with music but which would look well in a sarong." (ibid)

Yma's life soon became one of managerial dictates. Provided with a primer of instruction, she was expected to follow the manual as a sort of catechism. This set of rules included everything from the color of her nail polish to the admonition that she sleep without a pillow in order (somehow) to maintain her chin line. In view of her fierce determination to have a career in America, it is not surprising that she followed the primer to the note.

Occasionally, she resented such an existence, complaining that her managers drove her "like mula." Generally, however, Yma complied with her managers' demands, although she often felt much of the fuss was senseless. "Everyone get jitters, do this, do that. He's important . . . she's big thing. Bah! . . . But Sunday is my own day. Every Sunday—every one—I can go to the movies." (James Poling, "The Most Exciting Voice in the World," *Collier's*, 4/14/51)

The deliberately concocted Incan legends and fabrications were merely a necessary ingredient in the mixture that Yma Sumac had become in the hands of her publicists, and in the imagination of Moisés, who provided agents with the pertinent information. Yma herself became so immersed in the magic of the fairytales that she began to believe them. When, in later years, Yma became difficult to work with, one of the reasons was that she felt she had been artistically abused and grossly misrepresented. In many ways she was. It must have been very painful for her to realize that while she had hoped to see her name become synonymous with artistic imagination and integrity, it had, at the last, become indiscernible from fraud and hype.

But there is another issue. Despite her tremendous initial popularity there was a crucial musical factor that limited Yma's continued public appeal. This was her inability to conform to accepted modes of musical expression. Part of the problem lay in her simple inability to comprehend the basic mechanics of the European singing tradition. But it was also due to her earliest training and guidance under Moisés. Always an imitator, during her vocal development and early career Yma was rightly encouraged to develop and perfect this gift. Unfortunately, this eventually prevented her from being able to sing a simple, prewritten vocal line without superimposing her own "ideas" over the melody. Her manner of singing was so rooted in an improvisational viewpoint that her entire technique of singing and breathing were controlled by it.

When confronted with music that had specific, accepted spots for breathing and phrasing, such as operatic arias, musical comedy songs or art songs, Yma was confounded by their structural requirements, which tended to be completely contrary to her particular method of singing. Undaunted, she sang them anyway, inaccurately. Musically she remained a law unto herself, governed entirely by her moods and whims. As extraordinary an accomplishment as it was to have single-handedly invented an entirely new way of performing popular music, it was at the same time extremely limiting. Everything that Yma Sumac sang, whether a Peruvian folk-song, an "Incan chant," an adaptation of a Debussy piano piece, an operatic aria, or a hit song from a musical comedy, was sung in the "Yma Sumac style." This was the paradox—the switchback, the dead-end—that was built into her career. Although the act of improvisation is a freeing of certain musical restraints, in Yma's case it also became seriously confining. Because of the tremendous emphasis she placed on her idiosyncratic vocal effects, Yma was never able to achieve a normal artistic balance that would enable her to sing in whatever music genre was current.

On the positive side, Yma's idiosyncratic way of singing lent to all her performances, whether in front of an audience or in the recording studio, an undeniably individual quality, a spontaneous freshness found nowhere else. With Yma Sumac the very act of singing, of expressing oneself through music, reached a peak of almost ecstatic immediacy. It is this ecstasy that is communicated to the listener and it is this that is unforgettable.

Imma Sumack had become Yma Sumac and the legends had begun.

In February of 1950, Yma went into the Melrose Recording Studios in Los Angeles to begin recording her first Capitol album. Les Baxter had composed and/or arranged music for the eight selections that had been chosen to be included in the album. The titles were indicative of the type of descriptive material that would soon appear on her concert and night club programs in the coming decades:

"Taita Inty" (Virgin of the Sun God, Hymn to the Sun)
"Ataypura" (High Andes)
"Accla Taqui" (Chant of the Chosen Maidens)
"Tumpa!" (Earthquake!)
"Choladas" (Dance of the Moon Festival)
"Wayra" (Dance of the Winds)
"Monos" (Monkeys)
"Xtabay" (Lure of the Unknown Love)

Although Baxter's original concept for the album was that it be a series of numbers that formed a suite, each piece is actually its own entity; they are of course linked together by Yma's unusual singing and Baxter's lush orchestrations. It was a concept that would also be maintained for her next solo album, *Legend of the Sun Virgin* in 1951. As David Troop wrote: "Baxter draws on his love of Maurice Ravel's sensual exoticism for the Yma Sumac arrangements. Though Ravel's exotica was inspired by slightly less remote sources, his attachment to artificial otherness can be likened to Baxter's. *The Voice of the Xtabay* is so clearly odd, a kitsch eccentricity that nevertheless endures through its originality, that the question of authenticity refuses to be heard. The music depicts a mystery that archeology and other sciences of disinterment can only spoil." (*Exotica*, Serpent's Tail, London 1999)

Though few know it, the sessions for these, Yma's first North American recordings, were complicated and controversial. About a week before the sessions were to begin, Yma was given a copy of the orchestral soundtracks of the songs so that she could familiarize herself with the accompaniment. Moisés and Hernán went over the music with her and suggested spots to ad-lib and the type of improvisations she could use. Yma entered the studio with some basic ideas that still had to be organized.

From reports, it seems that Moisés felt put upon. With Baxter in charge of the recording project, and Livingston in charge of Baxter, Moisés was no longer in control, and certain insecurities of his now came to the fore. As one colleague, who preferred not to be named, told me: "Moisés would always say things like 'I taught her this', or 'I did that.' He kept her apart from others so that they dealt only with him. That's why he didn't want her to learn English. He purposefully kept her ignorant of business affairs. She knew nothing about what was going on. Moisés could be ruthless in dealing with people about engagements and he always tried to out-connive them."

Les Baxter found Yma fascinating but exasperating—likable but temperamental. "She had a great talent and a fiery temper. She was child-like and very wise. She could read things in my personality instantly. Children can do that. She was, however, difficult to work with. It was very hard to convince Yma and Moisés of anything. It was a battle all the way. There was a great deal of pride there. To preserve that, there was a great deal of

1950—First ad for *Xtabay*

ceremony and mystery. When I would meet with them, or before a recording session, Yma gargled with white wine and knelt in prayer to the Sun God—either a gold image, or a picture they had on the wall." (Les Baxter, private conversation, 1981)

Baxter remembered Moisés' behavior during the sessions vividly. "Vivanco wanted to be considered the Gershwin of South America but I found he couldn't read or write music, even though he said he could. And when it came time to play the guitar, he always developed arthritis." (ibid)

In a January 24, 1995 interview with James Call and Peter Huestis ("Les Baxter: Godfather of Exotica," *Hypno*, Spring Issue 1995) Les Baxter further wryly commented: "(He) was a pain in the butt. . . . He had no ability whatever, in anything." In that same article, Baxter told of an incident between him and Moisés during the recording sessions concerning the compositions being used for the *Xtabay* recordings. (Baxter had related the same story to me in a 1981 phone conversation.) "One day [Moisés] said, 'You stole from me.' And I said, 'How did I steal from you?' He said, 'Well, you stole my note, B flat.' That's an honest to God true story. 'You stole my note!'"

Despite such problems, Baxter was fascinated with Yma's voice. "I liked the wild, unrestrained ad-libbing folk talent. It was so unusual and is what made the recordings possible. I don't think you could have done it with a trained soprano, it would have sounded too polished." (Les Baxter, private conversation, 1981)

When asked about the music he was given to work with to produce the songs on the album, Baxter said, "That's difficult. The tunes were highly derivative and mixed up; part 'Incan' [he means Peruvian] and part Puccini—but, you see, Yma had always wanted to sing Puccini. She talked about opera frequently and had always wanted to sing *Madama Butterfly* and *La Boheme*. 'Taita Inty', for example, is a mixture. Part of the piece is traditional, very old Peruvian melody, part is opera, and part is ad-lib distinctly based on South American music. Combined with this is a lot of Afro-Cuban influence in the ad-lib. Yma came out with some absolutely remarkable phrases."(ibid)

There were problems, however, from the beginning of the sessions. As Baxter remembers, "Yma was extremely independent. I don't know exactly why, but I suspect it had to do with a complicated mixture of insecurity, being in a new situation, not being able to easily communicate in English, and pride." Moisés, on the other hand, was simply "egotistical. No talent whatsoever." (ibid)

Alan Livingston remembers the communication problems vividly. "[Yma] was a very sensitive person and because the communication was so difficult, it was not always easy to get through to her. I had to be very careful not to make a statement which might upset her, or be misunderstood. I remember in one case I had asked for some kind of a document. I don't remember what it was, but it was a document—a proof of something. And she brought me this thing from Peru, which was a piece of very poor grade paper, brown paper with purple ink on it. It was supposed to be an important document. . . . I looked at it and made the remark without thinking, 'My goodness, they certainly use cheap paper down there!' She became very upset, took it as an insult to her and her country and wouldn't speak to me for a week!

"She was an extremely talented woman. She did not have any musical education. She did not have the advantage of being taught music or learning to read music, or anything else, it was just within her. She grew up with it. It was very hard to channel, but the talent was certainly there. She was a very sweet person, but so foreign to our way of life and to our music and to everything we were doing. It was very difficult to go beyond. Because of the relationship—I always spoke to her through an interpreter—it was very difficult to encourage her . . . to go beyond what she did." (Interview in *Yma Sumac, Hollywood's Inkaprinzessin* by Günter Czernetzky)

A number of arguments erupted during the recording sessions between Yma and Moisés, Yma and Les, Les and Moisés. But then arguments were not uncommon in the Vivanco household. As if baiting Yma's fiery temper and volatility, Moisés' practice at this time was to pinch her painfully just before she went on stage to sing. He felt she sang better when angry.

Being constantly told what to sing and when to sing it obviously did not elevate Yma's mood. Despite the importance of the sessions, which Yma recognized, she was irritated at all the outside musical supervision.

Les Baxter remembers definite musical and production problems. "It was hard to get her to do what we wanted. She was an instinctive musician but at the time we had trouble getting her to sing in the right octave! ... When we were rehearsing for *Voice of the Xtabay* Yma would sing a marvelous high phrase and I would say: 'OK! Now, Yma, could you do it again the same way for the recording take?' 'Oh yes,' she'd answer. Then we would start the taping machines and she would start growling—three octaves lower! It was impossible!" (Les Baxter, private conversation, 1981)

The recording sessions were long and seemed to take forever—Yma's problems with repeating vocal effects in sequence causing serious problems. Alan Livingston remembers: "Because she did not read music, we had to determine which portions of her music we were using and we would sit by the hour and record very small sections with the orchestra. We would do this bit, by bit, by bit . . . because there was no way to channel what she was doing into written music, as we were used to working with. I can't remember how many sessions there were, but we must have spent a total of at least 30 or 40 hours in the studio, recording her in sections with the orchestra and then sitting for hours afterwards, piecing them together." (Interview from *Yma Sumac, Hollywood's Inkaprinzessin* by Günter Czernetzky)

This situation caused great frustrations with the recording team.

"There were many, many takes and much editing," Les Baxter remembers. "We only took the best parts. Her talent, through Moisés, was great—but disorganized. All I did was organize it for her and give it those lush backgrounds, the voice and orchestra blending into one. We did hundreds of edits. For instance, Yma would run up a scale and have to hit a high F-sharp, which is a hard thing to do. On tape you can take each portion from different takes. Finally, we were just putting notes in and eventually spliced-in the high F-sharp. It is not the performance of a 'live' person. It was a performance put together on tape. That is why, at first, she had trouble doing it live.

Yma with Jerry Hopper, director of *Secret of the Incas*, c.1954

"But," insisted Baxter, "you must remember we now live in a world of 24 and 32 tracks. All the rock artists record on endless tracks, which provide multiple choices. It is also a world of endless editing so that only the best takes and sections are used to make the most perfect record possible. It is no insult to Yma to say, and to recognize, that we were really pioneers in that field. This is also not to say that *Voice of the Xtabay* is a false representation of Yma—that she could not do what was on that recording. Everything there is real. It is just that it had to be organized into some kind of cohesive musical form." (Les Baxter, private conversation, 1981)

Despite the tremendous problems in harnessing Yma's unrestrained singing, Les Baxter enjoyed producing the album. "There is a unique mystery in producing sounds and ideas you feel the public will want to hear. I presented Yma the way I felt she should be presented, and I feel there is an agelessness there in the Xtabay selections. I took the things Yma did that I felt were either commercial or vocally spectacular. Since I had a background in concert composing, Jazz and all that, I felt I knew the kind of things people would want to hear; the high staccati, the growling . . . ." (ibid)

Despite the problems Yma encountered making *Voice of the Xtabay*, of all her albums it remains her favorite, especially the chaste "Taita Inty" (Hymn to the Sun). "My favorite (album) is *Xtabay*. There are two songs which are my favorites, Hymn to the Sun and Forest Creatures (Chuncho)."

When the sessions were completed for *Voice of the Xtabay*, Alan Livingston was impressed. "(It) was . . . phenomenal—a very unusual album. We didn't know what to call it at the time. (Yma) came up with the idea of 'Xtabay' and we did not know what that meant. It meant something to her, so we called it *Voice of the Xtabay*." (Interview from *Yma Sumac, Hollywood's Inkaprinzessin* by Günter Czernetzky)

In an interview with Matt Groening, then a music critic for the underground paper *LA Reader*, 3/30/84, Yma tells a different story about the choosing of the title of "*Voice of the Xtabay*": "That's no Peruvian name. I don't know why Capitol records choose that, maybe for exotic name, you know. That comes from Mexico I think, meaning princess from the Azteca civilization."

After *Voice of the Xtabay* was completed and all the necessary editing done, Hernán Braña was given the responsibility of quickly transcribing the "new, after-editing" versions of the songs onto music manuscript. Because of the extensive editing done by Capitol technicians, listeners may notice that some songs have odd, irregular measures. As Hernán recalls, "Because of this editing, I had to set down the new added measures and then Yma had to relearn the pieces in their new form for her public performances." (A good example of this irregularity can be heard on the album in "Tumpa!" in the sequence containing the high F-sharp.)

For a while the recordings remained unpublished. Their release was preceded by an appearance Yma made at the Hollywood Bowl. This, too, has had a number of legends appended to it. According to Hernán, it was a prestigious job that Moisés managed to secure for Yma. It has also been intimated, however, that Capitol Records arranged for the appearance in order to introduce Yma to America and subsequently to get record sales moving. It was also rumored that after hearing Yma sing and examining Moisés' music, Sigmund Romberg arranged for the performance.

The summer concert was a pops-folk event that was to be conducted by the famous orchestral conductor, Arthur Fiedler. Moisés decided that for this important concert Yma should sing pieces that she had recorded for Capitol, banking on the fact that they would be shortly released. It was decided that she would sing three of her favorite pieces, ones that would soon become her most famous: "Ataypura" (High Andes), "Tumpa!", and the haunting "Taita Inty."

There was, however, an amusing incident shortly before the Hollywood Bowl concert was to go into rehearsal. "I'll never forget," said Baxter, "Arthur Fiedler, the conductor for the concert, called me on the telephone. He knew I had worked with Yma but he didn't know anything about her or her musicianship. He asked me if she could read music and whether she was a good musician—you know, would she come in at the right time for her musical entrances? I told him Yma couldn't even come in on the right octave!" (Les Baxter, private conversation, 1981)

On August 12, 1950, without any advance publicity, Yma appeared on the stage of the Hollywood Bowl and took the audience by storm. Standing in a rather plain, traditional peasant costume she sang her numbers—and everything changed. Yma Sumac had arrived. *Time Magazine* reported on August 28, 1950: "For the first few bars of a Peruvian folk chant called High Andes the full figured Peruvian girl on stage rumbled roundly at the bottom of contralto range. Then to [the audience's] astonishment, she soared effortlessly up a full four octaves, began trilling like a canary at the top of coloratura. At the end of her first song, the audience was still too surprised to raise more than warm applause. The second, 'Tumpa' . . . brought cheers; after the third, a pyrotechnical Inca Hymn to the Sun, the applause and cheers swelled to a roar for encores. Guest conductor Arthur Fiedler, who had a plane to catch, was obliged to break up the demonstration by launching his orchestra into Tchaikovsky's noisy Marche Slav."

Albert Goldberg of *The Sounding Board*, wrote: "It is difficult to convey in words just what this extraordinary singer accomplishes. The three songs she sang . . . obviously represent a type of exotic folk music that has not before been exploited on the concert stage . . . One instant she sings in the chesty, sensuous tones of a contralto, and the next moment she is caroling in the stratosphere in a species of birdlike coloratura that is as technically astounding as it is musically weird. Add to this the strange patter of a quick succession of babbling syllables, and you get a musical effect that has to be heard to be believed."

The August 28th *Time Magazine* review mentioned above also elicited some strong reaction concerning the photograph used. In April of 1988, JK of the online *Der Blauegeiger, A Journal of Gonzo Musicology from Vienna and America,* noted, "Even I find the picture of [Yma] in the 28 August 1950 issue of *Time Magazine* a little shocking. Not because I'm shocked by the sight of large amounts of cleavage, but because it's hard to believe she would have let someone give her quite this much of that kind of image, in the 50s, in America." He quotes from an interesting article by Hal Holly from *Downbeat*, October 20, 1951: "We told [her agent, John] Rose that Downbeat readers were old enough to see a photo of Yma like the one published in Time, but Rose, who still insists that the singer didn't know what that little box the man was pointing at her was a camera, said firmly that there will be no more 'art' of that type permitted to get around."

JK continues: "Sure. Like, 'Here, you lean forward, put your head back, and I'll point this thing down your dress. No problem, babe, right?' Happens every day, back home in Ichocán. I mean, Boucicault used that old 'child of nature, doesn't know what a camera is' routine in *The Octaroon* in 1859. It's getting a bit old."

Although not mentioned in reviews of this famous concert, I was told by Hernán Braña (who was present) that Yma's segment did not begin as smoothly as reported. In his account, during her first song, "Ataypura," Fiedler cued Yma to begin singing a number of times without success. Seemingly confused by what she heard from the orchestra and not recognizing the musical cue, or Fiedler's conducting, she could not find her way into the song. This went on until Moisés suddenly rushed onto the stage and "told" Fiedler that he was not conducting the piece correctly. Moisés then proceeded to conduct, beginning the song once again. Miraculously, this time Yma entered correctly.

Some important people were in that audience. N. Peter Rathvon, a former head of RKO Pictures production and now an independent producer, had had Yma in mind for a film version of the W. H. Hudson novel *Green Mansions*. He invited a number of the film industry's most influential people to hear Yma's concert. Their presence eventually led to the two movies in which she appeared ("Secret of the Incas," in 1954 and "Omar Khayyam," in 1957). But when a film of *Green Mansions* was produced in 1959, Audrey Hepburn was chosen for the role Rima.

The furor that Yma caused at the Hollywood Bowl concert did not abate. Soon, people were clamoring for her recordings. With the aid of John Rose, now Yma's manager, Capitol decided it was time to release the Xtabay disks, which had been on the shelf for 6 months. They were rapidly prepared—in some cases too rapidly: a number of blatant errors were made that later would haunt the recording firm. The original release was an album of 4 78-rpm disks, with 45 rpm disks, a 10" long-playing album and a double 45-rpm EP album following soon after.

One of the first problems that arose was that the listing of the album's contents on the record sleeve did not match the order of the songs as they played (at least on the 10" LP).

Listing on the Cover	Playing Order
"Xtabay" (Lure of the Unknown Love)	"Taita Inty"
"Wayra" (Dance of the Winds)	"Ataypura"
"Accla Taqui"(Chant of the Chosen Maidens)	"Accla Taqui"
"Choladas" (Dance of the Moon Festival)	"Tumpa!"
"Taita Inty" (Virgin of the Sun God)	"Choladas"
"Ataypura" (High Andes)	"Wayra"
"Tumpa!" (Earthquake!)	"Monos"
"Monos" (Monkeys)	"Xtabay"

This was especially annoying for listeners because of the unfamiliarity of Yma's repertoire, not only confusing but even to some degree undermining the establishment of recognition and familiarity that pop success partly depends on. To determine the right name of the songs you were listening to you had first to refer to the label on the disks, and then manually number the listing on the back of the album to reflect the correct playing sequence. It wasn't until 1956, when *Voice of the Xtabay* was paired with Yma's third album, *Inca Taqui,* and issued on a 12" LP, that this problem was corrected.

The color cover of the 78 r.p.m. first release of *Voice of the Xtabay* (and most subsequent releases) was one of the most famous and the most evocative of all the exotic photographs taken of Yma by the distinctive photographer, Tom Kelley (1914–1984). It was Tom Kelley who took the iconic photographs that are now indelibly associated with the singer. Through his own art, he took Yma's already striking beauty and transformed it into something almost unearthly.

Tom Kelley was born in Philadelphia, but it was in California, where he moved in 1935, that his fame as one of the preeminent photographers of celebrities was established with sensitive portraits of such people as Gary Cooper, Greta Garbo, James Cagney, Clark Gable, Winston Churchill, Bob Hope, Marlene Dietrich, Joan Crawford, Jack Benny, John F. Kennedy, Dwight D. Eisenhower, Franklin D. Roosevelt and, of course, Marilyn Monroe. Probably the most famous of the Tom Kelley photographs is the nude "red velvet" series of photos taken of Marilyn Monroe on May 27, 1949, which included the immortal centerfold photo in the inaugural edition of Playboy Magazine.

For *Voice of the Xtabay*, Kelley photographed Yma dressed in Peruvian high-ceremonial garb and much jewelry. The striking cover (probably her most famous portrait) shows Yma with arms raised, palms uplifted ritualistically. Her name appears as though hewn in rock and the effect is immediately arresting. The clever fantasy is enhanced by an angry, erupting volcano in the background and a partially visible ancient stone effigy in the lower right-hand corner. It was a superb creation with its riotous colors and exotic typeface, unlike anything seen in record stores before. Over the next decade, Tom Kelley took hundreds of photographs of Yma and today, many of them remain iconic. More than anyone else, Tom was able to capture (even in black and white) the mysterious allure that surrounded Yma.

The initial publicity for *Voice of the Xtabay*, which was released in September of 1950, was a tiny advertisement in an obscure journal. Produced by Alan Livingston, *Voice of the Xtabay* sold 5,000 copies in one day, thanks entirely to fevered word of mouth. The entire first pressing was sold out within one week. Capitol quickly issued another pressing. This was sold out by October and so another pressing was released at that time, and still another in January of 1951. Publicity for the records remained confined to small items in magazines. In early December of 1950, for instance, *The New Yorker* carried a tiny ad that boasted a photograph of the album cover but simply said "the album *everyone* is talking about. Acclaimed the most exciting musical event of our generation . . . Yma Sumac's album is again available at your record dealer."

Before long, almost everyone knew of the mysterious singer from Peru with the four octaves. One woman, not sure of Yma's name or how to pronounce it, went into a Madison Avenue record shop in Manhattan and asked for the records of "the girl with the alphabet voice; you know, it goes from A to Z." The clerk knew exactly whom she meant. The signature name "Alphabet Voice" soon became common when referring to the exotic Peruvian singer. Headlines in the Parisian *Samedi Soir* (5/12/51) inventively read: "The 'Alphabet' voice of an Incan Sun Worshipper Princess astounds Paris." (Translation, Anna Schumate)

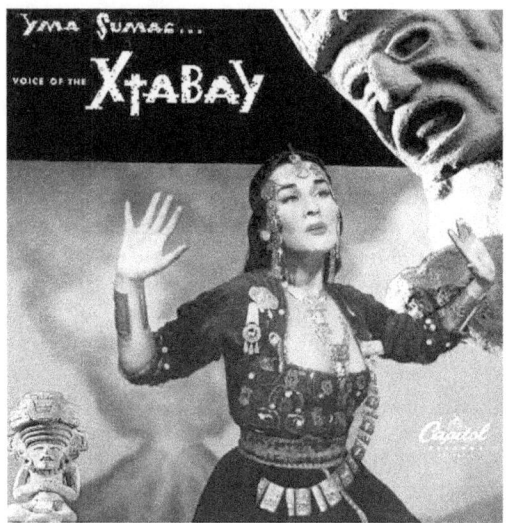

By the end of 1950 and after only a few months of its release, *Voice of the Xtabay* was #1 on Variety's best-seller list. Reviews of the album were generally good, although at a loss to describe Yma or her music. Baxter remembers a bad review that *Voice of the Xtabay* received from one of the technical magazines. "It was written by a very irate person who felt I had 'hollywood-ized' Yma with my 'movie-score' orchestration; that I had destroyed a good folk artist. My thought in retaliation is that I disagree. I don't feel I destroyed her. I presented her to the world and she was heard because of it. She sold no records in North America as a folk artist." (Les Baxter, private conversation 1981)

In his 1999 book, *Exotica*, David Toop disagrees: "Melodramatic tone poems, [the songs on *Voice of the Xtabay*] trade shamelessly upon the ignorance of record buyers by mixing Baxter's atmospherics—chiming percussion and piano, trembling flutes, shivering strings—with Hollywood Afro-Cubanissimo, either quasi-ritualistic or cha-cha-cha. Nothing musical can be traced to South America, despite the vivid sleeve-note descriptions of Incan hymns, Andean mountain grandeur, Peruvian monkey calls and Aztec Princes." (*Exotica*, Serpents Tail, London, 1999)

As one might expect, in time listeners began to become suspicious of traditional, ancient Incan chants being framed in a distinct cha-cha-cha beat. The suspicion quickly moved from the product to its creator. Often an artist must accept compromises in order to achieve the success they desire. These compromises may affect their private life, their art or, as in Yma's case, both. Artists usually find ways to accommodate the compromise. In Yma's case, however, she was never able to completely put aside her folk roots. As years passed, it seems as if both she and Moisés attempted to re-integrate into her singing and repertoire as much of her original folk roots as possible. Her greatest concessions, however, concerned the complete revamping of her singing style and the vulgar commercialism of her music, which smacked of American exploitation at its worst. When the era of the 1950s passed and a new musical culture took precedence, these compromises (originally made in good faith) were to haunt Yma.

Despite its success, after *Voice of the Xtabay* Les Baxter's name was conspicuously absent whenever the singer toured or recorded. In order to show that it was her talent that made her a success and not the trappings with which Baxter surrounded her, Yma broke away from Les and his influence. Baxter was not surprised at this: "Any great artist might do the same. I think it is only natural. We've used this director. I'm the artist, now I'll show him and everyone. I'll get a new director. It's another way of saying 'I'm in control, I can do it myself'." (Les Baxter, private conversation 1981)

Not surprisingly, Yma's new director was Moisés. The question as to whether Yma and Les would have made a viable team over the years is unanswerable. It is doubtful, however, that it would have worked for any length of time. Without a doubt there would have been irreparable clashes due to ego battles and the influence of the ever-present Moisés. Although Les Baxter was responsible for much of the album's contents, and thus its success, it seems that Moisés had had enough foresight to persuade Baxter to relinquish certain compositional rights.

Three days after the Hollywood Bowl concert, and *before* the *Voice of the Xtabay* recordings were released by Capitol Records, Moisés Vivanco and Les Baxter signed two hand-written documents. Yma's lawyer at the time, Alexander Borisoff of Hollywood supervised the documents. Both deal with the ownership of the music found on *Voice of the Xtabay*. This was important since eventually the question of royalties for these compositions would come into play. The first document states:

"Hollywood California
August 15, 1950
This is to testify that the following compositions as used in the Capitol Records album, "Voice of the Xtabay," and performed in the Hollywood Bowl, August 12, 1950, are the original works of Moisés Vivanco:
High Andes! (Ataypura)
Tumpa! (Earthquake)
Taita Inty (Virgin of the Sun God—Traditional Inca Hymn to the Sun)
The following additional numbers used in "Voice of the Xtabay" are also the original works of Moisés Vivanco:
Monos (Monkeys)
Choladas (Dance of the Moon Festival)
Signed:
Moisés Vivanco
This is to testify that I have no claims as to the original composition of the above numbers, but they were arranged by L. Baxter.
Signed:
Les Baxter"

The document was witnessed and signed by Alexander Borisoff, John C. Rose, Yma Sumac, and June Starr.

The other document is similar:

"Hollywood, California
August 15, 1950
This is to testify that the following numbers used in "Voice of the Xtabay" are the combined works of Moisés Vivanco and Leslie Baxter:
Wayra (Dance of the Winds)
Accla Taqui (Chant of the Chosen Maidens)
The song "Xtabay" (Lure of the Unknown Love) is the work of Leslie Baxter, with Quechua lyrics by Moisés Vivanco.
Signed:
Moisés Vivanco
Les Baxter
Alexander Borisoff"
This too was witnessed and signed by Yma, John C. Rose, and June Starr.

These documents are Les Baxter's agreement to relinquish any compositional rights for the songs listed in the documents, and thus relinquishing any residual royalties that might occur from record sales. Baxter, of course, was paid for his work but rather than residuals he was paid a flat fee for his arrangements—a not-uncommon arrangement in the popular music field.

Although there were many problems plaguing the recording of *Voice of the Xtabay*, the eight selections have stood the test of time. By any standards and in any context the album is a classic of its type. Since its 1950 international release, *Voice of the Xtabay* has never been out of print. (though in America, due to litigation brought against Capitol by Yma, the album was withdrawn from 1990 to 1996). *Voice of the Xtabay* is one of the few albums in the history of recordings to have that distinction. The timelessness Les Baxter spoke of is evident in each piece and is responsible for their continued appeal despite obvious dating to the 1950s. This timelessness combined with Yma's powerful, authoritative, fresh and amazing vocal filigree, make these recordings an unusual treat for listeners. As is true with any recording of distinction, the magic is not dimmed by familiarity.

After the Hollywood Bowl concert and the release of the *Voice of the Xtabay*, the life of the Vivancos changed drastically. Everyone approached Yma and Moisés with advice. The famous composer Manuel de Falla advised Yma to avoid any teachers who would try to alter her vocal style, urging her to sing only as she naturally felt. Similarly, despite the problems during her appearance with him, Arthur Fiedler was impressed enough by Yma's voice and potential that he sent her to his sister, Elsa, who was herself a concert pianist, for musical coaching. He warned, however, that Yma's voice not be tampered with. Elsa Fiedler became a rehearsal pianist for the young Peruvian and, importantly, helped to teach Yma how to talk and understand the idiom of professional musicians.

In addition to Ms. Fiedler, Alejandro Granda (1898–1962) was called upon to coach Yma in the music she had always wanted to perform—opera. Operatic arias were to be inserted into concert programs to demonstrate Yma's versatility. Granda, an operatic tenor born in Peru, had been sent by the Peruvian government to study in Milan with the famous vocal instructor, Alfredo Cecchi. Making his debut in 1927, in Como, Italy, in Mascagni's *Iris,* he soon became a highly regarded specialist of Puccini roles. In 1928, Granda made his debut in Milan at the famous La Scala, becoming a favorite tenor of the conductor Arturo Toscanini, who compared him to Enrico Caruso. Granda also took part in a number of solo and early complete opera recordings on Columbia (released on 78-rpm disks) including *Tosca, Madama Butterfly,* and the first complete recording of Ponchielli's *La Gioconda.* After long tours of South America, Granda accepted the position of first tenor with the San Carlo Opera Company in the United States. He remained with that company from 1945 to 1950. He left the company in 1950 to work with Yma. It was a working relationship which was to last the rest of his life.

Granda became an indispensable member of the Vivanco household in Hollywood and rehearsed Yma in arias from Puccini's *Madama Butterfly* and *Tosca,* as well as Ponchielli's *La Gioconda.*

Yma was now in great demand. More offers were coming in than they could possibly fulfill. For the first time in their careers Moisés had to choose which offers they should accept. Newspapers and magazines wanted to interview Yma and then there were the social obligations—more than Yma had ever anticipated.

In December of 1950, Yma made her first television appearance since her break into the national scene. This was on the Eddie Cantor Show, a part of the Colgate Comedy Hour televised at 8:00 pm on Sunday evenings. Very popular with audiences, the Comedy Hour rotated comedians every week and provided spots for new musical talent.

Another important person now began to make her influence felt in the Sumac arena, Pru Devon. Ms. Devon was the host of a half-hour radio show called "Nights in Latin America" which was broadcast Monday and Friday nights on WQXR (the classical-music station of the New York Times) in New York City. Pru was the first person to play Sumac recordings on the air and, in many ways, was responsible for much of Yma's initial popularity. Contrary to what one might suppose, Yma's recordings were rarely played over the radio. Classical stations would not touch her, and there were no authentic South American ethnic radio programs at that time. Yma's phenomenal popularity was due almost entirely to word-of-mouth publicity by people who had either bought her recordings or seen her perform.

Pru Devon was one of the few of the time who regarded Yma as a serious musician even though she recognized the singer's limitations as well. As she once said of Yma's music, "There's everything in it except the gong at Grauman's Chinese Theater." Devon's show boasted a rare combination of both entertainment and the esoteric and she always had a general thematic format: Planting time, The Harvest, The Jungle. She was sure to play at least one Sumac recording a month, accurately introducing the music as representative tone poems. Often she would provide very interesting comparative listening, like the time she offered excerpts from a Folkways disk of jungle sounds, following it with Yma's "Chuncho!" Devon noted for listeners that in Yma's version Vivanco's guitar represented the basic, ever-present rhythm found in jungle life. Interested in authenticity, Pru Devon went so far as to travel to Peru in order to tape the famous Inty Raymi Festival (Festival of the Sun), held every summer.

Pru Devon was also the first to play the early Argentinean disks that Yma made in 1943. These were very popular with listeners. Bob Covais, (1936–1998) one of those responsible for Yma's final commercial solo album, *Miracles*, remembers that during 1953, Pru aired two cuts from an album of folk songs. Prefacing the songs, called "Pokra" and Pitu," she expressed pleasure that Yma was at last singing the true music of her country.

In February of 1951, Yma accepted an engagement at the Roxy Theater on 50th Street and Seventh Avenue in Manhattan. A three-week stint, Yma was to be the opening act for the popular comedian, Danny Kaye. For her short segment Yma sang the three pieces from the Hollywood Bowl concert and the *Xtabay* album: "Ataypura" (High Andes), "Tumpa!" (Earthquake!), and "Taita Inty" (Hymn to the Sun). Since Hernán Braña had another, previous commitment and was not able to play the Roxy job, Moisés hired David Revera, a young percussionist he and Yma had met at a club date at the Waldorf-Astoria Hotel in New York. Revera played irregularly with the Sumac troupe during the 1950s. During that time, however, he was one of Yma's "approved" escorts for her favorite relaxation—going to the movies. Moisés specified, however, that she was never to see any Spanish-made films. He felt they were too passionate for Yma to view. Generally, however, David kept to himself and did not become overly familiar with the Vivancos.

During the performances at the Roxy, a former Vice President of Peru, Dr. Rafael Larco Herrera, "flew 10,000 miles to catch Yma's act, paid his own admission into the theater, presented (her) with a pair of gold Inca earrings and flew back the next day." (James Poling, "The Most Exciting Voice in the World," *Collier's Magazine* 4/14/51) Although Yma was only on stage for about ten minutes, her impact was sensational. Paul Ash who, at the time, had been conducting the Roxy orchestra for 14 years, said he had never seen such audience reaction.

Variety's critic said of the show: "[Sumac] has probably one of the most impressive vocal ranges of any femme singer currently on the circuits. This Peruvian looker has the depth of a low contralto and can trill in the upper soprano registers without any appreciable loss of vocal timbre on either extreme." (Jose, 2/7/51) As was typical, the critic was at a loss to describe the music or Yma's performance: "Her numbers, a trio of Peruvian chants, are tunes of fragile delicacy with minor overtones. It would take a skilled singer to deliver them in a straightforward manner even without the necessity of displaying an unusual voice. In doing both simultaneously, she handicaps herself, but comes out ahead on values by netting a huge mitt." (ibid.)

Because of Yma's new concentration on nightclub work some distinct differences were becoming apparent to audiences familiar with her recordings. The main one was the absence of a full, lush string orchestra. Her music was also modified, arrangements and accompaniments simplified. For instance, "Taita Inty" reverted to the original arrangement used in Inca Taqui Trio days, with only guitar, flute and percussion. This was a practice that Yma and Moisés carried into the concert hall as well. Yma had always preferred singing certain pieces, such as "Taita Inty," in their original, more pure versions. Understandably, this confused and disappointed some listeners who expected to hear what they knew from the recordings. Because of the unfamiliarity of her music, her peculiar style of singing, and the odd inconsistencies in her biography, these additional performing differences merely exacerbated a growing confusion and skepticism.

The situation was becoming serious; Hernán Braña remembered that at times it could be quite embarrassing. "We would finish 'Taita Inty' and the audience wouldn't applaud. It was terrible. They didn't know what it was. They didn't recognize it from the recording!" According to Hernán, to remedy the problem, Moisés came up with a clever solution. When it came time to perform such pieces as "Taita Inty" or "Tumpa!" live, Moisés (or Yma) would ask the audience if they wanted to hear the piece as it was on the recording, or if they would prefer to hear the very old, authentic, traditional version. Invariably audiences said they wanted to hear the "original," and the audience's discontent was averted.

Contributing to audiences' growing confusion about the Peruvian singer was the fact that Yma rarely performed a song exactly the same way twice. Certain vocal effects regularly appeared as charted by Hernán and Moisés, but much of her singing depended on her mood, the condition of her voice that day, and what inspiration gripped her when performing. It is a fact that there are days for women singers especially when the voice is less responsive than other times—especially around the time of their cycle, when the vocal cords tend to swell due to water retention. During the course of vocal study, singers learn to solidify their technique in order to deal with circumstances such as these so that there is no noticeable difference in their performance. Because of Yma's particular repertoire and the range extremes required, however, she was in a different and extremely vulnerable position. Her solution was simply to alter her ornaments or improvisations, modify her vowel sounds, or omit high or low notes. It is interesting that it was only much later, after about a decade of singing thousands of performances of her demanding "Incan" material, that Yma began to have various songs transposed lower.

Glorying in the egotistical aspects of self-expression, Yma simply did what she wanted; what her instincts told her. Musically, and in regards to her performing, she became a law unto herself and did as she pleased. Because of this Yma rarely faltered in performance. Her willful, improvisational work was never at the expense of the music, but rather was part of the aural fabric she created to surround the piece she was singing. Yma's vocal filigree twined in and out of harmonies like a fine tweed and, amazingly, always maintained a relationship with the musical form and accompanying instruments. This was her instinctive genius and it was this that gave her performances and recordings their air of spontaneity.

When Yma began her performances at the Roxy she did not have any billing outside the theatre since she was considered only the warm-up for Danny Kaye's act. Kaye was an avid fan of Yma's, however, and during the course of the run introduced a segment into his skit in which he shouted "Yma! Yma!" and did an elaborate take-off on the singer. Audiences loved the new segment and the added publicity certainly did not hurt Yma. Audiences arrived for the Kaye show unaware that Yma was performing and left with the new "Incan" singer's name on their lips. Soon, Yma received her own, separate billing.

According to Hernán Braña, however, it was after this particular advertising at the Roxy that the infamous "Amy Camus" canard became established. Hernán distinctly remembers walking past the Roxy with two musician acquaintances. One of them, glancing up at the marquee, noticed the new billing of "Yma Sumac" and cleverly remarked: "Oh yeah! Yma Sumac!" after which he paused for a moment while studying the theater's marquee, and then, laughingly said, "That's Amy Camus—from Brooklyn!" The suggestion that Yma had reversed the spelling of her original name for exotic, professional reasons was originally intended as a sarcastic but harmless joke at her expense. Unfortunately, it quickly assumed enormous proportions—it became what's now called an urban legend. By August 1951, the Amy Camus myth was appearing as a fact in major American newspapers. For many people it seemed at last to explain just who this strange woman was. The idea that a simple Brooklyn housewife had reversed her name in order to pursue a singing career in exotica was certainly more believable than the Incan priestess-princess story they were being fed by Yma's management, publicity agents, and Capitol records. The suggestion that Yma might not be what she claimed to be only served to fan the fires of suspicion even more.

Walter Winchell, kind of an extreme, 1950s version of today's New York Post Page Six and similar gossip outlets, soon got wind of the Amy Camus joke and virtually guaranteed its long-lasting effects by broadcasting it on his radio program and celebrating it in his newspaper columns. Within months, irreparable damage was being done to Yma's credibility.

Winchell (1897–1972) was generally considered a brilliant but loathsome human being. Tremendously powerful and influential, Winchell was the creator of modern gossip writing, at the peak of his success appearing in over 1,000 newspapers with 50 million readers, including his home paper, the tabloid New York Daily Mirror. Even more people supposedly listened to his weekly radio broadcast, which he opened with "Good evening, Mr. and Mrs. America and all the ships at sea! This is Walter Winchell in New York. Let's go to press."

Audiences and readers had been fascinated by this singer who seemingly appeared out of nowhere, had this phenomenal voice, strange music and (literally) unbelievable background story. The Amy Camus story provided a convenient explanation for people who were skeptical of such unprecedented talent and sought an explanation other than the certainly dubious story that she was a princess from an obscure, exotic country. Amy Camus took the mystery away from "Yma Sumac" and made her more accessible to the general public.

Strangely enough, and unfortunate for them in hindsight, nothing was said by Yma, Moisés or their agents to refute the stories circulating that she was Amy Camus, Brooklyn housewife. Possibly satisfied by the added publicity, Capitol Records also said nothing. Whether advised by Moisés or her agents Yma remained silent and blithely continued singing. If anything, agents and publicists began to build on the controversy that was growing at an alarming rate, even integrating it into Yma's biographical material in a tasteless example of shameless exploitation.

And in fact, for a considerable time no harm appeared to be done by this demeaning story. Hordes of people flocked to see and hear for themselves if she were real. Woolworth's contributed to her renown by selling effigies of Yma in her "Virgin of the Sun God" finery. Also at this time the first Yma Sumac Fan Club was formed by Marilyn Jesmain.

So Yma had become a "show-biz" personality. The public was interested in anything written about the unusual singer. Only rarely did a thoughtful, well-researched article appear, one that approached Yma as a person or performer of genuine importance. And so when the novelty wore a little thin, the relative tawdriness of the Brooklyn-hausfrauputting-on-airs tale contributed mightily to an easy scorn that came to be directed toward her.

One thoughtful piece that was written about her, perhaps the only one in the 1950s that seriously tried to address her credibility and worth as a musician, was the excellent article written by James Poling for *Collier's Magazine* that I have already quoted a number of times. This article superbly balanced Yma's complex personality with fact and myth and helped readers relate to the person who was Yma Sumac. At the same time Poling managed to tactfully point out the many inconsistencies that surrounded the singer and her "heritage." It was unfortunate that these inconsistencies continued to be repeated until the end of her international career. In the Poling article, while Yma was brought down from the airy heights of the "Virgin of the Sun" mythology, she was presented as a strikingly original, but normal human being. "Cesar Bustamente," Poling says, "an elderly relative of Yma who now lives in New York, says with commendable restraint, 'Always very strange girl'."

In early March of 1951, the *New York Times* announced that Yma was to appear in a new Broadway musical called *Flahooley*, co-written by E. Y. (Yip) Harburg and Sammy Fain. Scheduled to open in New Haven on April 9th, *Flahooley* was to move to Philadelphia for three weeks before settling in New York on May 14th.

By this time, Yma, Moisés and their now-two-year-old Charlie had chosen their home in New York—a large penthouse apartment at 340 West 86th Street, on upper Broadway.

March also saw the publication of an interesting interview with Yma for the *Los Angeles Times* (3/12/51): "Yma Sumac, the Peruvian singing marvel, goes into a kind of self-hypnosis when she sings. She completely forgets, she said, the 5000 people out front, the pale indifferent faces in the orchestra pit, the stage hands, chorus boys, managers and press agents crowding in the wings. 'I do not see the theater at all' she said. 'I sing and I am at home, among my own people. I see only the mountains and my own tiny village.'"

"'She is five singers in one,' Moisés Vivanco, her husband and composer, said during a backstage interview. 'Never in 2000 years has there been another voice like hers.' The extravagant praise brought lowered eyelids from the dark, shapely singer. She quietly explained that her range covers five octaves—all the way from 'B natural' three lines below the staff to 'A-sharp' four lines above the staff."

In this interview Yma maintained that she was born in 1928 (and is thus 23 years old at the time). A dig at operatic music strikes an odd chord at the end of the interview: "Miss Sumac plans shortly to appear in a Broadway musical. She has sung operatic arias but does not particularly want to appear in opera. 'I like music,' she explained, 'that makes me cry or makes me laugh. Opera has nothing here (she touched her heart). I like our old Inca folk songs. I like your Negro spirituals and your hillbilly music. That is from the heart.'"

April also found Yma on the Fred Waring Show, an hour-long television show that aired Sunday nights at 8:00 PM. This was an unusual engagement in that the entire show was built around Yma and used sets of various idols and mountains as well as a full orchestra. Yma's selections included her three most famous songs: "Taita Inty," "Ataypura," and "Tumpa!"

Flahooley, a now all but forgotten entry in the annals of Broadway musicals, was an unusual mixture of fantasy involving toys, dolls, American puppets, and an Arabian genie—a sort of magical musical. The story took place in Capsultani, Indiana, in and around the B. G. Bigelow Inc. toy factory in 1951. Yma's role (basically inserted into the musical and incidental to the plot) was that of the Arabian princess-seductress, Najala. Considering the publicity she had been receiving this was a logical casting decision. Although Yma got most of the publicity surrounding the show, the cast was excellent

Yma in *Flahooley*

and indicative of the quality of musical theater at that time. Most importantly, *Flahooley* was the stage debut of the great Barbara Cook, but it also included such Broadway luminaries as Irwin Corey, Fay Dewitt, Lulu Bates and Jerome Courtland as well as the famous Bil Baird marionettes.

Publicity preceding the opening of the show highlighted Yma's exotic qualities: "Yma Sumac, possibly the most enigmatic personality to hit show business since the Cardiff Giant, raises her multi-octave voice in several songs, including a number of her exotic, wordless rituals." (*Cue* Magazine 5/51)

Yma's appearance in the musical had much to do with its popularity. Even though (on the cast recording at least) her musical contributions last only seven and one-half minutes, Yma was spotlighted well in both acts. Her first appearance was Act I, scene 5, where she sang "Najala's Lament," which was prime exotica. She reappeared in scene eight where she sang "Arabian for Get Happy" (also billed as "Najala's Song of Joy"). Act II scene four, however, contained Yma's showstopper, "Enchantment" (also called "Birds"), a tour-de-force that displayed Yma's imitative genius and which was soon to evolve into her most famous number, "Chuncho!" (Forest Creatures).

The young Barbara Cook found Yma fascinating. In an interview with Ken Mandelbaum for the first, Capitol CD re-release of *Flahooley* she remembers, "Yma was actually just stuck into the show—I believe it was Yipper who had heard her and thought she was wonderful and decided to use her. She did such unusual things musically. I remember standing in the wings every night waiting to make an entrance during one of her numbers. While there was a vamp underneath, she did this slide up, went as high as she could go, then did a glissando down. As she did the glissando, Maurice and I couldn't believe how she actually worked in two notes an octave apart, like singing a double note. We thought, 'What has she got in there instead of vocal cords?'"

Understandably, the original 78-rpm and LP releases of *Flahooley* have become collector's items, especially now with the ease of the Internet. (Don Pierson, the webmaster of Yma Sumac Home Page, www.sunvirgin.com, noted in an email to me: "One of the other collections here in California has "the 78 rpm set (of Flahooley) autographed both by Barbara Cook and Yma Sumac. Both were done in more recent years and, apparently

Yma Sumac's was after Barbara Cook's. [on seeing Barbara Cook's autograph] Yma asked, 'Who is she'?" private email, 7/25/1999)

When the show premiered in New Haven, *Variety* commented that the "show can materialize as an exceedingly novel, appealing tune-and-dance concoction, or as an exceptionally beautiful flop." After the show moved to New York, however, problems arose. Constructed as a fantasy, *Flahooley* was unmistakably a satire of contemporary social and political matters. Because of its mockery of the American economic system, many thought the show anti-American, or at least inappropriate during wartime (this was early in the Korean conflict).

Flahooley was, for whatever reason, short-lived. It only played at the Broadhurst Theater on New York's Broadway for just 40 performances, (about a month) and closed suddenly on June 16, 1951, with people still waiting in line for tickets. Although it was originally announced that the show was only closing for the summer, for revisions, during that time *Seventeen* moved into the Broadhurst. *Flahooley* never reopened. Despite attempts (1952, 1964, 1998) at revising and reproducing the musical, it has remained a failure.

In *Flahooley*

Reviews of the show were mixed. Robert Coleman of the New York *Mirror* commented, "The materials are there for a delightful, captivating fantasy, but, alas, they have been subordinated to lengthy passages critical of our politics, economics and ethics." Although a number of reviews applauded the score's originality, others found the show tedious and overcomplicated. Mark Barron of the *Associated Press* found Yma "an enchanting Latin beauty, (who) won applause in her first Broadway stage appearance with her extraordinary voice, which ranges from the low contralto to A above high C."

Today it is widely believed by Broadway theater historians that *Flahooley* succumbed to the political pressures of that era. This was not only the time of the Korean war, it was also the McCarthy era. The red-baiting senator from Wisconsin was at the height of his influence, and paranoia about the threat of communism and its possibility of reaching and infiltrating America was at one of its periodic high points. It was, in this stage, peculiarly focused on the entertainment industry especially. The infamous Hollywood black list was in force, but many artists, musicians and other artists throughout every part of the entertainment business were also losing jobs and positions in the community, not being able to obtain work for years.

Fortunately, on May 27, while in the midst of performances and before the show was prematurely closed, the cast of *Flahooley* assembled to record a cast album of highlights

from the show for Capitol Records. Despite the precarious New York reviews the show had received—and since Yma, who was one of the main draws of the show, was a Capitol artist—it was decided to go ahead with the planned cast album. Interestingly, when the album was recorded, it was decided to omit the controversial final song, "Sing the Merry," a satirical comment on the commercialization of Christmas in America. The last line of the song had already been cut in Philadelphia performances and had never been reinstated: "And for Christ's sake, may this nation soon give Christmas back to Christ."

Although not all the music from the show was included on the recording, all three of Yma's numbers were. They represent some of the finest singing Yma ever put to disk. The first two pieces were operatic in their structure and technical requirements, and perfectly showcased her voice. The third underlined her imitative abilities and was a stunner. Cleverly, each selection highlighted a different aspect of Yma's vocal witchery.

The cast album sold well and was the third top selling record in Philadelphia, where the show was first performed. In his notes for the CD release of the cast album, Ken Mandelbaum noted: "From its beginning, with a March of Time announcer inviting us into 'the greatest toy factory in the world' over the sound of industrial noises, to the final rather eerie giggles of a laughing doll, this recording sounds like no other. There are songs sung by the purely beautiful soprano of Barbara Cook; recording star Yma Sumac's four-octave warbling, hissing and grunting; and a great deal of singing about a doll called Flahooley. Once beyond the strangeness of it all, one notices that E.Y. Harburg's lyrics are brilliant, and that Sammy Fain's melodies are consistently beguiling."

Shortly after *Flahooley* closed, Yma made a guest appearance on the Arthur Murray television show. This was the first of several guest appearances the Peruvian soprano was to make in front of television audiences that year.

In June, Yma took part in a popular TV show called "This is Show Business," a panel show where guest stars presented various problems to a panel of celebrities and asked for advice. Yma's "problem," or dilemma, was whether she should continue singing her usual "Incan" chants, or concentrate on popular music. Of course, she was required to demonstrate her music and so she sang a fiery performance of "Tumpa!" The panel emphatically decided that she should continue in her present vein. Although contrived, the show was fun and entertaining for viewers and served to introduce a number of artists (including Yma) to the growing television audience.

Also in June of 1951, the *Melody Maker*, an English publication, printed an article by Claude Lipscombe called *Is she an Inca Princess—or just a smart girl from Brooklyn?* (6/2/51) During the course of the article Lipscombe reviewed the Xtabay album. "Of the eight titles on LP, 'Earthquake' (Tumpa) is possibly the best, and is a superb example of the simple mode of musical story telling. Other outstanding titles on the long-player are 'Virgin of the Sun God' (Taita Inty), 'Dance of the Moon Festival' (Choladas) and 'Lure of the Unknown Love' (Xtabay). In the remaining titles ... Yma sings in a typically Brazilian rhythmic manner, a little like Carmen Miranda. She even says "Chic-a-chic-a-boom"—once!"

In the same issue, discussing the release of the 78-rpm single of "Virgin of the Sun God" and "Dance of the Moon Festival," Laurie Henshaw stated: "Whether Yma Sumac will merely prove a 'nine days wonder' or be acknowledged as a singer of lasting merit remains to be seen. There is no disputing, however, that hers is the most startling voice ever to break into the popular record catalogues." (ibid)

During July of 1951, Yma, Moisés, and Hernán took part in one of the most important broadcasts in the history of American television—the first commercial color telecast (RCA). One show was aired live, every day, for one week on channel 4. For her segment Yma sang "Tumpa!" to the backdrop of an Incan set. Those who saw the performances have said that Yma's singing, which was not dubbed, was identical in content to the famous Capitol recording.

In August, Yma traveled to Chicago for an hour-long concert at the Chicagoland Music Festival. For her stage entrance a touch of eccentricity was offered. The audience was given matches to light after the house-lights had been lowered. In this atmosphere of the eerie, Yma entered, carried on a litter by a number of men. As was now typical, she wore a large cape which was reverently removed by an attendant. Her selections were well received and included "Ataypura," "Suray Surita," "Taita Inty," "Tumpa!" and "Montana."

In early September of 1951, Yma, Moisés and Hernán again entered the Capitol studios to record a second solo album for Capitol Records, the now famous *Legend of the Sun Virgin*. For this album, at least twelve selections were recorded.

"Karibe Taki" (written by Hernán Braña)
"Witallia!" (Fire in the Andes)
"Lament"
"Zana"
"Kuyaway" (Inca Love Song)
"Suray Surita"
"No es Vida"
"Mamalloy"
(Also *recorded but not released until 1956, when pressed onto 12" LP*):
"Kon Tiki"
"Montana"
"Panarima"
"Ccori Canastitay"

(Most probably, one other song, "Inca Waltz" was recorded during these 1951 sessions. For some reason it was rejected for the *Legend of the Sun Virgin* album and remained unpublished until 1995 and the release, *Voice of the Xtabay and Other Exotic Delights* by Revola (Creation Records)—United Kingdom: CREVO 34 CD

As was the case with *Voice of the Xtabay,* there were inconsistencies in the documentation of *Legend of the Sun Virgin*. Although Les Baxter's name does not appear on more recent releases, it seems he was involved in this second album, since his name does appear on early pressings of each format of the album. Interestingly, both Yma and Les vociferously denied his involvement.

Alan Livingston, however, remembers: "After a meeting at Capitol Records, Les Baxter was again selected as arranger and conductor for the first session. Moisés presented them with a list of songs he wanted on the album. Les worked with Moisés, who gave him the lead lines with guitar. At another meeting, Baxter showed the arrangements he had put together to Yma and Moisés and showed her what she would be doing and gave her a lead sheet. Moisés rehearsed her with guitar so she could learn and memorize it." (Interview from "*Yma Sumac, Hollywood's Inkaprinzessin*" by Günter Czernetzky)

Like those for *Voice of the Xtabay,* the recording sessions for *Legend of the Sun Virgin* were strained, although technicians found Yma pleasant to work with. By this time she had gained enough self confidence and knowledge of her craft that she basically just got down to business and created music. The main problem seems to have been Moisés. He was always at Yma's side in the studio and it was he who would stop sessions to tell Yma that she was not singing the melody correctly at spots. He would then sing it to her and she would say "Oh, yes." The next time she would be fine. There were other times, however, when Yma stood her ground. She felt the melody should go one way and Moisés would say no, it went the other way. Standing her ground, Yma would insist it went her way. The sessions would stop until they finished arguing.

The main problem with these internal disagreements between Yma and Moisés was the fact that the producers had planned to complete three or four sides within the 3-hour recording time limit set by the musicians union. Anything after that went into overtime, at significant added hourly cost. Usually overtime did not occur during such recording sessions because the orchestral musicians in Los Angeles were excellent; most of them playing for the big movie studios. They could look at a piece of music and read it perfectly. Because of the problems encountered during *Voice of the Xtabay* and *Legend of the Sun Virgin* sessions, however, Yma's subsequent recordings were all made with the orchestra laying down their music first, as a background track. Yma would then come into the studio afterward (accompanied by the ever-present Moisés) and record her tracks.

Alan Livingston commented: "Many questioned Moisés' managing credentials since his scope of managerial abilities was limited to Yma and he was a jealous person. He did not want any other person or company to manager her. He wanted sole charge and control of her at all times. It was suggested to Yma that it might be a good idea for her to concentrate more on concert work or even Light Opera, since, realistically, her recording life was only to be about four or five years and in order to continue using her voice she would have to branch out. Yma was not pleased with the suggestion." (ibid)

After the initial recording session, in any event, Les Baxter seems to have been conspicuously absent. Undoubtedly, he was taken care of as expediently as he had been in the earlier *Voice of the Xtabay* album. He had no more artistic contact with Yma until 1970, when they agreed to collaborate one last time to create the *Miracles* album.

Generally, the *Legend of the Sun Virgin* recording sessions went smoother than those for *Voice of the Xtabay*—at least in technical matters. Technicians found the singer better prepared for the recording microphones. Alan Livingston was impressed with the differences: "Because it was on tape, they could stop and start if Yma forgot the melody. But there were not many stops and starts. She now came prepared for recording sessions. In about three hours time, Yma often did three or four takes before having to stop. Usually there was a fifteen-minute rehearsal and then they would do takes. Usually there were 3 to 5 takes and then on to the next record. Rock artists at that time took much longer. Sometimes three to four months. Yma's recordings usually took three sessions, and were over within a week and a half." (ibid)

Like *Voice of the Xtabay,* this second album was given a colorful title and superb, imaginatively exotic cover art. Even so, *Legend of the Sun Virgin* was confusing and problematic from the beginning. As if ignoring the problems with the first album, where song titles were listed on the album differently from their playing order, there now was (and still is) no listing at all of the selections on the record sleeve of the *Legend of the Sun Virgin.* For the names of the songs, the listener is forced to refer to the record's label. None of Yma's other albums have this blatant omission of titles. The liner notes created for the album barely mention Yma, although Moisés now merits a paragraph heralding his compositional accomplishments. Instead of a contents listing, record buyers were treated to colorful, fantasy notes of the duties of the Virgins in Incan temples of the Sun—and what would befall them should they neglect their duties. Although tying in nicely with the title of the album, the notes had absolutely nothing to do with

the selections.

"Every year the most beautiful maidens were selected to become Virgins of the sun, serving in the convent which rivaled in splendor the Inca's palace.

"The sacred flame was entrusted to the Virgins and if by neglect, it was allowed to go out, it was believed that some terrible disaster would follow.

"The Virgin assumed holy vows which bound her to the temple service. Should she prove unfaithful to her vows, she was buried alive, while her lover was strangled, and the village to which he belonged, razed 'so that no stone stood upon another."

The cover of the album, however, was a stroke of commercial genius. Any record buyer would be drawn to this cover. It boasts an striking and intriguing head shot of Yma with an enigmatic expression on her face—at once seductive and vaguely menacing—with her hair severely slicked back and her name and the title of the album seemingly carved from stone arching above the photograph. Squatting near Yma is the familiar little Aztec (not Incan) stone god. It is a prepossessing cover and does its work well. Although not the most beautiful of Yma's album covers, (*Inca Taqui* wins that distinction), it is the most striking. The stunning photograph, like those for *Voice of the Xtabay* and *Inca Taqui* was taken by Tom Kelley, who always did superb, artistic and imaginative work. (Kelley played Yma's music during the sessions, having her move to the music as he took photographs.)

Like *Voice of the Xtabay*, *Legend of the Sun Virgin* can be considered a (very) loosely integrated vocal suite with orchestral accompaniment; each song a different movement and providing a different color or atmosphere. Moisés received full credit for all the music performed on the recording, with no mention at all of Les Baxter. Neither is any mention made of Hernán Braña, who in fact composed the opening song on the album, "Karibe Taki." Later releases of the album corrected this mistake—after Hernán took the matter to court.

(Don Pierson made an interesting comment on this, Yma's second album and its credits: "It turns out that [Baxter's] name was not on all 78 rpm sets, which is a surprise. I would have expected they were made before the 10" LPs so would all have it. Also, of my 7" records, [Baxter] is credited on the boxed set but is not on either my gate-fold or two-volume EPs. As I said earlier, he is on one of my 10" LPs but not on the other. I didn't bother checking the 12" LPs and would be surprised if he were there since they were issued much later."—private email, 7/25/1999)

This constant vacillating of composer credits was to eventually cause Capitol serious problems.

Yma's popularity at the time was most impressive when one remembers that artists did not go out for publicity appearances in support of the release of their records as they do today. Yma relied completely on Capitol's promotion department to do this. Branch offices were responsible for supplying local radio stations with new recordings to play. Disk jockeys, however, were hesitant to play Yma's recordings because they did not fit in with the other popular songs of the time. So branch offices had to visit record stores and get them interested enough to stock her records. Huge posters were made and put on display in stores.

Although *Legend of the Sun Virgin* sold well in America, generally the album was not considered as successful as *Voice of the Xtabay*. Even though the music was of the same style and format as *Voice of the Xtabay*, countless vocal effects were now being exploited with a heavy use of additional grunting natives to provide atmosphere. Emphasis was still on exotica but the technical devices used to enhance Yma's bizarre music and singing, were being used ad nauseam, which made the album slickly commercial—as if the selections were attempts to out-do anything ever recorded. The end result is manipulative, distracting, and occasionally straddles the border of good taste. Bombarded by all the additional effects, listeners tend to find themselves concentrating more on what is going on behind Yma, than on the singer herself.

Also in September of 1951, Yma fulfilled one of her most prominent nightclub engagements. This was at the famous Cotillion Room in the Pierre Hotel on Fifth Avenue in New York City. This prestigious engagement would be repeated in 1952 and again in 1955. It was to be a lucrative job since she was to receive $10,000 a week.

Advertised as "Exotic International Star and her company featuring Moisés Vivanco," Yma performed one show a night, at 9:30, Sunday through Thursday, with an additional show added at 12:30 on Friday and Saturday. The performances were filled to capacity and well received by ecstatic audiences who were shocked and startled not only by Yma's distinctive singing but also the spectacle surrounding her. The germ of the yet-to-come Sumac extravaganzas, those seen on the concert tours of 1954 and 1955, was born as Moisés began to expand production details. Now Yma was framed by unusual dancing numbers, instrumental solos and a very grand, well calculated, entrance to music and the crash of a gong.

By this time two important things had evolved in the Sumac show. First, the improvisational, extraneous grunts and exclamations of the accompanying percussionists. Both Braña and David Revera played the Pierre Hotel job. Revera enjoyed having more responsibility on differing instruments, including doubling on timbals, mallets, bongos, conga and kinto drums, castanets, and cymbals. Interesting additions to Yma's programs had been made by the time of the Cotillion Room appearances. Hernán remembers that during one of the numbers preceding Yma's entrance, he and David would improvise shouting nonsense syllables at each other as their percussive rhythms became more intricate. Yma loved these particular segments and often would quickly dress for her entrance and then hide behind the backdrop so she could listen and giggle at the silly sounds they were making at each other.

Hotel Pierre Ad

Secondly, Yma and Hernán had developed a subtle set of signals to each other that they used during performances. In the midst of her many tangents of coloratura improvisation, Yma would alert Hernán, who was usually providing the percussive foundation, that she was nearing her conclusion by using a set of preestablished, ritualistic-looking hand movements or positions. Hernán would interpret the signals she gave him and accordingly signal the conductor. Since Yma was in charge of the length of her improvisations, this was very important for smooth transitions during the course of a song. So subtle were they that the secret signals were never suspected or discovered by audiences. It is apparent that Yma never forgot those symbolic hand movements. As if forgetting herself, during her appearance years later at the Ballroom in New York City (1989), Yma was seen to strike various poses during her improvisatory passages that were obviously meant to signify to the conductor that she was going to continue with the rest of the song. The conductor, unfamiliar with her signals, had no idea she was trying to communicate with him.

To help make Yma more accessible to audiences, certain current "pop" songs were now inserted into her programs. They were not successful. Most critics agreed that it would have been better had she not sung them.

Also, the glamorous side of the singer was now being exploited for all it was worth. Yma now appeared in full concert regalia: sumptuous gowns, exotic jewelry, superb hairstyles all accentuating her natural beauty. Reviewing her performance on September 26, 1951, Russell Rhodes of the *Journal of Commerce*, wrote that Yma was strikingly attired in "a gold medallioned necklace, a gown of white and pink French taffeta with a bouffant skirt of partial rainbow motif." He frowned on Yma's one excursion into popular music, "Too Young," which she sang in unintelligible English. He hoped that "by now she has eliminated that . . . it is a distracting blur in a performance that needs not lower its standards to any audience compromise."

Variety's critic, Abel, noted that the "number about the birds in flight is a virtuoso item of rare value, as is her Peruvian love song, to the degree that when she essays 'Too Young' it is almost a broughtdown. Not that she doesn't endow that pop with unusual distinction . . . but . . . she might maintain the aura . . . better by remaining in Peruvian character." (sic) 9/26/51

The New Yorker succinctly commented, "In the Cotillion Room, Yma Sumac sounds weird and wonderful as she trills her native Peruvian mountain music, just weird when she essays Tin Pan Alley."

During performances at the Pierre Hotel, Yma found time to appear on the Milton Berle television show and the Jack Carter Variety Show. With the completion of the contract at the Cotillion Room, she participated in a benefit concert for the United Jewish Appeal given at Madison Square Garden, and then left for Toronto, for a concert for the Toronto Police Department. This affair was held at the famous Maple Leaf Gardens, home of the city's hockey team.

About this time the first of several serious managerial problems began to surface. *Variety*'s headline for an October 17, 1951 article states: "Yma Sumac Wants Out On John Rose Mgt. Pact That Floors Her Income."

John Rose, Yma's personal representative of the William Morris Agency, was still under contract to Yma for five more years, but she felt he was receiving an "excessive amount" for his services and complained to the American Guild of Variety Artists (AGVA) "in an effort to extricate herself from a pact which resulted in her netting $460 from her stipulated $1,250 salary." This meant that John Rose was receiving $790.00 each pay check rather than $312.50—more than twice his contractual amount.

According to *Variety*, Rose's percentage was 25%. "In addition, sundry undisclosed 'expenses' are allegedly involved." Because of this, Ben White, then in charge of AGVA's organization of artists, made arrangements that Yma be paid directly by the Pierre Hotel instead of through Rose, as previously arranged. Yma was advised by AGVA not to accept any work in which Rose was involved and the organization eventually resolved the problem.

Rose played a strangely undefined part in the Sumac promotion. Since he was her manager, one would expect his involvement. However, the added expenses never seem to have been explained. Neither were the reasons for his supposed involvement in the composition of two of Yma's songs. Although Yma seems to have been vociferous about the circumstances of her reduced pay, Moisés, at least in print, was oddly silent. Since Moisés controlled all the financial aspects of Yma's career, it is doubtful that Yma would have known anything about her salary unless told by Moisés. Since Moisés was typically the first to complain about Yma's fees, his silence was interesting.

Ludicrously, at the time Moisés was still trying to maintain Yma's allure as a single woman. Hal Holly, in Down Beat reported on October 20, 1951: "Vivanco is a guitarist and a sort of fountain of native Peruvian music. He is also said to be the only player of several ancient Inca instruments. Vivanco seems to have been close to Yma since her first concert and festival appearances in South America. He says that, contrary to published reports, they are not married."

Shortly after this, Yma appeared at the Cocoanut Grove in the Ambassador Hotel in Los Angeles. Only one show was given a night, at 10:15 p.m. with a cover charge of $1.50. Her debut on December 6, was a great success. So much so that the hotel's club, which had a seating capacity of 960, and had not been doing good business up to that time, suddenly found itself inundated with crowds that came to hear the strange Peruvian "Princess."

Generally, for nightclub programs Yma sang such things as "Taita Inty" (Hymn to the Sun)—often used as the final encore, "Ataypura" (High Andes), "Birds" (from *Flahooley*), "Tumpa!" (Earthquake!), "Babalu," "Zana" and other songs soon to be recorded. Her singing led audiences to distraction and according to reviews the addition of percussionists in a number of songs had an exhilarating effect on Yma's singing, which actually became frenzied. Most commentaries refused to make any judgments of the music or any detailed analysis of her singing. This was a constant problem during Yma's career. For example, *Variety*'s review by Helm (12/12/51) simply notes:

"Miss Sumac is presented with showmanly touches that set off her flights beyond the coloratura level. Vocal trick of rolling her voice in the lower register and then soaring to the heights with perfect control…sets her artistry apart from other stylists."

The critic from *Billboard* found Yma's show great entertainment. "Mixing Spanish and Incan, Miss Sumack stays in the high registers with virtual ease. Her rhythm and timing are tops. With the eerie 'Hymn to the Sun', the rhythmic 'Tumpa' and a breathtaking 'Birds,' the princess keeps ringsiders enthralled."

Listeners were fascinated with the ease and seeming limitlessness of Yma's top register and applauded her satin-trimmed, black velvet gown with red cape. It is amusing that in many reviews Yma's dress choices were more accurately described than her singing.

Things were going very well for Yma and Moisés despite the "Amy Camus" gossip. Yma was now one of the first of the American recording industry's album-oriented, rather than hit-singles popular artists. Royalty checks from "*Voice of the Xtabay*" enabled them to purchase a mansion in the exclusive area of Cheviot Hills in Los Angeles and Yma now traveled in a pink and black Cadillac with gold wheels. Yma, who was judged the possessor of a voice that could "freeze listeners in their tracks," was sitting comfortably on the top of the music charts and seemingly the world.

It was during 1951, however, that things began to go seriously awry with the Incan priestess/princess theme. Tired of the ploy, critics became more outspoken about the dubiousness of Yma's heritage and also the authenticity of Moisés' music. The operatic cadenzas of the "Incan" music with Yma's flute-like trills and odd, sultry growls were found highly suspect, especially as experts on Peruvian history were interviewed. All of them maintained that Incan music was never notated, so it was impossible to know what it really sounded like. Then there were the inconsistencies that cropped up with embarrassing regularity between press releases and interviews with the singer.

One of the main contentions was that Yma's music sounded too slick, too commercial to be what it claimed to be—authentic Incan chants. Her odd manner of singing with its obvious roots in an operatic or classical style housed within a popular music framework was also thought to be of questionable origin.

Then there was the exhibitionistic, exploitive way Yma sang and the questions concerning her actual vocal range, which was quoted in print as anything from three and-a-half to six octaves. It was at this time that Walter Winchell decided to drop his bombshell by intimating that Yma Sumac was really Amy Camus, a schoolteacher (some stories say housewife) from Brooklyn who decided to spell her name backwards and have an international singing career as an oddity.

All this tended to solidify the growing feeling that a hoax was being perpetrated. After the Winchell remark, things were never the same for Yma, who found she had to constantly defend her position and heritage. (Many years later Yma recalled meeting Walter Winchell. "I met him at a party in Los Angeles. . . . He looked at me, then looked away, like he wanted to hide. I went over and said, 'Don't be afraid. I won't sue!' And we talked." [NY Daily News 2/17/87]}

Reports soon surfaced that Yma had been born in New Jersey, Canada, France, Connecticut, Mexico. Another rumor suddenly sprang into being: that Yma did not actually sing all the high and low notes on the recordings herself—rather, two women went into the studio to record.

Foolishly, Yma and her agents remained silent, possibly misinterpreting the controversy as good publicity, which would increase her mystique. The rumors quickly grew to alarming proportions and finally all involved realized that a mistake had been made by ignoring them. Some sort of response was demanded. The situation was close to affecting Yma's popularity.

Yma has remained silent as to who, if any, of the nine managers and agents she had had by this time in her career was responsible for the Incan publicity campaign in the first place. With the Amy Camus scandal brewing stronger than ever, it was decided that some kind of formal statement had to be made. Unfortunately they were innocuous, ineffective and did little to change the minds of an already seriously doubting public. Instead of reassuring them that Yma was simply a gifted singer from Peru, publicists and agents, abetted, it must be admitted, by Yma and Moisés, promoted the story that Yma was not only Peruvian, but a descendant of the last of the Incan kings, a revered ritual priestess-princess singer deified by the Indians. This new twist and its emphasis only increased disbelief.

Nonetheless, by the end of 1952, Yma and her agents had convinced themselves that they had squashed the Amy Camus rumor. So comfortable were they that Yma was allowed to do an interview with a reporter from the *Brooklyn Eagle*. The interview shows the misplaced emphasis that was now being exerted on the Incan princess myth. Here, however, Yma hit new heights: now claiming that she was descended from the Incan Sun God:

I'M NOT FROM BROOKLYN—YMA

Singer says She's Incan Princess from Peru

Yma Sumac decided today she has convinced Americans she's not "Amy Camus" of Brooklyn, nor two ladies instead of one.

Yma is the beautiful singer who can hit bird-like high notes and then slither to low tunes. She claims she's an Inca princess and the last descendant of the Inca sun god too.

But when Yma first startled American music lovers with her voice . . . a few unbelievers raised their eyebrows.

They um-hummed that Yma Sumac is Amy Camus spelled backwards. Furthermore, in tight black suits and bright lipstick Yma looks more like a big city glamor girl than an Indian from the primitive Andes.

A few doubters who heard only her record albums were sure she was two people taking turns on the musical scale.

"Walter Winchell say I'm from Brooklyn, Bolivians say I'm from Bolivia, but I say I'm from Peru," shrugged Miss Sumac.

"It happens many times. People write or ask if I'm Amy Camus from Brooklyn, but when one magazine write about me they send someone to Peru to ask who was Yma. They went to my village and got proof.

"I speak the truth. Now everybody knows since I tour nightclubs. People come to see Yma at the Cocoanut (sic) Grove and they believe."

But the Inca princess shrugs. "I do not explain my voice. All I say is I am Yma from Peru." (Aline Mosby, 12/25/52)

There are some factual errors in the article—Moisés' name is frequently misspelled as "Divanco"—but the most egregious errors, in this and many other articles like it, are Yma's errors of judgment in refusing to drop the "descendant-of-royalty" theme and the religious appellation with which she was labeled: a sun-worshipper. Despite the emphasis placed on her perfectly authentic Peruvian heritage, which was meant to counteract the effect of the Amy Camus rumor, the Inca king story, unsurprisingly, did nothing to convince Americans of Yma's sincerity. In fueling the controversy by claiming that she was, of all inexplicable things, a "last descendant of the Inca Sun God," Yma Sumac completely undermined the last vestiges of her credibility.

Ill-advised by her agents and Moisés, Yma continued to state proudly that she was an Incan princess. It wasn't until the 1970s, some twenty years later and after her divorce from Moisés, that Yma admitted in public that there hadn't actually been any Incas for hundreds of years. A fact, it seems, that everyone except Yma had known all along.

Unpublished Voice of the Xtabay photo—Tom Kelley 1950 (used by permission of Tom Kelley Studios, Ventura, CA)

CHAPTER 4

"Accla K'ory"
(Chosen One of Gold)
1952–1954

In January of 1952, Yma made her debut at Las Vegas, Nevada at the El Rancho. Financially Yma and Moisés were doing better than ever before—she was now averaging $25,000 a week. She and Moisés were excited about the Las Vegas appearances because of their high profile in the music industry and because of the large crowds expected. The El Rancho had no cover or minimum charge and boasted a house orchestra of 10 musicians. Yma's opening shows (there were two a night, a dinner show and a late show) on January 9, 1952, were enthusiastically received.

Variety's critic found the "Peruvian thrush" an unusual presence in such surroundings but commented that "attention was rapt to pin-drop concentration." Yma's exotic appearance and aloof stage demeanor were considered novel but were as well received as her selections: "Tumpa!", "Birds," "Inca Love Song," and "Malambo." The favorite of audiences, however, was her encore, "Taita Inty" (Hymn to the Sun) which was magically sung to Moisés' simple guitar accompaniment. Pianist June Starr also participated in the show and would accompany Yma and Moisés to England.

Also in January, *Quick* magazine, then a popular publication, printed a short article about Yma dated January 28, 1952 that featured some lovely photographs—including a glamorous cover photo. Building on the mystery surrounding Yma, it noted: "The release of Yma Sumac's second album of "Inca" songs, *Legend of the Sun Virgin*, renewed a standing question about the exotic Peruvian songstress: Who is she? When her first Capitol album, Voice of Xtabay, appeared in 1950, the true identity of Yma Sumac was shrouded in mystery. That mystery, plus Yma's astounding, four-octave vocal range, has made the weird tunes one of the three best-selling albums. Yma has remained mysterious despite (or perhaps because of) a variety of explanations. These range from the claim that she is actually Amy Camus (Yma Sumac spelled backwards) from Brooklyn, to the tale that she is an Inca princess. Counters Yma, in slow, halting English: 'I am not from Brooklyn. But I hear it is beautiful . . . . .'

"After her debut at the Hollywood Bowl, the critic of the Los Angeles Times wrote: 'Miss Sumac did amazing things with an amazing voice . . . that has to be heard to be believed. The Andean Indians put it differently, says her husband. They call her low register "the voice of the earthquake," her high register "the voice of the birds."

"Music lovers and bobby-soxers alike flocked to Yma's subsequent performances in nightclubs, theaters and TV, and snapped up her album. No one has yet been able to prove anything about Yma. No one has really tried. The U.S. loves a mystery, and Yma Sumac is one of the best."

Because Yma's performance schedule was so hectic, her only television appearance during 1952 was in February on the Frank Sinatra Show. The tremendous audience response for her selections, "Inca Love Song" (Kuyaway), and "Tumpa!" prompted a

Legend of the Sun Virgin poster

request for Yma's return. Due to already heavy bookings, however, it had to be postponed until the summer of 1954.

The highlight of 1952 was a massive summer tour of England and parts of Europe. This was the first tour Yma had undertaken since her days in South America. It was an important tour since it introduced her to European audiences. The most concentrated branch of the tour was the crisscrossing of England. Within less than a month's span, Yma executed a feat that tested her emotional, physical, and vocal endurance by often performing night after night.

Aboard the Queen Elizabeth, 1952: (left to right) David Revera, Franklin Marks, Maureeen Shea, Moisés Vivanco, Alexander Borisoff, Hernán Braña. In the deck chairs, Yma Sumac, June Starr.

Below is the schedule of the English branch of the tour:

May 30 Colston Hall, Bristol
May 31 Royal Albert Hall, London
June 4 St. Andrew's Hall, Glasgow
June 5 Caird Hall, Dundee
June 6 Usher Hall, Edinburgh
June 7 City Hall, New Castle
June 10 King's Hall, Belle Vue, Manchester
June 11 De Montfort Hall, Leicester
June 12 Sophia Gardens Pavillion
June 13 Winter Gardens, Bournemouth
June 14 The Dome, Brighton
June 16 Royal Albert Hall, London (return)
June 17 Civic Hall, Wolverhampton
June 18 City Hall, Hull
June 19 City Hall, Sheffield
June 20 King George's Hall, Blackburn
June 21 Albert Hall, Nottingham
June 22 New Opera House, Blackpool

The tour was under the auspices of the Harold Fielding Concert Division and was in conjunction with the famous George Melachrino Orchestra. It was a tremendous artistic achievement for Yma, despite the dangerous frequency of performances. Carefully planned and programmed, however, certain things helped ensure that Yma avoided problems during the back-to-back concerts.

The concerts were in two distinct halves. Part one, which lasted an hour, was Melachrino and his orchestra, who performed numbers by such popular composers as George Gershwin and Cole Porter. Part two featured Sumac and Company. For her half, Yma sang between five and eight numbers, some with orchestral accompaniment and some only with guitar, flute and percussion.

The program below is what was given in most cities during the tour.

YMA SUMAC
with Original Music Composed on Ancient Inca Themes By
Moisés Vivanco
World's Foremost Authority on Ancient Inca Music

A. **Pachacamac (Overture)**
B. **Yma Sumac:**
Ataypura High Andes (Andean Enchantment)
Mamallay Mother's Sorrow
Najla's Lament
C. **Wiracocha (orchestral)**
Pok'ra Inca March (orchestral)
Inti Waccay Nostalgia of the Sun God (orchestral)
Cusi Joy—Andean Dance
D. **Yma Sumac:**
Urpi Challai-"The Bird Who Became Woman"
(one of the Yma Sumac Legends)

Yma Sumac and Moisés Vivanco:
Birds
Taita Inty—Traditional Inca Hymn to the Sun
(Forbidden music, dating back to 1,000 B.C.)
E. Orchestral:
Tuta Wayra: Chant of the Wind
F. Yma Sumac:
Tumpa!—Earthquake (Yma, the voice of the earthquake—Andean Legend)
Huayno—National Dance of the Peruvian People

From the program above one notices that there are some interesting new claims being made. Yma's "Hymn to the Sun" has become *forbidden* music And is said to date from 1,000 B.C. Moisés is now credited as "Composer and Musical Director." Yma's gowns have now become costumes specially designed for her "with Inca Motifs by Norman Maxon," her shoes by David Evins.

David Revera's participation on this tour provided Hernán with the opportunity to demonstrate his virtuosity on the flute in solos and intricate duets of improvisation with Yma. Also taking part in the rigorous tour were Franklin Marks (assistant conductor), cellist (and lawyer) Alexander Borisoff, and the pianist June Starr who had accompanied Yma at the Vegas club, El Rancho. (Older readers at least may remember June's sister, the celebrated pop organist Ethel Smith, famous for her recording of "Tico-Tico.")

Another name now appears quietly at the bottom of programs. In years to come it would play an important part in newspaper articles and scandal-sheets: Maureen Shea, "Secretary to Miss Sumac." Of the eight people connected with the Sumac tour, only Maureen was not a musician. She had met Yma and Moisés earlier in the year while they were performing in Reno, Nevada. Maureen was seventeen. At the suggestion of Moisés, who had been planning to hire a secretary for Yma, Maureen took the job and joined the Vivanco household.

Although the scheduling of the tour performances was concentrated and intense, in actuality Yma was only required to sing about one-half hour each night. Even so, her most taxing pieces were always included—"Taita Inty," "Tumpa!" and "Birds," all of which demanded over three octaves to execute.

When questioned about the tour, David Revera confessed that he purposefully did not spend a lot of time with Yma and Moisés. "They wanted everyone to be part of the family. But I wasn't interested in that. To me it was just a job. I only worked for them when Moisés called and hired me." When asked to comment on the Sumac tours he took part in, he replied, "I never think about them, only when someone else brings it up. I did enjoy working with Yma, though, at least most of the time. She was phenomenal. Yeah, she was fussy, but not difficult. I liked all her songs, but especially the improvisational segments when she sang and I would create various sounds on the timpani under her to frame what she was doing."

When asked about the Incan stories, Revera shrugged his shoulders, "Well it *was* different, and Yma certainly was different. I really didn't pay much attention to that kind of stuff. It was all hype. I just dealt with Yma as a person, another musician—a colleague. I just did my job." Generally, David found Moisés to be pleasant. He remembers that during the 1952 England tour he (David) sprained his foot. For a while, David just dealt with the pain and limped around. It was Moisés who noticed him limping and bought him a cane to use to help his foot heal faster. When asked about Maureen Shea, David said, "I don't really remember much about her. She had been with the company for a while. She was OK, but she didn't spend much time with the troupe."

2. HAROLD FIELDING presents

Yma Sumac

with Original Music Composed on Ancient Inca Themes by

MOISES VIVANCO

World's Foremost Authority on Ancient Inca Music

A. Pachacamac — Overture
    Ataipura — High Andes (Andean Enchantment)
    Mamallay — Mother's Sorrow
    Najlas Lament

B. Wiracocha — (Orchestral)
    Pok'ra — Inca March
    Inti Waccay — Nostalgia of the Sun God
    Cusi — Joy — Andean Dance

C. Yma Sumac:
    Urpi Challai — "The Bird Who Became Woman" (one of the Yma Sumac Legends)

Yma Sumac and Moises Vivanco:
    Birds
    Taiti Inta — Traditional Inca Hymn to the Sun
        (Forbidden music, dating back to 1,000 B.C.)

Orchestral:
    Tuta Wayra — Chant of the Wind

Yma Sumac:
    Tumpa! Earthquake (Yma, the voice of the earthquake — Andean Legend)
    Huayno — National Dance of the Peruvian People

Miss Sumac's Personnel:
Composer and Musical Director
MOISES VIVANCO
Assisted by
Alexander Borisoff and Franklyn Marks
Andean Drummers
Hernan Brana   David Revera

Miss Sumac's Costumes Designed with Inca Motifs by Norman Maxon. Shoes by David Evins.

Program, 1952, England

David does remember that when problems arose they centered around Moisés rather than Yma.

"It was really very strange. He kept her apart from others so they only dealt with him. That's why I was surprised when he said Yma could go to the movies with me. He usually didn't let her out of his sight. And he would constantly say to other people, 'I taught her this' or 'I did that'—he wanted credit for everything. He and Yma were always fighting because Yma resented being constantly told what to do. He had so much control over her that she would run and hide if any dignitaries came to see her because she was afraid she would say something wrong and upset Moisés."

An example of this clash of wills surfaced on the 31st of May, the day of Yma's first performance at the Albert Hall, in London. The company had completed a long afternoon rehearsal and a tired Yma was looking forward to a few hours rest before the evening's concert. It was a crucial performance because it was her first London concert and it was in an internationally famous concert hall. It was essential that she be at the peak of her powers. For publicity purposes, however, Moisés had arranged for Yma to sing on a radio program for the BBC. Because of time limitations, it could only be scheduled between the afternoon rehearsal and the concert that night. Moisés neglected to tell Yma of this obligation. Had she known of it, it is fairly certain that she would have paced herself differently during the rehearsal, allowing for the extra appearance on the radio. Instead, when the rehearsal ended around five o'clock Moisés told Yma that she was now expected at the radio studio. "What studio?" Yma asked, confused. When Moisés explained, she became furious and adamantly refused to go. Moisés found himself incapable of calming an enraged Yma and was forced to call upon the ever-diplomatic Hernán to try and placate her. As she finally understood, fairly or not, Yma really had no choice. Newspapers had printed information on the time, the radio station and the fact that she was to sing. If she did not appear it could create serious problems. By this time, Moisés and Yma were angrily conversing in a corner where Moisés had taken her, away from the others. Yma remained livid but went with Moisés to the studio and sang the two numbers she had been scheduled to sing. When finished, she concentrated on preparing for the concert, which was only an hour or so away. Despite the strenuous demands of the day, the concert was a complete success. The hall, which seats 8,000, was filled to capacity. Over 2,000 people stood and, according to what was reported, more than 5,000 others were turned away from the box office. English critics found Yma "magical."

This lack of communication between Moisés and Yma was not uncommon. People who worked intimately with both told me that Moisés often displayed a curious disregard for Yma—as if (like others) he expected her to demonstrate superhuman abilities at all times. Although Moisés was responsible for much of what had become "Yma Sumac," he too was capable of exploiting her just as heartlessly as other people. Plagued with his own demons and insecurities, Moisés was prone to equally passionate tantrums. Nevertheless, he viewed his wife's outbursts with almost clinical disdain.

By the time the troupe reached Sheffield on June 19th, they had already given fourteen concerts. A few weeks earlier, Yma and Moisés had celebrated their 10th wedding anniversary. Although cheerful, they missed their son, now three-year-old Charlie, who remained chaperoned in Hollywood. Yma called him long-distance three times a week.

The review of the Sheffield City Hall concert appeared the following day. The critic, G.F.L., wrote a more in-depth review than was customary, noting that Yma kept the large audience "spellbound with her ritual songs and vocal legends." Different from most other critics, he was meticulous in authenticating the vocal range that Yma used during the concert that night.

"[She] is said to have a range of four-and-a-half octaves. If that is so, then she must have kept an octave in reserve, because the audible compass of the songs she sang last night did not extend beyond three-and-a-half:—three octaves and two tones in 'Birds' and exactly three in the 'Hymn to the Sun God'." 6/20/52 (*Sheffield News [?]*)

After mentioning the lovely quality of Yma's voice and its exciting impact, he balked at trying to pin-down Yma's music: "Most of the music appeared to be a kind of wordless vocalise with some imitation of natural sounds and typically 'Moorish' vocal inflexions. It was all very exotic and in spite of the free arrangements of the Incan themes, all quite convincingly authentic."

The production effects surrounding Yma were now being seriously played with by Moisés, who continuously augmented the degree of display around his wife. Blazing headlines from reviews of the Sheffield performance prove their effectiveness:

"Cymbals Clashed For Emperor's Descendant"

Within the review was a colorful description of that evening and an amusing error about Yma's famous alleged ancestor.

"A thunder of drums, a clash of cymbals, and . . . with only a tom-tom muttering in the background, Yma Sumac, descendant of the Aztec [sic] Emperor Atahualpa stepped on to the platform of Sheffield City Hall last night.

"A splendid apparition in magenta and white, she made a slight obeisance to the grinning lions behind her, and then growled into the microphone. Yma 'the voice of the earthquake', was initiating Sheffield in the forbidden Inca music of 1,000 B.C."

Interviewed before the performance, Yma was found to be "an imperious beauty with raven hair and almond eyes . . . likable and tongue-tied." Moisés was described as her "self-effacing husband (dressed) in a white tuxedo (who) twanged a guitar softly in a corner, and sang to himself." Flanking Yma were Hernán Braña, who wore "an embroidered pixie hood, Indian shawl, purple trousers and beach sandals and glittered with Andean horse-brasses," and David Revera who wore a "beaded Balaclava helmet and a breastplate like a waxed lampshade."

Adding to Yma's mystique was the fact that although she would gladly sign autographs after a concert, she now rarely spoke, always covering her mouth with a handkerchief. Moisés explained to fans that Yma was not supposed to speak after a concert.

By the time Yma and Moisés embarked on the tour of England, Scotland and Ireland, the production surrounding her had become more involved, though still not as spectacular as it would become in America two years later. Although the production expansion

Moises, Yma, on tour feeding pigeons

had a definite, positive impact on Yma's relationship with audiences, there were other changes that did not sit quite as well. Some were decisions that unfortunately continue to damage the singer's credibility as a serious musician to this day.

The "Incan Princess" theme was now being exploited as recklessly as Yma's vocal range. Because this was Yma's first concert tour since her Hollywood Bowl breakthrough, imaginative program notes were created for concert programs. These notes were interesting as unusually creative and poetic hokum. Emphasis remained on Yma's exoticism, but a clear effort was now being made to bolster her credibility as an authentic "Incan" performer. There was now a subtly defensive note taken in her biography that was jarring. Most of the "facts" questioned by the critics and the public were ignored and left unanswered, which left many shadows in her biographical material. Unfortunately, inexcusable errors were now appearing *within* errors. For instance, this portion of the first paragraph of the program given to audiences during this 1952 tour:

"Yma Sumac does not claim to be a princess but she does claim she is an Inca, born and raised in the village of Ichocan, 16,000 feet up on the side of Mt. Cumbenayta [sic] in Peru . . . There is also a letter in the files of the Peruvian Consul in New York which supports her claim that she is a direct descendant of the Emperor Atahualpa . . . "

This "document" was the focus of much speculation when it first appeared. And throughout her career much emphasis was given it. Supposedly, it was produced by the Sumac management at the height of the Amy Camus controversy in 1951, as a defense. I suspect it actually arrived on the scene earlier. This was probably the official document that Yma gave Alan Livingston during the recording sessions of *"Voice of the Xtabay."* It reads:

"I hereby certify that to the best of my knowledge, and in accordance with the assertions of authorities on the History of the Incas and on Peruvian History in general (whose names will be furnished upon request), Imma Sumack is a descendant of the Inca Emperor Atahualpa, her mother having been Dona Emilia Atahualpa, direct descendant of the last Emperor of Peru."

May 23, 1946 Jose Vareka y Arias
Consul General del Peru"

Yet, later within the same program notes a contrasting claim is made: "There is no mystery about her. She is a beautiful girl from the Andes who happens to be born with the kind of voice which has occurred only a few times in recorded history."

One wonders at the necessity for such a document. Professor William P. Mitchell provides a possible reason: "In the 1930s and 1940s there was an indigenous movement in Peru where intellectuals were glorifying the Incan past of Peru. Yma was probably feeding into that since the Compañia may have been part of that movement. In the US and Europe Peruvians often try to claim Indian ancestry since such ancestry gives them prestige.

"If you notice," he continued, "the document states 'To the best of my knowledge' so the Peruvian Consul isn't really asserting anything. He is simply saying that people have told him… So actually, it doesn't mean very much—except for her claim for being a descendant of Atuahualpa, which would have contributed to her mystique here in the United States. You must understand that, in Peru, you can buy almost any document. I am not saying that that is what she did, but that is a reality."

As seen in the *Brooklyn Eagle* article, by December of 1952, Yma was again boasting that she was an Incan Princess. This constant vacillation between stories was a persistent theme throughout Yma's career.

Even so, the use of the Consul General's document is an example of grossly poor timing. The Amy Camus controversy began around February of 1951. By April this defense document had suddenly been produced for the media but with the date of 1946, though nothing had previously been claimed about the existence of such a document.

When Yma and Moisés arrived in America in January 1946, they were promoting Peruvian folk music, not Incan exotica. Nowhere can you find them claiming she was Incan. At that time, a document such as this would have been unnecessary. Yma was billed (or advertised) as "soloist," nothing else. During the years before their US arrival, they would not have needed such a document in South America. For all his bravado, Moisés certainly never presumed to present Yma to South American audiences as Incan. It wasn't until her national breakthrough in America in 1950 that Yma suddenly emerged as a personage of royal descent, revered by the mountain villagers of Peru, her voice worshipped by superstitious natives. Only then was there a need for such a document.

The timing of this document's appearance seems, then, to have been but another clumsy faux pas committed by managerial powers, concocted to authenticate—or prop up—their claims about the Peruvian singer. In hindsight, it can be seen as actually insulting to Yma as well as to popular audiences that managers, publicity agents and even her own husband had so little faith in her natural abilities that they felt it necessary to construct such fantasies.

Also confusing record buyers in 1952 was the release, on the Coral label, of eight of Yma's 1943 Odeon recordings. Although accurately proclaimed as Yma's first recordings, nothing was said about why they were so different.

It was also at this time (1952) that the hyperbolic publicity concerning Yma's vocal range reached its peak. Stunned European audiences read that on a good day Yma could vocalize through six full octaves—that is, almost the entire piano keyboard. Again, it is a sad commentary on Yma's management and press corps that they never seemed satisfied with Yma's truly awesome natural range boundaries. The constant toying with Yma's range is typical of a nonmusical, but very American, misplaced faith in "bigger must be better." Because of their constant desire to impress and because of the unique nature of her performances, Yma and Moisés allowed, even fostered, the liberties taken in the claims about her range. Indeed in many instances, they supported the fabrications vociferously—to the extent, indeed, that as late as the time of this writing—2007—Yma still maintains that she had five full octaves.

It is interesting, however, that during the 1940s (Yma's early career in South America) the question of range seemed to be of no particular importance; especially to Yma. Her attitude toward this changed once she reached North America. After that, she, herself, began to take an almost obsessive interest in her range extensions. Reviews in her private scrapbooks show eccentric tampering. Passages referring to her "four-octave" range are scratched out and replaced with a hand-written "five-octaves." The truth of the matter is that during her prime (1950–1955) and as proven by her recordings, Yma possessed four octaves. Throughout the entirety of her long career, however, Yma stubbornly insisted she actually had five.

Yma enjoyed touring, finding the experience exhilarating. Hernán Braña remembers that "Yma never got tired. She seemed to thrive on the tours. She was a tremendous source of energy and inspiration for the rest of the group." English newspapers reported every move the petite Peruvian made. In some cases, they concocted stories when none existed. For example, while driving between engagements, with all their instruments in the back of a station wagon, the car in front of them braked suddenly, forcing them to also brake abruptly. Because of the jerking motion, the instruments fell out of the car and splayed all over the road behind them. Newspapers turned this little incident into a serious accident with injured passengers. Although later it was remembered with humor, at the time it caused big headaches. Many phone calls and reassurances had to be made to frantic employers of forthcoming engagements.

The only note of dissatisfaction from English critics during the course of the tour was that Yma did not sing any operatic arias, as had been originally promised, thus removing any opportunity for comparisons with other singers.

After the conclusion of the English tour, the troupe traveled to Paris for a number of performances. During the last days of June, concerts were given at the famous Alham-

David Revera, Yma, Hernán, Paris 1952

Paris, 1952

bra, Rex Theater, and the Folies Bergere (with a young Yves Montand). Parisian audiences were thrilled with Yma's exotic singing of "Taita Inty," "Tumpa!", "Birds," "Monos," and "Ataypura" (High Andes). *Le Soir* wrote, "A vocal miracle! The first time you hear Yma Sumac you gasp, for this is the most unimaginable vocal phenomenon that has ever been revealed to the world."

By this time Moisés had settled on the program layout for both nightclub and concert appearances. Nightclub programs usually consisted of two sets of three songs with Peruvian dances in between and (occasionally) encores after each set. Yma would be required to sing no more than eight numbers. Concerts were more involved. Usually an orchestra of twenty musicians was hired, and Yma sang between 9 and 12 numbers. Whenever possible, Yma introduced the songs of each set.

During July, the troupe gave concerts in Belgium, Holland and Italy. After which they made preparations to return to the United States for an engagement in San Francisco, at the Peacock Room in the Hotel Mark Hopkins. This engagement was to stretch from July 30th to August 17th.

David Revera tells an amusing anecdote dating from the performances at the Peacock Room. It was Yma's practice to conclude "Taita Inty" with a long, chromatic descent from a sustained high F. It had been prearranged between Yma and David that he would gently smack a gong for punctuation as she neared the end of the descent. During one performance, while hemmed in by various drums and congas, he found he could not reach the gong. He finally managed to turn the gong on its side so that he could drop it for the effect they wanted. Unfortunately, the gong slipped and came down harder than he meant it to, producing a crash that visibly startled Yma, who lost her usual perfect composure.

When the show was over, David returned his costume to Yma's dressing room as usual, expecting to find Yma, understandably indeed, in something of a fury. Sure enough, there she was, surrounded by various VIP's and admirers, imperious as an empress preparing to order lackeys to drag an offender off for a beheading. Instead, though, as David made his apology and explained what had happened in halting, broken Spanish, she burst into giggles. To this day, he is not sure whether it was the slapstick sequence he was describing or something about the quality of his Spanish that evoked the fit of hilarity from Yma.

Reviews of the shows given in the Peacock Room were favorable. One in particular showed that the critic had done some homework. A number of years earlier, Yma had briefly performed at the Mark Hopkins as a Peruvian folk-singer. The current article observed that one would not have recognized her as the same artist. For emphasis two photographs were shown, one of Yma in traditional Peruvian festive garb taken at the time of her first appearance, the other of Yma in her Inca princess costume, resplendent in jeweled finery. Under normal circumstances this would simply have shown her growth as an artist. Coming so soon after the Amy Camus farce and the transparent Inca princess publicity ploys, it simply made it seem that Yma was something of a humbug—if a humbug with great talent.

This brings us, perhaps, to the point of facing the simple explanation of the origin and probable reasons for the continuance of the Inca princess motif even after it had become passé. It was a demonstrable, undeniable fact that the Inca Princess packaging sold tickets. When Yma first arrived in America, hotel and nightclub managers encountered great difficulty selling a show featuring a "Peruvian soprano." When advertising that an Incan Princess would be singing, however, the story was very different. As Bob Covais wryly commented to me, "At that time, what did American audiences know from an Incan Princess? They would go just to see what she looked like. Then, after experiencing that voice, well, word got around fast that she was something quite special."

For the most part, audiences adored Yma Sumac. Yet she continued to pay a price for slipshod publicity, organization and the continued empty boasting of her Incan heritage as her reputation slowly corroded and bits of her believability crumbled each time a well researched article appeared. Whether at the instigation of Moisés, her many various managers, or her own counsel, Yma remained almost entirely silent in response to doubters and scoffers.

After the Mark Hopkins performances, the troupe moved on to fulfill an engagement at the Mocambo Club in Hollywood. The Mocambo was still one of the most famous nightspots in the world. The September shows drew capacity crowds and idolatrous audience response. Yma's performances were of such caliber and originality that they were still spoken of in wonderment some twenty years later.

October 1952 found the singer returning to the Cotillion Room at the Hotel Pierre in New York City. While there, Yma, Moisés, Hernán and David recorded "Babalu" (Hernán's arrangement) and "Wimoweh" which were released as a single in both 78 rpm and 45 rpm. Recorded at the hotel, the recordings are unusual in that no over-dubbing of the singer was done. "Wimoweh," which Yma learned from the original recording made by The Weavers, was not an inspired choice or an inspiring rendition. "Babalu," however, drew some dazzling singing from Yma. Interestingly, "Babalu" bears a strong resemblance to "Tumpa!" (Earthquake!)—making the "Incan" origin of that number all the more suspect. (One person who worked with Yma was heard to mutter, "Everything Yma sang sounded like 'Babalu.' ")

In December, Yma rounded out the year with a successful first appearance at the Marine Room in Chicago's Edgewater Beach Hotel. Of the December 26th performance, *Variety* noted in their inimitable style: "Gal nicely overflows her off-the-shoulder gown and strengthens the natural interest of her unusual voice with effective, if slightly cool, salesmanship. . . . Miss Sumac's somewhat esoteric collection of native festive and religious song hits the peak with the 'Birds' number run off to a subtle Vivanco guitar background. It's an amazing display of vocal gymnastics and the canary exits with very large applause." (Dave, 12/31/52)

The shows in Chicago stretched over the better part of a month, into the beginning of 1953. Newspapers noted the success of such crowd pleasers as "Tumpa!", "Birds," "Malambo," "Ataypura," and a new concert piece, a stratospheric vocalise arrangement of Claude Debussy's piano piece, "Clair de Lune." As with audiences all over the world, the favorite remained the hymn to the sun, "Taita Inty."

On February 1, 1953 The Musical Courier carried an enticing announcement: "Yma Sumac will make her first concert tour next season under the auspices of Kenneth Allen Associates, Inc. (formerly James A. Davidson Management, Inc.) Miss Sumac . . . will have with her a company of 13 dancers, drummers and musicians in a program entirely Andean and Peruvian. The music consists of ancient Inca melodies and original music composed on ancient Inca themes by Moisés Vivanco, authority on Andean Music. The Inca costumes for the tour are valued at $50,000."

After the Chicago stint, the Sumac troupe settled at the Century Room in the Dallas Hotel Adolphus for a two-week engagement. A $3.00 cover charge was required at the door and the performances, which opened February 27th and extended through March 14th, were just as successful as those in Chicago. Advertisements for the show billed Yma as "The Peruvian Princess with the most exciting voice in the world."

Despite the constant performing schedule, Yma's voice was in good shape, its quality and use sending critics and audiences alike on a search for new adjectives to describe the effects of her voice and music. The show at the Adolphus was thirty-five minutes long and Yma sang seven numbers typical of club dates.

Programs were occasionally altered depending on current favorites but usually included the, by now, mandatory "Birds," "Kuyaway" (Inca Love Song), "Taita Inty," "Huayno" (National Dance of Peru), "Tumpa!", "Lament" (from the *Legend of the Sun Virgin* album), and "Malambo #1." Assisting Yma was June Starr (pianist), Hernán, Alejandro Granda, Yma's operatic coach, and Cholita Rivero, who danced two numbers.

An article promoting the Dallas appearances noted that the night before she opened Yma was the guest of honor at a press and radio reception given by the hotel management. A newspaper photo taken at the time shows a posing Yma flanked by Moisés and Randall Davis, the managing director of the hotel. After noting that Yma's grasp of the English language was very good, mention was made of the four-year-old Charlie, who was also present.

"The precocious youngster sings, dances and composes, but his big ambition is to be a conductor. According to the young man's father, every night he includes in his prayers, 'let me be a great conductor some day.'" (Fairfax Nisbet, The Dallas *Morning News*, Friday, February 27, 1953)

Charlie in cowboy suit c. 1953

In addition to noting that Charlie spoke English, Spanish and "Inca, the ancient language of his mother's forbears" (read Quechua) a rare mention is made of another member of the troupe. "Also in the Sumac entourage is the singer's cousin, Yolanda Rivero, a dancer known professionally as Cholita...."

Nisbet also reviewed the show a few days later. "The lady who is reported to be a descendant of Inca royalty looks every inch of it, with her inky black hair worn smooth over the head with a thick braid over one shoulder, her heavy-lidded dark eyes and high cheek bones." After commenting that "Birds" was the best demonstration of her abilities, he noted "There is also her husband . . . arranger-composer-guitarist who contributes a stunning guitar obbligato to counterpoint the Sumac vocal effects."

Variety found Yma's miniature review excellent entertainment. Special mention was made of Yma's exotic beauty, which was "enhanced via off-the-shoulder costumes, straight Inca hair-do with jet black, waist-length braid and (other) obvious physical assets . . . " (2/27/53) Also admired was Cholita's colorful dances and June Starr's pianistic contributions to "Tumpa!"

In March 1953, after the Dallas run had been completed, Yma returned to Los Angeles to record her third album for Capitol records, *Inca Taqui*. It was released six months later, in August, as a 10" LP.

This was a pivotal recording for Yma and the eight selections were chosen with care. It was also obvious that the album was meant to be distinctly different from the two earlier recordings. The cover had a beautiful color photograph by Tom Kelley of Yma and Moisés performing in authentic Peruvian garb and posed naturally. Ironically, the album included a number of songs that were never used after the recording.

The eight selections were:
"K'arawi" (Planting Song)
"Cumbe-Maita" (Calls of the Andes)
"Wak'ai" (Cry)
"Incacho" (Royal Anthem)
"Chuncho!" (Forest Creatures) (interestingly, "Chunchos" is the word Quechua speakers use to refer to the peoples of the tropical rain forest to the east of the Andes.)
"Lulla Mak'ta" (Andean Don Juan)
"Malaya!" (My Destiny!)
"Ripui" (Farewell)

Although *Inca Taqui* was well conceived and performed, it was not as popular with the record-buying public as the two previous recordings. One of the reasons was the album's distinct departure from the lush orchestrations and harmonic tradition of *Voice of the Xtabay* and *Legend of the Sun Virgin*. Gone were the juicy, Hollywood movie-score accompaniments. Instead, there was an attempt to return to more ethnic, authentic-sounding material. Although *Inca Taqui* more accurately reflected Yma's stage performances, the starkness of many of the arrangements and the hokey use of over-reverberant acoustics in some tracks often set up distinct conflicts.

Record buyers had grown accustomed to hearing Yma surrounded by the Baxter-lush orchestrations. After Yma's second album, *Legend of the Sun Virgin*, consumers would be confronted with a hodge-podge presentation of Sumac disks—each album with differing harmonic and structural priorities. The only constant was that listeners were guaranteed that Yma would deliver some unusual and often startling acrobatics.

In any case, *Inca Taqui* remains one of Yma's most important studio efforts if for no other reason than that the ever-evolving "Birds" was finally documented in its completed format as "Chuncho!" (Forest Creatures) During concerts in the next twenty years, Yma would still often refer to "Chuncho!" as "Birds," as though loath to give up the original concept of the song.

Inca Taqui was the last of Yma's records to promote "Authentic, ancient Incan melodies." No fewer than twenty-eight selections of Yma's Incan ritualistic flights were now available to the public.

Inca Taqui was also the first (and actually, only) album to include descriptive liner-note fantasies for each of the songs. These descriptions were soon reprinted in concert programs and although not related to the music performed, did offer some kernels of traditional Incan practices. When *Inca Taqui* was paired with *Voice of the Xtabay* on 12" LP in 1956, similar notes were created for the earlier *Xtabay* selections. By that time, the creative writers of the Sumac entourage had quite a backlog of legends they could call upon.

After the recording sessions, Yma and Moisés concentrated on plans for a massive concert tour that was to take place the next year. It was to be the most ambitious undertaking ever made by the Sumac troupe. The tour, under the auspices of the Kenneth Allen Associates, was to cover most of the United States and Europe. Nicely coinciding with this, in England Yma was voted, "Teenager's Favorite Recording Artist of 1953."

1952 Argentinean ad for records

"Accla K'ory" **81**

Sans Souci, Montreal, June 1953. Alejandro Granda, unknown man, Cholita, Hernán

April 1953 found Yma making a long overdue return trip to her Peru. While visiting with her family, she gave a concert in the ruins of Machu Picchu. An unusual event, it was one of the few times that Yma sang without a microphone. Generally, Yma was terrified of not having that instrument with her to aid in her subtle colorations. For the Machu Picchu concert, Yma offered a number of selections from the *Legend of the Sun Virgin* album, performing them for a Peruvian audience who enjoyed the fantasy of her music. Some of the songs, such as "Zana," "Montana" and "Kuyaway" (Inca Love Song), were recognizable to the audience because the melodies had their roots in Peruvian folk repertoire, though altered with differing titles and slick musical presentation. Other selections, such as "Lament," "Kon Tiki," "Panarima" and "Suray Surita" were admired for Yma's lyrical or bravura singing rather than for authenticity. This concert would appear to have been the only time Yma performed "Panarima" (from *Legend of the Sun Virgin*) live—unless, as in fact I suspect, it was sung in concerts under a different title.

Immediately following the Machu Picchu concert the troupe traveled to Venezuela, Puerto Rico, Argentina, and Mexico, giving performances to stunned listeners. Audiences in Buenos Aires were especially impressed. They had not had the opportunity to hear Yma perform since 1943, a decade earlier, and much had obviously happened to Yma and her music since then.

By the end of May 1953, the group was performing in Montreal's swank nightclub, Sans-Souci, where Yma broke all attendance records previously set by the French chanteuse, Edith Piaf. Yma's contract stipulated two shows nightly, at 9:30 and midnight. Also taking part in the show was the 55 year-old Alejandro Granda, who played drums and sang a song written by Moisés. During the May–June performances at the Sans-Souci, Yma reputedly had her own radio show in Montreal. Live, it boasted a narrator who supplied pertinent data on Incan history while Yma warbled her way through her most famous numbers. For the radio programs, she had the support of a full symphony orchestra.

Near the end of Yma's appearances (which were extended) *The Montreal Gazette* noted "Seldom has a performer had the impact on Montreal audiences that Miss Sumac has had.... She gives her audiences ample opportunity to judge her voice by giving generously of her talent on each show. Particularly outstanding is one number she does called Birds. In it she does abstractions of various bird and animal sounds, combining them all in an off-beat, gentle rhythm that is most effective." H. W. described Yma's singing as going from "a low whisper, through a husky, throaty tone to a high note that is almost felt rather than heard."

By mid-June, Yma and Moisés had returned to New York City to prepare for one of their most important appearances yet, their New York concert debut. This was a Latin American Fiesta that was to be given at the Lewisohn Stadium on the 25th of June. The first half of the program featured Leonard Bernstein conducting the Stadium Symphony in selections by Copland, Guarnier, and Villa-Lobos. This last, the Villa-Lobos "Concerto for Piano and Orchestra #4," was being given its New York Premiere and featured the brilliant Brazilian pianist, Bernardo Segall, to whom the concerto had been dedicated on its composition in 1952.

Yma and her group, Moisés, Cholita, Hernán, and David Revera, had the second half of the program. Yma and Moisés offered to the New York audience a typical Sumacian program of orchestral numbers, solo dances by Cholita and at least eight numbers by Yma, all conducted by David Mendoza. Yma's program included:

Kon Tiki (Wiracocha)—Suite for Orchestra in three movements
Ataipura (High Andes)—Yma
Montana Mama (Lullaby)—Yma
Tumpa! (Earthquake!)—Yma
encore: Vocalise on Clair de Lune by Claude Debussy—Yma (N.Y. Premiere)
Pitu-Serrania—Orchestra
Criollo Waltz—Orchestra
Tuta Wayra-(Chant of the Wind)—Orchestra
Huayno (National Dance of Peru)—solo dance by Cholita
Pachamama (Mother Earth)—solo dance by Cholita
encore: Puccini: "O mio babbino caro" (from Gianni Schicchi)—Yma
Chuncho—Birds—Yma
Taita Inty—Hymn to the Sun—Yma
Cholo Traicionero—Song of Youth—Yma

Thirteen thousand people came to hear the Peruvian singer exhibit her exotic material and reviewers made special note that everyone present certainly received their money's worth. Francis D. Perkins of the *New York Herald Tribune* wrote: "Her voice is hard to label; it runs from what seemed to be a tenor register to the highest soprano altitudes, and has an impressive array of colors and timbres at different points ... some of the lower notes had a darkly, husky quality which was well suited to the kind of music for which they were implied; the quality of some of the highest notes seemed almost instrumental; at one point, a steadily sustained crescendo told of notable dynamic control in expressively convincing singing....The instrumental works ... were appealing, but Mr. Vivanco's music at times combined them with a rather cosmopolitan atmosphere; the indigenous (flavor) was strongest in the guitar-accompanied songs."

Robert Bagar, writing for the *New York Post,* was very enthusiastic: "In Part II the sensational (can't help using that word) Yma Sumac, a beautiful Peruvian with an astounding voice, proved the star of the occasion. Miss Sumac, in fact, has several voices, one tacked on to the other from deep and rich contralto to light soprano. In any of these areas she does the most remarkable things—coloratura work, on pitch gargling, lip flutterings, trills of all kinds. She can leap from low to high, switch back halfway in one timbre and rise again in another. She can toss out notes thunderous enough to sound like broadsides . . . . What she does is artistic, it has purpose, the purpose of interpreting the folk songs of the Andes . . . . Certainly hers is a most exotic style of singing. It must be judged by standards of its own . . . "

Writing for the *New York Post* on June 26th, Harriet Johnson remarked that the "exotic Ima Sumac . . . not only sang but provided the most sultry growl . . . ever to tax the curiosity of my ear." Celebrating the singer's prodigious virtuosity, Ms. Johnson emphasized that Yma's throat "can turn from vocal depths to heights with the dexterity of a quick-change artist" and that she was "best throughout the evening in music that seemed closest to her ancient heritage. The more contemporary she became the less effective she was. Puccini's 'Oh mio babbino caro' gave the impression she had better stay away from opera. Her loveliest notes are those startling, bird-like high tones which emerge from the vocal stratosphere with more ease and beauty than what comes forth from normally easier registers . . . In addition to music there were colored lights for different moods, and a languorous if non-musical moon, serenaded by Miss Sumac in Debussy's 'Clair de Lune' sung as a vocalise. The . . . drummers were vividly costumed to match their vividly painted tools of expression. They grunted too while they drummed but not so effectively as Miss Sumac during her singing."

Ms. Johnson's assessment of the evening's entertainment was that the Latin American Fiesta "may have splashed more in flamboyancy than historic authenticity but the end result was an intriguing variety show which captured the eye if it didn't always intoxicate the ear." Moisés, introduced to the audience by Yma as "a great composer," was found to be a competent accompanist on the guitar, and Cholita "a fascinating dancer . . . who whirled her plentiful head of hair as well as the rest of her pliant body."

Yma's singing, still new to many New Yorkers, was not to everyone's taste. Douglas Watt, writing for the *New York Daily News* (6/26/53) did not enjoy it at all. "The Peruvian pouter pigeon with a four octave range drew 13,000 bird fanciers to Lewisohn Stadium last night to listen to her exercise her deep guttural tones, her high thin ones and all those in between . . . Her voice, like a human theremin, carried clear over to the bleachers to catch up with me halfway down the 136th St. hill to Broadway. It sounded as if it were right in my ear, where I didn't want it."

Mr. Watt conceded that Yma was "strikingly gowned in white and gold" for her first segment, and for her second appeared in "a bluish, billowing affair" but found her musical selections inane. "For an encore she did a piano piece, 'Clair de Lune' by Debussy, rearranged for orchestra and inhuman voice. She made it sound something like 'Carry Me Back to Old Virginny'. Nobody else can do that." But highest on his list of dislikes was the famous "Chuncho!," which he described as "a piece about birds, all sorts of birds. It was for the birds all right. It sounded as though she were wringing their necks."

He also did not care for Cholita's brand of dancing. "Pretty and small, like Miss Sumac, Cholita turned out to be a kind of tassel dancer. First she did the National Dance of the Peruvian People, which it developed, is a thing in which you Lindy while swinging a rope with a tassel on the end. Next she presented 'The whirling drama of Mother Earth', this time using her hair for a tassel and swinging her head as if it were a mop."

Wrapping up his review Mr. Watt concluded with amusing insight. "It's probably a nice accomplishment, Miss Sumac's, but I'm still glad I'm not Vivanco. Imagine coming home late some night and getting told off in all those voices!"

The most discerning comments, however, came from J.B. of the *New York Times*: "Advance publicity had claimed for Miss Sumac's voice a range of five octaves. Her voice is a remarkable instrument, but not as remarkable as that. The range she displayed last evening, and which probably approximated the useable limits of her voice, descended below Middle C and passed the high C two octaves above. This is of course an unusual vocal compass, but not a unique one. The peculiarity of Miss Sumac's voice is that it possesses both the deep chest-voice tones of the contralto and the high flute-voice of a [coloratura]. These are (characteristic) timbres that one listener had never before heard combined in a single voice. In special music composed for her . . . Miss Sumac showed herself able to produce an astonishing variety of coloristic effects . . . Miss Sumac's voice is a freak, as most really fine voices are. She might well become an artist of distinction if her tastes and inclinations are in that direction. On the other hand, her bird-calls and other vocal tricks are diverting enough in themselves to provide an evening of unusual entertainment."

Although most critics appreciated the many effects Yma was partial to display in her Incan music, without exception all agreed that the Puccini aria was not at all satisfactory, spoiled by scooping and an inartistic phrasing of Puccini's melodic line.

The Lewisohn Stadium concert was broadcast on WQXR radio and fortunately, a tape exists of most of Yma's half of the program. Missing from the tape are the orchestral overture, "Kon Tiki," Yma's "Ataypura" (High Andes), and "Taita Inty" (Hymn to the Sun), and Cholita's two dances. Of the nine selections extant, six are sung by Yma.

The tape is a fascinating document of Yma's concert performing practices at the time. This was also the first time "Chuncho!" was listed as such on concert programs, signaling the completion of its metamorphosis from "Birds." The sound quality of the tape is occasionally distant but is still invaluable for a number of reasons. Because it was Yma's New York concert debut, it was a pivotal performance in securing her popularity with that sophisticated audience. Also, the tape captures Yma's voice in its prime, under typical performance pressures, and just after an extensive, grueling tour of Europe. The voice is in splendid shape. Low notes are solid and rich while high Ds and Ebs are easily floated over the Stadium's amplification system. By Yma's standards, the range used for most of the concert was conservative. That is until "Chuncho!" (Forest Creatures), where she pulled out all the stops and covered almost three-and-one-half octaves.

The tape is also the only existing example of Yma singing an operatic aria. Puccini's "O mio babbino caro" (*Gianni Schicchi*) played an important in Yma's concerts. Despite adverse criticism, Yma often included an operatic aria on her concerts, usually either this aria or a bastardized version of Mozart's Queen of the Night's aria "Der Hölle Rache" (*Die Zauberflöte*) which was sung as a "Queen of the Night Mambo." Unfortunately, a performance of that has never surfaced on tape.

The Lewisohn Stadium tape is also invaluable because it shows the type of orchestral selections used to frame Yma's sets. For us today, it gives a clearer picture of just what kind of music was being offered to 1950s audiences and its quality.

I am sure other Sumac performances of the 1950s exist. Hopefully they will surface some day. Most probably, however, they are in collections of people who do not think they would be of any interest to anyone. This was the case with Phil Mealey, who kindly provided me with a copy of the Lewisohn Stadium concert and also a 1975 appearance of Yma's at the Chateau Madrid in New York. "I had no idea anyone would be interested in them," he told me. "They have been sitting around my house for twenty years!"

After studying Yma's live performances and the commercial recordings she made for Capitol, the fact remains that the commercial recordings caught the singer at her best. The Capitol disks perfectly represent Yma's vocal capabilities and provide concise examples of the best of her work. That being said, as with any performer, live performance cannot help but provide additional insight into their art and development. Yma was anything but a static singer and her songs and vocal effects were constantly undergoing revision.

For instance, "Chuncho!" (Forest Creatures). Aurally, the development of this piece can be traced through at least four versions, from 1951 to about 1961. During that decade of performances, the amount of intricacy and added dimension given to this number is astounding for its imaginative growth. Yma's selections on the Lewisohn Stadium tape include a "Montana" that is simple and idiomatic, differing little from the recorded version for Capitol. "Tumpa!" (Earthquake!), however, had begun its metamorphosis from an exotica centerpiece, to an uninteresting cha-cha dance number. The growl had been discarded (at least on the Lewisohn Stadium night) and phrase endings are changed at will. The famous climactic rise to high F-sharp (found on *Voice of the Xtabay*) has been altered so that Yma only ascends a third lower, to high D. This is most probably the way Yma most often performed the song. Staccati up to high E, however, still abound in the second, improvisatory section.

"Clair de Lune," Yma's C-major adaptation of Debussy's popular piano piece, is well suited to her gifts and the soaring lines span almost three octaves. It is no wonder her version was so popular with audiences since it allowed them to revel in her free, sweetly lyrical singing. It remained in her repertoire for another twenty years.

There was, however, a startling and absurd claim made for the Debussy number during the concert. During the tumultuous applause, the radio announcer, presumably reading from prepared notes given to him, says: "Yma Sumac has just sung the new vocal arrangement of Debussy's familiar 'Clair de Lune.' Mr. Vivanco, incidentally, tells us that this is the first time this music has been sung. The text is Incan." Yma's arrangement of "Clair de Lune" was a vocalise. There was no "text."

The three orchestral pieces attributed to Moisés are typical of the reams of program music heard in Yma's concerts at that time. Taken as such, they are melodic and enjoyable, without any pretence that they were written by Beethoven. Chromatic, atmospheric; alternately lush and stark, they framed Yma's exotic programs very nicely. Especially fine is "Pitu," a melancholy, honeyed number that tends to remain in the memory.

The famous Puccini aria from *Gianni Schicchi* suits Yma's voice very well. Her pronunciation of the Italian, however, is an embarrassment and her manner of singing is completely at odds with traditional operatic concepts. The Peruvian tradition of descending grace notes lends a distinctly off-kilter feeling to the aria that is as unappealing as it is wrong. Although Yma often asserted the opposite, she had no comprehension

Villa Rosa, Madrid, 1954 (Hernán on conga, floor at left)

of operatic *rubato* or the concepts of correct stylistic proprieties. Yma often boasted that if she took a year off to learn repertoire she could be one of the great opera stars. Granda's coaching obviously had its limits since Yma's concept of operatic singing remained rudimentary at best and entirely her own.

It is ironic that the timbre of Yma's voice was ideal for operatic music but the instinct simply was not there. It is an unfortunate paradox that Yma only approached a true operatic style in the midst of her own, specialized, Incan fantasies. In the lyricism or coloratura of such pieces as "Taita Inty" (Hymn to the Sun), "Kon Tiki," "Ccori Canastitay" (Golden Basket), "Kuyaway" (Inca Love Song), "Suray Surita," and "Najla's Lament" (*Flahooley*), Yma Sumac approached an operatic ideal epitomized by such contemporary artists as Lily Pons, Roberta Peters, and Joan Sutherland.

"Chuncho!", always the high spot of Yma's performances, is a different matter entirely. The performance at the Lewisohn Stadium concert is a fascinating combination of the best of the original 1951 "Birds" and the new novel effects that had been incorporated into the Capitol recording sessions four months earlier. In concert at least, Yma usually introduced the piece over quiet guitar accompaniment by Moisés, and "Chuncho!" became an obvious tribute to her Andean origins. The piece must have mystified listeners hearing it for the first time. There is nothing in the annals of Western music that equals its distinct combination of song and mimicry.

James Branciforti, who helped Bob Covais produce Yma's *Miracles* album in 1971, once asked Yma exactly what animals she was imitating during "Chuncho!" "Oh," she said, smiling, "No particular animals. We have very strange animals in the Andes. What do you think—that it's like the Catskills?"

Years later Yma explained to *Spin* magazine (5/87) "As a child, I thought that all of nature, including all kinds of animals, were my audience. I learned something from them. In Forest Creatures . . . I sing, but I blend it with very strange sounds." These sounds included the whispering of trees and wind, the buzz of insects, the growling of predatory animals and a host of birds. In this instance, the range Yma used to perform the song stretched from the C below middle C to high F-sharp—just under three and a half octaves.

Typically inconsistent, concert programs and Capitol reissues title the piece "Chuncho!" (Forest Creatures). Hernán Braña informed me that the correct title was really 'Chunch*u*!' (*Jungle* Creatures). Yma insists that it is Chuncho! (It doesn't help matters that the song was about equally often called "Birds.")

Professor William Mitchell of Monmouth University explains: "The different spellings represent an inconsistent orthography for Quechua, which one often finds in Peru. 'Chuncho' would be pronounced in Quechua just like 'Chunchu'—one often finds the two spellings used for the same word. It refers to the tropical rain forest people, not animals."

Both versions, whether called "Birds" or "Chuncho!" have an identical framework and certain vocal effects were carried from one version to the other. Generally, however, the piece was free in its structure with minimal accompaniment, which served to heighten and underline the exoticism of Yma's singing. "Birds/Chuncho!" remains Yma's nature piece; of all her repertoire it displayed her imitative abilities at their most outré.

When questioned about the exact form or structure of this piece, Hernán Braña compared it to a jazz musicians' jam session—essentially improvisatory, within a certain melodic or harmonic framework. In this case, everything was completely controlled by what Yma decided to do in the course of the performance. Because of this, there is an immediacy to both versions that is riveting.

"Chuncho!" (in any format—or spelling), does not appear on Yma's programs, or in reviews of performances, before the Broadway production of *Flahooley* in the spring of 1951. At that time, it went under the title of "Birds" and was recorded on Capitol

Records' recording of the cast album. Within two years, the piece had been expanded, reworked, retitled and rerecorded as "Chuncho!" on *Inca Taqui*. The earlier version was discarded; "Chuncho!" had become a mainstay of Yma's performances.

Despite the fact that no mention is made in reviews or concerts of such a piece before 1951, and despite the fact that such a piece was not chosen to spotlight Yma when she made her first recordings for Odeon in 1943, Moisés Vivanco insists the piece was composed—by him—much earlier. Moisés stated in private correspondence: "Mr. Braña is absolutely incorrect in his statement . . . that actually [Chuncho!] was very similar to (a) 'jam session' done in public. On the contrary, I composed 'Chuncho' around the year 1938, approximately 15 years before we ever met Mr. Hernán Braña. He was hired by Yma and myself as a drummer during some of my works, but not 'Chuncho,' where I played and led Yma with my concert guitar and then changed to other native instruments, and in the case of recordings, I doubled myself with these native instruments. I played my concert guitar for her on all the most famous stages of the world to lead her in 'Chuncho.' No European instrument, including the piano, is, as you probably know, adequate to accompany Yma for Chuncho. Only I myself know how to lead her with half notes on my concert guitar.

"'Chuncho' is amazingly enough composed in one chord, and Yma and I imitate the nature and the birds of the Amazones, both with my concert guitar and the voice of Yma. I taught Yma the highest note and the lowest note for the bird sounds."

"As a matter of fact, 'Chuncho' as a musical composition was already heard by the great Spanish composer Don Manuel de Falla, the Great Duchesse Maria of Russia, Dr. Rafael Larco Herrera, President of Peru at that time, and by all the other presidents and personalities of that time in South America, especially Argentina, as already said, before arriving to the United States."

Adamant that "Chuncho!" was composed in 1938, Moisés reiterated, "I must point out to you that this is my exclusive musical composition written at that time, in creation of the sounds of the inhabitants of the Jungle. I repeat I wrote it alone in that time, before starting my tours of Latin America, Mexico and then the U.S. I only changed the name for the American public.

"I repeat, I developed the sound of Chuncho by myself and alone and worked it into a written musical composition, in Lima, Peru, before starting any of our Latin American tours, and about 15 years before we ever met Mr. Hernán Braña."

The peculiar direction of Yma's career and aural evidence do not support Moisés' claims. In 1943, when she made her first recordings, there was no hint in Yma's singing of the novel effects later used in either "Birds" or "Chuncho!" The growl, quarter-tones, whispers, vibrato-altering, the extremely high "double-trill," insect mimicry, and the more overtly bizarre effects did not appear until 1950, and *Voice of the Xtabay*. If Yma had been renowned for her performances of such a piece during her early career in South America, it would seem likely that it would have been recorded in order to exploit her renown in that area. At the least, it surely would have been mentioned in reviews. The only mention of imitation that can be found was that she could imitate the sounds of the instruments surrounding her, especially the flute.

Despite Moisés' assertions, I suspect that "Birds/Chuncho!" along with "Taita Inty" (Hymn to the Sun), "Ataypura" (High Andes), "Tumpa!" (Earthquake), and "Kon Tiki" were composed after the United States migration, and after the changing of musical and artistic priorities had solidified. The Lewisohn Stadium performance of "Chuncho!" builds on the Capitol recording made just a few months earlier and not then yet released, but is about twice as long. It is also interesting in that it has Yma introducing the piece. After introducing Moisés as a "great composer," Yma explains the song to the audience, calling it "The Birds."

Paris 1952

Its effects include whispers, tiny, barely audible *pianissimi*, high staccati, register breaks, clicks, pops, menacing growls, wails, coos, and a climax of a trill on a sustained high F-sharp underscored by the soft crash of a gong. One passage appears that seems unique to this performance. It is an imitation of an Andean bird, a volley of high staccati up to high E flat that burst forth from Yma's throat like machine-gun fire. It is a stunning effect. Even though the rendering on the Capitol recording is an abridged version of what Yma sang in concert, it remains the finest, most cohesive and most stirring, almost harrowing version.

"Cholo Traicionero" is identical to "Lulla Mak'ta" on "*Inca Taqui*" and has its roots in Peruvian vocal tradition and folklore. The use of new or different names would remain a running theme through any history of the Sumac troupe.

Flush with the success of the Lewisohn Stadium concert, the Sumac troupe took off for a concert at the famous Red Rocks Amphitheater in Denver, Colorado. They then traveled to San Francisco for a four-week engagement at the Venetian Room in the Fairmont Hotel, returning to Hollywood for a return engagement of several weeks at the famous Mocambo Club.

While performing at the Mocambo, Hernán Braña contracted glaucoma, a disease of the eye, which leads to a gradual loss of sight. The doctors consulted had wanted to operate but were unable to due to the pressure in Hernán's eye, which had reached a dangerous 61 points. Moisés was extremely concerned about Hernán's condition. At his instigation, a consultation took place with Dr. Fields, the attending physician. At Moisés' suggestion, Hernán was given a specific medication (Pilocarpin) and intra-muscular injections. Until his death, a grateful Hernán maintained that this step, instigated by Moisés, saved his eyesight.

While the troupe was in Hollywood (August 1953) *Inca Taqui* was released to great fanfare. Yma now had three solo albums available to the public and was averaging an album a year. It was becoming evident to people in the industry that not only had Capitol scooped a major find in securing Yma but also that the covers of her recordings (with Tom Kelley's remarkable photographs) were quickly becoming classics of their kind for arresting photography, rich use of colors and inventive packaging.

Meanwhile, Moisés had made certain decisions concerning the course of the next few years and it was at this time that he began to put his plans into effect. By the end of August, Moisés had completed his preparations. Originally, the William Morris Agency had planned to book the Sumac troupe for an extensive return tour of Europe. This was to begin in the winter of 1953 and extend into 1954. Moisés, however, had other plans. In a letter to Hernán, dated August 27th, 1953, and typed by Maureen Shea, he explained.

> After hour-long conversations to Paris and London and after lengthy conferences with the Wm. Morris Agency, Inc. I have finally arranged to postpone our European contracts for next season. Everyone thought it would be impossible to arrange the postponement, so I managed all the negotiations alone. My plans for (America) are so great, and developing so tremendously, that I want to fulfill and realize my ideas here before going to Europe.
>
> Thanks to my revolutionary ideas and efforts, flutes are back in vogue again. If you can manage to prepare two new, exciting flute solos, I can give you a chance to work starting September 22nd in my new show. You've never seen anything like it in your life.

The letterhead Moisés used was one of Yma's, with a typewritten "Enterprises" after "Yma Sumac."

The planned result of Moisés' negotiations was that he and Yma would tour most of the United States before the European contracts would be executed beginning in the spring of 1954.

During the fall of 1953, Yma, Moisés and a recuperating Hernán took part in the filming of Paramount Pictures' adventure movie, *Secret of the Incas*, which starred a young Charlton Heston. Originally, Moisés was to provide new, original music for Yma to sing in the film. Because of their hectic performing schedule, however, this was not possible. Instead, previously recorded songs from *Voice of the Xtabay* were used: "Ataypura"—the melody of which also became the main theme of the movie—"Taita Inty," and "Tumpa!" These songs were incorporated into the soundtrack and Yma lip-synced her way (unconvincingly) through them.

Mel Epstein, the producer of "Secret of the Incas," got the idea for the film from seeing photographs of Machu Picchu and Cuzco in a National Geographic Magazine. The mysterious ruins of Machu Picchu have had an interesting history. When the conquistadors came and conquered Peru (1531–1535), they razed most of the great Incan cities. Throughout the centuries, however, there had been persistent rumors and hints that there were hidden cities that had not been touched by the Spanish conquerors. During the early part of the twentieth century, Hiram Bingham, a professor at Yale, traveled throughout the mountain ranges of Peru in search of such a city. In 1911, he followed the Urubamba River as it flows north of Cuzco, once the great capital of the Incan empire. The region of the Urubamba was reputedly a dangerous region, crawling with poisonous snakes. He and his team climbed the 2,000-foot peak, "a good part of the distance . . . on all fours, sometimes holding on by our fingertips," and found a small mountain peak nestled between two larger mountains. It was on this peak that he found the now famous ruins of Machu Picchu. These ruins are now the most famous tourist attraction in South America. Bingham found the remaining walls of granaries, houses and temples of the ancient Incas. There was also a magnificent stone altar (some refer to it as a sundial), which overlooked the mountain's precipice. This altar was called "Inti Huatana" or "hitching post of the sun" by the few families living at the site at that time. Just as impressive as the altar were the ten-foot-high terraces that were arranged in systematic tiers. The historic site was cleared and explored during 1912–1915 thanks to grants from Yale University and the National Geographic Society.

Why the Incas abandoned the mountain city and why it had never been discovered by the Spanish conquerors remain a mystery (for more information, see Appendix C on the CD Rom). Considering the altitude, it also remains a mystery how the Inca workmen hauled and moved into place the huge stones of the buildings found on Machu Picchu. In his book, *Peru, Bolivia, Ecuador, The Indian Andes*, Charles Paul May wrote, "Today visitors accustomed to low altitudes may gasp for breath because the air, a mile and a half high, contains less oxygen than air near sea level. Yet the Incas accomplished amazing feats requiring great physical effort and lived sometimes for more than eighty years."

Epstein had never seen such a location in films and was intrigued with the possibility of filming a motion picture in that milieu. He traveled to Peru and took a scriptwriter with him who worked on feasible story lines while Epstein checked out the possibilities of shooting at the site of Machu Picchu. After finding it was possible, preparations were made. While deciding on casting choices, it was decided to incorporate Yma into the picture because of the tremendous international publicity she was receiving at the time and because of her obvious relationship with the country.

The production manager went to Peru ahead of the cast to set up and to hire local help. Two crews of nine or ten people, one experienced crew and one inexperienced, were hired. This was because one of the conditions that had been set by the Peruvian government was that both experienced and inexperienced workers be hired for the shoot. Later, sixteen people from Hollywood traveled to Lima and flew to the site of Machu Picchu. A few passengers became ill on arrival because of the high altitude. This "soroche," or altitude sickness, consists of various bad reactions to the altitude, including headache and dizziness, fever and nausea.

Dorothy Hopper, the wife of Jerry Hopper, who directed the film, also made the trip. She remembers Yma very well, especially her green eyes. According to Ms. Hopper, Yma was very cooperative with Hopper and responsive to his direction. Socially, however, Yma stayed to herself and, surprisingly, did not talk to the Peruvians.

Unpublished Legend of the Sun Virgin photo (used by permission of Tom Kelley Studios, Ventura, CA)

CHAPTER 5

"Taita Inty"
(Virgin of the Sun God)
(1954)

Yma settled into Milan for a week's worth of engagements beginning November 3, 1953. After which she and the company traveled to Rome where, on November 9, they began another week's shows. Italian publications noted that she was a big "disk seller."

The new year, 1954, would be one of the most productive and strenuous years for Yma and the Sumac troupe. It was at this time that Moisés' grand production concepts came to fruition and Yma was spectacularly presented. Although still young, she was rapidly approaching her vocal and artistic maturity. This was made obvious by the introduction of a new quality in her singing—a clearly discernible degree of discretion. The over-embroidered vocalism on *Legend of the Sun Virgin* and *Inca Taqui* was now being more judiciously integrated throughout her work. She was becoming more discerning in her use of the vocal effects she had mastered over the last few years and was capable of calling upon at a moment's notice. Although the outré still predominated, emphasis now centered on more subtle coloring effects. These included the "growl" (always one of her favorites), high staccati, and a generous sprinkling of her pure, honey-like top notes, all delivered in a relaxed, strikingly professional manner.

A new, massive concert tour in three sections began in January. From January 16th to March 3rd, the company performed in the major cities of the United States. From April to July they visited nine countries in Europe. Then, beginning October 12, 1954 and continuing through March 7, 1955, they resumed their canvassing of American cities. It was a huge, complicated tour of outlandish proportions. Remarkably, during the three-section tour few concerts were cancelled.

Below is a listing of the concerts

Date	Day and Time	Location Theater
2/17/54	Wednesday 8:30	New York Carnegie Hall
2/18/54	Thursday 8:30	Baltimore, Lyric Theater
2/19/54	Friday 8:30	Philadelphia, Academy of Music
2/20/54	Saturday 8:30	Washington, Constitution Hall
2/22/54	Monday 8:30	Atlanta, Tower Theater

European wing of the tour begins April 24th 1954

Date	Day and Time	Location Theater
4/24/54	Saturday, 8:00	Bournemouth Winter Gardens
4/25/54	Sunday, 7:30	London Royal Albert Hall
4/28/54	Wednesday, 7:00	Bristol Colston Hall
4/29/54	Thursday, 7:00	Birmingham Town Hall
4/30/54	Friday, 7:00	Sheffield City Hall
5/2/54	Sunday, 2:30	Leeds Odeon Theatre
5/3/54	Monday, 7:00	Nottingham Albert Hall

5/4/54	Tuesday, 7:30	Manchester King's Hall, Belle Vue
5/5/54	Wednesday, 7:30	Scarborough The Floral Hall
5/6/54	Thursday, 7:00	Newcastle City Hall
5/8/54	Saturday, 8:00	Eastbourne Winter Garden
5/9/54	Sunday, 3:00	London Royal Festival Hall
5/11/54	Tuesday, 7:00	Leicester DeMontfort Hall
5/13/54	Thursday, 7:30	Wolverhampton Civic Hall
5/14/54	Friday,, 7:15	Blackburn King George's Hall
5/16/54	Sunday, 2:30	Bradford Gaumont Theatre
5/17/54	Monday, 7:00	Hanley Victoria Hall
5/18/54	Tuesday, 7:00	Liverpool Philharmonic Hall
5/20/54	Thursday, 8:00	Dublin Theatre Royal
5/21/54	Friday, 8:00	Cork Savoy Theatre

American wing of tour resumes after hiatus

10/12/54	Tuesday 8:30	Sacramento, CA Sacramento Memorial Auditorium
10/18/54	Monday 8:30	Calgary, Canada Stampede Corral
10/19/54	Tuesday 8:30	Edmonton, Canada Edmonton Gardens Concert Hall
10/25/54	Monday 8:40	Manitoba, Canada Auditorium—CANCELLED
10/26/54	Tuesday 8:40	Winnipeg, Canada Auditorium
10/30/54	Saturday 8:30	Duluth, MN Denfield Auditorium
11/4/54	Thursday 8:30	Minneapolis, Northrop Auditorium, University of MN
11/10/54	Wednesday 8:30	Topeka, KS Topeka High School Auditorium
11/12/54	Friday 8:30	Louisville, KY Memorial Auditorium
11/16/54	Tuesday 8:30	Kansas City, KS Music Hall
11/19/54	Friday 8:30	Tulsa, Municipal Theater
11/29/54	Wednesday 8:15	Houston, Music Hall
11/27/54	Saturday 8:30	Memphis, Auditorium South Hall
12/2/54	Thursday 8:30	St. Louis, Kiel Opera House
12/6/54	Monday 8:30	Toledo, OH State Theater
12/7/54	Tuesday 8:30	Indianapolis, Concert Hall
12/8/54	Wednesday 8:15	Milwaukee, Milwaukee Auditorium
1/22/55	Saturday 8:30	Los Angeles, Shrine Auditorium
1/24/55	Monday	Pittsburgh, Mellon Auditorium
1/27/55	Thursday	Ottawa, Canada Capitol Theatre
1/30/55	Sunday 8:30	Montreal, Canada Her Majesty's Theater
2/3/55	Thursday 8:30	Brooklyn, Brooklyn Academy
2/6/55	Sunday 8:30	New York, Carnegie Hall
2/8/55	Tuesday 8:30	New York, Carnegie Hall
2/10/55	Thursday 8:30	Charleston, WV Municipal Auditorium
2/11/55	Friday 8:30	Richmond, VA The Mosque-CANCELLED
2/20/55	Sunday 3:30	Augusta, GA Bell Auditorium
2/24/55	Friday 8:30	Montgomery, AL Lanier Auditorium
2/26/55	Saturday 8:30	Jackson, MS Municipal Auditorium
2/28/55	Monday 8:30	Asheville, NC Asheville City Auditorium
3/2/55	Wednesday	Chattanooga, TN Memorial Auditorium
3/3/55	Thursday 8:30	Atlanta, GA Roxy Theater
3/7/55	Monday 8:30	Savannah, GA Auditorium

Compiled by Don Pierson, 10/20/99 based on press reviews—there may actually have been more shows.

The Yma Sumac concerts in the United States during 1954–55 were full-fledged theatrical extravaganzas involving over twenty people. For the European appearances, personnel and extraneous sets were less lavish, to hold travel and shipping expenses under control. In North America Moisés seized the opportunity to expand, and exhibit his true genius in producing a unique showcase to frame his wife's idiosyncratic talents. The money they'd made during the last few years would now finally allow him to execute his production ideas to their fullest. He had been slowly expanding these ideas since 1951, but during 1953 he had designed something that was completely novel for American audiences. During the tour of the United States, the company achieved predictable success with their new production, which was aptly advertised as "The most exotic show in the world … brings a new dimension to the world of entertainment."

The new troupe performed in arenas, concert halls, auditoriums, theaters and amphitheaters, literally anywhere their agents could book them. Rooming accommodations were just as varied, ranging from the Plaza Hotel in New York City to college dormitories. There were a number of cosmetic and corporate changes. Yma was now incorporated, known as "Inca Concerts and Yma Sumac Enterprises Inc." Moisés was now credited as producer, director, and conductor of the concerts. The company traveled with their own orchestra, various stage sets, six dancers, a narrator, brilliant costumes and a lighting system that Moisés had carefully crafted during the last few years and that he worked himself when he wasn't on stage. Superbly planned, coordinated and executed, his lighting system was one of the glories of the show.

The Sumac concert now took at least two hours. Billed as a Peruvian variety show, the concert was divided into two halves with four or five sections each half. The most common breakdown for each half was: Orchestral selections, Yma, Dancers, Yma.

Saving Yma's grand entrance for the second set was a great theatrical stroke, which served to heighten the already palpable audience expectancy. Now stage sets and props included temple ruins, a village, volcanoes that spewed fire (during "Tumpa!") and flanking pots of fire and incense. The programs for these concerts were also imaginative and colorful, if not exactly authentic.

The dance sequences had become more involved than before and included a "Betrothal Dance" and a humorous, inventive dance for three llamas (in costume), two "males" competing for the attention of a "female." Costume changes for the dancers were as numerous as the gowns designed for Yma, which were superbly constructed and fashionably exotic with a clever use of chiffon veils, brilliant peacock feathers, smooth velvet of rich colors, and other materials threaded with strands of gold and silver.

Hernán Braña provided his own virtuosic flute solos as requested by Moisés in his letter. By this time Hernán was listed on programs as "Tata Siboney," an all-purpose stage name he used whenever he performed with the Sumac troupe. Amusingly, when Hernán was not performing with the troupe, his replacement assumed the name—as though "Tata Siboney" were somehow a character in the show, who might well be played by different actors. Moisés liked everyone to invent clever or exotic names when they performed with his company.

There were also new instrumental solos, including an intricate and atmospheric violin solo by a young and talented new member of the company, Elisabeth Waldo. Elisabeth Waldo participated only in the 1954–55 tour, leaving after that to concentrate on her own work as a musical archeologist. A scholarship student of the Curtis Institute of Music in Philadelphia, she was recommended to that school by the famous violinist, Jascha Heifitz. Waldo was invited by Leopold Stokowski to join the All-American Youth Orchestra which was then touring South America. Her stint with the Sumac troupe was part of an exploration that she was undertaking

Elisabeth Waldo with orchestra members. Hernán on right

to learn more about South American musical idioms. She eventually settled in Mexico City where she was a popular radio performer.

Soon after her time with the Sumac troupe, Waldo released her own recordings, for which she composed and conducted her own music (*Rites of the Pagan, The Realm of the Incas, Maracatú*). She was the first to record rare, pre-Columbian instruments and to recreate long forgotten music by study of the melodies and airs that still live with the Andean people. Waldo's compositions presented fascinating interpretive concepts of the music of the pre-Columbian era and used many ancient instruments. Remnants of her experience with the Sumac troupe can be found on her first two recordings by the occasional use of a very high, sweet, soprano who warbles wordlessly over the archaic instruments. Similar to other exotica albums released at the time, Waldo's compositions are enjoyable, if rather kitschy, fantasies. Refreshingly, they had historically accurate notes and musical descriptions.

In his book, *Exotica,* David Toop has a sterner judgment: "Waldo's late fifties music is quite as Hollywood bonkers as the Bollywood bonkers film music of Rahul Dev Burman, but cranked even higher on the crazyometer by her agenda to rescue 'the musical values of the Ancient Americas' and unveil 'the mysteries of a vast North-American Empire, silent for centuries.'

As Dean Wallace wrote in a concert review for the San Francisco Chronicle: 'The effect was slightly devastating.' What it sounds like, more than four decades on, is the kind of music you might expect Charlotte Vale [the Bette Davis character] to write, had she been a composer, after her trip to South America in *Now Voyager*. Though rhythmically banal, Waldo's fabrications of Aztec sacrifices and animistic chants are compelling for the sincerity of their fictions, the oddity of their sound world. Reminiscent of Baxter's work with Yma Sumac, Waldo's fantasy of pre-Columbian America creates bizarre juxtapositions of plodding 'exotic' rhythms, bird and insect imitations played on the 'authentic pre-Columbian musical instruments,' duets of alto flute and conch shell trumpet, and rhapsodic Jewish melodies played on the violin." (Serpents Tail, London, 1999)

In 1994, Waldo's two most popular albums, (listed above) *Rites of the Pagan* and *Realm of the Incas,* were released on one CD called *Sacred Rites* (GNP/Crescendo GNPD 2225)—although five selections from the two albums were inexplicably omitted. Elisabeth Waldo now has her own Web page at the American Music Center Web site, which presents information about her work, recordings and background. Curiously reticent about her time with the Sumac troupe, she declined to be interviewed for this book—preferring not to discuss that particular time in her life.

For the 1954 tour, Moisés also employed six dancers who were now given the formal title of "The Yma Sumac Dancers." Their professional names were Don Kiego, an excellent male dancer formally with the Japanese Imperial Dancers, Ula Kon, Teresita Hoefki, Sari Dar, Magana and Gualtiero. These artists were variably called upon, depending on the choreographic requirements of each tour division. There were also other new members: Mario Cortez, an assistant conductor to Moisés, and a narrator whose job it was to introduce the concert and create a suitable atmosphere of the eerie and exotic.

Generally, Yma sang twelve songs for concerts, sometimes more depending on the number of encores she decided to give. Without exception, however, the final set of every concert remained an unspoken, private tribute to earlier, simpler, "Inca Taqui trio" days. With only Moisés and Hernán on stage, Yma sang her favorite pieces, "Taita Inty," "Chuncho!", and "Suray Surita." As if recalling happy rehearsals in the cramped apartment in Greenwich Village, Yma, Moisés and Hernán recreated the sense of excitement and hope that was so much a part of their work in those early days. These sets were always the most impressive and magical of the evening.

Despite the familial problems that would eventually begin to plague Yma and Moisés, artistically they were well matched. Moisés was the complementary genius to Yma and the height of their artistic collaboration remains the 1954 production used for the American tours during the next two years. Following are the program notes taken from these concerts.

The Most Sensational Voice of the Century!
Yma Sumac
and her *Unusual Company* of **Dancers**, **Andean Drummers**, **Musicians**
A wardrobe of fabulous Inca costumes
Original Music Composed on Ancient Inca Themes by
Moisés Vivanco

AN EXOTIC MUSICAL EXPERIENCE!
PART I
1. **Original Music Composed by Mr. Vivanco**
A. **ADORATION** (The Temple Virgins and the Sun God)
A beautiful young virgin, torn between her human passions and her vow renouncing the world for the Temple of the Sun God, succumbs to her human desire in an ecstasy of surrender. The entreaties of the Temple Virgins finally re-unite the girl with the Sun God.
B. **ANDEAN IMPRESSIONS**
A moving medley of ancient Incan themes, skillfully woven by Moisés Vivanco, to capture the spirit of Incan culture.
2. **YMA SUMAC SINGS**
A. **ATAIPURA** (High Andes)
Only the enormity of Yma Sumac's talent could embrace the totality of the three-thousand year old Incan culture in all the varied facets of its daily experiences.

B. MONTANA
In the quiet of dusk, after a day's work, Andean mothers croon their babies to sleep with this haunting lullaby. It expresses the hope and love every mother feels for her child.

C. INCA LOVE SONG
Using the full scope of her magnificent voice, Yma Sumac gives a complete interpretation to this tender and moving song of love.

3. YMA SUMAC DANCERS
A. GOOD AND EVIL
A violent battle in dance form is waged between Good and Evil for control over the hearts and minds of men. Locked in fierce physical combat, two dancers strike blows which are starkly real.

B. ANDEAN MEDLEY
Musical interpretation of the strange exotic sounds heard in the Andes. By Siboney

C. MUNACAY (Betrothal Dance)
The embarrassment of young lovers is expressed in this delightful dance. The suitor offers wine to his beloved's father. After drinking the wine, the father gives his daughter to the waiting lover.

4. YMA SUMAC SINGS . . . SPIRITUALS AND ARIAS
A. NOBODY KNOWS THE TROUBLE I'VE SEEN
For the first time, Yma Sumac lends the great range of her voice and spirit to this famous Negro spiritual.

B. OUVRE TON COEUR (Open thy heart) by Georges Bizet
C. TUCCA NON QHIANE (Neopolitan Song)
D. TUMPA (Voice of the Earthquake)
The low notes of Yma Sumac are the deep rumble of the Earthquake! Her high notes are the voices of the birds rising above the holocaust below.

INTERMISSION
PART 2

5. A. KON TIKI (Orchestral Suite in three movements by Moisés Vivanco)
Pok'ra—Inca Soldiers announce the arrival of Kon Tiki, the God of Justice.
Inti—Sorrow of the Sun God—Ambition and greed have created injustices to the People. The k'ena (ancient flutes) reflect the sadness of the Great God.
Tika Kashwa (Floral Dance)—The Youth's dance of hope for all races, blending the ancient folk song with the native rhythm.

B. WAYRA (Dance of the Wind)
In a gay, flirtatious dance, an Andean boy and girl express the joy they feel in their youth and love. As they dance, the beating of drums heightens their excitement.

C. COQUETTES
Versed in the Incan Arts of Love, two coquettes, with subtle voluptuousness and a deft mixture of humor and passion, go through the flirtation ritual.

D. PACHAMAMA
This dance in Incan tradition is expressive of the state of the world. The dancers whirl their heads to symbolize the troubled earth. Their flaying hair represents the fears and distress of man as the world is driven towards its end . . . in chaos.

6. YMA SUMAC SINGS
A. YA ME VOY
A girl's farewell to her lover made more moving by its simplicity, embodying the wordless anguish of parting.

B. **YMA'S LAMENT** (by Moisés Vivanco and dedicated to Miss Sumac)
Mr. Vivanco wrote this tender and beautiful song to ease his wife's homesickness for her native Andes.

C. **JEALOUSY**
Tortured by jealousy, an Incan maiden turns to nature and joins the birds in song, but her sorrow soon returns. The K'ena used in this number is an ancient Incan instrument introduced to this country by Mr. Vivanco.

7. YMA SUMAC DANCERS
A. **WARI WARI** (Andean Dance)
The dance of love performed after an Incan marriage ceremony. The groom, declaring his love anew, woos his bride as they make their way to the bridal chamber.

B. **WIRA** (Chant of the Winds)
High among the Andean Peaks, the wind creates varied and mysterious sounds which intrigue an Incan maiden. The music and intimate caresses of the wind awaken her desire. Lost in delight and torn with overwhelming emotion she throws herself into a passionate dance expressive of all the sensuality of man.

C. **LLAMAS**
A lighter moment in the life of three llamas as two males out for a browse spy a lady llama. The males come to blows over the girl, but all ends happily with the three-some skipping off together.

8. YMA SUMAC AND MOISÉS VIVANCO
A. **SURAY SURITA**
To win the love of his princess, an Incan general sets out to win Chile for her. He is killed and the Chileans send his head to the princess. Yma Sumac brings the full power of her dramatic talent to bear in depicting the anguish of this princess who dies of a broken heart.

B. **VIRGIN OF THE SUN GOD**
The religious chant sung in the temple of the Sun God by the virgins of the temple. It is a hymn to the sun.

C. **CHUNCHU!** (Jungle Creatures)
The bird who became woman . . . a Legend of the Amazons. Moisés Vivanco's early recollections of the sounds of birds, trees, and the mountain winds, etched against the background music of a guitar, k'ena and tinya.

D. **MALAMBO**
Modern Peruvian music used in the National Dance of the Peruvian People.
[As one can see from the above, "Chunchu!" (Jungle Creatures) and "Chuncho! (Forest Creatures)" were often used interchangeably. Recordings always used "Chuncho!" while programs seem to vacillate between the two spellings.]

Program notes for the Sumac concerts often included an emphasis on peace and brotherhood that was expected to be universally appealing to audiences of the time. The specific notes were, of course, merely fairy tales intended to make audiences more receptive to Yma's exotic music.

As if in retaliation for the new excesses of the Sumac extravaganzas, reviews often contained an insinuating edge of sarcasm or amusement. In March of 1955, the critic for the *Musical Courier* commented: "With the array of instrumentalists, dancers and drummers, all in weird costumes, who join enthusiastically, if somewhat erratically in the proceedings on stage, one may have quite an evening of enjoyment . . . .If there were less distraction offered and a more focused concentration on the chief artist, Yma

Sumac, one would have a better idea of the singer's quality and feel less like the viewer of a live Hollywood production."

The 1954–55 Yma Sumac production certainly had a ripe Hollywood flavor; but they must be said to have achieved their end. Moisés, with his very acute sense of theatricality and popular taste, was trying to create an aura, an atmosphere of the unusual, to frame Yma's singing. He wanted to create a sense of mystery, excitement and theatrical satisfaction which would leave its impression indelibly etched in the audience's memory. Most critics disapproved, viewing the Sumac shows as embarrassingly ornate and fussy. Audiences were generally quite entranced by the otherworldly quality of the entertainment. People I spoke with forty years later vividly remembered the pleasure of those Sumac evenings—even if they couldn't remember what Yma sang.

As one critic wrote, "Costumes, scenery and lighting were all under the personal direction of Vivanco, who displayed a versatility sufficient to establish his reputation as a showman with an authentic feeling for sound theatre . . . " (E.J. Renk, Frenso, CA 10/11/54)

By the time Yma and Company began the tour on January 16th, her three North American recordings had topped the two million mark in sales. *Variety* (2/24/54) noted that, "Interest in Miss Sumac's trilling technique has been sparked and sustained by her Capitol Records albums."

On Wednesday, February 17, at 8:40 P.M., the troupe gave one its most important concerts of the year at Carnegie Hall in New York City. This was Yma's Carnegie Hall solo concert debut. (She had sung there as part of a South American Folk Festival in 1949, shortly after the birth of her son.) Exotic flyers and announcements preceded the troupe's arrival in Manhattan. These were clever tidbits to whet the audience's appetite and curiosity. The advertised program listed Yma performing twelve numbers, including two operatic arias. On the night of the concert, however, there were a few interesting substitutions.

1. "Mamalay" (Beloved Mother)
2. "Montana" (Lullaby)
3. "Inca Love Song" (Kuyaway)
4. "Yma's Lament"
5. "Inca Tears" (Waltz)
6. "Tumpa!" (Earthquake)
7. "Vissi d'Arte" (Tosca) by Puccini *replaced by* "Caminto del Indio" *(The Way of the Indian)*
8. "Deep River" (Negro Spiritual) *replaced by* "Waccay" *(Cry)*
9. "Chacun le sait" (*Fille du Regiment*) by Donizetti *replaced by* "Ccori Canastitay" *(Golden Basket)*
10. "Ataypura" (High Andes)
11. "Chunchu!" (Jungle Creatures)
12. "Marinera" (National Dance)

Such program changes were not uncommon during Yma's concert tours, for various reasons, many of them by no means peculiar to her. In this particular instance, it is not improbable that we see a simple case of discretion displacing valor. The idea of Yma performing operatic arias for New York audiences, in this world-class concert hall, just a few blocks from one of the world's foremost operatic companies—the Metropolitan Opera—must on consideration have seemed rather needlessly bold. It is also possible that the criticism of her operatic effort at Lewisohn Stadium, the year before, may have influenced the decision.

Whatever the reasons, Yma was obviously more comfortable performing her own unique "Incan" repertoire than attempting to exhibit her concept of operatic arias for an audience of such sophistication and artistic expectations. Whether calculatedly or not, the result was that Yma remained shielded by the singularity of her music. There were no comparisons to be made with other singers.

The Carnegie Hall concert was a great financial success, grossing $5,700 from an over-flowing crowd that paid a top ticket price of $3.60. Reviews of the February 17th concert were unanimous in their praise of the Peruvian songstress. The *Musical Courier* noted that "one seldom, if ever, hears potentials apparently so limitless." (3/1/54) *Variety* described the concert as "a colorful program of Peruvian song, dance and instrumentals" and misstated her range as "five octaves." The critic praised Yma saying, "she doesn't spare herself in giving the customers what they want to hear." (But he also felt that Moisés was "on [stage] too long.") (Gros, 2/24/54)

J.B., the critic for the New York Times, maintained initial impressions of the singer he received at the Lewisohn Stadium a year earlier. "Even though Miss Sumac's press agents cannot get over the habit of sending out stories about her 'five-octave range,' the voice actually is a rather unusual one. Miss Sumac has the coloratura soprano's trick of singing extreme high tones in 'flute voice', and . . . low tones of almost mezzo-soprano solidity. She sings these low chest tones with a pronounced break between registers . . . reinforcing the illusion that the distance between her topmost squeak and her lowest growl is an astronomical one. Should Miss Sumac take to Western-style music she could probably sing Violetta or Gilda quite prettily. Meanwhile, her repertoire of Andean birdcalls is an agreeable novelty."

In the same vein was the critical assessment provided by J.L. for the March issue of *Musical America*. "Those who go to enjoy a novelty, and who do not expect it to be studiously authentic in every aspect, could not but have a wonderful time. The vocal attributes for which Miss Sumac is justly renowned were amply in evidence. She sang higher than anyone I have heard, and downward from that altitude across three and a half octaves, and always beautifully. Since her repertory is her own, no valid criteria are available in these northern latitudes. It would be an interesting experience to hear this remarkable voice turned to music more conducive to comparative listening."

Louis Biancolli, writing for the New York *World-Telegram* (2/18/54), found the Sumac experience fascinating. "A packed house watched the pageant of native costumes and folk rituals at Carnegie Hall and listened to the music of Moisés Vivanco as slickly purveyed by David Mendoza and an instrumental ensemble.... Attention concentrated, however, on the high-flying vocalism of the sumptuously garbed Miss Sumac, whose voice can drop two octaves and more from the coloratura altitudes to the low registers.... It was quite a thing to hear these upper-tone twitters suddenly replaced by a deep contralto drone. You could have sworn they came from two separate sets of vocal cords."

The highest tribute, however, was a lengthy, extremely articulate review written by the regular music critic for the New York *Herald-Tribune,* who was the renowned composer Virgil Thomson (1896–1989). He devoted two full columns to Yma (2/18/54), in a review that Yma treasures to this day. Thomson was one of the few critics of his stature who ever approached Yma as a serious artist and reviewed her accordingly despite her unorthodox repertoire and manner of singing. His comments and observations were realistic and precise. Thomson was also one of the few critics qualified to accurately evaluate the music framing Yma.

Under the heading "Sensation Voice," he wrote:

Yma Sumac, Peruvian vocalist (all at the same time a female baritone, a lyric sopranco and a high coloratura) gave a concert last night in Carnegie Hall consisting entirely of music by her husband, Mosies Vivanco. Mr. Vivanco himself led an orchestra of some eighteen musicians in her accompaniments and in instrumental compositions of Peruvian inspiration. How far the melodic substance of these was authentic folklore and how far it had been merely dictated by the folklore premise I could not tell. The harmonic and orchestral texture of the music seemed to have been determined entirely by considerations of a facile effectiveness and by a thorough conditioning in the night-club world, where a smooth presentation and a will toward expressivity are more high prized (and payed) than originality, imagination and a clean communication of personal intensities.

Anybody could have known from the printed program . . . that the music itself was not likely to be very powerful. Its titles were too ambitious for that. And it was not very striking, for all its excellent sophistication and surprising good taste. Modest though it was, it was groomed to the teeth and presented with a professionalized perfection that no vaudeville public could have found anything but top-notch. What this reviewer went to hear was Miss Sumac's famous vocalism, and he was not disappointed.

Her voice is indeed one of great beauty, and her vocal technique is impeccable. She sings very low and warm, very high and bird-like; and her middle range is no less lovely than the extremes of her scale. That scale is very close to four octaves, but in no way inhuman or outlandish in sound. She is a pretty young woman (thirtyish perhaps) with a very, very fine voice, a pleasing personality and a perfect ear. No tone she uttered was displeasing or off pitch. Indeed her natural advantages, physical and musical, are so great, and her schooling is so sound that one could only regret the lack of their application to the great repertory of music. One regretted also, if she feels impelled to exploit them through a repertory especially created for their unusual breadth, that the repertory she had adopted for this concert was so inefficient to the purpose.

For Mr. Vivanco, in folklore vein, is not comparable in imagination or composing skill to a Villa-Lobos, a Smetana, a deFalla, even a Stephen Foster. Whereas Miss Sumac, if she put her mind to it, could, I am sure, make many an opera star sound amateurish. Her voice, essentially a lyric soprano with a baritone extension and a coloratura top, is a very lovely voice; and her use of it is in every way what we call "musical.". As the Queen of the Night in Mozart's "Magic Flute" or as Lucia di Lammermoor, possibly in many other roles, she might have a glorious career. Singing folklore (if that) in sleek arrangements, she is merely an exhibit in the zoos of show business. In a time when fine voices are as scarce as they are now, this reporter regrets that Miss Sumac is not working more ambitiously. If her mental capacities are even reasonably comparable to her musical gifts, she belongs in the great houses of opera.

The questioning of many critics of Yma's refusal to direct her gifts towards more classical arenas prompted Yma to supply a weak defense in *Time Magazine* (3/1/54): "It's too late for me to do it . . . (Besides) I make much more money than if I sing in 2 or 3 operas a year for the Metropolitan." Then, in April, in an interview with Art Buchwald for the *New York Herald Tribune* (4/22/54) Yma stated that she would very much like to sing at the Metropolitan Opera. ". . . (but) I want to show the world what I can do with my voice. Why not opera? But if you only appear 3 or 4 times a year, how can you live? I'd have to sing popular songs . . . on television in order to pay the rent."

Yma's unrealistic concept of an operatic career seems too deliberately defensive to be the entire story. It does suggest, however, that Yma may have instinctively realized and accepted her artistic limitations but preferred not to publicly admit them. The Metropolitan and other famous opera companies obviously recognized this as well since no offers of operatic roles were ever proffered the singer.

The evening (Thursday) after the Carnegie Hall concert found the troupe in Baltimore for a performance at the Lyric Theatre. Tickets for the performance at the famous Lyric Theater ranged from $1.20 to $3.60. Considering the tremendous success of the Carnegie Hall concert the day before, it is surprising that this next concert was clearly a disappointment—certainly to its most prominent reviewer, whose impression does not seem mean-spirited, but judicious.

Janetta Somerset of Baltimore's major newspaper, *The Sun*, took the Sumac experience to task. "Seldom has advance billing led to more disappointment than it did with Yma Sumac, the Peruvian songstress who appeared at the Lyric last night.... Senora Sumac has been widely advertised as one of the musical phenomena of our generation, but only her beauty and fine stage presence survive a first-hand experience of her program unimpaired.

"Her famous 'five-octave range' proved last night to be that of a normally good contralto with deep groaning sounds in the lower register, and a superstructure of what can only be called vocal harmonics, if such a thing is possible. The vulgar word would be 'falsetto.' . . . It may be that she was tired or feeling unwell, but the fact remains that the top octave was no more than a squeak, and that in the normal high contralto passages, Senora Sumac's voice is not pleasant, but weak, breathy and inclined to be harsh."

She noted that the fourteen-piece orchestra consisted of two Andean drummers who were "inscrutable persons in picturesque native costume, and a dozen others who appeared to be ordinary members of the musician's union."

The orchestra played a number of pieces that "possessed a great deal of native charm and would have made useful music for the soundtrack of a film, but the cumulative effect in large doses sent our neighbor to sleep, and we could not blame him, for they were undeniably a shade monotonous."

She concluded: "It was, all in all, an entertainment more suitable for a small stage and a supper club audience than for the very large audience which was present at the Lyric last night. The Sumac voice is a fine one, but it cannot have been at its best for Baltimore." (2/19/54)

And yet, the next evening proved to be an entirely different matter. The Philadelphia Academy concert was a resounding success by every measure. Marion Kelley, writing for the Philadelphia *Inquirer* (2/20/54) stated that, "Yma, the legend, proved herself last night. Her voice is all it was purported to be. Her register is phenomenal and her tones exquisite whether soaring in coloratura range or sliding into the rich sonority of a contralto . . . .Though Miss Sumac has a vocal register of practically four octaves, each displays a remarkable richness of tone. A lilt from low contralto tones to high E is accomplished with great ease, birdlike purity of tone and no grimace. Incidentally she is a strikingly lovely creature, a picture last night in exotic costumes that set off her beauty perfectly."

The best selections on the program were considered "Ataypura" and "Chuncho!," which "was a superb exhibition of vocal gymnastics, honestly interpreted by a singer with a perfect ear for sound. . . . The packed Academy gave her and her company of singers and dancers a rousing ovation, all richly deserved."

Even more interesting were observations made by the famous critic and historian of vocal music, Max de Schauensee for the *Evening Bulletin* (2/20/54): "Vivid costumes, effective lighting and exoticism were the key notes of last night's proceedings and, of course, Miss Sumac and her extraordinary vocal feats were the central feature.... It is hard to evaluate Miss Sumac's voice in her present repertoire. She sounds, at times, like a lady baritone, and then, suddenly, shoots up into coloratura altitudes worthy of Lily Pons or Erna Sack. She makes strange cackling noises, and she produces an even stranger grating note to gain the effects she is deliberately after. Undoubtedly, Mr. Vivanco has written his striking, if rather superficial pieces, with his wife's remarkable vocal feats in mind . . . .

"Musically, she is very accurate—right in the middle of the pitch—and there is a vibrant power, when she so desires. I would like to hear her in some arias of the lyric-coloratura repertoire.... Outstanding were some duets that had the genuine folk quality, which Miss Sumac sang with another singer, Cholita. The two young women made a charming picture as they sang together. . . . A very large audience applauded Miss Sumac and her entourage, finding enjoyment in an art and presentation that are quite distinctive."

The next night, February 20, was the 4th concert in as many nights. The 8:30 concert in Constitution Hall in Washington, D.C. was another success. No fewer than three reviews appeared in Washington papers. Unfortunately, we now find the first mention of a problem that would persist throughout the extensive tour—inadequate amplification systems. Melvin Altshuler of the *Washington Post* wrote: "Miss Yma Sumac, a sort of Peruvian Sonja Henie of the vocal cords, presented an all Peruvian concert last night . . . . as far as it went . . . it was a harmless novelty of a concert. . . . The reference to Miss Henie goes to the heart of the matter. What Miss Henie does on skates Miss Sumac does with an extraordinary voice—slide, glide, glitter, twirl, change directions. . . . The trouble is that when Miss Sumac has accomplished these vocal quick changes you begin to wonder why.

"She has an interesting voice, but the amplification system was inadequate and the value of her voice therefore was difficult to ascertain.... Miss Sumac has concentrated on nightclub engagements. The talents she displayed last night show better in that small arena of presentation. Little of last night's music . . . has much beyond supper club interest." (2/21/54)

More conflicted were the observations of Homer Ulrich of the *Sunday Star*. "Last night's concert . . . was a disturbing thing. First of all, it contained only unfamiliar music. . . . Then Miss Sumac produced sounds not native to the human throat, and this reviewer's musical vocabulary falters in trying to describe them. To say that she gurgled [and] whispered . . . at times is to draw attention from the authentic coloratura and the rich baritone tones she produced at others.

"Miss Sumac sang sensationally. The element of the unexpected loomed large in her performance for the listener never knew when she would shift two octaves up or down, or move from a raucous style to one of unearthly purity. But with the unexpectedness came the awareness that she had been coached by experts and had become a tremendously accomplished showman. Her performance last night was a long way from that of an Andean mountain girl."

Ulrich found the selections accompanied by orchestra "artificial and somewhat faked," but applauded the more modestly accompanied numbers. "In the second half, when she sang to Vivanco's guitar . . . the artificiality disappeared, and she gave what seemed an authentic performance. Miss Sumac must be heard to be believed. There is no one like her on the stage today." (2/21/54)

Glenn Dillard Gunn of the *Times-Herald* wrote "[Her] voice is beautiful in quality and, except for the extreme upper register, it has substantial volume. Mme. Sumac has all the technical virtues. She has such breath control that one never observes her respiration. . . . Like a bird, she never seems to draw a breath, and the song continues. . . . Her habit of tone production is completely natural and completely correct. Her vocal temperament includes every aspect of the emotional address. She can be grave, gay, can stress sentiment, can paint a picture with poetic implication. Finally, she has one indisputable advantage. She is a beautiful woman."

As did others, Gunn found "Chuncho" to be the apex of the concert but he also liked "Tumpa!" which "exploited her remarkable lower register and introduced a curious fluttering vibrato which was echoed by her flutist."

After a day of rest (at last! one can't help thinking), the troupe performed at Atlanta's Tower Theater on February 22. Advance publicity not only boasted of Yma's "five-octave voice" but also that the superb Incan costumes were valued at $50,000.00. Alex Joiner of the *Atlanta Constitution* (2/23/54): "Yma Sumac, the singing star from Peru with the variable voice, drew warm and lengthy observations from New York critics after her Carnegie Hall concert last week which one Atlanta concert-goer summed up in a sentence last night at the Tower Theater: 'She looks like Hedy Lamar and sings like Lily Pons and Ezio Pinza . . . with a little Libby Holman thrown in.'" Mr. Joiner adds a very endearing observation; after mentioning that Moisés had accompanied Yma during some numbers on the program, he reports, "Both were eyeing their six-year-old son, Charles, who was playing peek-a-boo in the wings, looking like he was trying to muster the courage to join the act."

By March 22, the group, trimmed of many of its sets, production effects, and all but about seven of its cast, left on a Pan American Clipper for a concert tour of Italy, England, Germany, France, The Netherlands, Switzerland and Belgium. This part of the tour would end about three months later, in June. Although the base of the European operations was in Paris, the concerts actually began in Italy.

While in Paris, however, Yma gave a single performance at the Empire Theater (near the Arc de Triomphe) sharing the bill with Maurice Chevalier. Originally, Moisés had wanted this particular concert to take place at the famous Lido. Other managerial powers, however, had scheduled it for the Empire because it could accommodate larger crowds and reap more money. The performance Yma gave that night was not well received.

The first concert of the European tour was to be at the Theatro Nuovo, in Milan. Arriving in Milan, Moisés immediately hired fifteen instrumentalists to supplement the company during the Italian leg of the tour. All the musicians hired were associated with the famous La Scala Opera orchestra. Arduous three-hour rehearsals revealed distinct problems in musical communications between Moisés and the musicians. Meanwhile, having a free evening at their disposal, the company decided to attend the famous La Scala Opera where they saw Wagner's *Die Götterdämmerung*.

From Milan, the troupe traveled to Palermo, Calabria, Bari, Naples (where, according to reports, Yma's operatic selections were rapturously received), Rome, Florence, Pisa, Bologna (a near riot occurring due to the troupe's refusal to provide more than the planned two-hour concert), and Torino. The *Musical Courier* (8/54) noted that during the Italian wing of the tour Yma "surprised her Italian audiences into a state of shock with her unique programs."

In Germany performances were given in Frankfurt, Berlin, Hamburg and Dusseldorf; Swiss audiences were treated to the Sumac mystery in Geneva, Bern, Zurich and Basel. On arriving in Geneva, however, Yma contracted laryngitis, a rare occurrence for this singer, and a full week's concerts had to be cancelled and rescheduled while she was treated and recuperated. During this hiatus, David Revera left the troupe, finding agreed-upon financial agreements with Moisés not met. Returning to Paris, David immediately found work and never again performed with the Sumac company.

A short tour of the Netherlands and concerts in Belgium (Brussels, Ghent and Liege) marked the conclusion of that segment of the tour and a return to Paris. While staying at the Hotel Modern, the company performed their unusual show at the famous Alhambra Club and made preparations for the "new" tour of England. This was inaugurated by a gala return to London's famous Albert Hall on April 25th.

Coinciding with performances in Great Britain, the British music magazine *Melody Maker*, published a scathing article by Ernest Borneman called "The Inca Grocer." (The title apparently a sardonic allusion to Moisés' failed tuna-fish-importing venture in their struggling first days in North America.) Appearing in the May 1, 1954 issue, the contentious article caused quite a stir in England. Borneman clearly found the entire Sumac experience deplorable. The brunt of the disparaging article fell not on Yma, however, but rather on Moisés and the nameless publicity agents that surrounded her.

It seems that Ernest Borneman first met Yma in August of 1946, during a party given by Dr. Luis Alvarodo, Consellor to the Peruvian Embassy in Ottawa, Canada. He distinctly remembered that, at the time, Yma considered herself a folk singer: "She called herself Imma Sumack . . . and formed part of the 'Inka Taqui trio.'" But, Borneman observed, with the original release of the *Voice of the Xtabay* in 1950, "all pretense at folk music was . . . shelved . . . except in the album notes which turned Yma into 'an Incan Princess' and described her highly skilled coloratura trills as 'the exotic folk music of a lost civilization'."

Most of the article consisted in a diatribe against Moisés' musical contributions. Reflecting on the performance Yma gave at the Hollywood Bowl in August of 1950, Borneman noted that there were "some startling anthropological discoveries. 'Taita Inty', for instance, a harmless musical confection in the Kostalanetz manner, was described as 'a traditional, authentic version of forbidden Inca music dating back to 1,000 BC'—although of course it happened to be played that day by a symphony orchestra under Arthur Fiedler of the Boston 'Pops'."

Borneman also had opinions about some other Sumacian pieces. "'Pachamac,' a bit of hybrid corn seeded from Puccini and Rimsky-Korsakov strains, emerged as 'The Legend of the Great Creator—the Destruction of the Golden Temple.' 'Mamallay,' a theme that was more than a little evocative of 'My Yiddische Momma' was described as 'strange mystic intervals in a chant.' 'Tuta Wayra,' a competent piece of modern cinema music, was said to 'recreate the melodic beauty and strange rhythm of the Andean wind at night.'"

As to the music's authenticity and that of Yma's Incan heritage, Borneman stated flatly, "It would be cruel to take any of this literally—but what lies behind it all? . . . Sumac . . . is a genuine Peruvian name. Similar names—Capac and Tupac—are among the most honored in Peruvian history. . . . *As for the 'forbidden music of 1,000 BC', the earliest records of Inca rule begin roughly 2,200 years later and include no evidence whatever from which we can deduce anything at all about the nature of their music.* The American Museum of Natural History has a collection of old Peruvian instruments which include pan pipes, triple flutes made of human tibia, conch shell horns, whistling jugs, harps made from hollowed tree trunks and leather thongs, seed-pod rattles, metal bells and gongs, and various kinds of drums—*but no one knows what sort of music they produced.*" (italics in original)

Ernest Borneman was certainly not the first, nor would he be the last, critic to call attention to the ambiguity of Yma's Incan music and Moisés' adamant claims as to its authenticity. In March of 1955, a *Musical Courier* critic stated, "Some of (Sumac's) songs are rare items and evidence a deal of research and selectivity. The original music, composed on alleged ancient Inca themes by Moisés Vivanco, holds audience interest. How much of the operatic material is authentic is for the musicologists to decide."

Variety observed that Yma's repertoire consisted of many songs "completely unfamiliar to her audiences. There are two reactions to this: one of respectful attention to the unfamiliar and one of questioning skepticism." (Gabe, 4/20/55)

Even stronger were the opinions of the *Jerusalem Post* in November of 1957. "Miss Sumac's vocal acrobatics, the unoriginal commonplace music of Mr. Vivanco and the rather doubtful folklore programme of the Inca group could eventually be enjoyed in the framework of a cabaret." (Variety, 11/13/57) (sic)

Then there were such claims as "Original music composed on Ancient Inca Themes by Moisés Vivanco." Moisés claimed to have used various Incan chants extensively in his composition of Yma's songs. Supposedly he incorporated the thematic fragments into an expanded scale. Unfortunately, only the smallest possible fraction of this claim is true. It is true that in a few of Yma's songs (when performed live) there are certain rhythmic patterns, harmonic progressions and melodic fragments that are old and indigenous to Peru. However, these fragments are all but invisible, submerged as they are in the commercialized arrangements and slick harmonic structures that surround them.

It is also true that a number of Yma's most popular numbers were *based* on Peruvian folk songs. But in most cases they are too over-dressed in their arrangements to be considered representative of the people or their musical culture. It would have been more accurate for Moisés to have claimed that Yma's songs were free interpretations of Peruvian melodies rather than actual Incan chants. For example, below is a list of songs Yma recorded (or performed live) that have some small portion of authenticity (sometimes very small).

1. "Ccori Canastitay" (Golden Basket on *Legend of the Sun Virgin*)—Huayno Puneno
2. "Cholitas Punena"—Huayno
3. "Incacho" (Royal Anthem on *Inca Taqui*)—Huayno
4. "K'arwawi" (Planting Song on *Inca Taqui*)—has fragments of ancient planting chant.
5. "Marinera"—Marinera
6. "Mi Palomito" (My Pigeon on *Fuego Del Ande*)—Huayno
7. "Montana" (*Legend of the Sun Virgin*)—Melodia Andina
8. "La Pampa y la Puna" (Plains and the Mountains on *Fuego Del Ande*)—Cancion Andina
9. "Que Lindos Ojos"—Marinera
10. "Taita Inty" (Hymn to the Sun on *Voice of the Xtabay*)—in live performances Yma usually sang fragments of "Wifala," a traditional Peruvian chant in praise of the sun.)
11. "Virgenes Del Sol" (Virgins of the Sun on *Fuego Del Ande*)—Danza. This piece was first written down by Carlos Valderamma and is a popular song sung by most of the soprano "flute singers" in Peru. It remains highly popular with Andean harpists, flutists and instrumental ensembles in Peru to this day.
12. "La Benita"—A Pampeña

Borneman was absolutely correct about the lack of documentation of Incan music. It was never notated in any type of musical manuscript. Peruvian music, and music of the Andes more generally, has always had the tradition of being passed down to succeeding generations by word of mouth. Naturally this made the material subject to the modifications of the transmitter. This is similar to the system that provided early Christians with their music, which originated from altered but traditional, ancient Hebraic religious motifs. Although modified or embellished upon in structure or harmonics, the essence of those fragmentary themes remained—many of them can still be recognized to this day.

In the case of Incan music, the suppression of recorded information by the Spanish conquistadors was due to two principal reasons. One was a complete lack of understanding of, or interest in, the involved musical form that was used by the Incan people. There also was a strong attempt to prohibit the use of "traditional" music because of the emotional response it prompted in the people. At the time, the Spanish were forcing Christian religious practices on the Peruvians and any emotional reaction caused by the old music seemed to threaten their control of the natives. Because of the stringent suppressing of musical expression the nature of the Incan performance practices and music was never documented.

In some respects, nevertheless, the old music never died. There has always been the living tradition found in the small villages high in the Andes. In places such as Pisac (located near Cuzco, once the capital of the Incan empire), or Auyacucho (Moisés' birth place), the old music has survived through the medium of folklore, or folk music. If you were to travel to villages in these areas today, you would hear music that has been handed down through the centuries, its roots firmly secured in the tradition of the "old music." The question that cannot be answered by any of the authorities, for lack of sustained research or any documentary record at all, is just how old this music or its tradition really is.

After the Spanish conquest, there were a number of augmentations to the native instruments of Peru: guitar, violin, accordion, and the European harp began to be integrated. Subsequently, tradition was augmented more generally, as the priorities and modes of Spanish music slowly infiltrated the ancient traditions. Moisés and the publicists would surely have been wiser to state that Yma's music was composed from "Andean" rather than "ancient Incan" melodies, and to bill Moisés as an authority on Peruvian music rather than the "World's foremost authority on Ancient Inca music." That means absolutely nothing.

Although I'm sure it was felt that promoting Moisés as an authority of ancient Incan music was more colorful for advertising in popular media, by not correcting this, Moisés invited skepticism and adverse criticism from music critics who took Yma's vocal abilities seriously and viewed her as a potent force of the music world. However unorthodox her repertoire, her voice and its capabilities were definitely a reality. Perhaps Moisés felt that no one would bother to give serious thought to his claims. If that was the case, he seriously underestimated the effect his wife's talents would have on the world's musical sensibilities.

The most comical humbug the publicists created is to be found in the fanciful concert program notes written for Yma's songs. "Taita Inty" (Hymn to the Sun), for instance, is proclaimed to be a "traditional Inca Hymn to the Sun [of] forbidden music dating back [to] 1,000 BC." It was "the religious chant sung in the temple of the Sun God by the Virgins of the temple." To picture an ancient Incan temple thronged with Sumacs howling this forbidden paean of praise is to be struck forcefully with the thought: No wonder the music was forbidden.

Another contribution to the ever-growing disbelief in everything surrounding Yma—especially her musical material—was the fact that Moisés was also credited with writing "lyrics based on authentic Incan legends." Where in most of Yma's wordless, jazz-like improvising, does one find text of any sort? When James Poling wrote his article, "Most Exciting Voice in the World" for *Collier's Magazine*, he quoted the "text" of "Taita Inty" (Hymn to the Sun). That text, although authentic Quechua and an actual hymn to the sun, had nothing to do with Yma's recorded version of the piece—in which there is absolutely no lyric. Neither does any text occur in the two live performances I have heard. In one of those live performances fragmentary lyrics do appear, but they come from "Wifala," not this poem.

As far as I can ascertain, only one recording of this chant with this title exists. This is a 78-rpm disk made sometime between 1920 and 1930 by a researcher in South American cultures during that time. This was Elsie Houston, granddaughter of the famous Sam Houston. During that decade Elsie spent a number of years in South America researching various cultures. One of the results of her studies was this chant, which she sang to a traditional Peruvian melody.

The version of "Taita Inty" that Yma Sumac performed was a personal expression, a very free artistic conception of an ancient Incan musical form: a hymn to the sun. In a word, it was a fantasy. The subject of fantasy brings up a few more questions. Since the original Quechua title of "Taita Inty" translates as "Father Sun" one marvels at the English title given it in Yma's performances: "Virgin of the Sun God"—obviously chosen purely for evocative purposes rather than authenticity. Descriptive titles and program notes were mandatory for all Yma's "Incan chant" compositions, and few would dispute the fact that "Virgin of the Sun God" conjures a more tantalizing air of mystery than "Father Sun."

This in turn leads one to ponder the origin of the pivotal "Xtabay" legend. There are many ways of pronouncing "Xtabay." Some say it is "Th-tabay", others say "Eks-tah-bay." According to Yma, the correct pronunciation of the word is "Eks-tah-bye." Publicity agents obviously felt that Xtabay was important since the word was not only the title of her first North American recording (as well as a song in that album) but also because it was boasted that the native Peruvians regarded Yma as an incarnation of that famous legend.

The word "Xtabay" does not exist in the Peruvian language of Quechua. Neither does the legend appear in Incan history or folklore. Actually, it originates in Aztec legend; one version is described in the deeply researched historical novel *Aztec* by Gary Jennings. The original legend seems to have arisen in the marshlands of the Totonaca area of the Aztec empire and concerns a horrific ghost-woman "wrapped in a garment that emits an eerie light" who walks the marshes, seeking lost travelers like some sort of vampiric succubus (not such an attractive myth with which to be identified, one might have thought.)

"According to the stories, any man who approaches her finds that the garment is only a hood to hide her head and that the rest of her body is bare—and seductively beautiful. He is ineluctably tempted to come closer, but she keeps backing coyly away from him, and suddenly he discovers to his dismay that he has walked into a quicksand from which he cannot extricate himself. As he is sucked down by the sand, just before his head goes under, the Xtabai at last drops the cowl and reveals her face to be that of a wickedly grinning skull." (Jennings, 1980, NewYork: Atheneum,)

Not daunted, Sumacian writers rewrote the legend, moved its locale to Peru, and did away with its horror and bite, replacing it with syrupy romanticism. The Xtabay legend was of extreme importance to Yma's agents, publicists, and copywriters. Seemingly, it was so important that it merited two, distinct versions (neither, of course, faithful to the original Aztec). Record buyers in 1950 were told that "in the faraway world of her native Ichocán, the natives still regard [Yma] as a reincarnation of Xtabay, lovely and mysterious woman of Incan legend." The unnamed writers then provided this legend:

> The Xtabay is the most elusive of all women. You seek her in your flights of desire and think of her as beautiful as the morning sun touching the highest mountain

peak. Her voice calls to you in every whisper of the wind. The lure of her unknown love becomes even stronger, and a virgin who might have consumed your nights with tender caresses now seems less than the dry leaves of winter. For you follow the call of the Xtabay ... though you walk alone through all your days. (Liner notes from original 78 r.p.m. pressing of *Voice of the Xtabay*, 9/50)

By 1956, however, this romance had been found wanting for color. It was magically replaced by:

Xtabay, a lovely Incan virgin, fell in love with a high prince of an Aztec kingdom. It was a forbidden love, however, for he was high born and she was but a simple peasant. The young girl, unable to keep the secret in her heart, sang to the mountains, the winds, whoever would listen to her song. Her voice was so penetrating and enchanting that ultimately it reached and killed the far-off prince. (Liner notes, 1956 re-pressing of *Voice of the Xtabay* and *Inca Taqui*)

This cheerful tale was of great importance during the years that Yma was controlled by publicity agents and inventive managerial powers. Although a fleeting reference is made to the Aztec empire (from which at least the word Xtabay actually arose), of course the "legend" itself remains a fabrication from whole publicists' cloth.

Like a maze, this leads to other questions. Whatever were they thinking (whoever they were) in dragging in a reference to the Aztecs in the first place? The only thing the Aztec empire had in common with the Incan empire was that it, too, was ancient—oh, and that it, too, existed somewhere south of North America. There was never contact between the warring Aztecs and the very different, peace-loving Incans.

The careless, probably simply mindless confusion of the two actually began with the cover layouts chosen for the initial album release in September of 1950. Those in charge of the cover layouts for both *Voice of the Xtabay* and *Legend of the Sun Virgin* made some gross historical errors when they flanked Yma with an idol of Aztec, not Incan origin. Or, perhaps, it was to help cover-up some foolish and unfortunate vague references Yma made during interviews to an Aztec influence. It is interesting that after *Legend of the Sun Virgin* none of Yma's covers boasted her little idol. Whether due to misinformation given to Capitol staff, or just careless, overhasty execution, this type of error remained a blight on Yma's reputation for authenticity. Extremely unhelpful in this regard was the fact that whether by intent or folly, the little squatting, smiling stone effigy soon became the singer's mascot. It appeared on flyers, programs and publicity releases. But it was a mascot that sat grinning in open derision of its own use.

While Yma was touring Europe, Paramount released the film, *Secret of the Incas*. Previewed on May 17, 1954, it was publicly released on May 30th. *Variety* found the 100-minute long film satisfactory, an acceptable adventure-drama with excellent location photography in Peru, especially the beautiful ruins of Machu Picchu. The main characters were:

Harry Steele	Charlton Heston
Dr. Stanley Moorehead	Robert Young
Elena Antonescu	Nicole Maurey
Kori-Tika	Yma Sumac
Ed Morgan	Thomas Mitchell
Mrs. Winston	Glenda Farrell

The plot centers around the (appropriately named) Harry Steele, an adventurer who attempts to steal a sacred gold sunburst found in a newly discovered tomb of an ancient Incan priestess in the ruins of Machu-Picchu. During the course of the movie, he relents

Paramount movie *Secret of the Incas*, 1954

and returns the treasure to the native Peruvians and winds up with Nicole Maurey, (Elena) while Yma, standing atop Machu-Picchu, wails at the top of her lungs, rejoicing in ecstasy that the treasure has been returned to her people.

In her short scenes, which suggest that Hollywood was at a loss with what to do with her, Yma portrays Kori-Tika, formerly a native of the village of Machu Picchu, but now, after formal education in America, a lab assistant to Dr. Moorehead. Moorehead is the archeologist responsible for unearthing the tomb of the "Mama K'una"–once high priestess of the ancient city. Kori-Tika is, of course, well versed in Incan folklore and just happens to be able to sing the obscure, forgotten ancient chants with her beautiful (and phenomenal) four-octave voice. A fact that goes completely unnoticed by the other characters, who listen nonchalantly as Yma sails through her multi-octave music. Yma's three musical numbers: "Taita Inty" (Hymn to the Sun), "Ataypura" (High Andes), and "Tumpa!" (Earthquake!)—the latter of which is often cut from prints of the movie available today—were choreographed.

The most interesting and artistically inventive scene is the "Taita Inty" sequence, which shows Yma in authentic Peruvian festive dress, kneeling in homage before an effigy of the Mama K'una, offering an overflowing bowl of fruit as she sings the opening, high, chant-like phrases. As the music builds, Yma launches into various dramatic gestures (like those she used in concert performances of the piece), which fit in nicely with the mood created by the music. The "Tumpa!" sequence is also fascinating because it shows authentic Peruvian dances as well as shots of the accompanying musicians (including Hernán) while Yma trills and dances her way through the number. (One sweeping, bowling gesture is distinctly odd, though.)

Yma has an interesting dramatic (or serio-comic) scene. Elena visits Dr. Moorehead in his laboratory, where he is working on the tomb findings with Kori-Tika (Yma). Elena has come to have him sterilize a wound she has just received from a slight fall. After introducing Elena to a silent, disapproving and stone-faced Kori-Tika, Moorehead begins to examine the wound. He is obviously quite taken with the beautiful Elena. When he asks Kori-Tika for some antiseptic, she replies stonily, "Iodine? Lots of Iodine!" "No," he replies, "something gentle." "No Iodine?" asks Kori-Tika. She leaves to get the medication. She returns, silently hands a bottle to Moorehead and stands by, watching expressionlessly as he applies it to Elena's wound. "Oh!" cries out Elena in obvious pain as Kori-Tika, with a satisfied smile, says, "Iodine!"

The Washington Post wrote that the soundtrack was able to "pick up some of [Sumac's] notorious thrusts at the sound barrier," while the *Christian Science Monitor* commented, "One striking figure emerges, that of Yma Sumac, the Peruvian singer . . . .both the upper and lower reaches [of her voice] are exploited here, along with her darkly dramatic appearance."

The New York Times reviewed the film on May 29, 1954 noting:

> (Secret of the Incas) is basically interesting because of its authentic and truly colorful locales. . . . It is the location camera work of Irmin Roberts that is the film's highlight. The towering Andes; the actual ruins of Machu Picchu, the Inca city rediscovered some forty years ago; the hundreds of Indians in exotic costumes and headgear who were filmed in ceremonial dances and wending their way up the lush mountains, and the spectacular singing of Yma Sumac, whose multi-octave range runs the gamut from baritone to coloratura keening, are visual and aural treats.

Now sometimes shown on late-night television, the colorful background of Peru and the incredible ruins of Machu Picchu make it worth the effort to stay up and see. As of this writing (2007), it has not been released on DVD.

It was around the time of the movie's release that the comedian Imogene Coca did her now famous impression of Yma singing "Lament" on the Show of Shows television program. Done in good natured fun, Coca mimicked Yma with startling clarity while dressed in her own version of "Virgin of the Sun God" robes.

The Yma Sumac company completed the English phase of their tour with a performance in Liverpool, after which they took a ferry to Ireland. Concerts were given in Dublin (at the famous Royal Theater), Galway, Waterford, and the European tour was completed with a gala concert in Cork on Friday, May 21, 1954.

In the meantime, Moisés had been busy booking engagements on his own. Without the aid of their agents, he arranged for a four-week stint at the Pavillion in the Villa Rosa in Madrid, Spain. The engagement was to begin immediately following the conclusion of the tour and the many shows given during the end of May, and June were greeted with enthusiasm by capacity crowds.

Yma re-entered American waters on July 6, 1954. She had returned to New York via the great liner, *SS United States*. Before disembarking, however, the singer was interviewed aboard ship by the radio personalities Tex Mex McCrary and Jinx Falkenberg. It was Yma's first interview alone (Moisés had returned to the U.S. earlier) and the first to be conducted entirely in English. To add an exotic flavor to the interview, "Xtabay" was played quietly in the background. Despite her efforts and obvious enthusiasm, it seems to have been a polite disaster because of her linguistic shortcomings and the unfortunate, confused references she made to fictitious Aztec influences.

Yma's lack of English vocabulary may seem rather strange considering that she had been living in America for eight years. But, as we have seen before, it seems that Moisés kept a tight rein on Yma, preferring that she not master the language. In this way he could be in charge of what was said during all interviews, financial discussions and publicity related matters. This is why he also preferred Yma not spend a lot of time talking with fans after concerts, pretending she had to protect her voice. It would seem that Yma, shy by nature, and preoccupied with her singing, welcomed such protection.

It is interesting in any case that no live interviews with Yma occurred after that unsuccessful Tex and Jinx episode, only written interviews or articles which could be easily controlled or edited by Moisés and/or other managerial powers. It was only after Yma was on her own that live interviews reappeared. By that time, her repetition of the old legends was simply ludicrous.

Landing on United States terrain proved to be more difficult for Yma than she had anticipated. Problems arose during an odd sequence of events, which would influence not only the rest of her career but would also dictate the type and quality of newspaper coverage allotted to her from then on. From this time forth, journalists gloried in exploiting the private affairs of Yma Sumac to the exclusion of all else. With the adverse "Incan" criticism and the "Amy Camus" stories still making the rounds, this type of publicity toppled, once and for all, the careful image of "Yma Sumac" that Moisés and others had so sedulously created and presented to the American public.

It remains the tragedy of Yma Sumac's career that although Moisés was responsible for much of what she had become, he was also responsible for her artistic destruction. All this happened as Yma stood by, confused and seemingly unable to rectify poor choices and problems created by Moisés and her artistic management. Although the Amy Camus scandal in 1951 presaged things to come, July of 1954 signaled the beginning of the end.

Before being allowed to enter New York City and the United States, Yma was detained by Immigration authorities for questioning. According to newspaper stories at the time, this centered on a question of what was vaguely characterized as subversion. Moisés had returned to the United States by air on June 15th, three weeks before Yma. At that time he was detained overnight on Ellis Island for questioning. He did not inform Yma that this had happened. When he met Yma at Pier 86 on West 46th Street, he took with him Ricardo Goytisolo, the Peruvian Consul General. His vague excuse was that " . . . in my country . . . women are very home lovers. Some things are a little embarrassing to them because they are not accustomed to these things." (*New York Herald Tribune,* 7/7/54, sic)

Yma was mortified and utterly bewildered. Practically incoherent, she frantically said: "I didn't kill . . . I didn't rob. I didn't nothing. What?" she said when met by officials, "lifting her hands in a gesture of dismay." (ibid.) Taking charge as usual, Moisés insisted that Yma had never taken any interest in politics. "Art never leaves time for anything. She's busy working, keeping her home, creating new repertoire for new tour." (ibid.)

Moisés received his second papers and Yma was paroled in the custody of the Peruvian Consul in New York City pending further questioning. While they were staying at the Plaza Hotel, Moisés informing reporters dramatically that Yma intended to apply for American citizenship. Interestingly, he said nothing about his own desire to do so. Obviously still in shock, an embarrassed Yma posed for unflattering pictures that show her tired and haggard-looking. Her main concern, she said, was to be able to return to her home and her son. On July 12th, Yma was officially admitted to the United States after a closed hearing on Ellis Island. All present were reticent about speaking of the circumstances, although Moisés maintained "that someone envious of Miss Sumac's career may have been responsible." (Ibid.)

Weak, defensive news stories now appeared, fostered by Moisés, containing veiled hints that Yma had been the victim of a poison-pen letter because of a rival's jealousy. Yma's only reply to *The New York Times,* (7/13/54) was one of relief that the problem had been resolved. "I am very happy now. Everything was a mistake." *Musical Courier* magazine made their opinion known by stating that Yma had been " . . . a caged bird temporarily when some unkind person . . . accused her of subversive tendencies . . . Well now, we never knew it was subversive to tear singing technique to tatters . . . " (8/54)

It is not known to this day what was behind the subversive story, and there is even reason to doubt that there really was such a story. A different problem emerged, which was kept extremely quiet but which suggests that the the real reason Yma and Moisés had been detained had to do with the Internal Revenue Service of the United States and concerned taxes not paid by Yma and Moisés. It seems, in fact, that Moisés had neglected to pay any taxes to the I.R.S. since their arrival in America in 1946. These taxes constituted an enormous sum of money since they not only reflected their work in the United States during the eight years from 1946–1954, but also all the royalties from three million-seller recordings, and all moneys accumulated during the massive concert tours both in America and abroad. Until negotiations were concluded, the remainder of the United States tour was in serious jeopardy.

What Yma's thoughts were concerning this disastrous episode has never really been explored since, to this day, the affair remains too embarrassing to her for her to publicly address. In any case a settlement was reached, and Yma's managers quickly began to arrange for additional bookings during the next year to accommodate a new set of financial responsibilities.

During the summer, Yma appeared on the Jackie Gleason television show, singing her famous "Chuncho!" (Forest Creatures). It was her only televised performance of the piece. She also finally returned as a guest star to the Frank Sinatra show. Tremendous plans were underway for the new tours. In October, the new, expanded "United States troupe" began another extensive touring of the country.

In September, before they left for the tour, Yma and Moisés collaborated with the swing bandleader Billy May to produce what was to be her final great recording, called *Mambo!* Superbly organized, arranged and sung, the recording captured Yma at the zenith of her vocal and imaginative powers. For once, Sumacian legends were discarded by Capitol Records in favor of a more realistic presentation. The cover of *Mambo!* showed Yma mid dance step, arms outstretched, and in one of her attractive décolleté concert gowns. The brief liner notes only talk about the Mambo as a dance form.

In an interview in the jazz journal *Metronome* magazine (4/56), Billy May pointed out that Moisés' concept for the recording was to utilize Yma's voice as an instrument within a group. May defined Yma as a classically-based concert singer with "a strong native feeling" and a "wonderful sense of rhythm" and found the collaborating experience "really enlightening."

Treating Yma's voice as an integral part of an instrumental ensemble, Moisés and May finally offered the Sumac voice in an almost ideal musical framework. The only other disk Yma recorded that approaches this one's quality an ideal is *Miracles,* recorded some 17 years later. Like a breath of fresh

Recording *Mambo* at Capitol, 1954 (used by permission of Tom Kelley Studios, Ventura, CA)

air, *Mambo!* was presented to the listening public sans program notes and Incan trappings. Finally the reality of Yma's voice took precedence over biographical fantasies and publicist's dreams; authenticism had finally been achieved. Unfortunately, this concept was short-lived; eventually it would be dropped for yet another "angle."

October 11, 1954 found the troupe giving the first concert of the new American tour in Fresno, California. Eldred J. Renk, reviewing the performance at the Fresno Memorial Auditorium, made special mention of the Inca Taqui trio "tribute" segment at the end of the program. "The greatest moment of the concert arrived near the end, when Vivanco appeared with his guitar to accompany Miss Sumac in a series of songs involving careful teamwork. The dynamic plasticity displayed by both guitar and voice in this series was memorable and produced an almost endless variety of fresh effects ranging from a suggestive twang to a full roar."

Renk wrote that Yma was "a gorgeous creature who (combined) personal beauty and an instinctive feel for the appropriate in drama. . . . Her low contralto tones are rich and buttery (while her) high register exhibits a purity of tone and sheer agility which must be the despair of conventional bel canto sopranos who twitter in vapid thirds with Italian flutes." He found the music "off the track, spontaneous and exciting, full of unexpected effects . . ."

Programs for this new section of the American concert tour show that Yma's repertoire centered on audience favorites such as:

"Ataypura" (High Andes)
"Montana" (Lullaby)
"Inca Love Song" (Kuyaway)
"Tumpa!" (Earthquake!)
"Mamalay" (Beloved Mother)
"Lament"
"Zana"
"Jealousy" (probably "Kon Tiki")
"Marinera" (National Dance of Peru)
"Suray Surita"
"Taita Inty" (Virgin of the Sun God; Hymn to the Sun)—often the final encore
"Chuncho!" (Forest Creatures)
"Mambo" (Malambo #1, Goomba Boomba, or Queen of the Night Mambo)
"Ccori Canastitay" (Golden Basket)
Bizet: "Ouvre ton Coeur"
Debussy: "Clair de Lune" (Vocalise)

The next evening found the troupe in Sacramento, at the Memorial Auditorium. William C. Glackin, of the Sacramento Bee (10/13/54) noted that the Sumac voice "has been called everything from a freak to a miracle but words seem a little pale and unimportant in the presence of the living article. On the strength of the sounds it made in the memorial auditorium last night, Miss Sumac's voice is certainly the most unusual these ears have ever heard and its owner is a real musician who knows how to use it to spectacular effect." Mr. Glackin felt, however, that a non-Peruvian group of songs was less successful.

"In these last, she seemed out of her element. She did them intensely but a little stiffly. But when she got into her own element, she was something to hear—now weird, now beautiful and often wonderful. . . . She moved her voice freely and expertly, tossing conventional technique and tone aside whenever the effect demanded it."

Patricia Paine, of the Sacramento Union (10/13/54), noting that Yma had performed for an audience of no fewer than 1,500, observed that one of Yma's "favorite vocal tricks is to pick a super-sonically high note out of nowhere, expand it as loud as it will go, pull it to a barely audible silver thread and drop to a note at the very bottom of her range. She did this several times."

October 18th found the Sumac troupe in Calgary, Canada. Yma's Canadian concerts coincided with concerts being given by the famous Metropolitan Opera coloratura soprano, Lily Pons. Pons was the first concert of the season's celebrity series at the Stampede Corral Concert Hall. Her concert (given October 15th) included such favorites as "Caro nome" from Verdi's *Rigoletto* and the Bell Song from Delibes' *Lakmé*. Yma's was the second of the series. The review by Louise Laverie, a *Calgary Herald* staff reporter, was headed, "Sumac's Range, Power Astonish Concert Crowd." After mentioning that Yma's range was promoted emphatically, she commented that whether singing in the lower or upper reaches of her instrument, "her voice maintained its power, its tone color, its mood-creating quality . . . the quality of her performance did not rely solely on mere shows of range; it was rich in tone, and her singing was notable for ease, and control of breath and pitch." She had the fairly common critical reaction to Yma's performance of an operatic aria: "With Peruvian orchestration and altered rhythm, [it] sounded incongruous." Laverie concluded: "The stage room did not permit the dancers much freedom, the choreography was not very inspired, but the dance interludes were rightly kept brisk and brief, as background to Miss Sumac, indeed an unforgettable performer."

The next night the Sumac troupe was in Edmonton, Canada performing for an audience of 3,000 at the Edmonton Gardens Concert Hall. (This time Lily Pons preceded the Peruvian soprano by one week.) J.B.P. of *The Edmonton Journal* reported: "For many it was an occasion to hear in person the amazing vocal capabilities of an artist they had listened to on recordings and on radio. Their enthusiasm for her program was shared by those who were hearing her for the first time. . . . Even shorn of the imaginative Peruvian atmosphere, colorfully established through costumes, dances and music, the artist's voice would merit the enthusiasm of any concert audience. Yma Sumac proved equally able to execute the unique Peruvian native songs, a grand opera aria and a Negro spiritual. To this she added her clever sense of the dramatic, the potent illusion of effective lighting and unrestrained savage rhythms."

Elisabeth Waldo garnered some praise as well. "Miss Waldo and her violin were featured in two of the dance offerings. . . . Her familiarity with the instrument, expressed with tonal eloquence, added greatly to the portrayals."

Although the next performance scheduled on the Canadian wing of the tour was to be at the Wheat City Arena in Brandon, Manitoba on October 25, the show was cancelled. In a divatic display of willfulness, Yma cancelled the show due to a "lack of public support. . . . She was, it seems, miffed at Manitobans for what was considered a lukewarm reception by the city of Brandon." (Rhoda Feldman). Understandably, managerial powers of Winnipeg (the next stop on the tour) were a bit concerned. Bill Gee, who was sponsoring the tour, emphatically said the performance in Winnipeg would happen and admitted "he was 'bewildered' by the whole thing . . . (and) couldn't understand what was happening. 'I haven't had any trouble with her so far.'" (ibid)

As if in an effort to ensure that Yma didn't feel slighted again and to ensure that an audience would be present, newspaper advertisements now carried a "quote" from a telegram sent by A.K. Gee: "Yma Sumac and her unusual company completely thrilled 3,000 people in Calgary Monday night (Oct. 18). Her voice is absolutely unique–almost unbelievable. Her four costumes gorgeous and the supporting company of fifteen Andean drummers, dancers and musicians gave a superb, colorful show."

The Winipeg show took place as planned on October 26 at the Civic Auditorium. Frank Morriss' review in the Winnipeg Free Press had the headline: **"Sumac Vocal Acrobatics Spectacular, Fascinating."** Morriss found the Sumac experience somewhat limited. He noted that she "is a lady of spectacular, if limited, attainments. When she is operating in her own vocal territory, which is manipulating the exotic passages of songs devised for her . . . she is fascinating. It is a voice at these times, of phenomenal quality and surprising agility. It shines with myriad colors from dark contralto to flutelike coloratura. When, on the other hand, she tries to sing the conventional concert songs, she descends to a far lower level."

Referring to the segment of the concert in which Yma performed a spiritual and a Bizet aria, he continued, "It was then that the drastic limitations of her art were revealed, because the voice was badly out of focus, a distressing vibrato crept in, the rhythm was faulty and the lack of pitch downright distressing . . . (She) must rise or fall, then, on her freak vocal chords and this is not enough to fill a program of more than two hours."

As was typical of her critics, he found the final set with Vivanco the best of the night. Although dressed "in four exotic gowns obviously of Paris origin . . . (she) seemed rather ill at ease on the stage until the latter part of the program when she was joined by Mr. Vivanco on the solo guitar. It was then that the evening took on its most exciting aspects. Under the spell of his persuasive playing, and minus the orchestra, she responded with some bravura vocal acrobatics that were nothing short of astonishing."

He concluded by recognizing and naming the central problem with the current Sumac presentation: "If Miss Sumac is going to continue to succeed as a concert artist she needs to have a presentation that is better devised than the one that was offered last night. It was plainly hastily put together with people who didn't have the appearance or the real ability, to give you the color and flavor of Peru."

October 30th found the Canadian wing of the tour ended and the resumption of American cities began. On the 30th, it was the Denfield Auditorium in Duluth, Minnesota that heard the warblings of Yma. Yma was interviewed on October 29th by Earl Finberg for the *Duluth News-Tribune*. During the interview mention was made about the Amy Camus story and the supposition that she was really from Brooklyn.

Yma's reaction was coy. "I would be proud to be from Brooklyn . . . but I am already from Peru." Charlie's absence was also explained: "He is in Hollywood, our home, because it is time he went to school . . . before, he always went with us, but now he must go to school."

Mention was also made of Yma's sumptuous gowns, designed by Dior, Fath and Don Loper. "What does she think of the new Dior profile? 'It is not for me,' she explained. 'I tell them what I want, and they give me the Sumac look.'" (Ibid)

The Denfield Auditorium was sold out the day before the concert, except for standing room. Mr. Finberg also reviewed the concert for the *Duluth News-Tribune*. Not ashamed to admit the fact, he stated, "I liked her." He also liked the dancer, Don Kiego, who "was controlled, lithe and brought an oriental perfection to the rather rustic proceedings." He did, however, notice some odd goings on back stage. "Besides playing the guitar, Vivanco produced and directed the show . . . Backstage last night he cued the assistant director from the wings and told the man at the switchboard which lights to turn on and off. . . ." Commenting on Sumac, Finberg said, "After you have heard the vocal acrobatics, you can settle down to enjoy the effortlessness of her breath production, the perfection of her pitch that makes her exotic repertoire anything but outlandish."

As far as he was concerned there was really only one serious fault with the Sumac show. "The musicians take up most of the stage, leaving little enough room for the dancers and destroying the setting for the singer by virtue of their presence, especially when dressed in costumes which make you wonder if they are not out for tricks or treats."

The next show, on November 4th at the Northrop Auditorium at the University of Minnesota in Minneapolis, was not as well received. Paul S. Ivory wrote, "It was a good show, calculatedly well presented and likely to trap the unwary into thinking it was some item of high art. . . . Miss Sumac herself is so unbelievable as to be uncanny. It was worth the trip to the university just to hear that voice and see her marvelous costumes and lovely person. The extremes of her mile-long range are hardly musical notes at either end, but it is something to see that they can exist at all."

He did not care for her forays out of the Peruvian repertoire. "This kind of thing is not her dish, since it was done with truly outrageous hamminess and with no signs of a vocal line." Mr. Ivory took especial objection to the sound system used that evening, "which appeared to have been manipulated by some descendant of an evil Incan deity."

Writing for the *Minneapolis Star*, John K. Sherman noted: "Shifting light effects, gorgeous costumes, Inca love songs and Negro spirituals all went into the act, making a mixture that at times seemed more Hollywood than Andean. . . . Sumac's voice is an amazing natural endowment and it does some amazing things in its guttural depths and twittering altitudes. But it is not trained, or at least doesn't sound so, and this lack limits her versatility as an interpreter and produces a monotonous effect intensified by a heavy throb in most of her tones. The result is a trick voice involved in over-elaborated show, sometimes impressive and even awesome when evoking the primitive and ancient world of her Inca ancestors, at other times, over-emotionalized and downright corny, as in 'Nobody Knows the Trouble I've Seen' . . . More artistry and less showmanship, more consistency in style and subject matter, would pull the show out of the vaudeville character it assumes from time to time."

Next on the Sumac schedule was an appearance at the Topeka, Kansas, High School Auditorium on Wednesday, November 10, 1954. Advertisements in the local newspaper promoted Yma's recordings. At that time, the 10" LP disks of *Legend of the Sun Virgin* and *Inca Taqui* were selling for $3.98 while Yma's classic, *Voice of the Xtabay*, went for $2.98.

A hint of uneasiness possibly carried over from the Canadian wing of the tour might be detected in the newspaper advertisements, where is found a little block that states brightly, "It's been a sellout in every city so far! Topekans will call it the show of the year."

A review of the November 10th show, by M.E.M. for *The Topeka Daily Capital*, stressed that the best part of the show came near the end. "The entire group of songs which Vivanco accompanied were by far the best of the evening. The last half of the program was a great improvement over the first part…Costumes…were varied for each act. Even the instrumentalists were in costume. Sumac chose to appear in modern evening dress."

By November 12, the troupe was in Louisville, Kentucky for an 8:30 PM performance at the Memorial Auditorium. In an interview for *The Courier-Journal*, Phil Querido, commented that Yma was "touchy" about her birthplace. He quoted her as having said: "Oooh, what they are saying about thees in Brooklyn. And een Hollywood it is even worser. They say I am an Indian from New Mexico who leev eenside of cleef."

The next day, William Mootz, Music Editor of *The Courier-Journal*, reviewed the concert given on November 12, 1954 in the Memorial Auditorium. "As one who has listened in rapt fascination to the 'Voice of the Xtabay' on records, I can only report that the first part of the evening was an experience of strange disenchantment. For the truth is Yma Sumac, until well into the second half of her program, was but a pallid shadow of her recorded self. . . . I have seen it written that Miss Sumac, if she chose, could sing in the great opera houses of the world. I think her performance of Bizet's 'Ouvre ton Coeur' should put to rest that myth."

He concluded: "The rest of the program last night left me feeling woefully out of touch with the Incan temperament. To my jaundiced eye, the dancing was on a level of accomplishment that no self-respecting amateur would dare display in public. The orchestra, which consisted of a violin, cello, flute, piano, and assorted Peruvian instruments, played passionlessly throughout the evening. I even overheard one disgruntled soul during intermission express willingness to take bets that few, if any, of the troupe had ever been south of Florida. . . . Nevertheless, there was that final moment of wonder when Miss Sumac erupted in all her glory, and this was enough to make the evening a unique theatrical experience."

Kansas City followed on November 16—a return visit to the Kansas City Music Hall. And, on Friday the 19th, the Municipal Theater in Tulsa Oklahoma. Audiences in Tulsa were informed that Yma's gowns were "by Jacque Fath and Don Loper, (and) are styled in the Inca motif and made entirely by hand. The average dress takes ten months to complete. The materials as well as the gold and silver threads and the beads are imported from Peru."

Different from other cities, boiler-plate promotion appeared in Tulsa newspapers promoting Moisés instead of Yma: "The work of [Moisés Vivanco] is widely known throughout the world and leading music critics have named him the foremost composer of exotic Peruvian music. . . . Credited with discovering and recognizing the exceptional talent of Yma Sumac, Vivanco has guided her career to the point where today she is a world figure in the field of music. There is no yard-stick by which to judge the lovely Peruvian songstress. The incredible five-octave range of her voice ensures her place in musical history. . . . During the time he was furthering Miss Sumac's career, he gradually built up his own reputation in esoteric music circles where he is today regarded as a brilliant composer of Incan music, and the creator of a new form of music based on Incan themes. He has created, conducted and arranged all of the selections which comprise Miss Sumac's Capitol record albums. . . ."

"With the completion of the songs he has recently written for Miss Sumac's next album, Vivanco's immediate plans are to finish a symphony he has been working on for the last two years. He feels it will be the best he has ever done and hopes to present the work next year."

Yma's singing on November 19th was admired, and so was the addition of Don Kiego to the dance troupe. M. deV. felt that the dancing had been immeasurably improved with the addition of Kiego "who is a great young dancer and a master at pantomime."

The Sumac troupe next performed for 3,000 people at the famous Music Hall in Houston, Texas, on Wednesday, November 24th. It was their first time in Houston. Hubert Roussel, writing for *The Houston Post* noted that "we have a new cult in the land [(and] the high priestess of this mystic society is Yma Sumac." Commenting on the attendance, he noted, "this was surely the most tight-fitting audience the new municipal tabernacle has held." Of Yma he wrote: "The sounds she produces at the extremes of her register are not sounds I would describe as exactly musical, but they are strikingly true, for she has absolute pitch or thereabouts, and it is a wonder to hear some of them. The all but incredible range of five octaves is claimed for this interesting lady. She did not cover that span in this program, if my ears are to be trusted, but she did operate over more than three octaves with a flexibility and accuracy altogether worthy of cheers... It was a thoroughly unusual entertainment, an evening of charm and vocal novelty, and I imagine everybody took home what he went to the temple to get."

Three days later (November 27, 1954) found Yma in Memphis, Tennessee at the Auditorium's South Hall. Advance notices carried some startling (but false) news. In addition to her Incan chants, Yma would sing a group of Negro spirituals "plus a medley of Gershwin and Cole Porter tunes."

The review appeared the day after the concert. Ben S. Parker, in the *Memphis Commercial Appeal*, headed his review: "Sumac, Vocal Phenomenon, Provides An Eerie Evening." Mr. Parker noted that an audience of some 1,500 came out to hear the Peruvian singer and found the experience disquieting. "Many of her tones are rich and musical; many others have the quality of a musical saw in pitch and timbre—not necessarily unpleasant in moderate quantities, but hardly human. There is a strong suspicion that some of her weird echo-chamber effects and disembodied pianissimos were given an assist from a tape recorder and other electronic devices partly concealed in the orchestra pit.

"She was at her spellbinding best in (the) native-sounding weirdies . . . in which she can do her own special brand of vocal gymnastics to the full. . . . She was least effective in her conventional songs, where the familiarity . . . showed up her weak points, including a tendency to slide off pitch, labored tonal production, and some faking of runs."

Thursday, December 2, 1954 found Yma singing in the Kiel Opera House in St. Louis to excellent effect. Thomas B. Sherman, writing for the *St. Louis Post-Dispatch* on December 3, found the Sumac voice a marvel. "For whatever it's worth, Yma Sumac is indeed a unique phenomenon and in an exact sense of the word. [Her various registers] were interesting in timbre, well-focused and thoroughly agile. So if she had chosen to do so she could have sung the 'Queen of the Night' aria, the 'Saphische Ode' or the Toreador's Song from Carmen with equal facility."

Concerning her music: "Supposedly these songs were derived from native material; but the absence of any suggestion of a primitive scale and the persistence of a generalized Latin-American night club coloring made it all sound rather synthetic. In any case it had little artistic consequence. The large audience liked the show and was mightily impressed as it should have been, by Miss Sumac's piping highs, rumbling lows, her amazingly sudden changes from a roaring fortissimo to a whispered pianissimo, her bird calls, shouts, whistles and slides. Truly she was miraculous. But even miracles . . . repeated often enough, run into the law of diminishing returns and we begin to take them for granted."

Monday, December 6th found Yma singing at the State Theater in Toledo, Ohio. A new type of gimmick now began to appear. It was one that would be be dragged out of the closet for an airing every couple of decades or so. **"WHO IS YMA SUMAC"** (reads a large square now inserted into pages of a newspaper).

"Answer on Postcard to Flora Ward Hineline, Commodore Perry Arcade

Prize of Value for first 100 correct Answers

Do Not Delay"

Just what that valuable prize was is never mentioned in the advertisements.

Pat Eberhart waited for more than 45 minutes for Yma to honor a scheduled interview. She was told by a stagehand that she would be lucky if she got in. But the time was not wasted. During those 45 minutes, Moisés managed to fill her in on Yma's story, and Yma did then show up. When she did, she confessed that she was tired and looked forward to some time off once this section of the tour was completed. After resting she would travel to Japan and appear in Europe.

Young as she was (though as we've seen it's hard to be sure exactly what her age was—she's given as 26 in this article, which would be in the ballpark—it appears that Yma was already becoming preoccupied with the aging process. "Sometimes flying, sometimes riding with the rest of her troupe by bus, the 26-year-old woman appeared beautiful but weary but admitted that she does not get the 10 hours of sleep that she would like for her voice. ''I am still young . . . how old do you think I am.'"

Reviewing the performance, J.S. found it "bewildering." "The lady has a freak voice, totally devoid of musical instinct or texture, which romps from the mosquito range down to the cellar. Her diction is unintelligible in any language but English, and that is accented noticeably. . . . Her idea of a Negro spiritual, 'Nobody Knows de Trouble I've Seen,' was hardly convincing in the light of troubles at hand. She sang the Bizet song . . . in a foghorn voice, strident and tasteless, and in questionable French. Her troupe of dancers, musicians and such, had a great deal to do and some trouble doing it. I thought the ensemble better suited to a night spot of intimate rapport."

Reviewing her next concert, the next night in the Murat Concert Hall in Indianapolis, Walter Whitworth found the Sumac experience baffling. "There certainly are four octaves and more in the range of the voice. It is rather like being Marian Anderson, Irene Jordan and Roberta Peters rolled into one person. . . . Anyway the singing is startling. It isn't artistic singing and sometimes not very good singing, but, to repeat an adjective, it is incredible singing. The songs, of course, were devised to display the four octaves, and it was sort of a game with us to wonder in which octave Miss Sumac was going to sing next, whether a single note or a whole phrase. The last song of all, an imitation of jungle noises, was one of those things you'd never believe from any description of it. You'd have to hear it. It was, indeed, the epitome of the singer's strange gift."

Writing for *The Indianapolis Star* (December 8, 1954), Corbin Patrick noted that there was "a modest gathering of devotees at the Murat last night."

December 8 found the Sumac troupe performing at the Milwaukee Auditorium. Here too, the audience was somewhat meager. "Her audience was not large, but listeners were properly startled by the singer's celebrated range. Actually Miss Sumac was more a delight to the eye than to the ear. Patrons who sat near the reporter, at any rate, exclaimed more frequently over her regal beauty than over the fact that her voice could cover five-octaves. It is a little difficult to write learnedly about a singer who can progressively sound like a line-man for the Chicago Bears, an ordinary soprano, a birdling and a mosquito." (Richard S. Davis, *The Milwaukee Journal*, 12/9/54)

The American tour continued to be incredibly arduous, one of the most difficult and intricate the Sumac company had ever undertaken. Although concerts were slated to begin at 8:30 in the evening, they invariably started late, since 8:00 would usually find the group still in transit from the previous engagement. Hernán Braña recalls that, more often than not, they would literally jump out of the cars and buses, get things set up and run on stage.

The success of the tour is all the more impressive when one takes into consideration the conditions the performers were subject to—inadequate performing facilities and amplification systems and inconsistent rooming accommodations. Although the schedule was a dangerous one for Yma, she was careful and concentrated on preserving the freshness of her voice and health.

Yma and Hernán 1954

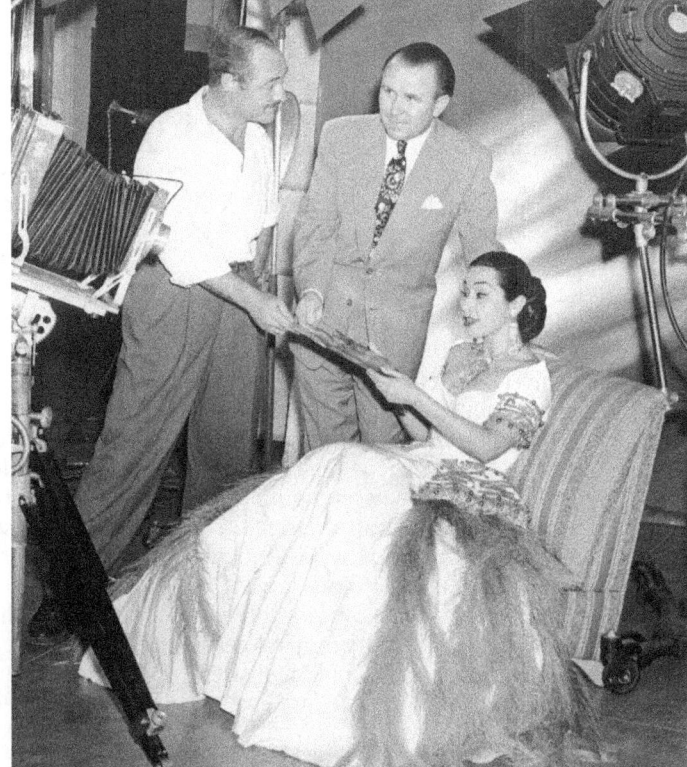

The photographer Tom Kelley and Glen Wallich, one of the founders of Capitol Recors, with Yma

Chapter 6

Lament
1955–1957

On January 22, 1955, Yma and the expanded company gave a concert at the Shrine Auditorium in Los Angeles. Ticket prices ranged from $1.10 to $3.85 and the crowd that gathered to sample the singer's Incan chants was impressive, especially considering that the popular musical satirist, Anna Russell (1911–2006) was performing at the Wilshire Ebell Theater the same evening.

Although the Sumac concert was scheduled to begin at 8:30, it opened twenty minutes late, a fact that seems not to have bothered either the audience or the critics. Alma Gowdy, of the *Los Angeles Evening Herald Express* wrote : "Sumac's entrance was worth the wait..(she was) . . . an imposing and beautiful sight." Ms. Gowdy found Yma "sloe-eyed" and "double-voiced" and was both fascinated and puzzled by the voice, which sounded like "two different instruments." Most intriguing was the tonal quality of Yma's voice, which Gowdy found "eerie . . . from its deep resonant lower voice to the coloratura bird sounds at the extreme top." Gowdy's summation of the quality of the evening's entertainment was that "it was show business for the sun gods."

On January 24th, the touring company gave a gala concert at the Mellon Auditorium in Pittsburgh. This was Yma's first appearance in that city; the concert was followed by a formal reception given at the Gateway Plaza by the Board of Directors of Music for Mt. Lebanon. Newspaper articles announcing the arrival of the Peruvian singer showed unmistakable signs of overenthusiastic publicists being indulged.

Headlines for the *Times Herald* read: "Miracle Singer To Perform Here." At least two inaccurate mentions were made of Yma's "five-octave" voice. The issue of her range arose in a pre-concert interview with her. "'I only sing, she says, 'I'm the interpreter of the music. Somebody else must interpret the range,' she remarked somewhat disinterestedly."

Donald Steinfirst reviewed the concert for the Post Gazette. He commented that the audience was one of the largest ever seen at the Mellon Auditorium. "It is rather difficult to give any appraisal of the other qualities of (her) voice since Miss Sumac uses a microphone. She croons into it, whispers and sings forte, all at about the same distance from the mike. However, the voice seemed to be fairly clear and to be delivered cleanly."

Another reviewer, Ralph Lewando, of *The Press*, unfortunately, left at the intermission. But he did note: "Dignity of manner, serious and non-expressive visage and carefulness of procedure characterized all of Miss Sumac's endeavor up to the time we departed at intermission."

January 27th found the troupe back in Canada, this time in Ottawa. *The Ottawa Citizen* reported that "the house was sold out to capacity, including standing room and the audience good-humoredly accepted a wait of 40 minutes for curtain time. Antonio Tremblay the impresario, explained that at two o'clock yesterday (the 27th), traveling by bus, (they were) stranded in Niagara Falls and he outlined the emergency means–chartered bus and chartered plane–which were used to get (them) into Upland by 7:30 PM."

The Ottawa Citizen reported: "While every part of the show was of interest in itself, the performance as a whole did not have strong theatrical quality which one had

1955 Concert Ad   1955 concert ad, reverse

expected. The audience was responsive but seldom excited, and it was tempting to puzzle over the reason for this. It would hardly be fair to lay all the responsibility at the feet of the orchestra, though it was largely made up of our civilization's concert grand piano, double bass, cello, etc. which were at odds with the primitive Inca songs and supposedly primitive dancers."

January 30th found Yma at Her Majesty's Theatre in Montreal and readers got some real news. *The Montreal Star*, promoting Yma's visit, told readers that not only did Moisés discover and train Yma, "He has also prepared four ancient Incan operas in modern form and hopes to star Yma in them."

The day before the concert, this was further explained: "(Yma's) largest ambition, as yet unfulfilled, is to sing an Inca opera at the Metropolitan Opera House. She is intensely proud of the fact that four operas, remnants of the era of Incan glory, have survived through generation after generation and are intact today in their original forms. Vivanco, who is half Spanish and half Quechuan, has adapted the operas to modern musical forms and hopes to star Yma in them. The couple believes that the operas would be exciting musical adventures for American audiences as well as tributes to a once-great civilization. 'They will help to show everyone what a highly developed culture the Incas possessed and to increase respect for the Indians,' says Vivanco." (1/29/55)

The Montreal show did not go well. Trouble with the amplification system seriously hampered the ability of the audience to enjoy the more subtle aspects of the Sumac show. Jacob Siskind wryly noted: "Miss Sumac ran the gamut of her extensive and expensive wardrobe, and sang a few songs. She seemed thoroughly uncomfortable every brief moment she was on the stage, and seemed too to be making a special point when she surprised the company and her audience by singing Nobody Knows the Trouble I've Seen. Vocally, Miss Sumac did not seem to be in top form last night and was not helped by the public address system which had to be shut off for the second half of the program. In fact Miss Sumac's fabled top octave or two were nowhere in evidence."

On February 1, 1955, Yma performed in Boston; the review that appeared in *The Boston Daily Globe* the next day expressed typical reactions of audiences: "Yma Sumac Warbles Both High and Low" by John Wm. Riley. "Just what this Yma Sumac business is all about I'm sure I don't know. [but] No matter how you slice it, Miss Sumac is a remarkable performer."

The company returned to the New York City area for a series of performances. Two concerts were scheduled at Carnegie Hall, on February 6th and 8th. These were prefaced by the troupe's first appearance at the famous Brooklyn Academy of Music on the 3rd (Yma's first visit to Brooklyn) and one-night stands in New Jersey and Connecticut. Coinciding with the New York-based engagements was the commercial release of her new 10" LP disk, Mambo! with the Billy May band.

True to form, the Sumac management preceded Yma's arrival in the tri-state area with exotic, tantalizing flyers. These advance notices were intricate affairs made available at concert venues. In one version, Yma's name appeared in oversize letters as though hewn from solid rock riddled with age. This framed a central photograph-drawing of Yma in her Sun Virgin vestments with outstretched arms and up-turned palms, as if in supplication to the Sun God. A colorful but preposterous geographical error was made by having an erupting volcano looming behind the singer. Another version boasted much of the same but included a line drawing of the ruins of Machu-Picchu surmounted by this same wildly misplaced volcano.

To excite ticket-buyers further, special Yma Sumac souvenir booklets were now available throughout the tour. These booklets gave the address of the recently incorporated Yma Sumac Enterprises Inc. as 3065 McConnell Drive, West Los Angeles, the address of the singer's home. The creating of a corporation provided Yma and Moisés some protection from tax payment pressures. Although Yma was being artistically represented by Kenneth Allen Associates Inc., of New York City, the concerts were being presented by "Inca Concerts, Inc."

Moisés was both manager and director of Inca Concerts Inc. As sometimes happens in situations like this, the quality of the finished product eclipses its creator. Moisés, a proud Spanish man, now found that he was of secondary importance to everyone except Yma.

One of the most difficult marriages to sustain is a marriage where both partners are public performers. This is one of the reasons why divorces are so common between artistic personalities—especially if one person (or talent) seems to overshadow the other. This can be especially sticky if the personality left behind is male. Depending on what culture one is brought up into, being the male half of a relationship that includes a highly successful female can wreak all sorts of emotional and even physical havoc–both in and out of the bedroom. For a marriage to work, both parties have to be extremely sensitive to the feelings and "baggage" of the other and work hard to keep the honesty and sincerity of the relationship. In both North American and Spanish cultures, which are both patriarchal societies, most men are brought up to believe that they should be the bread winner—the one making the most money—and also the one in charge. This set of assumptions tends to provide very little guidance for how they should deal with personal issues or emotions that can be devastating. Men are just expected to deal.

Whether Yma and Moisés ever had any such private discussions will never be known. But from all the evidence it does not seem that any such discussions were held with any great sensitivity or tact. At least from the outside it seems that Moisés always had issues about his own worth once Yma skyrocketed to international importance in 1950. Although I suspect he tried, he never quite managed to make the necessary adjustments. Instead, much of his time was spent in repeated, futile efforts to accentuate (read exaggerate) his own importance.

According to many who worked with both Yma and Moisés, this was done with what was seen as obnoxious aggressiveness, or stubborn belligerence. His domination over Yma was interpreted as inordinate jealousy and a revealing of deep insecurities. Moisés guarded Yma like a rare hothouse flower. Even regular members of the company remarked that it was practically impossible to see or speak with Yma alone. "You had to get past Moisés first."

Whether consciously or not, Yma allowed herself to be put into this awkward and precarious position. She became completely dependent on Moisés, to such an extent that later, when managing her career on her own, she was practically helpless without Moisés' guidance. In turn, Moisés was dependent on Yma to constantly feed his ego. Despite their success and renown and Yma's constant stroking of Moisés' ego, (even on stage) his sense of worth seemed to silently crumble. Ill-advisedly, probably—futilely, in any case—Yma took to introducing Moisés to audiences as "a great composer." Audiences couldn't have cared less; they came to hear her.

Most of Moisés' and his agents' efforts centered on this publicity material. The 1955 Sumac booklets represent an intense, calculated final exertion to promote himself—if not over Yma, certainly alongside her.

As early as 1952, publicity material contained information that only the naïve would believe "Moisés Vivanco . . . is recognized in the field of creative music as one of the outstanding composers of the 20th century . . . His music is standard repertoire in the great symphonic orchestras of the world. He is one of the few young composers today whose works are included along with such men as Brahms, Schubert, Tchaikovsky, Mozart, Beethoven . . . By giving new life, new brilliance to an ancient musical form Vivanco has won himself a place of inestimable importance in the world of great music."

Perhaps, since Yma's music originated in Peru, Moisés thought American audiences would not know the difference. It seems that Yma's only concern during her career was performing, so her naïveté was essentially of a harmless nature—except to herself. Moisés' however, grounded as it was in egotism, was dangerous and only led to complete dissolution.

Yma delivered what was expected of her because, in reality, her talent equaled the extravagant claims of the publicity releases. In Moisés' case, however, the competence and quality of what was offered failed to measure up to the publicity praises. Audience reaction to the "Kon Tiki" Symphony, which occasionally opened concerts, was only polite. Audience interest centered only on Yma—a situation Moisés himself had fostered. As Yma became more famous, Moisés became more adamant about his own importance. Unhappily, we're about to see that Moisés' feeling around this time that his needs were not being met seemed to drive him to seek satisfaction elsewhere.

The 1955 Yma Sumac concert booklets consisted of twenty thick pages of Sumac and Vivanco propaganda. Superbly designed by Bruce Hopper and lavishly illustrated with photographs, the booklet featured outrageously fantasized biographical commentary. Not surprisingly, nowhere does a name appear responsible for originating the text. Close examination, however, shows it to be a compilation of previously released publicity material all jumbled and thrown together. Of the fifty-some photographs, many are fascinating since they show Yma in various theatrical poses on and off stage. There are also a few, rare shots of Yma performing with the original "Compañia Peruana del Arte," back in 1942 (when she'd have been somewhere in her teens). In these, she is colorfully dressed in authentic traditional Peruvian festive costume, with bobby-socks and sandals.

The biographical and analytical prose of this booklet is embarrassing. Yma's voice is described as though it was some kind of health food—"virile, subtle ... vitamin-packed [*sic!*] ... loaded with a rare animal magnetism that has caused men and women of all ages all over the world to forget their everyday problems. To step outside the four walls of their narrow lives, to experience new emotions." Readers are told that Yma's voice was capable of freezing listeners in their tracks. Nothing having been learned, apparently, from the ill effects of the controversy in 1951 and 1952 surrounding the authenticity of her "Incan" heritage, blatant and vulgar emphasis was now re-applied to that claim. (Many of these photos are reproduced in the supplemental CD available from the publisher, as is the full text of the egregious 1955 "souvenir program.")

By 1955 no one believed Yma was a "last descendant of Incan kings." In fact, doubt was widespread that she was even from Peru. No matter, publicists ground out the same old story. Instead of tactfully trying to heal and rectify the tenuous relationship between Yma and her audience by reverting to, and incorporating, believable facts, they poured salt into still open wounds and smacked readers on top of the head in attempts to convince them of what could not be proven—discrediting in the process much that was genuine.

Still maintained was the insipid impression that Yma was a woman of superhuman qualities. As if she were a reincarnated goddess, or a revered priestess reminiscent of H. Rider Haggard's 2,000 year-old "She." A being who descended from her mountain-top aerie to share her magnificent talent with mortals of the lower lands. Then, to even out the balance, writers went to great lengths to describe Yma's temperament in terms of kindness, simplicity and honesty—especially honesty. This created impossible and grossly unfair contrasts.

The 1955 souvenir booklet remains the apex of publicists' frenzied absurdities. Legend and nonsense are freely and indiscriminately interwoven with threads of fact. Unfortunately, the handbook emphasizes several flagrant inconsistencies. The most blatant one concerns Yma's vocal range. This was a matter that seemed to vary depending on what country she was in. On page 5, her range is said to be four octaves. Ten pages later, it is stated that she has "the only five-octave voice in the world." This illogical discord is made all the more embarrassing by appearing within the very same text, suggesting not only arrogant charlatanism but simple incompetent proofreading.

Perhaps the most regrettable thing, however, was the downright perverse winking insinuation that, as long as Yma continued to sing "as she was born to," what difference did it make whether she was really an Incan Princess, a fulfillment of an age-old prophesy, or in fact, Brooklyn's Amy Camus? This teasing reference to a deception that actually didn't occur is made worse by the contrived, open-eyed manner in which it is presented—presumably an attempt to defuse this canard by treating it lightly—but at what cost to its object's dignity? Publicity agents now used the "Amy Camus" motif without reserve and in spite of the repercussions it visited upon its subject. It would not matter if Yma Sumac denied its validity until the world ended. The continued use of this negative, exploitative device simply poured acid into wounds that were not sufficiently healed. Today, over fifty years after its inception, Amy Camus remains a taunting lie that pursues Yma Sumac wherever she goes. Like the Aztec Xtabay legend, it is a silently grinning specter.

Both Carnegie Hall concerts were well attended. Compared to the reviews of the year before, however, New York critics' reviews show a distinct change in attitude. A clipped, inarticulate critique from *The New York Times* (2/7/55) said of the first concert: "An audience of 2,000 assembled last night for the show presented by Yma Sumac and her husband Moisés Vivanco. Miss Sumac was assisted by four dancers and a nine piece orchestra." Nothing was said of Yma's voice, its comparative condition to the year before, or of its use. Mention was made, however, of a theatrical device used during "Tumpa!" (Earthquake), when "two miniature volcanoes on either side of the stage . . . burst into simulated eruption."

Reviewing the same performance, the *Musical Courier* objected to the extraneous grunting and wailing of accompanying musicians. Finding the supplemental expressions of primal ecstasy distracting, the critic commented, " . . . what [Yma Sumac] might achieve in straight concert, unimpeded by noisy competition is anyone's guess." He admired her vocal prowess, however, and was amazed at her technical facility. "[Her voice has] an enormous range of almost unbelievable colors and textures. She can sing a wide open chest production and skate blithely to a flute coloratura in less time than it takes . . . to type this."

Musical America reviewed the final Carnegie Hall concert of February 8th. It was to be the last time Yma would perform on the stage of that august hall. The review gives a wonderful, tongue-in-cheek image of the entertainment that night; a taste of the grand theatrics with which Moisés framed his wife's unearthly warbling. "With an ominous gong and some mysterious marimba music from behind the curtain, the mood was set. As the curtain opened . . . one saw two volcanic mountains on either side of the stage and a band consisting of cello, violin, oboe, flute, piano, and an assortment of drums manned by people in native costumes. As a prelude to the entrance of Miss Sumac, a chant was sung telling of the 1,000 year old prediction that a maiden of miraculous voice and beauty would be born in this age, and would carry to all parts of the earth the story of the great and glorious past of the Inca civilization. In this aura of mysticism [she] appeared." (M.L., 2/25/55)

Of Yma's performance, the critic wrote that although "vocal trickery may be involved, the unusual thing is that (she) handles her voice with consummate control from top to bottom." It is not explained what was meant by "vocal trickery" but I suspect the critic was referring to Yma's emphasis on using her register breaks and her ability to quickly switch between them.

From reviews, it is obvious that Yma's voice was healthy and responsive to her demands despite the rigors of touring. It seems that over the years, the only throat remedy she used with any frequency was a common mixture most singers use to keep the throat relaxed and moist, a concoction of honey and lemon, the honey acting as a soothing agent for the throat when it is tired or irritated, and the lemon helping to cut through phlegm. (In the 1955 booklets readers were assured that this remedy was "a traditional compound made by her mother in the mountain village of Ichocán.")

Richard Westenburg, founder and conductor of New York City's famous professional chorus, Musica Sacra, remembers when Yma visited his college in late 1954 during her tour of the United States. At that time, he was at the University of Minnesota working on a Masters degree in musicology. In order to make ends meet, he took a job as stage-left-door guard, three or four nights a week at the University's theater. During this time, he saw and heard many artists perform including Mary Shearer, Roberta Peters and Yma Sumac. "I can't remember exactly what she sang," he said, "but it was the ethnic material one had come to expect. But then, one hardly expected a voice like that to sing Bach or Mozart!"

Interviewed more than thirty-five years later, Westenburg remembered Yma being preceded by a "fascinating publicity machine" and that she was a "strange and interesting performer, who certainly knew her craft and seemed to be an attractive and warm person. She looked terrific wearing the colorful costumes that one always saw on posters and I remember that her singing knocked me out!"

By February 10th, the troupe had settled in Charleston, West Virginia to perform for 1,600 people at the Municipal Auditorium. According to Bayard F. Ennis, Staff writer of *The Gazette,* the "Inca Singer (was) Well Received." He had somewhat mixed feelings, however, concerning the Sumacian troupe. "For one thing, few of her musicians were Peruvian as advertised. It seemed somewhat incongruous to have native North Americans attired in the exotic costumes of the Andes. In addition, only two or three of the instruments played could be considered indigenous to (Yma's) land."

The next night (2/11/55) they were to perform at The Mosque in Richmond, Virginia but weather forced the concert to be cancelled. Yma and the company had attempted to fly from Charleston to Washington, DC but the plane had been forced down prematurely by the weather conditions. They switched to cars and tried to get to Richmond that way but finally had to give up. The concert was not rescheduled.

During the course of the tour, Yma performed at the famous Symphony Hall in Boston. *The Boston Herald* found the trappings surrounding Yma banal. "The program of Yma Sumac and her troupe of Andean dancers, drummers and musicians begins as the ensemble takes its place between two gnarled papier-mâché objects resembling elephant-foot scrap baskets. Later in the evening these sprout a synthetic flame and are, presumably, to be taken for volcanoes." (R.S.T.) The critic did, however, find Yma and her voice to be everything that had been boasted, commenting: "She is also an excellent musician. Her voice is a slightly restricted one in volume, but at every level it is pure, well-placed and capable of the most astounding tones whether she wishes to essay a flute-like soprano or a dusky lower register." Yma's music was found to be "... authentic enough via European modes, and the highpoint was a duet with Cholita, a contralto, and with Moisés Vivanco, an accomplished guitarist. It is Spanish in style with fiery hand-clappings and guttural shouts heightening the accelerations."

Sunday, February 20th found them performing at 3:30 pm to enthusiastic crowds in the Bell Auditorium in Augusta, Georgia. Four days later found them in Montgomery, Alabama in the Lanier Auditorium. Some 1,200 people listened to Yma on the 24th and J.M. in *The Advertiser* noted: "High light of her part of the show was 'Chuncho,'....In a word, the song is elemental. A hushed audience sat breathlessly as the weird, indescribable tune, unfolded, accompanied by guitar and a flute. Also, Yma is a showman. Her reaction to the audience's applause began with the first number, with an icy disdain. When she finished her last number she bowed deeply, almost prostrating herself on the stage."

Clearing weather permitted the troupe to land in Jackson, Mississippi for a Saturday, February 26th concert at the Municipal Auditorium. Tommy Herrington, the Music Editor of the *Clarion-Ledger,* commented: "Her program of Incan music got off to a late start, but by the time the finale came she had them clamoring for more!"

Elisabeth Waldo again merited special praise: "Miss Elisabeth Waldo, violinist with the accompanying instrumentalists, was popular with two violin solo excerpts."

Asheville, North Carolina was the next stop on the tour. Writing for the *Asheville Citizen,* W.D. underlined certain problems with the concert's presentation: "The Yma Sumac voice trills and sighs against probably the most elaborate theatrical display of any singer appearing on the American stage. The production even includes twin 'volcanoes.' To perhaps belabor a comparison, the show is a bit like highly seasoned sausage—there is so much spice it becomes a bit difficult to evaluate the basic ingredients. But spice, volcanoes and all, the audience warmly responded to Miss Sumac and her troupe, particularly during the second half of the program."

Unfortunately, amplification problems were evidenced. "Miss Sumac and a woman violinist for a while fought something of a battle with the auditorium sound system. Often as not, the electronic device answered their high notes with high pitched 'feedback' as if not to be outdone. Between times, it emitted a frying egg sound a bit disconcerting to members of the audience in the front part of the auditorium." (2/29/55)

Wednesday, March 2 found the troupe at the Memorial Auditorium in Chattanooga, Tennessee.

Headlines in *The Chattanooga Times* the next day read: *"Yma Sumac Gives Pleasing Concert*
With her 4-Octave Range, She Fulfills Legend and Expectation"

Unfortunately, the next concert, a return to Atlanta, Georgia, on Thursday, March 3 was an all out disaster—although the blame did not fall on the Sumac Troupe. Reporting for the *Atlanta Constitution*, the next day, Alex Joiner, Jr. wrote: "There was static in the Andes Thursday night and it was difficult to tell who was exasperated most, Yma Sumac or her Roxy Theater audience. "The microphones the singing descendant of Inca emperors depends on were on the blink, making a near fiasco of what was to have been a triumphant engagement here. Biggest applause of the evening it turned out went to the singer's husband and the producer of the show, Moisés Vivanco who courageously approached the footlights and announced: 'I have to apologize for the little attention the house management has paid to the sound system. It is absolutely terrible.'

"Maintenance men ran hither and yon, urging the audience to be patient and trying their best to remedy the situation. It was a losing battle.

"Miss Sumac, working without mike during the greater portion of the evening, was inaudible beyond the first few rows. Using it, as she did to recreate bird sounds in 'Chunchu,' she sounded like a tired Florence Foster Jenkins.

"It is useless to go into the production in detail because, under the circumstances, one selection sounded pretty much like the next one . . . It was just, as they say in show business, one of those nights."

Sarah Myrick, writing on Friday, March 4, had much the same to report. "A sympathetic but slightly perturbed audience seemed to have enjoyed what it heard of Yma Sumac in performance. . . . The Peruvian singer might have spanned her advertised range of five octaves, but the inadequate sound-system denied the Atlanta audience the delight of fully hearing it. What the microphone couldn't catch, the spotlight did. Miss Sumac definitely won her audience with her Peruvian beauty, a low cut red velvet gown and a form-fitting Parisian green velvet dress."

Monday, March 7, was the last concert of the tour and found the company in Savannah, Georgia. The day before the concert at the Municipal Auditorium, the *Savannah Morning News* (Sunday, 3/6/55) ran an interview Yma and Moisés gave with Anna C. Hunter. The operatic question once again reared its head. "Declaring that she can sing any operatic aria but prefers to bring to the world songs from an ancient civilization which are unique and beautiful, Yma Sumac discussed her repertoire in Savannah yesterday. " 'People ask me why I do not sing more operatic arias,' said the glamorous star with the five octave range. 'I can sing all these arias, but I do not care to compete in this role. I want to show to the world the Incan melodies and native songs. This music is something new and beautiful.'

"Also operatic arias are in one color and demand only the conventional range, whereas the Incan songs cover a tremendous range."

Ms. Hunter also reviewed the concert under the headline *"Audience Is Spellbound by Yma Sumac."* "A pin could have dropped . . . . last night as Yma Sumac, glamorously gowned and veiled, imitated woodland creatures with an astounding variety of strange sounds—hissing, guttural, rasping, raucous and softly cooing. The audience sat in stunned silence and wonder, so phenomenal was it for a beautiful woman to so deport herself as an artist.

"It was disappointing to those who have heard some of her records that she did not give more high-pitched songs in her repertoire of Andean music, for in these and the imitation of woodland sounds she excels. It was also regrettable that she elects to wear Paris and American creations, as exotic as she appears in them, as the Indian costumes worn by the dancers were strikingly beautiful in color and pattern."

Interestingly, Hunter is one of the few critics to support Moisés' compositional claims. "But the program bears out what Moisés . . . states, that he composes with American themes combined with ancient Andean traditional folk tunes, and the combination of Indian pipes, piano, xylophone and strings was evidence of this."

Finally, with the American tour completed, Moisés again re-organized the company. April and May found Yma, Moisés, Hernán and three dancers (Don Kiego, Ula Kan, and Margala) performing at the Empire Room in the Palmer House Hotel in Chicago. Advance publicity boasted "Peruvian Princess with an unbelievable voice range of more than four octaves . . ."

The *Chicago Daily News* described Yma as being arrayed " . . . as if for grand opera in Lima. Her white satin bouffant gown is set off by a waistband, seemingly of gold. Her fetching brunette hair is ornamented by gleaming metal pendants as big as shoehorns. Her personality is eye-catching before she has sung a note."

Reviewing the April 13 show, the critic from *Variety* commented: "Reaction to this type of show will always be mixed: there are them what digs it and them what don't. Miss Sumac, of course, dominates the scene with the quality of her voice and an air of queenly hauteur . . . (she) amazes the customers with the clarity, volume and great modulative control of the voice she projects. She creates an atmosphere of exotic, distant and wild lands, and this too is the flavor of the production she and her husband have created." (Gabe; 4/20/55)

Of a later performance, *Where Magazine* made the interesting comment that "night clubs normally don't go in much for culture. But the Empire Room of the Palmer House . . . makes an exception in its current show." (4/30/55)

This confusion as to what type of artist Yma was defines another fascinating, and impossible paradox created (without intent) by Yma and those who wrote her music. Concert critics felt her show more appropriate for nightclubs and nightclub critics felt it more suited to the concert hall. Not only that, but classical music (or culture) fans tended to relegate Yma to the popular music idiom because of the format of her music, while many popular music fans felt her to be a "culture" item because of the smooth classical sound and polished, operatic use her voice. This situation was never correctly balanced. On the other hand, perhaps, because of this very situation, Sumac devotees came from both sides. And they still come from both sides. Classical enthusiasts appreciate the beauty and athletic control of her voice while popular music fans identify with her music and its rhythmic structure.

The review from *Where Magazine* went on to single-out various dance routines and Hernán's exceptional flute work, all of which were found to be particularly inventive and entertaining. As expected, Yma's numbers were especially enjoyed. Her sets at the Palmer House Hotel included:

Xtabay (Lure of the Unknown Love)—a rare occurrence in nightclubs and concert halls
Montana (Lullaby)
Kuyaway (Inca Love Song)
Taita Inty (Virgin of the Sun God; Hymn to the Sun)
Chuncho! (Forest Creatures)
Ya Me Voy. (This is probably the "Ripui" found on *Inca Taqui*. Both songs have the same central text and the program notes used for "Ya Me Voy" resemble those of "Ripui.")

On June 27th, 1955, Capitol Records corrected an error in a composition credit for which Hernán Braña had been fighting for years in court. On that date, Capitol released an "immediate correction" release confirming that the composer of "Karibe Taki," the first song on Yma's second album, *Legend of the Sun Virgin*, was Hernán Braña—not Moisés Vivanco. At that time, rights for the piece were transferred from Moisés to Hernán. Another battle, for the compositional rights of "Taki Rari" on *Mambo!* were lost. Contention over composition rights and credits was not an uncommon occurrence between Moisés and Capitol Records. As one might expect, however, Hernán's court battles strained his relations with Moisés to the extent that within a year his performing relationship with the Sumac troupe had ended.

Although at the time Yma and her company had no idea of its importance, June 29, 1955 was a crucial day in the history of popular music. It was on that day that Bill Haley's rock and roll song "Rock Around the Clock" hit number one on the music charts. This single circumstance was to forever change the course of American popular music. Rock and roll soon became the standard for American pop music. Before long, Yma would find it difficult to fit in with the rapid changes happening all around her due to the popularity of this musical form. Rock and roll also instituted other changes in America's culture. Yma's Incan fantasy-music quickly became less intriguing as new musical vistas suddenly opened up to the American public and consequently the audiences of the world.

In June and July Yma returned to the Cocoanut Grove supper club in the Ambassador Hotel in Los Angeles. While performing there, she made a special guest appearance on the Steve Allen television show, which was filmed live from the supper club. For her selection, Yma sang her infamous "Queen of the Night Mambo" her only televised performance of the piece. This peculiar mambo remained in Yma's repertoire for another decade. Unfortunately, the piece was never recorded.

Yma and Moisés were in the news a good deal during July, 1955. On July 22, Yma became a naturalized American citizen at the age of "twenty-eight." Photographs showed a smiling Yma being given a kiss by her six-year-old son. Although little mention is made of Charlie, it seems that he accompanied his parents during most of their tours, his education being taken care of by private tutors. From reports he was an avid (and good) swimmer. He later went to live in Spain with Moisés, where he went to college studying engineering. Information about Charlie is scarce—even today. It seems that, as the years passed, he retained good relations with both parents, though it seems he chose to live with Moisés in Spain.

Although Yma had become an American citizen, nothing was mentioned of Moisés' desire to do the same. During the entire process, he remained conspicuously silent.

Although Yma's performances were going well, her life would soon fall apart. On July 31, 1955 news dominated the papers that 38 year-old Moisés Vivanco had been named in a paternity suit brought against him by former employee, Maureen Shea, Yma's twenty-one year old personal secretary. Maureen, who had occasionally filled-in as a dancer for the Sumac show, stated that Moisés had fathered her nine-month old twin daughters. She demanded monthly support in the amount of $500.00.

Having heard the news, Yma collapsed at her home in Cheviot Hills and was under a doctor's care. Coming so soon after the tax scandal and the additional pressures created by those problems, Yma was completely devastated. With a little simple calculation, Yma was able to figure out that Maureen's twins were conceived during a very high point of her career—a time when Yma had felt most happy and secure.

Plans for future concert tours were shelved. Engagements for the rest of the year, however, had to be honored. Despite tremendous emotional strain between them, Yma and Moisés managed to fulfill a 14-week return to the Cotillion Room in the Hotel Pierre in New York City. Beginning in September, this three-and-a-half month stint was only their third appearance at the prestigious supper club; it was also their last.

It was decided that only two female dancers would be used for the Cotillion Room engagement. Ula Kan, a Hungarian-born dancer who had been currently performing with the troupe agreed to do the job. The other girl, a newcomer to the troupe, was chosen from an open audition held in Hollywood. She was a talented fifteen year-old girl named Vilma Rizzo.

Vilma had studied dance in her native Cuba and at the time of the audition had been visiting her brother, Marco Rizzo in Hollywood. Marco was the musical director of the television show, "I Love Lucy." Originally Vilma had intended only a two-week visit. At a party that Marco took her to, however, she was introduced to Ruth St. Denis, a great figure in American dance, famous as (among many things) the first American to specialize in Oriental dance. Vilma was fascinated by St. Denis as well as oriental dance. When St. Denis heard that Vilma was a dancer, she invited her to study in her studio. As Vilma discovered that she had a natural aptitude for oriental dance, her visit with her brother stretched into months. During those months she arduously worked with St. Denis three times a week, mastering the new dance form.

With Charlie c. 1955

One morning Vilma spotted a notice in *Variety* about dancer auditions for the Yma Sumac company. She knew of Yma Sumac and was familiar with her recordings. For a lark, she decided to go and see what the audition was like. She did not intend to actually audition. That was reinforced when she arrived and saw the competition. "I saw all these gorgeous girls in their leotards (I hadn't brought any) and there I was—in the corner—frightened!"

Even though she had come completely unprepared, Vilma was persuaded to audition. Her memory of it is quite vivid. She was asked to perform an interpretive dance to a recording of Yma singing one of her famous Incan songs. "I was so nervous that to this day I can't remember what it was that I danced to. I didn't know if there was any similarity between oriental and Peruvian dance but I figured I might as well incorporate my studies with Miss St. Denis."

As happens in most auditions, the comment was "Thank you. Next!" Vilma returned home, pleased with herself, that at least she had the nerve to audition. It had been an interesting, rather fun, experience.

Two weeks later, an unsuspecting Marco answered the telephone and was surprised to learn that Vilma had been selected to join the Sumac troupe. At Yma's invitation, Vilma and Marco went to the Beverly Hills mansion to meet Yma and Moisés. Yma and Vilma took to one another right away and soon grew quite close. Marco was not at all sure what his parent's reaction would be since Vilma was only 15. Vilma could not join the troupe without their permission. Again, at Yma's invitation, Vilma's mother was flown to Hollywood to meet and discuss the situation.

Despite a successful meeting with Yma and Moisés, Vilma's mother did not approve of her daughter traveling cross-country un-escorted. Yma, perhaps remembering her own parental experience concerning un-chaperoned events, invited Mrs. Rizo to accompany Vilma for the duration of the engagement at the company's expense.

Asked to select an exotic professional name, Vilma chose "Sari Dar."

The Cotillion Room engagement was typical of its kind and consisted of two shows a night, six nights a week. The program breakdown was:

Dancers
Yma
Hernán (flute solo)
Yma
Dancers
Yma and Moisés (Inca Taqui Trio Tribute)

Yma and Vilma Rizzo 1955

The Armenian choreographer, Karoon Totikian was responsible for the dance sequences and Vilma remembers rehearsals being long and arduous. For Vilma, however, they were exciting. "They were a workout, I can tell you! Of course at that age one doesn't get as exhausted as you would if you were older, and I was so happy to be part of the show that I never felt tired."

The two dance sequences chosen for the Cotillion Room were performed in excellent costumes designed by the famous Edith Head. One dance was an interpretive dance of exoticism and the other was called "Carnavalito" in which Vilma and Ula were dressed like Peruvian dolls.

During this period of emotional strain, Yma and Moisés kept their private problems to themselves. Vilma comments: "It is hard for many people to realize that Yma truly worshipped her voice and her art. She was very strict with herself and fussy about all the details concerning her singing. During rehearsals, she was very serious and preoccupied with her work. Although she was cordial to others in the troupe, she remained conservative in her relations. Both my mother and I were close to Yma. I considered her like an older sister and I think she felt the same. But, you have to understand that, at the same time, Yma was a very proper person, and was very private.

"In front of an audience though, she blossomed. She literally became another person. And the magnetism! Yma hated it if people talked when she was on stage. They didn't dare talk, her magnetism was so great. She was very energetic and, at least for me, she was a definite source of inspiration. I can remember the way she would perform 'Chuncho!' It was very concentrated with very little physical movement—it was incredible. You know, she and Moisés were quite a couple. Artistically they were perfect for each

Cotillion Room, Hotel Pierre (Vilma Rizzo on left)

other. He was the mind behind Yma and he certainly understood how to project her voice and her image. I was so young at the time that I didn't realize this, but—as so often happens in situations like this—they destroyed each other."

The performances at the Pierre Hotel went well and were favorably received. There were the expected mishaps, however. For the dances, Vilma danced barefoot. She remembers one night in particular when during an energetic dance sequence she stomped down on a stray shard of glass on the stage. Although in pain, she finished the dance. Noticing Vilma leaving the stage in obvious pain, Yma asked what was wrong. After she found out what had happened, Yma went to her dressing room, got her eyebrow pluckers and removed the sliver from Vilma's foot. Vilma never forgot Yma's thoughtfulness whenever it came to herself. "She was very kind to me, a good friend." Occasionally Yma seemed a bit distant "but she was a real lady. She was very distinct and extremely honest."

Reflecting on her experience with the troupe Vilma said, "It was a beautiful part of my life and I have no regrets at all. I loved every minute. Perhaps, because I was so young, I was protected, only exposed to the beautiful aspects of the company. I don't care. I would have preferred it that way anyway."

After the Cotillion Room, Vilma was supposed to remain with the company for the Las Vegas engagement that was to follow. The job was canceled, however, and so Vilma's parents decided it was time for Vilma return to Havana to complete her education. She left the company with an open invitation from Yma and Moisés to rejoin the group when she was finished.

Over the years Vilma and Yma lost contact. The last time they saw each other was when Yma returned to Manhattan in 1975. "At that time Yma wasn't performing as much as before and she resented the fact that the public didn't recognize her art. We didn't seem to have very much in common anymore—so much time had passed. We both had changed, and she was very moody and difficult to be around."

Due to parental pressure, Vilma did not pursue dancing as a career. She took an academic BA degree and worked in public relations—for some years at the Hotel New Yorker, later for the public relations department of AeroMexico, which gave her ample opportunity to travel, which she loves. She remains a charming, modest woman.

"I think of that time often." Ms. Rizzo said cheerfully. "It was thrilling for me to be a part of such a company. I was so young and very honored to be asked. Yma was a great artist. I don't understand what happened. Her dedication to her work was something I have never forgotten. It inspired me. I still listen to her recordings sometimes. But you know, I prefer the old ones, the ones with the native instruments because that was the real Yma."

While appearing at the Pierre Yma performed on the famous Woolworth Hour radio program with Percy Faith, which aired on Sunday mornings. For her selections, Yma sang "Montana" (Lullaby) and a long, involved version of "Chuncho!".

It had been planned that after the Pierre Hotel engagement, the company would perform for a number of weeks at the famous Caesar's Palace in Las Vegas. Moisés, however, decided to cancel this engagement. One reason for that decision was probably a pending paternity test. Moisés had agreed to support Maureen Shea's twins, pending the test. On October 15, in Los Angeles, Judge Lewis Drucker ordered both parties to report back to him a week later after the tests were completed. *The Daily Sunday News* (10/16/55) commented: "The former secretary, Maureen Shea, 21, now a dancer, charged that Miss Sumac's husband, Moisés Vivanco, made love to her many times while she worked for the singer. The twins, Mary and Catherine, are a year old. Vivanco agreed to pay $200 a month support pending trial of Miss Shea's paternity suit, unless the blood tests show he could not have been the father. His attorney told the court: 'There is no admission of paternity.' "

The year 1955 was ending on a definite low note for Yma. One of the last jobs of that year was a concert for a BMI convention in Washington D.C. Tired and under persistent emotional strain, Yma and Moisés decided to remain in the nation's capital as tourists for a week of sight-seeing.

There was another sharp disappointment in store for Yma in 1955. It was apparently a matter of bad timing. Capitol records gave a gala celebration when they opened their new building. All the great Capitol artists were asked to be present—Jo Stafford, Kay Starr, Dinah Shore. Yma did not attend. Either she was not invited, perhaps due to the recent unfavorable publicity, or perhaps Moisés had declined the invitation without informing Yma. (It is true in any event that by this time relations between Capitol Records and Moisés were quite strained) Yma's disappointment was great. Her absence from the gala was conspicuous, considering that her recordings were a significant source of revenue for Capitol during this period—it hardly overstates the case to say that her revenues had practically built the new structure that they were celebrating.

In February of 1956, almost as an anti-climax to all the turmoil in the Vivanco household, Yma got her star on Hollywood Boulevard, the celebrated "Walk of Fame." It is unfortunate that such an honor came at a time when Yma was preoccupied with depressing personal matters.

The year 1956 also saw the cancellation by Yma and/or Moisés of many engagements. A few were honored for financial (tax) and publicity reasons including the Patti Page television show. On August 13th Yma sang "Tumpa! (Earthquake)" on the Ernie Kovacs television show. Recording commitments with Capitol Records were also unavoidable. In September, Yma and Moisés entered Capitol's studios and produced her fifth solo album, *Legend of the Jivaro*. This album was Yma's first 12" disk and was purported to be based on melodic and rhythmic fragments culled from the Amazonian head-hunting tribe, the Jivaro.

Cynical listeners probably thought that since the Incan idea was under attack, Yma and Moisés figured they would try on another culture for size. Unfortunately, the album has always smelled of cheap exploitation. It seems little coincidence that one of the most popular adventure films of 1954 was a jungle film called *Jivaro*.

The cast included Fernando Lamas, Brian Keith, Lon Chaney Jr., Rhonda Fleming and Rita Moreno.

The colorful album-cover of *Legend of the Jivaro* boasted a menacing photograph of a wild-eyed Yma in what we might take for tribal dress, looking quite dangerous, crouching over a bubbling cauldron full of nameless, boiling items. The little, squatting stone idol that used to make a regular appearance on her record albums had been replaced by a withered, shrunken head.

David Toop, also enjoyed this particular Sumac album cover: "Dry ice froths out of the pot and Sumac, in an unaccustomed state of undress, flashes the spectacular white of her eyes at a shrunken head that hangs in front of her. Behind her, naked Indians are throwing up their hands, either in ritual dance moves or dismay." (*Exotica*, Serpents Tail, London 1999)

Although the recording is well executed for the most part, it was not the authentic item that was so heartily boasted. Also, the music and singing are too outré to meet standards set by Yma's earlier disks. As if mirroring the emotional turbulence she was experiencing at the time, a few of the bands are disturbing for Yma's rather frenzied, almost psychotic singing.

Unfortunately the effusive liner notes continue the trend of fantasy that had been refreshingly dropped on the previous *Mambo!* disk. The *Legend of the Jivaro* notes were the last that were supplied by the seemingly inexhaustible Capitol staff. As if finally exhausted, after this album they fell blessedly silent.

Considering the problems caused by earlier liner notes and programs, those for *Legend of the Jivaro* were especially ill conceived—to the extent that they can be seen as insulting the intelligence of the record buying public. Yma and Moisés are portrayed as having taken time off in the middle of their performing schedule (and personal problems that were being reported on daily in newspapers) to travel into the Jivaro territory in order to gather fragments of melodies that Moisés then adapted into more commercially viable products. This is an interesting boast since one of the songs had already been used two years earlier for the album *Mambo!*, while two other songs originate in the Andes, not the Amazon. The liner notes are clever in their shameless way. Although authenticity is brazenly boasted, the only thing that is authentic about the recording is that Yma Sumac is singing—sometimes howling—throughout the unholy rituals.

In November, Yma performed on the Woolworth Hour, and also during that year performed "Birds" on the Jackie Gleason television show. She also made an appearance on the Ina Ray Hutton television show. Ms. Hutton had been known during the 1940s and '50s for her all-women band, and now her TV show boasted only women guest artists. For the Hutton show Yma sang an arrangement of "Autumn Leaves" and "Jungla," from the Mambo recording. An unusual effect was provided by photographing the singer through a waterfall during "Autumn Leaves." Yma's singing was well displayed by her two selections—sweetly floated high register work marked the former and brilliant high staccati and low notes the latter.

During the winter months of 1956, Yma made her only television appearance in a dramatic role, in a play for the prestigious and popular Playhouse 90 series. Yma played Sari, a singer in a night club where most of the action took place. Yma's opening scene was typically theatrical and tempestuous. Hands full of suitcases and followed by noisy poodles, Yma entered a hotel and began berating the receptionist for some mishap. During her few scenes of dialogue, she acquitted herself well. Yma only sang one piece, "Cha cha Gitano" (from the *Mambo!* recording). This was during a night club sequence where Yma made an impressive entrance through transparent hanging streamers.

By 1956, the 12" LP had firmly established itself as the recording industry standard in America. Because all of Yma's disks before *Legend of the Jivaro* had originally been issued as 78 rpm sets, 45s and 10" LPs, Capitol decided it was time to re-master and reissue the earlier disks on 12" LP. Because the first album, *Voice of the Xtabay* and the third, *Inca Taqui* were self contained—something like what would later be called "concept albums"—and had no extra tracks in the vaults, it was decided to pair the two on one disk. This combination album remains in print to this day (new on CD, of course), bearing just the first title, *Voice of the Xtabay*.

In the case of *Legend of the Sun Virgin* and *Mambo!*, however, the Capitol staff was able to produce previously unreleased cuts from the vaults. These additions enabled time requirements of the 12" LP format to be met, and of course provided an incentive for owners of the original disks to buy the recordings for the "new" tracks. Covers remained the same except that the lovely photograph that graced *Inca Taqui* was dropped.

It was around this time that it became apparent that Yma's novelty was beginning to wear thin. American audiences were becoming less susceptible to the magnitude of her mystique. Reflecting the confusion audiences found themselves in is the following quote from *Current Biography 1955,* released in 1956:

> Probably no other singer before the public today has received more flamboyant publicity than Yma Sumac, who specializes in Peruvian songs. She has been described as a Brooklynite who spelled her name Amy Camus backwards, and as an Incan princess directly descended from Atahualpa, the last emperor of the Inca Empire. Imaginative publicity writers have shrouded her past in mystery, have set her aside as one of the chosen "Golden Virgins," a Sun worshipper, and marked her singing as the work of Indian sorcerers evoking from her throat the spirits of birds and jaguars. Her good looks and dignity, her use of heavy Peruvian silver and gold jewelry of ancient design, and most of all her remarkable vocal range from contralto to coloratura high C's have brought her world renown . . . Capitol Records has sold well over a million of her albums (4,000,000 records).

Commenting on Yma's "Incan" music, *Current Biography* gave the most accurate assessment to date. "Rather than authentic Inca music, this is music in modern form reminiscent of the days of Peruvian pomp and splendor."

Unfortunately, simultaneous with the diminishing public appeal was the crumbling of Yma's marriage to Moisés. On December 20, 1956, they were separated. It was generally held, and there seems no reason to doubt, that the paternity suit was the cause.

While in the midst of this turmoil Yma participated in her second and final film for Paramount Studios, *The Loves of Omar Khayyam*. Directed by William Dieterle and categorized as an Action/Adventure film, it starred Cornel Wilde, Sebastian Cabot, Raymond Massey, Michael Rennie and Debra Paget. The film utilized Yma even less than the earlier *Secret of the Incas*. Artistically, the 101 minute movie remains a forgettable event, as much for the fans of Yma as for cineastes in general. What remained of Yma's musical contributions for the entire movie was finally about four minutes of trite and generic music. Only one recognizable Sumacian theme emerged—a single phrase from her "Lament."

Things continued to deteriorate for Sumac and Company. During the first half of 1957, newspapers rehashed the gory details of the Vivanco's personal problems with relish. Coinciding with Capitol's January 1957 release of *Legend of the Jivaro*, were news items concerning the progress of Maureen Shea's paternity suit against Moisés. Maureen, then living in Dallas with her two daughters, testified in a Los Angeles court that Moisés had lured her into intimacies with promises of glamorous world tours. She maintained that her twin daughters, born October 4, 1954, were fathered by Moisés, which Moisés formally denied.

The twenty-two year old Maureen stated that she had met Moisés in Reno in 1952, when she was a seventeen-year-old student at the University of Nevada. Moisés hired her to be Yma's private social secretary. Intimacies began in Los Angeles that year and continued for two years. (The twins were conceived in February of 1953.) *The New York Daily News* quoted Ms. Shea as saying, "He said he had fallen in love with me, and that it was destiny that we had met. He said I reminded him of his mother, who was dead. It all seemed very wonderful and I was overwhelmed." Estimating Moisés' monthly income at $10,000, Ms. Shea asked for $500 for monthly support of her daughters.

Moisés lost the paternity suit. By early March of 1957, rumors circulated that Yma wanted a divorce. The couple were also now under some financial stress. The tax-arrears payment burden was enormous and now, added to this were the monthly payments Moisés had to pay Maureen Shea.

Except for Yma, those who knew Moisés were not surprised. Although Yma may have not been aware of the fact, or chose not to admit the truth, Moisés had a lurid reputation. Hernán Braña confided to me that as early as the late 1940s, he had been approached by Moisés' sister Rosita, who pleaded that he take Moisés to a priest or a church to try and get some counseling or to calm down his seemingly uncontrollable libido. Although sympathetic to Rosita's plea, Hernán felt that it was really none of his business and it would be presumptuous of him to speak so intimately to Moisés. It was obvious to me, speaking to Hernán about this some thirty years later, that the subject still made him very uncomfortable.

Despite shock at the court's decision, Yma traveled with Moisés to Las Vegas for a month's series of performances at the Venus Room in the New Frontier Hotel. Yma arrived early for the rehearsals, giving herself time to adjust for the performances, which were slated to begin March 11th.

The show that surrounded Yma was extravagant. Her segment was preceded by a lavish production number by Shaw-Hitchcock called "Mystic Shrine of Love". It was considered by the critics of the time to be one of the most startling, colorful production numbers seen in Las Vegas for years. Yma's set was thirty-minutes long and included five of her most popular songs, "Ataypura" (High Andes) now the traditional entrance number for her, "Kuyaway" (Inca Love Song), "Tumpa!" (Earthquake), "Chuncho!" (Forest Creatures) and her distinct vocalise on Debussy's "Clair de Lune". Yma now used an echo chamber as a vocal and theatrical device and had adopted a new coiffure, her hair streaked with white. *The Hollywood Reporter* felt this new appearance "added to her hauteur and magnetism" and was impressed by the instant attention Yma commanded when she began to sing. Maurice Leonard commented in his article for *Records and Recording* (11/79), "Sumac sometimes went over the top and bordered on the eerie, as when she appeared in a recital with an incense burner smoldering away and her hair dramatically striped black and white, zebra fashion."

Audiences at the New Frontier Hotel were fascinated by Yma's Incan pieces. The adaptation of "Clair de Lune" was described as "an interesting lyric exploration." (*Variety* 3/20/57).

Variety felt that, although Yma "may falter as a drawing card on the Strip, since she's stacked against a powerhouse lineup of magnetic night club names . . . her act . . . is offbeat enough to start a multiple word-of-mouth raves which should help fill the room for the next 3 weeks." (ibid.)

In spite of the ever-present personal problems weighing down on Yma, these Las Vegas shows were a triumph. Her music, always her great love, provided her with some temporary emotional consolation. Importantly, it allowed her to momentarily forget her problems as she performed songs that she had always enjoyed.

The *Las Vegas-Review Journal* neatly summed up the shows by remarking that "her voice is one of the most fantastic ever presented to the American public." After the completion of the shows, Yma returned to her home in Los Angeles.

Problems between Yma and Moisés continued. On April 17, 1957, less than a month after her return from Las Vegas, Yma filed for divorce, charging Moisés with general cruelty. She entered that particular charge to squash rumors that the divorce was due simply to the unfortunate results of the paternity suit.

Although she loved Moisés, Yma was a South American woman, reared in strict Catholic traditions. She was a fiercely proud person, and one of conventional moral attitudes. She had single-mindedly dedicated herself to her career and her voice, to which she had from the beginning felt a powerful sense of duty. From all recorded evidence, this mindset was vehemently encouraged by Moisés as well. The situation she now found herself in was more than a slap in the face. She felt profoundly betrayed by Moisés first because, after keeping her ignorant of all their business dealings, he had managed to put them into so much debt that she couldn't even imagine when they would be out of it.

The Shea affair, then, to compound her situation, was morally disillusioning and intensely degrading, especially since it seems to have occurred right under her own nose, and probably in her own home. Most humiliating of all was the fact that her private hurt and embarrassment was now news fodder for the general public. Yma wanted above all for audiences to respect her for her artistry; instead they were titillated by the shenanigans of her husband. Because of all this and in order to put some distance between herself and Moisés, Yma decided she had to move out of her home.

Filing for divorce under her real name of Emperatriz Chavarri Vivanco, Yma demanded custody of eight-year old Charlie, one-half of the community property, and $500 monthly alimony. Ironically, whether or not this was by conscious design, Yma requested the same amount of alimony as the monthly sum Moisés had to pay Maureen Shea.

The situation reached a head on Wednesday, the 24th April. On that day, major newspapers carried stories of a massive altercation that took place at the Vivanco's home the evening before. It seems that two days earlier, on April 22, at Yma's request, Fred Otash and another private detective attempted to remove some of Yma's belongings from the mansion in Beverly Hills. Moisés, who called the police, said that the detectives had twisted his arm and threatened to shoot him if he did not cooperate—which he refused to do. The next night, April 23, Yma arrived at her former home accompanied by Fred Otash, Norman Placey and Bill Lowe. The last two were also private detectives. It is not clear now whether Yma had already moved out, but in any event it seems that she was surprised to find Moisés there; she believed that all the locks were to have been changed. Noticing that her Cadillac was missing, Yma is reported to have screamed, "This man stole my house, my car and everything." Insisting that the house was his, Moisés ordered the private detectives to leave. They refused. Moisés called the police.

When she entered her home, Yma found that Moisés was not alone. Also present were Jose Farfan, a harpist who spoke no English, Esmila Zaballos and Yola Rivero. Esmila and Yola had been guests, staying with the Vivancos, although Yma snarlingly referred to them as her "maids." Esmila Zaballos was in fact a Peruvian of repute, a highly respected and popular singer of traditional Peruvian folk music in South America. Esmila sang some of Yma's older repertoire, including the traditional, altitudinous "Virgenes del Sol" (Virgins of the Sun). Esmila could also easily travel in the area of high E natural. Although her voice and range were not as formidable as Yma's, she was an excellent musician. Her recording of the intricate "Payas Shanan" is a performance of great vocal elegance. She was a magnetic and vivacious personality.

Shortly after Yma entered the house, she got into a heated argument with Esmila. This climaxed with Yma slapping Esmila. A free-for-all followed. During this mêlée, everyone was screaming, punching, tugging and pulling at each other—the detectives attacked Moisés, Ms. Rivero attacked the detectives, and the resident collie dog barked hysterically. Dark glasses Yma had been wearing were knocked off and fell to the floor, revealing a ripe black eye. Yma, when questioned, explained that this had been provided her when Moisés had hit her in the face during an argument a few days earlier.

The police finally arrived on the scene and broke up the fight. The Vivanco's dispute was referred to the District Attorney's office. While being dispersed, one of the private detectives was heard to mutter, "It's a bum beef. Vivanco's trying to get some sympathy for the divorce action."

But considering with more care, one can't help wondering just who was trying to elicit sympathy. For it seems that by some chance no fewer than eight newsmen and photographers were present at the house when Yma arrived. The photographs of Yma are by far the least flattering, most un-princess-like ever taken. Included is one of Yma, pouting, swathed in a heavy fur coat but displaying an ugly bruise on a shoulder.

Newspaper headlines and articles required little exaggeration to turn the out-of-control dispute into a mad circus act. "Yma Sumac's Party Hits High Note" is a headline in the staid *New York Times,* 4/24/57. The World Telegram of the same date reported: "The five-octave screams of singer Yma Sumac provided the sound effects for a clothes-ripping, head bumping, family brawl noisy enough to win the envy of film land's best domestic battlers." Sadly, the entire "showdown" has the distinctive look of a publicity stunt to elicit sympathy for Yma—but one that went ludicrously awry. Instead of emerging as a wronged heroine, Yma is made to look (or even—if my speculation is accurate—made herself look) pathetically ridiculous.

Newsreel footage taken during the melee—yes, there were also newsreel cameras present—reveal something else as well, something that Yma's fans do not have a chance to see: Yma in a rage. The film shows a disbelieving Yma listening scornfully to a babbling Esmila. Reacting to what is being said, Yma seems ready to explode with fury. Though she is not physically violent in this scene, an energy of tremendous force and power seems to radiate from Yma.

As if a final stroke of destruction to the image of a regal Princess of the Incas, the unflattering news footage disintegrated any residual believability in the legends that had been fed to audiences all those years.

The myth that had corralled America's interest in Yma Sumac had at the same time steadily undermined Yma's artistic integrity. The fact that much of this may have been self-inflicted makes it all the more tragic. Had an honest angle been introduced earlier, it might have been possible to salvage her reputation, to bolster lagging interest. In that case, this domestic brawling might have been the source of some sympathy for Yma. In fact, though, by this time readers just didn't much care. Yma became the brunt of snickering at posh parties, rude jokes, and general ridicule. Maintaining the confusion, newspapers in the same city gave her age as both 29 and 35.

On April 26th, the couple was given three weeks to privately settle their pre-divorce squabble out of court. Moisés' attorney filed a petition to "prohibit the singer and her friends from harassing him." The *New York Daily News* (4/27/57) quoted Moisés as saying "I and the members of my household are in fear for our lives."

On May 14th, Yma was granted a divorce. No mention was made of the paternity suit or its consequences. Yma did say, however, that Moisés had "called her names so vile she refused to repeat them in court." (*New York Herald Tribune*, 5/25/57) Judge Edward R. Brand approved an unusual agreement under which Moisés was to pay $200.00 a month for the support of his son. He was also, however, to continue to manage Yma artistically. For this he was to receive 50% of her earnings. After the session in court, Yma and her former husband traveled to Greece for a series of concerts.

The end of August saw the public release of Paramount's *The Loves of Omar Khayyam*. Reviewing the movie for *The Daily Mirror* (8/23/57), Frank Quinn found it "rich in trappings but paltry in story." A single mention of Yma's contributions noted that she yodeled her bird-like tones successfully. The movie soon faded into obscurity and now is rarely seen, even on late-night television.

In September and October Yma, Moisés and a company of six traveled to Paris to perform at the large Alhambra Theater. It was their first return to that city in a number of years. The show was again headlined by Maurice Chevalier, and except for him and Yma, was generally considered weak by reviewers. *Variety* found Yma "poised and elegant." Although she drew considerable crowds, it was felt she would have fared better had she been surrounded by a more suitable production. Yma made her appearances in two gowns and sang her Incan chants and vocal extravaganzas to responsive crowds. While in Paris, Yma celebrated her birthday–according to *The Daily Mirror* her 36th.

Meanwhile, in America, newspapers continued their coverage of the Vivanco scandal. Now Yma was being sued for the odd sum of $1,180.22, by Fred Otash, the private detective in Santa Monica. Otash claimed the money was due him for shadowing Moisés before the divorce. At the same time, odd rumors began to circulate that the couple was being reconciled while in Europe and were contemplating re-marrying.

In early November, Yma and the small group were in Tel Aviv for a series of concerts. Yma's first Israeli performances were to be given in the newly opened Fredrick R. Mann Auditorium, which seated 3,000. Ticket prices ranged from $1.10 to $5.00 (which was high by Israeli standards at the time). *Variety* reported that people "lined up from the cool hours of dawn until the still burning-hot hours of noon" to buy tickets. Only once before had such a thing happened. That was when the comedian, Danny Kaye had performed.

Despite the public's anticipation and the tremendous publicity surrounding Yma's first Israeli appearance, her performances proved to be a "bitter disappointment" to audiences. They were of such disappointment that unflattering cartoons of Yma appeared in the press and reviews complained that the show was not even fit for a cabaret. Yma's voice and idiosyncratic singing did not endear her to Israeli listeners and critics were especially suspicious of Moisés' Incan music.

By the third show, on November 5, it was obvious things were not going to improve. After a few numbers, Yma halted the show "with an announcer telling the audience (she) had contracted Asiatic flu." (*Variety* 11/13/57) The rest of the performances were cancelled.

She returned to Los Angeles.

Ironically enough, it was during 1957, one of the darkest years in Yma's personal life, that she accepted a presentation (for publicity purposes) from the Borough President of Brooklyn. In yet another apparent attempt to de-fuse the "Brooklyn housewife" canard by embracing it as a joke, Yma became an "Honorary Citizen of Brooklyn."

Chapter 7

"Kuyaway" (Inca Love Song)
1958–1970

The first months of 1958 were artistically unproductive. Yma's divorce was finalized in Los Angeles on May 20, and the former couple began their new professional relationship. Moisés agreed to pay $200 for the monthly support of nine year-old Charlie. Despite brief periods of musical equanimity, the new partnership was not a success.

The only engagement of any importance during 1958 was a series of shows given at the famous Casino Parisien nightclub in the Hotel Nacional de Cuba, in Havana. This hotel's reputation was similar to that of New York City's Plaza Hotel; it was the rendezvous of Havana's "society." Yma's performances were well received by patrons of the Casino. A photograph taken at a party given for the press of Yma being greeted by Thomas J. Kelley, resident manager of the hotel, showed her to be cheerful and elegant in a strapless gown, which exposed her lovely shoulders.

In early 1959, Yma and Moisés returned to Capitol's recording studios for what was to be her first stereo disk but also her last recording project with that firm. Produced by Bill Miller, *Fuego del Ande* (Fire in the Andes) was a flop. The album was a distinct departure from all Yma's earlier disks. Here, Yma was offered in a buffet of real South American folk songs and popular music. Ironically, although it was the first of Yma's albums to contain authentic indigenous music, the record had to be quickly withdrawn after its initial release in April of 1959 due to inaccurate composition claims and resulting royalty disputes. After corrections it was re-released. Compared with Yma's other recordings, vocally *Fuego del Ande* remains a disappointment.

Fuego del Ande provided a fascinating paradox for the singer. Because of the recording's unquestioned authenticity it was the only one of Yma's records that sold well in South America. In North America, which was home to some of her most vociferous fans, there was little interest in the new recording. There were things, however, that contributed to North America's lack of interest. First, it is obvious that the record was put together perfunctorily. The arrangements and accompaniments used were unimaginative, pedantic, and occasionally tasteless, rarely providing anything but poor support for Yma's talent. And as if mirroring this, Yma's singing was tentative, uninspired and uncomfortable. Duets and trios with herself are poorly organized, under-rehearsed and limply sung. Many listeners were disappointed that few of Yma's famous vocal effects made an appearance. Of them, only the "growl" and an occasional, tremulous, high note emerge. Most of her singing centers in her middle, mezzo-soprano register and is much less inventive than what one had come to expect from this artist.

Hernán Braña supplies the reason, explaining that during times of emotional stress, Yma characteristically reverted to the comfortable safety of her middle register, rarely venturing on her famous high note tangents. Whether consciously or not, this instinctive husbanding of her resources provided unique protection for her instrument. Yma's improvisatory singing demanded unclouded connection between her mind and her physical instrument. Preoccupied with private problems, emotionally drained and under duress, it is doubtful that the correct combination of support and energy would be in place. By reverting to a safer register, Yma ensured that she would not strain for high notes that were insufficiently supported and risk damage to her voice. Because no undue pressure was put on her instrument, especially her high register, Yma was able to retain her unusual range for an inordinate length of time.

Taken as a whole, *Fuego del Ande* wrongly suggested that Yma's days as a high-flying singer of exotica were numbered. One band does offer a taste of virtuosity. This was a remake of the 1940s favorite, "Virgenes del Sol" (Virgins of the Sun). Transposed down a third, unfortunately, the new arrangement is inane and vulgar–and Yma's performance is no better. Her singing is constricted, there are serious pitch problems (rare for Yma) and coloratura is sloppy. One sustained high C is particularly painful. This was the first evidence of Yma transposing in order to accommodate the natural aging of her voice.

There are a few redeeming aspects of *Fuego del Ande,* beginning with the distinct attempt to return to authentic material. Also, Yma crisply delivers rapid, tongue-twisting texts of Spanish and Quechua with impressive nonchalance, showing her linguistic gifts.

Despite these pluses, *Fuego del Ande* remains a dismayingly contrived effort. It is ironic that most of Yma's previous American made recordings made great boasts of authenticity for their contents—yet for this, the most authentic of all, no such claim is ventured. Although the musical material is poorly presented and uninterestingly sung, it was an authentic part of Yma's real culture and heritage. But the album was not what the North American record buying public expected from Yma Sumac and sales reflected this.

In June and July, Yma and Moisés undertook a concert tour of Brazil, a country they had not visited for many years. While stopping in Rio de Janeiro on June 6th, the couple informed reporters they were planning to remarry. The reason given was that they both loved and were concerned for the welfare of their son. They were in fact re-married later that year.

The "new" couple faced a number of serious problems that became increasingly difficult to cope with. For one thing the exorbitant taxes owed to the Internal Revenue Service remained an ever-pressing issue. New jobs had to be secured to meet this demand. But there was a new problem that was slowly creeping into prominence and this was trying to keep Yma current in the American musical scene. By 1959, the situation was serious. Audiences in the United States had begun to lose interest in the exotic warbler.

Since the pre-divorce squabble in early 1957, Yma had made few appearances in America. Although newspapers occasionally carried items about her, few dealt with performances.

Moisés decided that a new concert tour should be arranged. Unfortunately, America did not show great interest and Moisés realized that if this was to be done, it would have to be for unconquered audiences for whom Yma remained a novelty. The solution to this dilemma came from Russia. The Ministry of Culture offered Yma a four-week concert tour of the U.S.S.R., which Yma and Moisés eagerly accepted. The tour was a milestone in Yma's career, and as an added bonus (instigated perhaps by the clever Moisés), Yma was to be paid in hard American dollars. In terms of Yma's artistic ego and her financial needs, the tour could not have come at a

better time. It was a stroke of luck in a period of near-inactivity that was becoming dangerously arid.

The tour of Russia was to begin in early 1960 and preparations put the Vivanco household into turmoil. It was decided to take ten-year old Charlie with them to Russia so that he could experience another culture and so that they could have him near them. They had not attempted such a concert tour since the 1955 American extravaganzas and much had to be reviewed and decided. Orchestral musicians and instrumental soloists had to be hired and a solid program planned. Yma and Moisés invited Cholita and the ever-faithful Hernán Braña to re-join them and a newly formed troupe of musicians for the Russian expedition. Because of his problems with glaucoma and under advice from his doctor, Hernán declined the invitation. (As it turned out he could have joined them; the Soviet government provided the company with a private jet and a medical team to travel with them, to ensure the health of the entire company at all times during the tour.)

The tour was to be a four-week canvassing of major Russian cities. Because of the unexpected reaction of the Russian audiences, however, the tour was greatly extended. In all, they visited and performed in some forty cities:

Leningrad	Rostov	Voronezh	Yerevan
Moscow	Tashkent	Kharov	Kirovabad
Balka	Stalinsk	Odessa	Astrakhan
Riga	Kiev	Stalino	Stalingrad
Kaunas	Zhitomir	Kirghiz	Baku
Vilnyus	Vinnitsa	Novosibirsk	Samarkand
Tartu	Tula	Kraznodar	Alma-Ata
Minsk	Kursk	Tbilisi	Gorky
Smolensk	Tallin		

Since Yma would be singing for a new audience—one not familiar with her particular gifts—it was decided to resuscitate her famous "Incan" repertoire. This was a wise decision and responsible for much of Yma's tremendous success and popularity in Russia. Most of Yma's Incan songs had been abandoned three years earlier due to the introduction of more current popular music into her programs in a (relatively unsuccessful) effort to keep her current, and because of her concentration on nightclub work. For the tour of Russia, however, it was decided to offer her most famous selections. These included:

"Taita Inty" (Virgin of the Sun God, Hymn to the Sun)
"Ataypura" (High Andes)
"Chuncho!" (Forest Creatures)
"Tumpa!" (Earthquake)
"Lament"
"Kuyaway" (Inca Love Song)
"Montana"
"Cueca Chilena" (Entry of Mendoza in San Juan)
"Goomba Boomba" (Mambo)
"Ccori Canastitay" (Golden Basket)
"Marinera" (National Dance of Peru)

There were also typical orchestral pieces, instrumental solos and dance sequences for Cholita. These selections re-created programs offered to the American public a decade earlier and the reaction of the Russian people mirrored the phenomenal response of the Americans then. Audiences were delirious whenever Yma sang and the beauty and accuracy of her singing reflected this massive adulation. Most responsible for this was the fact that Yma had returned to musical material which best suited her talents, both musi-

Yma, Charlie, Moisés take bow in Bucharest, Romania

cally and artistically. She was relaxed and assured and her singing regained a freedom that had seemed lost in previous years.

Treated like royalty, Yma sang accordingly. Secure in her art and music she provided some of her most inspired singing in a decade.

Recordings released in Romania show that, compared with *Fuego del Ande,* recorded two years earlier, performances at this time prove Yma's voice to be healthy and pure, finely spun and limpid, with the famous Sumacian high-voice float very much in evidence, free from strain and pressure. The authority and vocal allure missing on the disk of authentic South American music were regained when her voice was featured in the less authentic but more favored Incan repertoire.

As a matter of fact, little seemed to have changed in ten years. Although the highest notes were a bit more diaphanous than ten years earlier, they were still produced with ease and facility. Her improvisations, clever to a fault and often quite ornate, still incorporated the delicate top Ds, Es and Fs that drove American audiences wild. All the famous vocal effects were unearthed and exhibited with uncanny accuracy. The "growl," high, pointed staccati, tiny, hairline *pianissimi,* wailing, whimpers, laughter, whispers and other touches that had been her trademark, were all offered now framed by more mature musicianship than ever. The range used for the concerts was generally over three full octaves. The coloratura technique, which had always been brilliant, was still capable of eliciting gasps from listeners. Yma's enjoyment in returning to her "Incan" repertoire was palpable.

While in Russia, 186 concerts were given for an estimated audience of sixty million. In Moscow alone, the troupe gave seven concerts at the famous Tchaikovsky Hall and Lenin Stadium. Moisés' orchestral forces were supplemented by musicians lifted from the famous Bolshoi Symphony orchestra.

Publicity releases for the Russian concert series, regrettably, regurgitated the Incan propaganda fed to audiences in the United States—and now there were some startling additions. Yma had now acquired a new title: "Fire Priestess". Yma's father, who was rarely mentioned in her biographical material, now emerged as a full-fledged Incan priest, reminiscent of Lakmè's religiously fanatical father, in Delibes' opera, *Lakmè*.

Galina Shergova, writing for the evening edition of the Moscow *Izvestija,* provided her readers with examples of the Sumacian legend—some of which were new additions. "Newsmen have reported that the daughter of an Incan priest was abducted by a wandering youth, a musician, who arrived in the mountains on a horse covered with lather." The musician, readers were informed, was—Moisés! It seems he was seeking new members for his Compañia while traveling on horseback through the wilds of Peru!

According to this most fanciful of all versions of the Sumac biography, Moisés had been told by a member of the ensemble, "Come to our region. A girl with the voice of an angel lives there. Subdue her with the golden strings of your guitar." Heeding the advice, Moisés found Yma in the midst of a huge religious festival. "She sang with her face veiled as was the custom . . . in what seemed to be four voices." Later he again heard Yma as she "stood in a field, a frail little stalk . . . (11 years old) . . . standing as though she had thrust herself up among the rocks, and she spoke with her eternal audience—the mountains, trees and grass."

Ms. Shergova stated that such fairy tales were created by "dozens of journalists," yet cannot refrain from trying her hand at creating her own version. Ms. Shergova's entry for the Sumac legend depicted Yma as a priest's daughter, singing a hymn to the sun in an ancient Incan temple, as a rising sun bathed her in its light. Ms. Shergova admitted that, after hearing Yma sing in concert she was tempted to believe the legends of her unusual origins. Her article concluded with a different sort of extraordinarily contrived story evidently intending to emphasize Yma's humanity—and, of course, her solidarity with the workers.

> Having stepped back a small distance from her, I see Ima Sumac not in green attire, taking upon herself the color of Amazon thickets, but in a simple costume, stepping up on candy boxes in a Leningrad confectionery factory. There she sang a sad song about Indian women for the workers surrounding her. Before that she had walked about the shops, and the workers told her—just as they would have told any woman—about themselves, about what they were proud of and what they were interested in. It seemed to me that she looked at everything with widely opened and slightly saddened eyes. I knew that she, a woman from legend, was stirred by an earthly longing for home and a simple happiness in having made the acquaintance of good people, to whom she said, "I am delighted with you. You know I shall leave the Soviet Union loving all of you!"
>
> No I would not want you to meet Ima Sumac on the road leading into legend, this noisy and inhuman road on which drums boom out publicity. If you succeed in hearing her when she sings 'The Wail of Ima Sumac', a song about the injustice in the world, you will understand and love her because she is not only a beautiful artist, but a woman as well. She is a woman telling the world about the bitter grief of her people.

So the Sumac experience that had been presented to the American people ten years before was being duplicated for the Russian people, its musical virtues and its publicity-hype vices side by side. Instead of discarding—or even lightening a bit—the silly legends in response to her genuine enormous success, the fabrications became ever more baroque. Yma became not only the Queen of Exotica but also the Queen of Publicity Hype.

Regardless—Russian audiences and critics adored her. "The Russian people have never experienced such a variety of emotions or heard such music. Yma Sumac is more beautiful than the legend. She has dominated the artistic sensibilities of the U.S.S.R. with her magic and divine voice." (*Izvestija*, Moscow)

The newspaper *Pravda* stated that audiences were "captivated". Other reviews accented the beauty of Yma's high register, agility in intricate coloratura and the surprising richness of her lowest tones, multiple octaves beneath the high ones. Audiences were so enamored that at one concert, patrons in the gallery released a fleet of doves during Yma's curtain calls. Celebrated wherever she sang in the Soviet Union, Yma was presented to Premiere Kruschev and honored by tributes presented by composers Shostakovich and Katchaturian, and the premiere ballet dancers Ulanova and Plisetskaya.

Coming during a time of artistic aridity and personal anguish, the Russian tour gave Yma a tremendous surge of confidence, which was reflected in the caliber of perform-

Yma, Charlie, Moisés with Kruschev gift (Russia 1961)

ances she gave to the Russian people. Completely preoccupied with her performances, her music and voice, Yma was happy for the first time in a long while. Her performances were taped, broadcast and even put onto disk. Black and white film footage exists from the Russian concerts. One sequence shows a concert given in a huge arena, the size of New York's Madison Square Garden. Filled to capacity, the audience, originally rather formal in demeanor, soon goes completely berserk.

In addition, more than 130 concerts were given throughout Eastern Europe, including 10 in Czechoslovakia (for the Ministry of Culture for a total of 300,000 people), 40 in Poland, 55 in Romania and 30 in Germany. After one of the Czechoslovakia concerts, Yma was presented with a huge bouquet of roses from a group of students. The young spokesman for the students would re-appear in connection with Yma in 1975. His name was Yosef Synovec. Although not widely known, for a brief period of about two years, Yosef had begun to establish himself as a unique cabaret singer in New York City, his specialty being Yma Sumac imitations. It was Yosef who smuggled a recording of one of Yma's Romanian performances–a recording that circulated for decades among New York City collectors.

It was during this time that Thomas Meehan wrote his now famous, much-anthologized humor piece "Yma Dream" for *The New Yorker* magazine. A brilliantly written nonsense article, it actually had nothing to do with Yma Sumac the person, but all to do with an endlessly proliferating array of oddly named, otherwise wildly mixed, celebrities, all of whom had to be introduced to each other by first names: along with Yma Sumac, Ava Gardner, Ali McGraw, the Israeli statesman Abba Eban, the stage actress Uta Hagen, Eugene O'Neill's widow Oona, the theatrical director Ulu Grosbard, and more and still more. Alan Eichler, Yma's agent during the 1980s explains:

"It all began in the comic mind of Thomas Meehan, who conceived a totally off-the-wall 1962 article for *The New Yorker* magazine entitled 'Yma Dream,' based on the premise of his having a recurring dream that he is giving a cocktail party in honor of singer Yma Sumac and as the celebrity guests begin to arrive he has to introduce them to each other: 'Oona, Yma; Oona, Ava; Oona, Abba.' Meehan later adapted the piece for Anne Bancroft's 1970 TV special." (*Los Angeles Times*, 8/31/97)

By August 1963, Yma was comfortably settled in Tokyo for a two-and-one-half-month series of performances at the famous Mikado Theater in Akasaka. Advance notices heralded the first Asian appearance of the "Virgin of the Sun God." The seventy shows ran through Wednesday, October 9, and were presented as the first of a series at the supper club called "Nights of the World."

The Japanese were delighted with Yma's brand of singing and her programs, which included favorites "Taita Inty," "Tumpa!", "Chuncho!", "Kuyaway", and "Ataypura." Before leaving Japan, Yma gave two benefit concerts for the remaining victims of the atom bomb.

By the first weeks in January of 1964, Yma and Moisés had returned to the United States. They had been gone from America almost four years. By January 28th, *Variety* had reported that the couple was planning a new concert tour of America, which would finish with a gala concert at the 1965 World's Fair in New York. Charlie obviously had accompanied his parents to Russia since pictures were taken of them together. As to his presence in the other countries they visited at the time less is known.On February 19, 1964, after a long absence, Yma made her first public appearance in America on the television show, "Hollywood Palace," hosted by Gig Young. Fresh from the triumphs in Russia, Europe and Asia, Yma sang "Kuyaway" (Inca Love Song) and "Tumpa!" (Earthquake). Although in good voice, Yma's singing that evening was tame compared to what American audiences had been used to a decade earlier. The musical arrangements were lamely updated under the influence of the now dominant pop music, rock and roll, and Yma's singing was shorn of some of its highest notes.

"Kuyaway" (Inca Love Song) had turned into a mock-pop number, similar to a passé foxtrot, which had nothing to do with either the early (pure) version of 1943, then called "Amor Indio" (Indian Love), or the busy, sexually-tinged and interesting version of 1951. The new version remained in Yma's repertoire until the early 1970s when she laid it to rest. "Tumpa!" (Earthquake) had been watered down to such an extent that it was virtually unrecognizable as a once virtuoso display piece. Both songs had lost their exotic flavor through updating and inferior arrangements.

Although the Hollywood Palace appearance was considered a success for the returning diva, as it turned out her timing was off. While she had been away conquering Russia Europe and Japan changes had been underway in America. This was made clear only ten days earlier (February 9, 1964) when the Liverpool group, The Beatles, first appeared on the Ed Sullivan television show. Some 73 million people watched the Sullivan show that night. It was an event that irrevocably changed the course and emphasis of American popular music. The rock and roll movement initiated by such artists as Little Richard and Elvis Presley had arrived with a vengeance.

In July, Yma traveled to Rio de Janeiro to help inaugurate the International Popular Music Competition. Held every year, the first competition boasted a remarkable panel of judges: Amalia Rodriguez from Portugal, Les Baxter from the United States, and, representing Peru, Yma Sumac.

Sitting as a judge on the panel for this competition must have been an extraordinary and educational experience for Yma. It was apparent to her that much had changed within the American music scene since her 1960 departure for Russia. She must have found it ironic that folk music had entered a new, popular phase. "Hootenannies" (often with audience participation) were now very popular. Singers like Joan Baez and Bob Dylan were very successful concert and recording artists. A new generation had arrived—a generation unfamiliar with the name Yma Sumac or her mysterious Incan legends. The mambo and the cha-cha-cha were dances of the past. The movement to rock and roll had completely taken over the sensibilities of the American public—especially its youth, where the cutting edge of pop entertainment was always located. For the time being, popular music had two main streams: rock and roll and the folk and "folk pop" music of performers such as Peter, Paul and Mary and Odetta.

America had also undergone change in other areas. The decade of the 1960s was a time of artistic and political upheaval for the American people. Now protest-conscious, there were demonstrations for civil rights, as well as a surge of new interest in the American space program. Both these things were constantly in the news and on the minds of most Americans. No longer fascinated with little known or forgotten countries on earth, Americans were now obsessed with the new and exciting possibilities of space travel. Concentration, previously centered on the mysteries of earth exploration, now switched to the mysteries of outer space. The lull-like atmosphere of the 1950s gave way to a tremendous progressive surge that permanently altered the lives and priorities of the American people.

In a sense, the audiences that Yma had once performed for no longer existed. Yma and her legends no longer fit in with the current standards of popular music or the artistic expectations of the American public. If Yma was to continue to perform in the United States, drastic changes had to be made. Once again, Moisés and Yma had to review their situation, select a solution and then alter her material to conform to another new set of musical expectations.

Yma was, in fact, faced with an impossible incongruity, one that would cripple her ability to completely regenerate public interest and from which she would never recover. This time the compromises she and Moisés made did nothing to further her career. Despite efforts to reinvent her music and singing, audiences (and critics) continued to expect to hear her unusual vocal effects—those for which she had become famous. Because of the new repertoire, these "tricks" could only be incorporated into specific songs. By 1975 and her Town Hall appearances in New York City, Yma had become a cult figure.

Yma had, of course, little choice in the matter, at least if she wanted to continue to sing. Had she kept singing her "Incan" songs, audience response would soon enough have turned to amused disbelief and humor at Yma's expense. Ideally, Yma should have retired after the triumphant tour of Russia, Europe and Asia.

There was another consideration that made the altering of her repertoire mandatory. This was the preservation of Yma's voice. At the age of thirty-eight (or forty, or forty-four), it had become time for her to settle into a less strenuous style of singing, one more conciliatory with the inexorable advance in her age and the resulting changes in her instrument. Although not old by any means—even for a singer—Yma had been performing very difficult music for twenty-three years. Even if her unusual range was a gift of nature, if not protected it might well deteriorate even more rapidly than most. As Bob Covais once commented to me, "How long could she keep up the Incan music? She sang it for decades. Who else could have done the same? That alone was a remarkable accomplishment."

It was decided that Yma would continue to sing but would retire her Incan music. To this end, gradual changes were instituted in 1964. Concerts and nightclub programs were now called "Yma Sumac Sings Songs of the World." A grandiose title that allowed Yma to select, at whim, from a large area of music. In reality, her selections rarely ranged beyond Spanish, American, and Italian sources—quite a narrow concept of those boundaries. Also used was a rock and roll number, "Good Lovin," (originally made famous by The Rascals) which Yma turned into a virtuoso display piece. that was, unfortunately, never recorded. As gradual as the changes in program contents was Yma's use of her still unique vocal range. Vocal gymnastics were now reserved for particular songs to ensure their impact. Otherwise, songs were performed in normal regions of the voice and centered on simplicity of delivery. It was a delivery that contrasted the florid accents of years before and was decidedly less successful.

The projected concert tour—which was to feature the new song recitals—never materialized. Instead, during the next decade, Yma gave few concert appearances but rather concentrated on the nightclub circuit, preferring their intimacy to the large theaters and auditoriums that required more demanding repertoire and singing. Instead of the tour of American concert halls, it was decided to tour the well-miked and amplified clubs of Las Vegas and summer amphitheaters.

The most important of these appearances was at a gala concert given August 6, 1965, at the Hollywood Bowl. The gala was called "South American Fiesta," and the concert was Yma's first appearance in fifteen years at the site of her first American triumph. Both Yma and Moisés agreed that because of the nostalgic feelings this concert invoked she would include a few of her most famous "Incan" chants, or "sounds of nature" as Yma called them. Newspaper articles proudly noted that the show marked Yma's 3,000th performance. The exact basis for that calculation was not announced.

Yma told Margaret Harford, of the *Los Angeles Times* (8/5/65) that "singing at the Bowl again (was) like a home-coming." The program was unusual in that fourteen year-old Charlie would be taking part. According to the *Los Angeles Times*, he had scored quite a success with Czechoslovakian teenagers when he got a rock and roll band together in Prague.

Advertisements in Los Angeles newspapers noted that "fabulous Incan costumes and jewelry" would also be featured. A curious boast was made that Yma now had "five operas in her repertoire." When questioned about the old Amy Camus legend, Yma told Ms. Harford "I don't resent it. It's a marvelous story. But Yma Sumac is a real Incan name. I can prove it."

Reviews generally agree that, though she was surrounded by an ensemble of 40, what triumph there was belonged solely to Yma. Her selections included "La Molina" (The Mill Song), "La Pampa y la Puna" (The Plains and the Mountains), "Taita Inty" (Hymn to the Sun), "Tumpa!" (Earthquake), "Moscow Nights," and the "Queen of the Night Mambo." Reviewing the concert, Patterson Greene was unforgiving of the group of performers who surrounded Yma, commenting: "Even in her more startling moments, [Yma Sumac] has been an artist of dignity, and she should never have been surrounded by such a raggle-taggle company as appeared with her at the Hollywood Bowl. In fact, such a company should not appear in public anywhere, except possibly at an amateur night in some salon in Gardena." The various dance groups which represented Trinidad, the Pampas, and other regions, were judged "amateurish and gauche;" an artistic embarrassment.

Yma herself, however, was an unqualified success. The non-Incan songs were "amply voiced and pleasantly phrased." One of the high points in her performance was her singing of "Tumpa!", which "brought the first ripple of the singularly sweet notes in altissimo that have made the record buying public all but forget Miss

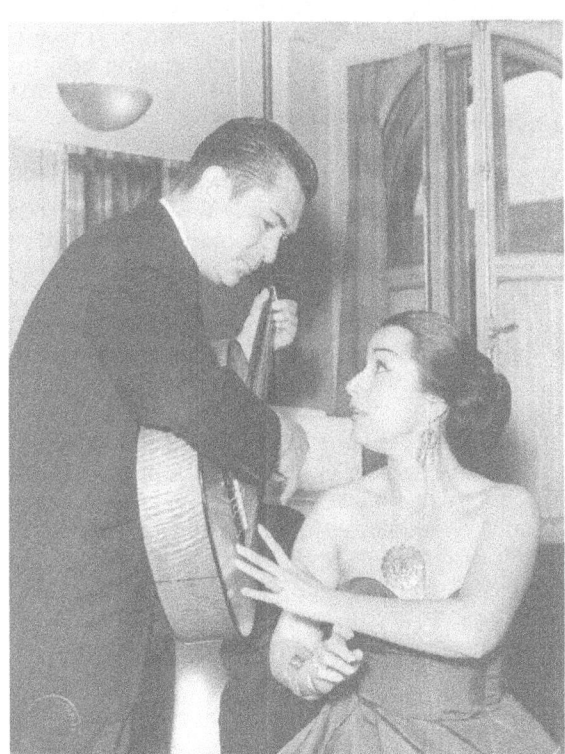

Yma & Moisés while in Russia

Sumac's prowess in the lower altitudes." Greene was also fascinated with Yma's "mildly polluted version" of the Queen of the Night's second act aria, "Der Hölle Rache" from Mozart's *Die Zauberflöte*. Wordless, the piece was sung to guitar accompaniment by Moisés. Greene noted, "Some day I hope to hear (her) sing it as written. She could do it." Unfortunately, the Hollywood Bowl performance was the last time Yma sang the piece.

Directly following the Hollywood Bowl return, Yma performed for the 1965 Santa Barbara Fiesta. Called "Old Spanish days in Santa Barbara," the festival took place throughout the city. Yma's show, called South American Festival, was performed in an amphitheater, the Country Bowl, on August 12, 13, 14 and 15. Her show was extensive and featured other musicians (including the dancer Cholita) from all over South America.

Despite the buoying of the very successful Russian tour and apparently brightening American prospects, the relationship between Yma and Moisés was deteriorating beyond repair. The decision to remarry had been a mistake and a final divorce was granted to Yma in 1965.

Although she received offers for appearances in 1966 and 1967, few, if any were accepted. On March 23, 1967, however, she did appear at Bimbo's in San Francisco. The singer had entered a difficult period of adjustment.

Ironically, Yma Sumac had come full circle. Her first appearance at the Hollywood Bowl in 1950 signaled the beginning of her international career. The return appearance in 1965 signaled its end.

This situation improved somewhat in the beginning of 1968. Preceding Yma's first appearances that year, *Variety* (10/28/67) printed an impressive, full-page advertisement that included a partial list of cities and countries in which Yma had performed. This was a list that had grown to staggering proportions since, by 1967, Yma had sung in virtually every corner of the world.

The list included 47 states of the United States as well as:

40 cities in Russia	24 cities in Latin America	23 cities in England
20 cities in Poland	20 cities in Italy	20 cities in Canada
16 cities in Africa	8 cities in Switzerland	8 cities in Holland
9 cities in France	4 cities in Germany	4 cities in Japan
4 cities in Ireland	4 cities in Greece	4 cities in Belgium

In the first months of 1968, Yma and Moisés returned to Japan and the Mikado Theater, in Akasaka, Tokyo. It was to be the last time they worked together. According to reports, her shows continued to be popular with the Japanese public, despite the instability of her personal life and her artistic situation.

Shortly after the Japanese engagement, Moisés left the United States and moved to Spain, where he remained until his death on September 19, 1998. According to reports, Charlie went with him, as he was expected to attend school in Spain. Little is publicly known about Charlie after this time, though he and Yma kept in touch on a regular basis.

Now an American citizen, Yma was left with the sole responsibility of the remaining unpaid taxes. It was a burden that she would carry until 1987. The grotesque tax problems encountered in 1955 took over 30 years to rectify. Moisés never returned to the United States, even for a visit so far as is known—not even when asked by Yma to help with her 1975 Town Hall appearances.

With Moisés' departure, Yma's life changed drastically. All career decisions were now left to her, ill-prepared as she was to handle them.

From the end of May until June 15th, Yma settled in Sydney, Australia for performances at the nightclub Chequers. These performances were the first she had attempted

Charlie c. 1958

on her own. Patrons paid $2.75 for the dinner show, Monday to Saturday, $3.00 for the supper show, Monday to Friday, and $3.50 for the Saturday supper show. Billed as a "Descendant of the Incas," and "the most exciting voice in the world," Yma shared the bill with the comedian Don Lane, who was giving his first Australian shows since a tour of America. Lane's reception was phenomenal and was the focus of most articles and reviews. *The Sun* wrote, "Inevitably it was an occasion that tended to overshadow the appearance of the show's star, famous Peruvian singer Yma Sumac. Understandably unnerved by this and the fact that illness had overtaken her own conductor, she nevertheless gave a splendid performance in what is anything but an ideal setting for her artistry." (5/26/68)

Although Yma was billed as the star, her segment was brief, consisting of only six songs: "Ataypura" (High Andes), "Sunrise, Sunset" (from "Fiddler on the Roof"), "La Molina" (The Mill Song), "Nights in Moscow," "Kuyaway" (Inca Love Song), and the audience favorite, "Good Lovin" with which Yma "won the room completely (as she) exploited her voice astonishingly." (ibid.) Critics found Yma "handsome and gracious" and charming as she promised to "be better tomorrow." During her sixteen nights at Chequers, Yma gave more than twenty-five shows.

Toward the conclusion of the engagement, the *Sydney Daily Mirror* reviewed her performance. After praising Don Lane's hour-long turn, the newspaper stated that Yma "was on stage for a mere 22 minutes but those minutes were an experience to remember. Her voice is exquisitely pure as much in the lower register as in the highest." (6/3/68) The special favorite with audiences remained the pyrotechnical "Good Lovin," which the singer introduced simply as "a happy song." Judged "perfect," the critic for the *Sydney Daily Mirror* felt Yma "undoubtedly [would] be heard to greater advantage in an auditorium but in the nightclub, the voice [was] something to hear." (ibid.)

Faced with various pressures, Yma decided to secure new representation. She chose Coast Artist's Management of Beverly Hills. Perhaps Yma expected the same treatment she had received from previous management, or Moisés' clever, but often ruthless manipulations. For whatever reasons, she soon grew dissatisfied with the new management, and they with her. Within a short time, Yma was flitting from one management firm to another as if in a futile attempt to find a new "Moisés."

Immediately following the stint in Australia, Yma left for New York City. This was to be her first performances there in a decade and her debut at the then popular new nightclub, Chateau Madrid, which had opened in the Hotel Lexington in April of that year.

Although at this time Yma was with Coast Artists, Inc. she needed additional artistic and musical guidance. With this in mind, she contacted Hernán Braña and asked him to help with the shows. Prior musical commitments made this impossible but, as a favor to Yma, Hernán agreed to rehearse the band. Yma's program was similar to that used in Sydney. The music for "Ataypura" (High Andes) was used, but only as Yma's entrance music. "La Molina" (The Mill Song) was reserved for her encore and a new song was included—"Filigrana" written by Hernán for Yma to display her virtuosity in duets with flute.

Variety found the Peruvian singer as impressive as before. "Miss Sumac still excites listeners with what she can do with her pipes [and] her ability to be at home on any range adds color to her offerings. Its not used as a freaky display." (Jose 6/26/68) Like reviews from seventeen years earlier, the periodical did not approve of Yma's "concession to pop taste" by including such songs as the "Sunrise Sunset" and "Moscow Nights," commenting that "apparently she feels it necessary in order to establish more rapport." (ibid.) Her voice was considered to have held up well to the demands of the last two decades. "Although her volume has diminished during the interim, she is still able to perform vocal acrobatics with high melodic content and musical validity." (ibid.)

Writing for *Cue Magazine*, Eugene Boe found Yma sporting a regal air while "Swathed in billowing chiffon, eyelids and lips and nostrils a-glitter with sequins." (2/29/68)

Coinciding with the Chateau Madrid appearances, *Variety* printed full-page ads boasting of Yma's success and "her five-octave voice." In them, Yma was dressed in one of the chiffon creations of which Boe wrote, adopting a theatrical pose, complete with diamond tiara and large, dangle earrings.

People I've spoken with who caught the Chateau Madrid performances remembered the voice being amazingly resilient and fluid. High notes were delicate but pure, and coloratura was attacked bravely and with élan. Even so, it was apparent that Yma was out of her element without Moisés beside her. It would take a number of years before Yma grew comfortable on her own.

By the end of July, with the Chateau Madrid engagement successfully completed, Yma returned to Beverly Hills to take care of an unpleasant financial task—that of selling her home. Tax pressures demanded this be done, as well as the fact that with her son and Moisés gone she no longer needed the large house.

Although publicity notices stated that Yma was planning another concert tour, it never materialized. She did appear on the Rosie Grier television show, singing "Good Lovin" and "La Molina" (The Mill Song). During 1968, she was approached by the small recording firm, ESP-disk founded by Bernard Stollman. Interested in producing a recording featuring Yma, Stollman sought her out in Beverly Hills and met with her. After much discussion a contract was signed.

The next year, 1969, was uneventful. Asked to return to the Chateau Madrid, Yma declined. Unhappy with the course of her life and career, Yma began to reject offers. The only appearance of any merit was a television appearance on the Della Reese Show, aired on December 26th. Again, Yma sang "Good Lovin" and "La Molina" (The Mill Song).

Yma's career was winding down at an alarming rate. With the departure of Moisés, Yma was left in an awkward position artistically. For twenty years her only concern had been her singing. Not versed in the ways of managing a career she found herself faced with countless things that had to be taken care of—screening of engagements, contractual rights, travel arrangements, hiring of musicians, scheduling of rehearsal time, hotel accommodations, distribution of music to musicians, programming. For an artist of Yma's background and lack of experience in such matters, it was a tremendous, and in many ways overwhelming, responsibility to undertake.

Compounding the problem was the fact that Yma stubbornly expected the same treatment she had received twenty years before—and the same fees. Not sure of how to correctly handle many of the situations she found herself in, Yma began to make serious mistakes in her dealings with managers and producers. Unused to compromise and lacking the slick tact needed at such times, she began to be branded "difficult." Trapped by the conflict between what her career had been and what it currently was, it seems that Yma grew frustrated and resentful. When situations arose that angered or threatened her feeling of artistic superiority she became temperamental and defensive about her artistic worth and her position as a major American popular music artist.

In fact, by 1970, most Americans did not remember or had never even known who Yma Sumac was. Not helping this situation was the very unusual nature of her artistry and the near-camp nature of her resultant reputation. Occasionally humorous articles appeared about the elusive singer. *The Sound* (Vol. 1, #20) a Seattle, Washington based publication, printed an obviously unresearched article about her records and her career: "Yma Sumac. Doesn't that name spell magic? Those of you born after '48 or '49 have probably never heard the name before. Those of you born before then might recall—The Legend. What a voice she had! Three full octave singing range. Practically from a female baritone all the way to a true coloratura soprano, capable of reaching some notes called 'inhuman'. . . Poor Yma. Here is the tragedy: overworked and exploited by the US merchandisers, Yma did too much, too fast and after 5 or 6 years her voice gave out. She was forced into retirement at a rather early age. She spent a few years in Los Angeles, where it is rumored she opened a South American restaurant. Can you believe it? The voice of the century slinging tacos in plastic-fantastic land? . . . . And whatever happened to Ms. Sumac herself? No one seems to know for sure. A very reliable source told me she died two years later over a bowl of chili. Oh, Yma, I weep for you! . . . That's it folks. The sorry story of a vocal phenomenon that is still talked about years after her unfortunate disappearance from the musical scene. Sad, ain't it?"

By 1970 Yma had become a lonely woman, haunted by memories of world tours and idolatrous crowds. No longer in the limelight that she had once dominated, she became a "monstre sacre" and was avoided by booking agencies whenever possible. Her career seemed to crumble around her while she stood watching, uncomprehending, not knowing what to do, and unable to undo mistakes made by herself, Moisés and others. She was no more than 48 years old.

Chapter 8

"Miracles"
1970–1974

The following year, 1970, was no more productive. Yma's only performance of any significance was on August 16; Yma had a spot in a variety concert at the Hollywood Bowl. The program, called "Nosotros" (meaning something like "all of us") was a night-of-the-stars sort of program, a hodge-podge celebrity concert featuring such major and lesser luminaries as Jose Ferrer, Charlton Heston, Tony Martin, Dionne Warwick, Ricardo Montalban, Frank Sinatra, and Jack Webb. For her segment, Yma sang the virtuosic rock and roll "Good Lovin'" and the lyrical, folk-oriented "La Pampa y la Puna" (The Plains and the Mountains).

For Yma, the experience was not a pleasant one. By this time in her career, the artists she shared the bill with were almost always more current. Her name still attracted audiences to solo concerts, but in distinctly lesser numbers. In box office terms she was no longer prime audience draw. Because of this and the resulting "supporting artist" position to which she was relegated, it came to seem of crucial importance to Yma that she appear in a choice spot during any program in which she took part.

An artist's position on a variety program can have much to do with their impact on an audience. The producers of Nosotros had promised Yma the closing spot on the first half—a strong position, one for a star. The night of the show, however, Yma found that she was scheduled next to the last on the first half—a spot generally considered much weaker, even though the change was of only one "slot". Although a seemingly minor change, to Yma it was of paramount importance. She was, despite strenuous efforts, unable to have her position in the program altered.

Yma now found this to be typical of the way she was being treated. Used to royal treatment wherever she sang during the 1950s, she found the new attitude lackadaisical and resented the lack of respect she felt was hers by right. She grew suspicious, mistrusting, cautious, and bitter.

By 1970, many people were unaware of Yma's continued existence as a performing artist. Not seeing her name in newspapers, or seeing her on television talk shows (now a staple of America's TV diet) or in concerts in major cities, the general American public assumed Yma had retired. Rumors circulated that Yma had left music; gone into self-imposed seclusion, died.

Of course, she continued to be part of the discourse on popular music, even though she was treated as a historical figure rather than a current one. In discussing recordings of Andean music, *The New York Times Guide to Listening Pleasure* (MacMillan, 1968), judged Yma's "Chuncho!" (Forest Creatures) elegant and "superb."

In 1971, the German author Kurt Pahlen gave the early, original Imma Sumack a poignant if judicious tribute in his magisterial *Great Singers from the 17th Century to the Present Day*. In this remarkable book, Pahlen traces vocal art through the centuries with an emphasis on classically-based singers. Yma's inclusion was a compliment of the highest order.

[T]he pipetones of the super-high register cannot be associated with words; at best they form a staggering extension of coloratura, a *tour-de-force*—one might almost say a circus number—and as such to be highly respected, sometimes admired. Art, however, is more than a particular form of ability. Voices like these make no appeal to our aesthetic judgment, nor do they touch the heart.

Yma Sumac is probably the most interesting modern case of such a freak voice. From the age of fourteen she toured with a company of American Indians, conducted by the Peruvian Moisés Vivanco. More by instinct than intent he gave her vocal effects which, at least for the white public, were literally unprecedented. She was a very beautiful girl, her gleaming black hair setting off the bronze skin, and her warbling was as high and as lovely as the rarest song-birds in her native Andes. The fascinating thing was not only the height she reached—starting where Queen-of-the-Night voices end—but the sound too. You felt you were hearing some pristine sound from long-forgotten ages. Artistic considerations did not come into it, for Yma Sumac never sang anything from the classical repertoire, in fact she had probably never heard such singing. She did not distort or spoil anything, or sacrifice art to effect, she was equally far removed from both art and effect. She was a piece of Nature, as music can sometimes be in especially lovely moments; that is until Hollywood discovered the simple Indian girl, made her into a diva and dressed up her voice as artificially as its owner, so that nothing more was left of the age-old power of a primitive race and a mysterious world. (Stein and Day, 1974)

One thing of consequence happened for Yma in 1971. This was the recording of her final solo album, *Miracles,* released by London Records. Within two months of its release (in 1972), Yma was back in the consciousness of the American public. *Miracles* was her first recording in twelve years—since *Fuego del Ande* in 1959.

Why did she not make any recordings during that twelve-year span? The success of the Russian and Asian tours of 1960 to 1963 would certainly seem to have supported new recordings which, with expert and appropriate promotion and publicity, might well have sold extremely well. It seems that Capitol Records had had enough of the Peruvian singer–and her husband/manager. Their contract had been terminated after *Fuego del Ande*. The reasons are many and complicated, and began with her first album, *Voice of the Xtabay*. One problem was, simply, what to record. The Sumac recordings show a constant search for new promotional concepts, and recording sessions were often strained and unpleasant. And of course, in purely practical, financial terms, Yma's selling power as a recording artist had steadily declined since 1955. Only the early Capitol disks (1950–1954) sold in any quantity while the two following, *Legend of the Jivaro* and *Fuego del Ande,* were, to put it politely, disappointments. Coinciding with this was Yma's adverse publicity during 1957.

There was, however, yet another matter that was at the crux of the break with Capitol Records. This was a problem that originated in relations of Moisés and Les Baxter rather than anything directly to do with Yma. On a number of occasions, Yma has spoken with touching poignancy

London Records *Miracles* advertisement

and resignation about the artistic and musical changes she had to make before her recordings were considered suitable for North American audiences. When one considers, first, the folk-oriented, authentic concepts she and Moisés originally meant to promote when they first came to North America, and then the final product of Yma as queen of vocal exotica, one begins to understand Yma's disappointment and hurt feelings at being taken advantage of. She and Moisés certainly did make the conscious decision to go along with the publicity. When it comes to Capitol Records, however, the question of who took advantage of whom becomes a close one.

The firm took a gamble when they agreed to record and promote the unknown singer; she, for her part, never failed to deliver what was asked of her. Evidence supports the conclusion, however, that Moisés took advantage of both Capitol Records and Yma. Most of the time this was done subtly, but, in at least one instance, quite crudely. The main reason for Capitol's break with Yma stems from inaccurate information that was constantly being supplied by Moisés to the recording company about songs' composition credits—and royalty rights. It is a matter of law that every time a song is recorded the composer is entitled to a certain, pre-designated royalty.

An examination of the pressings of Yma's disks on 78 rpm., 45 rpm and LP show distinct, and odd, discrepancies in composer credits. This varied not only from release to release—even pressings released simultaneously but in different formats (LP and 45-rpm).

During the recording of *Voice of the Xtabay* in February of 1950, the situation was compounded by the strained nature of the relationship between Moisés and Les Baxter. There was a constant battle for supremacy. Moisés, accustomed as he was to being in full charge of Yma and her music, was being relegated to a subsidiary position.

The evening before one recording session for that album, it was discovered that an extra song was needed to flesh out the album. Les went home and wrote a new, atmospheric piece, had it orchestrated and copied and brought it to the recording studio for the next session. When it came time to teach Yma the melody (note by note), Moisés accused Les of stealing his song. When Les explained to Moisés that he had just written the piece, Moisés retorted, "It is mine. It is one of the pieces I brought from South America that you didn't hear." Les dropped the subject and just ignored Moisés. Indeed there were other problems with these recordings. Les Baxter insists that the only recording he participated in before *Miracles* was *Voice of the Xtabay*. Yet initial releases of Yma's second album, *Legend of the Sun Virgin,* lists him as the conductor for a number of the selections. On later releases his name disappears, replaced by the meaningless "with orchestra."

Moisés' outbursts did little to promote his self-claimed position as a serious, accomplished musician. Nor did it endear him to colleagues. The situation concerning song credits is very complicated. Occasionally only small alterations occurred from release to release. Often it was a reversal of a name's position—when crediting music and lyrics for a song, the composer is listed first and then the lyricist. "Ataypura" (High Andes) for instance, was originally credited "Baxter/Vivanco." Later releases omit Baxter's name. "Wayra" (Song of the Winds) was originally credited "Vivanco/Baxter." Again, Baxter's name was later omitted. In a number of cases, names appear in one order and then, on a later pressing, the order is reversed, then, later, reversed again.

Of special interest is the song "Xtabay." In September of 1950, when the recording was first issued, the piece was credited to Les Baxter and John Rose. The 10" LP release, just a month later, lists only Baxter. Subsequent releases have reverted to the original "Baxter/Rose." The original manuscript supports the claim of a Baxter/Rose partnership. Yet there is a problem. There can be little doubt that Baxter composed the music—it is prime Baxter exotica, similar to the rest of *Voice of the Xtabay*. As to Rose as lyricist, however: there are no lyrics on the manuscript, and Yma's recording of the piece is a wordless vocalise. An alternate version of the song was recorded by a male singer, with text written to the music—but that recording remained "in the vaults" until it was finally released in 1995!

At the time of the recording John Rose was Yma's agent. One wonders what his contributions might have been to warrant either royalty rights or the immortalization of his name on every printed label of the song. I have been told that during the 1950s it was "generally understood" that John Rose was the one responsible for the entire "Incan" myth fed to publicists and audiences—as well as the pivotal title and legend of "Xtabay." I have not, however, been able to pin down any confirmation. In any case, it may well be that Rose is responsible for the lyrics sung in the long-unpublished version of "Xtabay."

Because of the extent of her range and her diverse abilities, most of Yma's music had to be specifically composed or arranged for her voice. In popular music it is a common practice to "farm out" music (or themes) to arrangers/composers who, for a flat fee, will write a piece around the material given them. The composer/arranger gives up his or her rights to the music and any royalties. Despite creative drawbacks and the anonymity involved, it can be a welcome source of quick money. This is essentially the reason Moisés and Les Baxter signed the document reported on in Chapter 3.

Practically all of Yma's music went through this process and Moisés had little to do with any aspect of it except in a supervisory position—supplying the themes and the final claiming of royalty rights to the music. It would have been logical, with the addition of Hernán Braña to the group in 1949, that most of this work would have been handed over to him. When I repeatedly questioned Hernán about this specific detail, he vacillated between admitting and then denying that this was so. There is, however, an undeniable consistency in the 1950s Sumac arrangements—something that could not have been achieved with a host of indifferent, independent arrangers.

Occasionally an arranger/composer will enter into legal action in order to claim rights to a piece of music. This happened with Hernán, who, in 1951, composed the song "Karibe Taki" (*Legend of the Sun Virgin*). When released, the song's composer credit was assigned to Moisés. In 1955, however, Hernán Braña won a court case to recover the rights to his music. "Karibe Taki" was an original composition, not an arrangement. A similar situation concerns the song "Taki Rari" on the album *Mambo!* Like the previous piece, credit went to Moisés. When the album was pressed onto 12" LP, the credit was changed to "Hernán Braña." Most subsequent releases, however, find the credit reverted back to Moisés, since Hernán originally lost his lawsuit.

Then there are songs of questionable origin. "Chuncho!"(Forest Creatures) from the *Inca Taqui* album, and its earlier version, "Birds," are more than a little reminiscent of a flute solo Hernán wrote called "Andean Medley." "Calls of the Andes," also from *Inca Taqui* is the same piece as "Snake" written by Hernán in the 1950s and resurrected for Yosef Synovec's cabaret act, years after Yma had left most of her exotica behind her.

The situation became more complex as time went on. In some cases the problems were negligible.—a sometimes very slight misattribution, rather than an issue of legal substance. In the case of the 1959 album, *Fuego del Ande*, however, Moisés overstepped his bounds and involved Capitol Records in a slew of lawsuits, a situation that finally resulted in the severing of Yma's ties with that firm.

Some Examples of Varying Composer Credits

Song Title	First Pressing (78 rpm)	Later Pressing	Later Pressing
Voice of the Xtabay			
Ataypura	Baxter/Vivanco	Vivanco (12/51, 78 r.p.m.)	Vivanco (1956 LP)
Choladas	Baxter/Vivanco	Vivanco/Baxter (10/50, 10" LP)	Vivanco (2/51, 78 rpm)
Wayra	Vivanco/Baxter	Vivanco (12/51, 78 rpm)	Vivanco (1956 LP)
Xtabay	Baxter/Rose	Baxter (10/50, 10"LP)	Baxter/Rose (2/51, 78 rpm)
Flahooley			
Najala's Lament	Vivanco/Fain	Vivanco (1977 LP)	
Legend of the Sun Virgin			
Karibe Taki	Vivanco (with orchestra conducted by Baxter)	with orchestra	Hernán Braña (1956 release)
Witalia	Vivanco (with orchestra conducted by Baxter)	with orchestra	
Lament	Vivanco (with orchestra conducted by Vivanco)	conducted by Vivanco	
Zana	Vivanco (with orchestra conducted by Baxter)	with orchestra	
Kuyaway	Vivanco (with orchestra conducted by Baxter)	with orchestra	
Surray Surita	Vivanco (with orchestra conducted by Vivanco)	conducted by Vivanco	
No es Vida	Vivanco (with orchestra conducted by Vivanco)	conducted by Vivanco	
Mamallay	Vivanco (with orchestra conducted by Vivanco	conducted by Vivanco	
Mambo!			
Taki Rari	Vivanco Hernán (10" LP, #564)	Braña (10"LP, T 564)	Vivanco (12"LP, 1979)
Jungla	May (10" LP #564)	May (12" LP T 564)	May/Vivanco (12" LP, 1979)

Bobby Kreppel, Yma, Bob Covais, New York 1971

The first American release of *Fuego del Ande* listed Moisés as the composer of all selections. The recording was quickly withdrawn and corrected for re-release after lawsuits began to pour in from irate composers. Moisés' reasons for the many inconsistencies remain his own. Musicians who worked with him maintain, however, that it was simply an egocentric audacity on his part.

In September 1971, twenty-eight years after her first Argentinean disks were released, Yma recorded her last solo album, *Miracles*, at the instigation of Robert Covais, James Branciforti (aka James O'Maoilearca) and Robert Kreppel, three New York businessmen who were acquainted with the singer. Bob Covais and Bob Kreppel had both attended St. Raymond's School, near Parkchester in the Bronx. Jim Branciforti met Bob Covais years later in college, when his sister married Bob's brother. Bob and James eventually became life-partners.

Bob Covais (1936–1998), the driving force of the three, first heard Yma on television in 1949, when he was a youngster. He later saw her at Carnegie Hall, in 1954. He was completely smitten with the Peruvian singer. "She was absolutely the most incredible being I had ever seen! She was stunningly beautiful. I mean unflawed beauty, and a voice that was extraordinary. Truly amazing . . . " (Interview with Gino Falzarano for *DISCoveries*, 2/90)

Miracles' genesis dates to 1968, when Yma first appeared at the Chateau Madrid, in New York City. Covais, not missing the opportunity, went to every performance and sent flowers backstage to Yma every night. Finally he went backstage himself to meet her. An immediate rapport was established and they soon became friends. A high point of the relationship was when Bob attended Yma's Hollywood Bowl appearance in August of 1970. On March 3, 1971, Yma wrote a letter to him:

"My dear friend:

I wish there were a better word than 'Thanks' to express my appreciation for coming from New York to Los Angeles to see my performance at the Hollywood Bowl on August 16, 1970. And also I want to thank you for the lovely flowers you brought to my dressing room personally, they helped cheer me up on that night, not only because they added color to my dressing room, but because they reminded me of a good friend's thoughtfulness.

All my friends were commenting that 'Flowers have more scents than people.' As for me, I like both flowers and people like you!!.

Once again I want you to know that I am deeply grateful and I warmly appreciate your kindness

Sincerely

Yma Sumac" (hand-signed)

We saw earlier that Yma had signed a recording contract with the small firm, Bernard Stollman's ESP-disk. Stollman had since advertised in the *Village Voice* announcing that Yma was making a new recording and supplying a telephone number for interested readers to call for further information. Covais called the number and found that what Stollman was really trying to do was elicit donations for the project. It was Stollman's idea to back Yma with jazz musicians and have her record a scat album. That recording never materialized. Eventually, Yma, frustrated and irritated, asked out of the contract. Stollman, finding the project beyond his capabilities and tired of Yma's demands and complaints, was only too happy to release her.

Covais, Branciforti and Kreppel decided that they would pool their money together and undertake the recording project themselves. "We did this as a gift for Yma," Bob Covais explained to me. "To help her get back on her feet because she hadn't been in a recording studio since 1959."

Numerous phone conversations ensued until Yma eventually agreed. Originally, the plan was to record Yma in a grab-bag of numbers from South America and Africa. The program, suggested by Covais, was to include such songs as "Barco Negro" (The Black Boat), based on a hauntingly beautiful African folk song. Also to be included was the "Bachiannas Brazillieras #5" for soprano and eight celli by Villa Lobos, and the song, "Mahna de Carnival" from Black Orpheus, Daniel Robles' version of the Peruvian traditional song "El Condor Pasa" and perhaps one of the themes from the film Zorba the Greek, which would be done as a vocalise. Ultimately, none of this repertoire except for "El Condor Pasa" made it on the finished product.

Yma, cautious, yet eager to make a new recording, suggested that the new "producers" contact Les Baxter explaining, "He's one of the few people who understands my music." Covais, impressed by her apparent high regard for Baxter, decided it would be the best choice. Since none of the producers were musicians, it was important to have someone on hand who was familiar with Yma's peculiar brand of singing. Moisés, still incommunicado in Spain, was, of course, out of the question.

While verbal negotiations went on between Bob Covais and Yma, (Covais was the spokesman for the three, and always the one who dealt with Yma personally), Jim Branciforti undertook the responsibility of finding out about the legalities of producing a recording and also of locating Les Baxter. According to the musician's unions, AGMA and AFTRA, Baxter was in London working on incidental music for a play. Calls to London failed to produce him.

Unable to locate Baxter, the three producers decided to travel to Los Angeles and meet with Yma in person to make further plans. Suspicions that they were dealing with an extremely odd person were confirmed almost immediately. For one thing, Yma refused to acknowledge exactly where she lived—although they already knew. Whenever they were to pick her up to go somewhere, she would meet them near, but never at, her home. The strangest incident was the evening Yma brought her scrapbooks. Bob Covais had asked Yma if she had scrapbooks or if they were in storage. "Oh! I have many scrapbooks," she told him. That night they were to take Yma out for a fancy dinner. She had told Bob Covais that when he saw her that night she would look "very Yma Sumac." The three men drove up in a white Cadillac, formally dressed for dinner, "...and standing around the corner from Robert's [a department store in Culver City, where she lived] standing there in this beautiful yellow dress with all her jewelry on, and holding two big, black, plastic trash bags filled with scrapbooks, was Yma Sumac!"

Another evening added to Bob's understanding of the modus operandi of the singer (and of show business in general). They took Yma to dinner one night, by her request at a club where Jack Jones was appearing. When they arrived, the waiter recognized Yma and began to reminisce with her about her concerts, after which Yma spotted Les Baxter at a nearby table. Bob Covais was preparing to go to Baxter, but Yma stopped him, saying, "No, it is his place to come to me."

In the middle of Jack Jones' act, he paused to introduce Yma to his audience, "One of the greatest voices in the world—Yma Sumac!"

Bob Covais remembered that night vividly, "She was beautifully dressed, all in white with a lot of white makeup on—like a porcelain china doll. When she stood up to accept the applause, the image was really incredible—all white and radiant. She looked like an apparition. I remember thinking, 'Gee, isn't it amazing that Jack Jones knew Yma was here, and how quickly the spotlight found her.' Then Jim clued me in to the fact that she must have called ahead to let them know we were coming. She had set it up for herself. I felt so stupid, so naive."

And more: Like a scene in a Hollywood movie, Les Baxter came over to their table and greeted Yma and, being invited, joined them at their table. During the course of the evening, Baxter was approached about the possibility of making a recording with Yma. It was agreed that the four would meet at Baxter's home a few days later to discuss the project further.

Initially, Yma did not want to go to meet with Baxter, telling Bob and the other producers to go to Les Baxter's home without her and represent her interests. Bob thought that odd. "Actually, I should have realized that it presaged things to come." Eventually, Yma was persuaded to go and all four went to Baxter's beautiful home, which overlooked the Pacific Palisades. Les played Yma some selections on the piano and they discussed possibilities.

Les' initial idea of re-recording *Voice of the Xtabay* in stereo was immediately and emphatically vetoed. Bob suggested the songs he had come up with as the initial contents for the album, but Baxter seemed less than impressed, and so the rest of the day was spent in the music room going over ideas. Bob, however, was insistent that "El Condor Pasa" be included because it was very popular at the time (especially in Paul Simon's variant with Simon and Garfunkel) and fit in nicely with Yma's heritage.

At that time, Les was working with the rock group *Kansas* (akaThe Cowan Brothers, that happened to be living at his home at the time) that was providing background music for a play. The conversation eventually turned to the group and Yma began to be fascinated with the idea of doing an album of rock music. Both she and Les felt that, since rock was the dominant musical force in the popular music scene in America, an album of rock and roll would best serve as the vehicle to re-introduce Yma to the American public. At a time of Janis Joplin and Jimmy Hendrix, both felt that that musical form would be the most commercially viable. At the time the term rock and roll was a rather broad term used to encompass both the traditional music that grew out of the 1950s and the newer, "hard" or "acid" rock that had recently come into vogue.

Covais, Branciforti and Kreppel agreed, though with some hesitation. "I figured they should know best what would sell," Bob told me; "They were the musicians. But it struck me as odd. I mean, here was the King and Queen of exotica and they are going to do a rock album?"

Les Baxter was not—it seems a safe enough critical judgment to make—a rock musician and this product of the king of orchestrated exotica was pedantic, limp and, especially considering the singer at his disposal, utterly uninspired. Combined with Yma's odd, sometimes quavery singing, the album has always been bizarre—a curiosity conceived out of its time. (Perhaps even before its time—had it been created a decade later it might have crossed over into the "punk-rock" or "new-wave" experimental category.) And yet, for all its faults, it remains one of Yma's better "late" albums.

Originally, the suggested title for this recording was "Yma Sumac—The Second Coming." When that was discarded for *Miracles,* it became the key phrase for promotion. Yma wanted the record to be called, "The Vocal Miracle of the Ages." Bob Covais suggested it be called "Jungle Rock."

Difficulties arose almost immediately. Despite the intervening years and the initial cordial meeting between Yma and Les, their relationship was soon on shaky ground and quickly deteriorated. During meetings, arguments broke out and both grew edgy and defensive. Les was late in delivering the music, which he promised was newly composed. What he did supply was not new. Most of the songs had already appeared on an album called "African Blue" that he had released a few years earlier. What was new was only that they had been re-orchestrated, for a rock quartet of guitar, organ, bass, and percussion.

Provided with a tape of the pieces to work with, Yma began to plot the course of her improvisations. In September of 1971, Yma entered the Western Recording Studios in Hollywood and cut her first two songs. These songs, "Parade" and "Moses" were initially rejected and remained unpublished until June, 1998, when the album was re-released as *Yma Rocks*!

When "Parade," Yma's first cut was recorded, Bob Covais remembers that the engineers felt some extra voices would help set the mood, so he and Jim sang along during the first moments of the piece.

Because of the problems that were now beginning to plague recording sessions, Bob and Jim decided to spirit Yma away to New York to celebrate her forty-fourth (or forty-ninth) birthday. ("Who knew which birthday it was," Bob commented. "We just wanted to get her out of there before the entire recording fell apart.") They thought a change in scenery might be good for Yma, and a big party in her honor might help restore a better mood for the completion of the recording. That she and Baxter would get along was too much to hope for. At first Yma resisted the trip to New York. "How can I go to New York?" she asked, "when I don't have any luggage and no one to watch my dog!" Bob told her not to worry, just to agree to come and they would take care of everything. Yma decided to go.

Bob and Jim traveled to Los Angeles, bought Yma new luggage and arranged for a friend to watch her dog while she was away in New York. "The dog's name was 'Cholito,' or something," wryly remembers Bob. "One of those big, nasty, red chow dogs that eats the walls. He was just as temperamental as Yma."

Yma was flown out of Los Angeles first class. She also got first class treatment from the stewardess, who recognized her and was thrilled that Yma was on her flight. Asked about new recordings, Yma proudly told her about *Miracles* and, satisfied, settled back to enjoy the rest of the trip.

When she arrived in New York, Yma went directly to her hotel. Since she was in New York, there was other business that she might be able to see to. First, there was the possibility of an appearance on the Dick Cavett television talk show. Negotiations for this had been going on for a while without result and when it had been decided that Yma would be coming to New York, a preliminary interview had been set up. At the time (and to some extent, still, for new or inexperienced guests), this was a standard procedure, both to see how prospective guests handled themselves in an interview situation, and to discover and develop a productive line for the on-air conversation to take.

At 1971 birthday party

While on their way to the ABC studios, Bob and Yma ran into Hernán Braña. Yma, for whatever reason of her own, affected not to remember who Hernán was.

"The interview was a disaster," remembers Covais, "although, as far as Yma was concerned, it had gone beautifully. I went along because I knew what it was going to be like and I thought I might be able to help Yma; guide her through it, or help keep things running smoothly. "When we got there, a very nice woman sat Yma down and began to ask her questions to see how talkative she was. Yma was uncomfortable and not sure how to get the interview rolling. I tried to prompt her, but that didn't go over well, so I just kept quiet and let her fend for herself.

"At one point the woman said, 'I understand you've been to Russia, that you were the first American citizen asked to tour the country.' So, Yma told the Russian story, but it was very dry, more like statements than a running commentary. There were terrible dead spots and frankly, the way she told it, it was boring. Finally Yma stopped the conversation and told the woman she would need at least six months notice before she could appear on the show—she had to lose weight because of the horizontal lines on television. Then she told this woman that she would give Dick Cavett a list of the questions that he could ask her. The woman was very nice to Yma, but I knew right away that she had crossed Yma off. Yma, however, thought she had done marvelously.

"I didn't dare say a thing. Too much was pending on the *Miracles* album and I didn't want to make any more problems then there already were. Yma thought she had the situation under excellent control. She felt so magnanimous that she condescended to recognize Hernán when, surprisingly, we ran into him again after the interview.

Another business matter that had to be taken care of was the retrieval of Yma's recording contract from Bernard Stollman. This was basically a formality, a safety measure to protect the *Miracles* recording, and it was taken care of on the afternoon of Yma's birthday, September 10.

The contract secured, plans were finalized for Yma's birthday party that night. About thirty people were invited and the party was a great success. The celebration was culminated by Yma demonstrating traditional Peruvian dances. Private photos of the event show Yma to have been in a high mood, but still favoring fake, theatrical poses whenever in front of a camera.

Later that night, after Yma had been returned to her room at the Hilton, Bob received a frantic call from her saying that she had been robbed. He told her to call Hotel Security and that he would be over as soon as he could.

"When I got to her room at the Hilton, it was immaculate—nothing strewn on the floor, everything neat and tidy. Yma was sitting there calmly. I immediately thought it looked suspicious. I remember saying to myself: 'She's up to something.' Sure enough, the first thing Yma did was to urge me to call the *New York Daily News*. At first, I was alarmed. I asked her if her music had been stolen. 'No,' she said, 'They stole personal things.'

"By this time the police had come. Yma insisted I call the newspaper, so I did. The person who answered said it was too late to get it in the next morning's edition and suggested that I call back in the morning. I never did. I began to strongly suspect that the whole thing was some sort of publicity gimmick that Yma had dreamed up. The police were very kind and asked Yma what had been stolen. She said, 'Pantyhose.' The police asked how much they were worth. Yma said, 'Very expensive, they were designer pantyhose, Pierre Cardin.' They then asked her for an estimate of their worth. '$500.00.' she said. I couldn't really see her face or its expression because her hair was obscuring it, but it looked to me like she was having trouble keeping a straight face. I wasn't amused. 'And they ruined my suitcase', she said as she pulled out the suitcase we had bought her in Los Angeles. It had a number of neat, straight slashes on the top cover." The police gave Yma a paper to give to the Hotel management that authorized payment to cover her loss.

The next day, Yma was to fly back to Los Angeles. Covais and Branciforti and Kreppel went to the Hilton to see her to the airport. When they got off the elevator on Yma's floor, Yma was standing in the middle of the hallway ranting at a maid.

"Finally, we got her ready to go," remembers Bob, "She went downstairs to collect her reimbursement money and a new suitcase, and we hurried her off to the TWA terminal. We were running late. But, I said to myself, 'no way is she going to miss this plane!' We had to take her to the very last gate and the plane was about to leave. It must have looked hysterical,—the three of us grabbing a part of Yma and running down the aisle to the gateway all the while dragging a panting Yma. I was determined she would be on that plane."

"In the car on the way home, the three of us realized we had gotten ourselves into a mess. As we got further into the project, I for one began to feel overwhelmed. I think she thought of us as dummies."

After Yma returned to Los Angeles, Bob Covais had the photographs taken at her birthday party developed. He immediately sent copies, special delivery, to Yma's home in Los Angeles. He naturally addressed the envelope to Miss Yma Sumac. But it was Yma's custom to use "Yma Sumac" only for her PO Box in Beverly Hills. "Mrs. Vivanco" was used for any mail directly to her home. The delivery man, seeing the name the envelope was addressed to, and being a fan of Yma Sumac, asked her when she answered the door, if she was THE Yma Sumac. Yma denied it and said she was someone else. The envelope was, of course, returned to Bob. Later, she called Bob on the telephone and yelled at him. "When you write me at my home, only use Mrs. Vivanco, in care of 'Urquiola'." Urquiola was a secret name that Yma, Moisés and Hernán had used during her career to refer to Yma when they didn't want anyone to know who they were talking about. Like a game, the name was constantly used. Bob found out about Yma's secret name from Hernán who let it slip during a conversation. Picking the right time, Bob called Yma Urquiola and watched her become flustered and amazed that he knew about the "secret word."

Bob remembered that when Yma called him and explained why the pictures would be returning, he thought the whole thing pathetic. "Of course I redid the package the way she wanted," he told me. "And I sent it again. But I really didn't understand why she did that. Maybe she felt she had to keep up the fantasy that Yma Sumac was a very rich woman who lived in Beverly Hills, rather than some obscure apartment in Los Angeles. But, how pathetic. Here is a woman who performed all over the world, was honored by presidents and kings, adored by millions of people, whose records are in countless homes all over the world. Yet she felt it was necessary to lie in order to preserve this fantasy."

"But then," he continued, "her whole career was surrounded by fantasy. You know, she even did it with Jim and I. It was really strange. When we were down in Los Angeles with Bobby Kreppel for the *Miracles* disk, we could never meet Yma at her house. I don't think anyone has ever been in there. Yma was adamant about meeting elsewhere. Even though she knew that we knew exactly where she lived.

"If we were going out to dinner," he continued, "and were supposed to pick Yma up, we were told to meet her a block or so away. We never picked her up at her home. It's silly, I know, and really eccentric. But, I'll tell you, if you knew Yma, you would understand. If she wanted you to meet her six miles out of *your* way, you would. She can be impossibly stubborn and very proud. At that time, all she had were the memories of world tours and performances…and Moisés. She guarded them carefully.

"As far as I know she rarely listens to any of her records. I remember one time I played her some of her early 78s. They were some records that she didn't own. She began to cry as we listened and asked me to stop playing them. They brought back too many memories. I thought it odd too, that she thinks of her Capitol recordings by song titles, not album names and when I wanted to play a few of those for her she said she was tired of hearing them. But, her reaction to those early 78s was very sad to see. As far as I know, she hasn't spoken to Moisés for years. I have absolutely no idea whether she still sees her son—his name never comes up in conversation. For all I know she could have been a wonderful mother—the best. Or, she could have been 'Momita dearest.' To be honest, I found the whole thing depressing."

Although Bob Covais never acted as Yma's manager, there was one time when he did intervene and halt a potential job offer before it reached Yma's ears. "When people heard we were producing the *Miracles* album, they would contact me, thinking that I had access to Yma." In this instance Bob was told that the famous—or notorious—Continental Baths in Manhattan was interested in securing Yma for a 1972 New Year's Eve performance. This lavish bathhouse, located in the basement of the famous old Ansonia Hotel on Broadway, was for several years in the '70s the Mecca of gay New York. Bette Midler (accompanied by Barry Manilow, as her pianist—Barry sometimes dressed, as did nearly 100% of the patrons, in only a white towel)—had gone on to fame from there, and had made the place famous outside its original demi-monde. The Metropolitan Opera diva Eleanor Steber later peformed there, as well; the RCA LP recording of that performance has since become a coveted collector's item.

It was asked that Bob broach the subject with Yma. He immediately refused emphatically, saying "She thinks of herself at the Bolshoi. Can you imagine her singing for a bunch of naked men running around in towels? No. That is not her style, believe me."

It was then suggested that he just not tell her the true nature of the situation. "But, I told him they must be crazy if they thought I was going to do that. 'Do you think she is stupid?' I asked, 'do you think she would not notice that her audience was all men and that they didn't have any clothes on? No. That is not for her. I don't think she would be flattered. I think she would be highly offended.' And that was that."

Meanwhile, in Los Angeles, the recording sessions were almost over and Yma had yet to record any of her famous high notes. Up to this point her singing had centered in the mezzo-soprano register and the "growl." Covais and Branciforti, apprised of the situation, were commuting between New York and Los Angeles, and were growing very concerned. Les Baxter was also becoming concerned and was ready to bring in one of his recording sopranos, "Tiki," to lay down high note tracks.

(In 1962, Les Baxter released an LP album called *The Primitive and the Passionate* on the label Reprise (6048) now on CD. As though attempting to recapture the feeling and success of *Voice of the Xtabay*, the liner notes, by Peter J. Levinson, read: "Added to the distinctive, romantic quality of the instrumentals is the truly amazing high soprano voice of Tiki, a recent discovery of Les'. 'Tiki's' remarkable 4 octave range lends itself to being used not only as an instrument but also to simulate the unusual sounds of birds.")

The relationship between Yma and Les grew worse and Yma canceled a recording session, pleading illness. "By this time," recalls Covais, "Yma was an encyclopedia of excuses. The cold was the most frequently used, but there were others too. As far as I can tell, Yma's had a cold for at least ten years."

Whether at her own instigation or because Yma got wind of the possibility of Tiki's arrival, Yma finally re-entered the recording studio and, for two days, supplied all the high coloratura work now heard on the disk. "It was really amazing," remembered Covais, "after all the low singing she had been doing, she comes in and lets out with those famous multiple-octave swoops and coloratura of two decades earlier. I remember that at one point she was so pleased with herself that she threw the hat she had been wearing up into the air in triumph. It really was wonderful!"

The only piece that did not receive this treatment was "El Condor Pasa" which was left in its raw state. Originally, Yma was to have returned to make the final contributions for that song, but she never returned to the studio. Joseph Sidoro, the recording engineer, did a superb job of examining all the tracks and extracting all possible singing and blending or mixing them into a presentable product.

Returning to New York City with a copy of the master, Bob and Jim spent one full day taking the tape to various record companies: London, RCA, MGM, Capitol, Elecktra. They took it to London Records first and played the tape for Walter McGuire, who remembered Yma from her Capitol days. Despite problems, he liked what he heard and expressed an interest in pressing it.

Nonetheless, Covais and Branciforti continued taking the tape to other companies. "Capitol," recalled Covais, "was really an embarrassing experience. I couldn't even get to see anyone of importance and those people that I did speak to hardly knew who Yma Sumac was." All companies, except London, said thanks, but no thanks, complaining that Yma was too difficult to work with. Her reputation in the recording industry was not good and companies had no time to waste worrying about lawsuits that the singer now threatened at the slightest provocation.

Returning to McGuire, they contracted the tape to London Records. McGuire explained that for their purposes, they would need the "Mother" or master tape, which

Jim Branciforti,
unknown friend,
Yma,
Bob Covais,
Bobby Kreppel

contained all the original tracks. After much effort and a divatic intervention from Yma, Bob and Jim were finally able to secure the tape from Les Baxter.

The "mother" tape was taken to McGuire, who called in an engineering specialist to work with the tape and prepare it for pressing. "I didn't want Walt to hear the unmixed tape," remembers Covais. "If he heard it and thought it was a bomb, he might not want to do another disk. I knew Yma's voice at the time and I knew what to expect. So I went with the engineer and together we played through each track of the unmixed tape—all sixteen tracks. It was horrible, half of them were dead. Yma was only on about five or six tracks. Joe Sidoro did an incredible job of gathering everything Yma had done and using it, but even so, the London staff had little to work with."

The engineer prepared the tape (which included everything except "Parade" and "Moses") and eventually it was played for McGuire who liked the result. "Parade" and "Moses" arrived later that week but were discarded.

Problems surfaced immediately. The photograph Yma submitted for the album's cover was vetoed by London who felt it too posed and dated. Wanting something fresh they sent their own photographer to capture Yma in a relaxed, realistic setting. The photo session took place at the Century Plaza Hotel and was a complete disaster. Yma arrived for the session in a hooded, tent-like ensemble complete with a wide-rimmed black hat. The photographer, frustrated, found Yma blending in with the earth-tone color scheme of the Hotel and could not convince her to abandon the posturing that she had so favored decades earlier. The photos that he took were completely unsuitable for an album cover.

London Records decided to forget the photograph concept. Instead, a fantasy motif was chosen. The result was an unusual, imaginative drawing of Yma rising out of the sea in full Virgin of the Sun God regalia and feathered headdress, with her hands positioned as if in supplication. Near her floated a huge electric guitar. To the side sat massive palaces àl la Babylonia with two speakers perched in their midst. Ferns and jungle growth finished the exotic effect. Originally, this was to have been in gold leaf over a rich blue, foil background. Due to budget constraints, however, by pressing time this had been discarded for regular album cover cardboard.

Bob Covais, who liked the concept, nonetheless warned Walter McGuire that Yma would not. "She expects her photograph to be on the cover. Her photograph was always on her record album covers." Eventually Bob could not put it off any more. Knowing Yma would not rest until she had seen the cover, he sent her a copy. When Yma called him (collect as always) he asked her what she thought. Yma, thinking that what Bob had sent to her had been a first draft, commented that although she did not much care for it she realized that it was just a first effort and that it would be improved as time went on. Bob decided not to say anything to contradict Yma's impression. His main objective at this point was "to keep the lid on her so that London would release the record. We had spent three times the amount of money that had been originally estimated for the making of the album and were only concerned with pacifying Yma so that she would not begin calling up London records and screaming at McGuire. If she had done that he would have dropped the project immediately." So Covais endured Yma's penchant for calling collect at all times of the day and night to complain. "I just wanted to get the damned thing out and then forget about it!"

Bob had also supplied London with liner notes for the album. Although only a slight variation on the usual Sumac biography, London rejected them. Instead, nine short lines were written and inserted on the back cover in the bottom, right-hand corner. Brief, uninformative and inaccurate, these few lines were to cause intractable problems for the recording firm, which eventually was forced to withdraw the disk from circulation.

Making matters worse, the three producers found that the credits for the recording listed Les Baxter as producer. Both the record jacket and the label boasted that the recording had been produced *for* Bob Covais, Jim Branciforti, and Robert Kreppel *by* Les Baxter. "We were the producers of the damn album, not Les Baxter. He was the Musical Director. We had sold the recording to London records and were paid as producers."

Bob and Jim took their contract to McGuire and asked him what was going on. It seems that Baxter had convinced London that it was he who had produced the recording for the other three.

By this time, both Bob and Jim were too tired to fight and decided to just leave it alone. But, they had made a decision. They met with McGuire right before the recording's release and asked him to put Yma under contract to London Records. Even if *Miracles* was a success, the project had been too much for them to handle. They did not want to be bound by a contract that stated that they had to produce an album a year. McGuire explained that it no longer worked that way. Recording companies rarely made contracts with individual artists, only independent producers. McGuire explained, however, that if *Miracles* sold anything like *Voice of the Xtabay*, they would have a lot of money in the bank. If it sold 50,000 copies, London would do a second disk.

By November, 1971 Bob Covais, Jim Branciforti and Bob Kreppel were being emotionally bombarded not only by Yma but also by Les Baxter. Mailed on November 21, 1971, Baxter hand-wrote the following note to them:

Dear Friends,

Needless to say, I have been very badly hurt by Yma's behavior. I always look at the good side of things and never expect something like that.

You all are aware of what I have done for Yma but somehow it escapes her. If it is in your power to enlighten her regarding my work, please do so!

As you all now participate in all of her albums for the duration of the contract, which I think is entirely proper, could you make up a letter with me giving me 2% or 3% based on your 10%, or whatever you think proper?

Word it anyway you wish perhaps:

We the undersigned agree to pay Les Baxter an amount equal to -% for services rendered (better say -% of the sale price or whatever the contract says) for the duration of the London contract dated —signed .....

I think you would be doing Yma a favor to straighten her out on this matter. I got her the Capitol contract with great difficulty, my musical contribution was obvious. Her lack of loyalty only hurt her (those other albums!! No sales). Now a London contract, my work with her, and the loyalty sags again. For her own good protect her future, great albums lay ahead! I should think she should know that other record artists remain loyal to their producers, conductors, friends, etc.

I'm sorry I lost my cool with Yma. One can never be prepared for her. I try my best and think I have done well and whap! The Inca princess strikes again!

I forgot, you wanted a bio. Just say Les Baxter composer conductor, has written the music,—that I understand her style—you know what I've contributed….."

Most fondly,
The King of Exotic Music
Les Baxter

Miracles was finally internationally released around Christmas of 1971 with Boston as the marketing center, complete with Yma Sumac buttons and a contest. Because of additional budget cuts, the publicity campaign in America was minimal, but did include a full-page advertisement in Billboard magazine. The ad, which included a free, 7" plastic sample disk of two songs from the album, cost London Records $60,000. The headline boasted, "Give us just 6 minutes and 15 seconds. We'll give you an unexpected surprise. Yma Sumac, the lady with the voice so incredible that it's been called the 'Eighth Wonder of the World.'"

Originally, an ad was printed in the *Village Voice* newspaper in New York City which used the logo: "Yma Sumac—The Second Coming" and had a photo of Yma in her monk-like outfit.

Although McGuire had originally wanted to bring Yma and Les together in Boston for the promotion and "festivities," Covais told him frankly that it was doubtful McGuire would be able to get them into the same room civilly.

In February, 1972, as part of the promotion for the album, London released "Record and Artist Info" to record stores. Written by Peter Hay, the 11x14 sheet described Yma and the new album. "There is a certain primeval quality to Yma's tones. She seems to summon ancient and mystical daydreams especially where the arrangements are most abstract.

"From the first cut on *Miracles*, "Remember", she aptly fills the role as the most extraordinary singers ever recorded. She slips from a deep contralto voice to a trilling soprano with coloratura, stopping off at two mezzo-soprano parts in between. With glottal twists and growls she uses her voice like a fuzz tone for an abrasive sound. The high registers sound very much along the lines of a synthesizer.

"The production effects here, as throughout the album, add dimensions. The use of echo makes for a tumescent effect as her voice goes into one ear and the echo comes through the other. She is also heard duetting with herself because of double-tracking. Two "YMA SUMACS"!

"One of the most impressive productions on *Miracles* is a Les Baxter composition called "Magenta Mountain". Over a flamenco guitar introduction she soars to an incredibly high line. The rest of the band then comes in as an organ places a wall of sound around her. The rendition has an eerie and unearthly quality.

"Similar conditions flow through the album. One never ceases to be amazed by the woman's powers. She stands, in an industry crowded with 'cast-from the-same-mold' follow-ups, as a truly original performer." (sic)

In New York City, you could not pass a record shop where the disk was not being prominently displayed. *Miracles* sold very well in such countries as Yugoslavia, Japan, Germany and England. It did not sell well in the Americas.

It was at this time that all hell broke loose in the form of an enraged Yma. At the end of February 1972, Bob sent Yma an advance promotional copy of the recording; by March 1, Yma had written an angry letter to Walter McGuire.

Showing that there was no love lost between her and Les, Yma wrote:

"During my recording for my first album, Mr. Baxter tried to appear as being the composer of Mr. Vivanco's compositions of "Xtabay" album, thinking that we were some ignorant naïve people, who did not understand his malicious intentions. However, when he realized that this would mean serious legal trouble for him, he was afraid to face our attorney, and as a result, signed the acknowledgement a copy of which I enclose."

[This is the document dating from the Hollywood Bowl concert, in which composition credit was acknowledged by Les Baxter to belong to Moises, as quoted in full in Chapter 3.]

Yma was indignant (not unreasonably, it must be acknowledged) that Baxter was receiving credit for everything to do with her career while she was not even being credited for what she felt were her special musical contributions (improvisations) to the songs. She was especially enraged about the line in the liner notes that stated: "Miss Sumac achieved world fame during the fifties with the use of Mr. Baxter's productions." Still vociferously defensive about anything to do with Moisés, she demanded that this be corrected "before continuing to release" the album. She concluded her note to Maguire with the following paragraph:

"I want you also to know that the music on the "Miracles" record, was not written as I sung and recorded it. This means that I "enhanced" Mr. Baxter's compositions with my own musical improvisations, and the vocal introduction in "El Condor Pasa" as the end of this song, is my truly inspiration also. And my musical contribution in this regard should not be ignored."

In regard to "El Condor Pasa" London records had in fact made a startling gaffe by crediting this classic of Peruvian folk music to Paul Simon (who had, of course, written lyrics of his own to it for a Simon and Garfunkel recording).

The cost to withdraw an album in order to correct a few lines of copy was, of course, prohibitive, and so nothing was done. Furious, Yma slapped a massive lawsuit on London Records and the disk was withdrawn from circulation by early 1974.

Disappointed and completely disillusioned with the situation, Bob Covais wrote Yma, telling her that he no longer wanted anything to do with any recording projects. He soon received a letter from Yma's lawyer demanding that Bob release Yma from her contract. Bob got the release from London Records in June and sent it to Yma for her signature. Six months later it had yet to be signed or a copy returned. Covais, contacting her lawyer, was told that he no longer represented the singer and knew nothing about her whereabouts or the identity of her new lawyer. The document seems never to have been signed; in any event it was never returned to Bob Covais.

As was becoming a common practice by those who had prolonged contact with Yma, Bob Covais changed his telephone number.

The idea of doing another disk was of course shelved before anything concrete could be developed—a regrettable outcome, considering that the second project was envisioned as a tribute to the Inca Taqui Trio and was to present Yma in authentic folk music and South American music with only strings, flute and percussion.

During 1972, Yma's most important appearance was in February, on an American television special called "Fol-de-Rol." Again cast as a supporting artist, Yma was surrounded by Ann Sothern, Cyd Charisse, Howard Cosell, Totie Fields, Rick Nelson, Guy Marks and Mickey Rooney. Cast as a witch, Yma's brief contributions emphasized an aura of the circus tent that was cheapening. This was underlined by the decision to have her sing a truncated, modernized and barely recognizable version of "Taita Inty" (Virgin of the Sun God, Hymn to the Sun). Her exotic Incan chant was basically subsumed by Classical Gas. And although it was a unique opportunity to hear Yma sing with the accompaniment of a harpsichord, the song was oddly disjointed. As if to prove her continuing vocal prowess, Yma sustained a final high E flat for measures. "Fol-de-Rol" would be Yma's last appearance on American television for fifteen years.

During 1973, Yma traveled to Peru and Argentina for appearances, including a five-month engagement at the El Palmero nightclub in Lima. Probably the most important event of 1973, for Yma, and the most sadly nostalgic, was her return to Cajamarca, Peru to receive an award for her work as a Peruvian singer. On May 13, 1973, she performed in concert for the throngs of people that had come to hear their famous countrywoman. It was, however, a bittersweet occasion both for the singer and for her countrymen. As David Espena remembers:

"It was kind of a disappointment to the people because by that time she had become an American citizen and because of this she did not get as warm a welcome as she deserved. At the time I was the director of the National Institute of Culture in Cajamarca and I was chosen to head the ceremony. Well, some people clapped, some were silent, some booed, and some whistled. This was because many of them were hurt that she had adopted American nationality. In this case, I feel that all artists belong to the world at large and when you have a talent like Yma's it transcends the boundaries of being tied to just one country. I would have liked for her to have said (to the people) that she would always be a Peruvian and a Cajamarcan, but she has her own interests and she can do whatever she wants." (interview for Rubicom film, *Hollywoods Inkaprinzessin* (translated by Gianncarlo Cifuentes.)

During one of their trips to Peru, Bob and Jim met two of Yma's schoolmates who were also professional singers at El Chalan, one of Lima's top night clubs. They were mightily amused to hear that the *gringos* were saying Yma came from Brooklyn. They knew better.

On July 18th, radio station WBAI in New York broadcast an interview of Yma by Richard Lamparski. This was unusual since Yma rarely granted interviews. Working on a specialized book, *What Ever Became of...?* which contained updated biographies of former celebrities, Lamparski contacted Yma through Bob Covais and then traveled to Los Angeles to meet with her. The interview, done as a follow-up to *Miracles*, disclosed Yma's eclectic musical taste and expressed Yma's fondness for Delibes' opera *Lakmé*, while admitting to a secret desire to record country-western music. Although still cautious, Yma was articulate and surprisingly candid about the changes she'd had to make during her early career from folk music to exotica. She was, however, still not exactly fastidious with the facts, and one hears a subtle, yet definite attempt to defend her former husband and mentor, Moisés Vivanco.

A few years later Lamparski's book was published. Yma's section (pages 54–55) was predominantly accurate and sensitive to Yma's artistic compromises for acceptance. Unfortunately, he ended the article with a humorous attempt at squelching the Amy Camus question by commenting: "It is doubtful that anyone who has ever spoken with her went away believing it. Her English is like a parody of Carmen Miranda." Yma was highly offended.

In 1974, Yma spent a number of months with her family in Peru. During a Sunday afternoon in June, Yma made a guest appearance in a huge collective concert given at the damp and drafty Amatu Coliseum (an old bull-fighting stadium) in Lima. Yma sang three numbers, reportedly in good voice, but had a lot of trouble with a costume she had decided to wear. The outfit had "... black velvet that was generously studded with a ton of rhinestones accentuated by pearl sequins. The ensemble was supported by a hoop of hemispheric proportions, and with the help of her two arms and what must be Herculean hips she swirled and swayed her way across the huge stage right into the audience's heart. She wore a wig..(with) several feet of teasing and enough corkscrew curls to keep a sausage factory going for years. A garden full of daisies highlighted and gave an airy look to the coiffure. Marie Antoinette, were she there, would have paled by comparison." (Frank Schmitt, *Michael's Thing*, 8/12/74)

Frank Schmitt had traveled to Peru specifically to see Yma in this show. He also commented that Yma's voice had improved with age. "The high notes are still thrilling and nobody, not even that Sutherland lady, can do what Yma does when she 'talks' to the birds." (ibid.) During her second number, however, the hoop to Yma's outfit sprung and the "diva developed a definite right sided list . . . .With great effort, and surely at the risk of developing a hernia, she made it off stage and finished the number from there. The third song was completely sung from the wings and after that was over there was no more Yma." (Ibid.)

A company of 200 dancers took part in the concert, as well as another singer from Peru who had gathered quite a following during the 1960s and '70s. According to biographical information, her name was Judith Acuña, Professionally she went under the name of Wara Wara and counted Moisés as her mentor. She sang and recorded some of Yma's former repertoire and specialized in copying some of Yma's vocal tricks and effects. Wara Wara coached with Moisés and her recordings use a number of his "arrangements." Wara Wara's reception at the concert was tremendous. Wara Wara was the first of a number of Sumac imitators that began to appear over the years. (for more information on Wara Wara and other flute singers see Section II.)

Yma seemed to view all of this with a complex emotional combination of amusement, pride and resentment. It certainly created an unfortunate (and awkward) situation for Yma who stood by and watched as audiences showed more interest in the copies than in the original.

A few weeks previous to the concert, Yma had appeared on a Peruvian television show. Instead of singing or discussing her career, she made the tactless mistake of commending herself for the fact that, as she believed, before her, no one had ever heard of Peru. She also berated the Peruvian government for their lack of suitable compensation for her graciousness. She was cut off in the midst of her tirade.

When interviewed on the Rosita Peru Television show and repeatedly questioned about Moisés, an irritated and impatient Yma got up and began to leave. She was persuaded to remain only when Rosita promised not to ask questions about Yma's personal life.

Chapter 9

"Remember" (Miracles) 1975–1985

1975 included Yma's most important concert appearance in years, a return to Manhattan. Although she had fulfilled various night club engagements in New York City as late as 1968, she had not given a solo concert since 1955, at Carnegie Hall. Much had happened in twenty years, both to Yma and to the popular music scene. Compromises in program selections reflected both those changes. Produced by Jose Bovantes, and with Marco Rizzo (of *I Love Lucy* fame and the brother of Vilma Rizzo) as the musical director, two concerts were given at the famous Town Hall, located at 123 West 43rd Street on March 22 and 23.

Because of Yma's constant difficulty in securing what she considered suitable artistic representation, she contacted Hernán Braña and asked him for help. He, in turn, approached Gerard Della Chapell, a New York City copyright lawyer he knew, suggesting that Della Chapell represent Yma. Intrigued, Gerard contacted Yma and began to discuss possibilities. After much bantering back and forth, and despite his hesitancy, an agreement was reached between Della Chapelle and Yma that he manage her from February to April, which would cover her New York City engagements.

The concerts were to be called "Music Around the World," a safe if vacuous title. In addition to various solo piano pieces to be played by Rizzo, it was planned that Yma would sing eighteen songs. Her selections included "Ataypura" (the only song retained from the original Incan repertoire) and "Manisero" a pyrotechnical piece written by Hernán that boasted a voice-flute "contest." Tickets sold weeks before Yma's arrival in Manhattan.

Yma began her stay in New York at the Esplanade Hotel but soon found it too expensive. With Della Chapell's consent, she moved into his Manhattan office. This was a small space on West 58th Street, near Columbus Circle, and proved to be unlivable. Yma ended up staying with Della Chapell's secretary at her home on Long Island.

There were immediate problems with the concerts. Because of their importance, Yma had wanted Moisés to return to America and take charge of the music. Although doubtful as to a successful outcome, to his credit Della Chapell personally wrote Moisés, inviting him to take part. The reply from Moisés, however, demanded conditions that could not possibly be met, including that he be credited as the producer. The subject of Moisés was quickly dropped and never mentioned again. Yma, hurt and offended by Moisés' reply, grew sullen and uncooperative.

When questioned seven years later, about the period when he had represented Yma, Gerard Della Chapell was guarded and reticent. One of his few remarks was that "It was all rather cruel. The main drawback to Yma's career was that she was married to her manager. He was an excellent manager. She should have realized that he was more important to her in that context than he was as a husband."

In fact, and despite this, Yma remained loyal to Moisés as a manager, and with typical tenacity, as though harboring the thought that he would return one day. His failure to appear for the Town Hall concerts at all—even as a "surprise guest" to be supportive, was bitterly disappointing to her. Gerard Della Chapell said that in her naiveté, Yma thought that Moisés would return because the concerts were important to her.

As though striking out at others for Moisés' obvious disinterest, Yma began making outrageous demands on Gerard, who remembers her with little affection as a "monstre sacre." It became obvious to observers that Yma and Gerard heartily disliked each other. It seems that from the beginning, Gerard had formed an unrealistic, idealistic concept of who Yma Sumac was. Unfortunately, this often conflicted with the truth.

As though blaming Yma herself, he seemed to take it out on her. Bob Covais overheard Gerard muttering, "I wanted to bring a young, beautiful Yma Sumac to the world. And look at what I got." Bob Covais commented to me, "Well, what the hell did he expect for Christ's sake? It had been twenty-five years since "Xtabay". She had been through a lot. I thought she looked sensational. It was an unfortunate and cruel attitude to have."

It became apparent to those concerned with the concerts that Yma was as much in love with the Sumac legend as her former audiences had been. As in the past, Hernán acted as a buffer between Yma and her source of irritation, this time Gerard, trying to maintain a semblance of peace. As Yma's and Gerard's true feelings for each other became clear, this proved to be a difficult task.

It seems to have become clear by this time that only Moisés had had the power to successfully harness this very complex woman artistically and personally. I suspect that Yma knew this, although she often boasted otherwise. As if in defiant defense she developed the misconception that she had the savvy to decide what was best for herself without listening to the suggestions of other, more trained and qualified people. Mixed in with this was her complete conviction that she still was the queen of popular music. She adamantly refused to abdicate her throne and expected top fees.

Buried somewhere under all this, however, must have been the gnawing, frustrating realization that things would never be as they were in the 1950s. Yma was now moving in a totally different musical scene from the one that she had entered in 1950. Desperately fighting for her artistic survival, Yma demanded her way in all matters concerning her music. Although advised not to, she deliberately included the American songs, "Sunrise, Sunset" (from Fiddler on the Roof) and "Try to Remember" (The Fantastics) on her Town Hall programs. Her "reasoning," reflecting her magisterial concept of herself: if they were hits, Yma Sumac should sing them. The results were ludicrous.

The only person who could occasionally calm Yma, or to whom she would deign to listen at all, was the ever-faithful Hernán—who, despite Yma's flare-ups and often-dismissive attitudes had been loyal to her for almost thirty years. Nonetheless, it depended on Yma's mood whether or not she listened to what Hernán had to say. Her treatment of Hernán during the preparation of the two Town Hall concerts was atrocious. At a whim, she threw some of his compositions out of the program, replacing them with inferior material, never thinking of the hurt or offense it might cause.

Hernán deprecatingly explained the situation: "She was mad at me, that's all. She had wanted me to be the musical advisor for the concerts, but I had been called for jury duty. I could do little more than get some musicians for her. So she was mad at me."

Hernán never heard from Yma after the Town Hall concerts of 1975.

Much publicity was done to promote the concerts. *Newsweek* (3/17/75) accurately remembered the Yma Sumac of the 1950s as one of "the curiosities of the popular culture . . . (an) exotic looking, elastic-voiced singer . . . " Commenting that Yma's age was one of her secrets, *Newsweek* also quoted one of the musical arrangers concerning the extent of Yma's range in 1975, which supposedly, still covered five-octaves: " . . . two octaves below and three above middle C—depending on the day and the weather." (ibid.)

1975 Town Hall program cover

Interviewing Yma for the *New York Post* (3/20/75), Jan Hodenfield observed "Intact is . . . a certain primitive grandeur that in its time lent splendor to her rainforest trills underscored by a mountainous basso. And if now the waist is a bit thickened, the upper lip somewhat unyielding, her movement less sweeping, she is still a presence."

During the interview Yma reminisced about her reviews and the critics. "[everywhere] the [criticism] was very good—even Walter Winchell—and you remember how difficult he was—was saying nice things about me."

(Although Winchell promoted the Amy Camus fabrication, he had a genuine respect for the Sumac talent if not the person. He often told aspiring young entertainers that if they wanted to see a really great entrance onto the stage or a superb exit, "go see Yma Sumac.")

Yma also said that she felt the failure of her last album, *Miracles* was because *her* role in the production was not sufficiently promoted. Two television interviews were set up for Yma preceding the concerts. Although meant to attract audiences and promote interest, they did the opposite. For reasons we have seen, generally Yma avoided interview situations. Considering the way she was often presented, it is no wonder. The art of the interview had undergone many changes, however, since the 1950s. At that time, the public was more interested in the *image* of an artist rather than in the true emotional make-up of the person. When a fabricated, or created persona crumbled, attention centered on the scandal surrounding the breakdown not on the emotional trauma, sorrows or disappointments which led to it. By 1975, emphasis was on honesty, and interest focused on the artist as a person rather than the artist as a metaphor.

Yma's early interviews did not help clarify her complicated persona and were often thwarted by frustrations, many of which stemmed from an inability—her own—to understand who she was—which could vary depending on whether she was on or off stage.

Yma's dislike for interviews stemmed from the kinds of questions she was inevitably asked, about her voice and her personal life. She did not like questions about her voice for the simple reason that she had no intellectual understanding of it—its workings were as mysterious to her as they were to her audiences. Interviews throughout the years show that she never had clear, technical answers to such questions. She just didn't know. A shy woman, without a ready, articulate grasp of the English language, Yma's responses were often vague and hidden within the shadows of fragmented sentences. A private person, she also resented personal questions and often became defensive. Yma feared that interviewers only wanted to explore the "scandals" in her career—even though, compared to many others, her scandals were quite tame. Nonetheless, she preferred not to discuss these intensely personal matters in public. Consequently, she avoided reporters whenever possible. As a result, the public was never given an opportunity to know the woman behind the singer. Primed since the beginning of her career in North America, in 1950, to spew out the Incan Princess story, Yma soon knew no other story to tell and eventually began to believe much of it herself.

Freeman Gunter, who took charge of Yma when she performed at The Ballroom in New York (1987) said that he felt it was because of Yma's fear of someone getting to know her as a real person. If they did, she felt they would realize that everything was a fabrication, that there really was no "Yma Sumac." It wasn't until the late 1960s that Yma began to relent and imply, very subtly, that much of what had been written about her was not true.

Ironically, Yma enjoys talking about herself and her "accomplishments," but the language barrier has remained troublesome in the tension of interview situations. Interviews from the 1970s show the singer to be charming, rather formal, in an old world manner and engagingly flirtatious at times. Serious statements are often offset by sweet, girlish, embarrassed laughter.

One of the interviews scheduled in preparation for the Town Hall concerts was for the Joe Franklin Show on WOR-TV in New York. Mr. Franklin's late-night talk show dealt primarily with minor, offbeat, or cult celebrities. The decision to have Yma appear was a poor decision. She seemed uncomfortable, was inarticulate and exhibited more than a touch of defensive eccentricity. The other guests that evening first approached her with interest, and then, after Yma paraded her typical "Incan" story, amusement. Yma's reaction was haughty indignation.

Two weeks before the concerts, the reporter/humorist Chauncey Howell taped an interview with Yma in Gerard's office, to be shown as a self-contained feature in the Channel 4 news. This was the type of interview Yma would have avoided, had she known how she was going to be presented. Mr. Howell, as was his wont, found his subject matter highly amusing. The tone set for the interview was deprecating and the humor was at Yma's expense and was insulting. Hernán was asked to take part in the interview because they wanted to have some footage of Yma rehearsing. For this interview he was given the fictional title of "Consulting Musical Advisor" even though he was hardly involved in the concerts at all.

Part of the segment was obviously filmed without either Yma or Hernán realizing that the camera was rolling. In this context, Yma's odd, non sequitur singing suggested the insecure wanderings of an aging, rather dim operatic diva rather than the rehearsing of a specialist of improvisation. At one point, Yma had trouble finding her place in the music (Hernán's "Karibe Taki"). Hernán, trying to show her where they were, was immediately countered by an irate Yma lashing out in a childish, petulant tone, "No! You changed it!" In actuality, the entire sequence was pure misrepresentation. Hernán was not involved in the concerts, Marco Rizzo, the actual musical director, was nowhere to be seen, and even the song being rehearsed was never meant to be on the program.

Yma's singing was tentative and made little sense. Although her range was still extensive (close to three octaves, belying the fact that she had made her professional debut thirty-two years earlier), she wandered aimlessly through Hernán's music as if she had never heard it before and at times her voice seemed completely out of control. In conjunction with Howell's flip comments the whole sequence left one with the impression that it had been in very bad taste to air the thing at all. Howell's closing remarks best illustrate the pervasive air of sarcasm during the entire news clip. He referred to Yma's Town Hall appearances as occurring some twenty years after she had "resigned her job as priestess of the Inca Sun God and had packed up her jewels and high notes and moved to Hollywood."

The Town Hall concerts were crucial for Yma. They could help re-establish her public appeal. It is interesting that around this time a new emotion seemed to be appearing in her make-up—paranoia. This now began to appear in public. It was a fear that audiences felt she was too old to sing her famous songs. Because of this fear, more often than not, she relied on an ever-useful "cold." (The "cold" had great life; it appeared as late as 1997 when she appeared at the Montreal jazz festival.)

On March 31, 1975, the *Village Voice* printed an article/interview Yma gave to Jack Hiemenz in which she emphatically stated that songs from her albums would appear on the program for the Town Hall. "People expect that of me. If I don't sing (them), people say I can't sing anymore. I don't want people think that, because I'm still young, I still sing high notes."

Actually, the only song from her famous "Incan" repertoire that Yma sang in the concerts was "Ataypura" (High Andes)—her signature tune. By this time, however, the song had undergone a drastic, disastrous re-arrangement and had metamorphosed into a weak, limp song—tentatively sung by Yma.

Other interviews covered Yma's eclectic musical tastes and her plans to open a school of singing for girls in New York City, where the emphasis of the teaching would be on breath control.

Gerard, present for one of the interviews, was described as charming, but more interested in talking about Yma's soul than any artistic or musical matters. This observation is crucial in understanding what went wrong between the two. Not surprisingly, disillusioned by Yma in her current vocal and physical state (she had gained a good deal of weight since 1950), Gerard soon lost interest in continuing her promotion. (Later to satisfy his Sumacitis, he attempted to promote a talented Sumac imitator, Yosef Synovec.)

The Town Hall concerts had some surprises for audiences. Three of the songs offered were written by Yma. "Pa' Donde Vas," "El Trinar de las Aves," and "Señor!" This was a new development and one that would be exploited by the singer ad-nauseam during the next two decades. Also, for the concerts, Yma had a special wardrobe designed by Lloyd Lambert of Hollywood and Las Vegas, treating the audience to no less than four costume changes.

The printed program was an unruly hodge-podge of music. In addition to at least six non-vocal numbers, the overly ambitious program included contributions by Yma accompanied by either the seven-piece orchestra or Marco Rizzo on the piano:

Vivanco: "High Andes" (Ataypura)
Bock and Harnick "Sunrise, Sunset"
Perez Freire: "Ay, Ay, Ay"
Traditional Italian: "Fenesta Che Lucive"
Traditional Peruvian: "La Molina" (The Mill Song)
Valderrama: "La Pampa Y La Puna"
Sumac: "Pa' Donde Vas"
Sumac: "El Trinar De Las Aves"
Soloviev-Sedoi: "Nights of Moscow"
Traditional: `"Nobody Knows the Trouble I've Seen" *(Cut)*
Debussy: "Clair De Lune" (Vocalise)
Vert: "La Leyenda Del Beso"
Chaplin: "This Is My Song"
Simons: "Manisero"
De Curtis: "Tu, Ca nun Chiagne"
Traditional, Spain: "Clavelitos"
Sumac: "Senor!"

Actual concerts showed pruning of a number of selections, though not enough, and although three intermissions were listed in the program, the concerts had four. At Gerard's instigation, Hernán contacted Columbia Records in an effort to secure a recording contract. Representatives came to the concert but were not impressed.

It had also been planned to record the concert with Town Hall's house system. At the last minute, however, Yma vetoed that idea. No professional recording was made. Bob Covais did, however, make a private tape as did popular music "pirates". The surviving tapes of the concerts show cautious singing contrasted by occasional flashes of brilliance, all framed by unfortunate, provincial musical arrangements. The most distressing thing, however, is Yma's general lack of vocal authority, something that had never surfaced before. She was heavily miced for the concerts, sometimes very much to her disadvantage. In the "Clair de Lune", for example, dynamic changes from forte to pianissimo came across as harsh and abrupt, although her basic musicality was never in question. "El Manisero" boasted a duet with flute where Yma growled and took off in stacatti flights up to high C#. One of the most successful pieces, surprisingly, was the Italian "Funeste che lucive," where Yma's timbre and line suited the piece especially well. Except for a few breaths grabbed in the middle of words, the performance was quite moving. Another was a piano-accompanied vocalise on a famous theme from the Zarzuela *La leyenda del beso* by Reveriano Soutullo and Juan Vert. Aside from a false, hesitant entrance during the second half of the piece, Yma slithered through the graceful melody with a good legato and some imagination.

The New York Times review, on March 24, 1975, was headlined, "Yma Sumac Returns To Roar of Crowd." Robert Sherman gave an articulate, accurate review of the proceedings. He commented that the original *Voice of the Xtabay* album, "sold in the millions, and for some five or six years thereafter, the Peruvian singer with the range of four (some said five) octaves and an uncanny ability to imitate exotic bird and animal calls was a major box-office attraction. It was, then, a highly emotional moment when Miss Sumac strode onto the Town Hall stage Saturday night and 1,100 listeners stood to roar their welcome. Nor did the audience enthusiasm wane during the course of the evening. Prolonged applause forced Miss Sumac to repeat a bouncy tune of her own composition that traversed vocal textures from Louis Armstrong to Lily Pons. It would be lovely to say that the incredible purity of tone and impeccable technique that Miss Sumac displayed here in the nineteen-fifties are still as intact as her ability to negotiate multiple octaves. Her voice lacks resiliency now. It is grainier and far less controlled. Some of the top notes sound pinched and there frequently is an element of strain in her singing."

With Marco Rizzo, 1975

Bill Zakariasen, writing for the *New York Daily News,* (3/24/75) felt that "she managed some potent and occasionally haunting notes above and below the staff. While I think I counted only one high F all evening, it was nice to know she was singing for us humans this time, and not just for dogs. She tired a bit in the stretch, probably due to the length of her program, and possibly to the frequent and obvious struggle she had with the tacky arrangements and generally sloppy playing of the band under Marco Rizzo—Les Baxter he ain't."

Freeman Gunter, at the time writing for the gay publication *Michael's Thing,* commented that Yma "attracted large audiences who seemed starved for the kind of star trip she represents; they gave her standing ovations and lapped up everything she did. The concert was uneven, to say the least. The program was rambling and poorly sequenced. The musical direction . . . was tacky in the extreme, belonging in some low cocktail lounge and not on the concert stage." Freeman noted that Yma looked quite beautiful "and if her voice is a little drier and slower to start than it was 25 years ago (and whose isn't) it is still a lovely and unique instrument and when she is singing congenial material there is no one who can touch her. When singing the wrong material, which happened a lot in the earlier portions of the program, she was grotesque."

Variety judged her program "a mistake. What the audience had come to hear were those freaky sounds that rose four octaves from subterranean rumble to fire-siren wails. What they got were mangled syllables and dropped words in 'Sunrise, Sunset' and 'Try to Remember' and much of the style of an aging operatic diva in such songs as 'Ay, Ay, Ay' and 'Moscow Nights'."

According to Bob Covais, the most moving part of the evening came after the concert when the house lights were brought up and a chair and table were brought on stage, and Yma sat down to sign autographs. "It was a kind of love-in," recalled Covais, "and just what Yma needed so much—that feeling of adoration that comes from an audience." Another moving moment, although private, was the reunion of Yma and Vilma Rizzo, who had not seen each other in years. Unfortunately, Vilma never saw Yma after this.

After the autograph session was completed, Yma and fourteen others went to the Chateau Madrid to celebrate. That, recalled Bob Covais, was terrible. "This was supposed to be a dinner to celebrate the concert. I don't know what had happened to Yma—she had been so happy signing autographs—but her mood had changed drastically. She wouldn't speak to Marco Rizzo, and she and Gerard glared at each other all night. It was so depressing. I was sitting between Yma and Gerard. One minute Yma was leaning over and telling me how she hated Gerard and the next minute Gerard was leaning over and telling me how he hated Yma. It was a very long night. After it was over I went home with such a headache. So I said to myself, 'I can't take this anymore! That's it! It's time to change the phone again.'"

Because he had promised, however, Bob took his cassettes of the concerts to Gerard. Gerard was depressed because the people from Columbia had declined to record Yma. He asked Bob to approach London records. Bob explained why that would not be a good idea. Eventually, he was able to convince Gerard to drop the idea of a commercial recording.

It was during the Town Hall concerts that Yma met Alan Eichler, a young concert manager. By 1984 he had become her personal representative. When I first tried to get hold of a copy of these Town hall concerts for research back in 1981, it was Alan Eichler who supplied me with copies.

During rehearsals for her Town Hall concerts, Yma was re-introduced to Yosef Synovec. Small and lithe, with dark eyes and black, curly hair, Yosef had been a medical student in Czechoslovakia when Yma sang in that country during her great tour of Russia and Eastern Europe. After one of her concerts in Czechoslovakia, Yosef, acting as representative of a group of admiring students, presented Yma with a huge bouquet of flowers.

Later, Yosef left Czechoslovakia and moved to New York City bringing with him a tape of Yma recorded during live concerts in Romania. Musically gifted, Yosef was proficient on the violin as well as vocally, and once in Manhattan he made the decision to drop his medical studies and concentrate on music. Working at Schirmer's Music Store, he joined the ranks of thousands of other free-lance musicians in the city, and tried to obtain jobs. Yosef was a protégé of Holly Woodlawn, the inveterate talent scout and female impersonator who had appeared in several Andy Warhol movies, "who heard (Yosef) vocalizing as he worked away painting a bathroom...Holly determined, then and there that he had discovered a future star." *(Michael's Thing* 4/76)

Yosef's singing talent was, to put it mildly, specialized. He had a voice of tremendous range and a startling proficiency in mimicry; he excelled at Yma Sumac imitations. He had always been a great admirer of the Peruvian singer and had assiduously studied her recordings for years. He had become amazingly adept at re-creating Yma's particular tonal quality and resonances. Yosef idolized Yma so much that he had changed the *J* of his first name to *Y* to further emulate the Peruvian diva. An eccentric and occasionally a fabulist, he often told people that it was he rather than Yma singing on the smuggled Romanian tape.

Because Gerard had represented Yma around the time that Yosef was perfecting his Sumac imitations, Gerard got wind of his unusual talent. After his foray into representing the original had so spectacularly failed, he decided to undertake Yosef's representation. Realizing that Yosef needed suitable musical arrangements to highlight his gifts, Gerard contacted Hernán Braña, explaining that he had something very special for Hernán to hear. After playing a tape of one of Yosef's songs over the phone, Hernán, baffled, asked, "When did Yma record that?" Gerard quickly explained and arranged for Hernán to meet with Yosef.

"He really was amazing," remembers Hernán. "He knew all her songs and could imitate her almost perfectly. I had never heard a woman—much less a man—do such a thing. The voice was strange. It had this long range and no perceptible break into the falsetto."

With Hernán's help, Yosef made a demo disc that could be used for auditioning. Made around Labor Day of 1975, Hernán provided the arrangements for the two songs chosen and hired the back-up musicians. (Gerard, who was in charge of the entire project, must have thought Hernán was working with Yosef out of love for the art; Hernán was never paid for his work and had to cover the costs of the musicians as well.)

The two songs recorded at the Abrahamson Studio on West 76th Street were "Sooner or Later," Hernán's adaptation of a theme from Tchaikovsky's ballet, *Swan Lake*, and the "Theme from Beethoven's

Yosef Synovec publicity shot

Fifth Symphony." Both pieces were wordless vocalises in the Yma Sumac style and displayed Yosef's virtuosity in elaborate runs, jazz-scatting, high soprano staccati, and low, contra bass notes. The demo disc, which has survived Yosef, remains as impressive as it is outré.

When Yma was reintroduced to Yosef, she ignored him.

After dropping Yma as a client at the conclusion of the Town Hall concerts, Gerard began to seriously concentrate on Yosef's career. On April 12, 1976, Gerard sent out a news release under the auspices of the "American Copyright Society," announcing Yosef's booking on April 18th for two sets at the See-Saw Club at Lexington Avenue and 81st Street (now defunct). The release had typical biographical magnification and an attempt to bind the names Synovec and Sumac together. "The range of his voice exceeds five octaves without the slightest falsetto, but goes without any effort throughout the entire range. This is the most extraordinary and unique vocal range existing throughout the world, without excepting the famous range of the lovely Inca singer, Yma Sumac."

Unfortunately, Gerard's power in important musical circles was as limited as his musical managerial abilities in general; there was little he was able to do for Yosef. Yosef did, however, make a few appearances during 1976 in small New York City cabarets. Because of the peculiar nature of his gifts and the way they were exhibited, Yosef's popularity was confined to the gay subculture of New York City. It was hoped that as he matured as an artist and expanded his repertoire, he would become more widely accepted. The few reviews he received applauded his voice and technique. The only fault found was his rudimentary stage demeanor.

Gerard Della Chapelle reluctantly agreed to play a performance tape of Yosef Synovec for me when I interviewed him at his office in New York City in 1982. It was made during Yosef's set at the Tijuana Cat Club on June 16, 1976. Performing with piano, flute and percussion, Yosef offered an eclectic program that leaned heavily on Sumacian material, including "Ataypura" (High Andes)—in faultless mimicry, "Sooner or Later," the tenor aria from Bizet's opera, *Les pêcheurs des perles*, "Send in the Clowns," "Invisible Love" (a Sumac-like obstacle course), "Snake" (the same song as Yma's "Calls from the Andes" on *Inca Taqui*), and "Chuncho!" (Forest Creatures)—patterned after Yma's performances in Romania. Listening to the tape was an eerie and unsettling experience, so perfect was Yosef's imitation. Yosef's gift was real. With uncanny clarity he reproduced mouth, head and chest resonances that Yma used, as well as her vocal effects, including high, pecked staccati, the celebrated "growl," and amazingly, even the "double-voiced" trill found at the climax of "Chuncho!" Listening to Yosef sing "Chuncho" sounding like Yma yet knowing it was not her was a "Twilight Zone" experience for me. He was impressive, amazing—odd. For some savvy New Yorkers who heard Yosef Synovec's work, Hernán's artistic assistance and musical contributions to Yosef's club acts underlined the connection between Yma's "Incan" songs and Hernán's contributions to her music during her heyday.

Despite the specialty flavor of Yosef's act, because of his obvious gift and his dedication to his singing, it was hoped that, with time, he would mature into a successful cabaret entertainer. Tragically, on May 27, 1977, Yosef was one of nine men killed in a horrific, four-alarm fire that swept through the Everard Baths on 28th Street in Manhattan.

In the middle of September 1975, Yma returned to New York City for a month-long engagement at the Chateau Madrid. Previous problems smoothed over, the management welcomed the singer back for a series of concerts. Her set for concerts was distressingly short, only about twenty minutes, and Yma realized soon enough that she had primarily been hired for her name. The main attraction of the show was a revue called "Brandall's Follies," which *Variety* described as "essentially transvestite entertainment, with a line of four small girls (genuine) for further atmosphere."

Variety's critic, Jose, reported that "at the outset of her act [Yma] apologized for having a cold, which naturally retarded her aims. However, she still roams a wide vocal range. Her natural voice seems to be in the deepest areas. She goes all the way up to falsetto, all of which is delivered with clarity. The bulk of her songs are Latin, which is Okay with the Chateau's audience." (10/1/75)

Although no printed program was offered to patrons of the Chateau Madrid, Yma's six selections included "Amada Mia," "Nights of Moscow," "La Molina" (The Mill Song), "Alma Solitaria" (Solitary Heart) and Hernán's virtuoso piece, "Filigrana." "Alma Solitaria" would reappear in 1987 when Yma returned to New York City for performances at The Ballroom. By that time, the song had a new arrangement, new English lyrics, and a new title: "Don't Let Me Die Without Love".

Although her set was brief, Yma sprinkled her music with high Cs, Ds and E flats of crystalline purity. Actually, her singing at the Chateau Madrid had more vitality and vocal sheen than the Town Hall performances, six months earlier.

While in Manhattan, Yma acted as Grand Marshall for the 11th annual United Hispanic-American Parade on October 12th. 1975 was the International Women's Year and a special dedication was made to women during the course of the parade, which celebrated the discovery of the New World in the name of Spain. Twenty-one countries were represented in the parade, which took place on Fifth Avenue between 44th and 70th Streets. An estimated crowd of 10,000 watched from the sidewalks as Yma led the hours-long parade and was congratulated by Cardinal Cooke.

Yma's engagement at the Chateau Madrid was over October 21. Yma immediately traveled to Santo Domingo for performances at the Sheraton Hotel.

Without adequate artistic guidance and protection, Yma's career was beginning to dissipate into nothing. Unhappy with the way she was being treated, defensive and demanding, Yma began to alienate herself from former colleagues who would not cope with her transient and undependable moods. Producers, finding that her audience appeal had lessened, and finding Yma uncooperative and unrealistically demanding could not be bothered with the incalcitrant Peruvian singer. It was around this time that Yma decided to visit her son Charlie in Spain, and following that make a return to her homeland of Peru for an extended visit with her family. This was essentially a decision to retire (or perhaps "semi-retire") as much as an opportunity to visit and care for her parents who were then ailing.

In November of 1979, the English classical records magazine *Records and Recording* published an article called "The Legendary Sumac," by Maurice Leonard, the author of books on such classical artists as the English contralto, Kathleen Ferrier and the Russian mezzo-soprano, Oda Slobodskaya.

The article came out of nowhere and for devotees of the Peruvian singer, packed quite a wallop. Although it was not generally available to American readers it is one of the most accurate and informative articles that has been published about Yma Sumac since James Poling's "Most Exciting Voice in the World" for *Collier's Magazine* back in the 1950s. Aside from a few, minor inaccuracies, the article was superb; well researched, and the first to seriously analyze Yma's recordings. Yma's projected concert tour of England, meant to coincide with the article, never materialized. Curious about how such an important article happened to suddenly appear, I contacted Mr. Leonard by email in 2006. He explained:

When I wrote the Yma article for Records and Recordings…I was reviewing records and interviewing various recording artists including Julian Bream, Yeleana Obratzova, Nicolai Ghuiaurov…."Miracles" had come out some time ago and Yma was not really in the remit of a "classical" magazine, and there were few reissues of her records at the time, so it was not easy for me to place an article on her. However, as the editor sometimes welcomed my suggestions I managed due to my longstanding association with the mag, by concentrating on the "authentic" quality of her songs and the uniqueness of her voice, and throwing in as many "classical" comparisons as I could to get the article published. I was pleased on several levels particularly, as at that time, there was a ridiculous snobbishness about her voice from many publications, who purported to have an interest in singing and should have known better.

When the article came out a few were curious as she was largely forgotten, in England at any rate, by that time. But I still, from time to time, get inquiries about it and Yma. (private email 4/14/06)

Inspired by Yma and her music Mr. Leonard made a pilgrimage to Peru a number of years ago. But he was in for quite a shock: "I was surprised to learn from the few people I spoke to about her (none had met her) that (they) were rather disgruntled. Peru has few world stars and they felt she had deserted the ship, so to speak, by throwing her lot in with America. The fact that it would have been difficult for her to have managed such a huge international career from Peru did not sway them." (ibid)

While in Lima, Maurice Leonard went to a restaurant and found the entertainment fascinating. "In came a pretty indiano girl singer in her 20s and a young male harpist. They were terrific but I nearly fell off my chair when the girl sang—it was the young Yma, not as sophisticated or polished, of course, and a folk repertoire [just as Yma used to have] but a beautiful clear soprano the same translucent individual colour and texture as Yma's. . . . If I were rich I'd have paid for her to be properly trained—what a voice. When I mentioned this to a Peruvian lady I was with she was unimpressed. 'They all sing like that,' she said disparagingly (referring to the Indians) 'Anyway she'll be dead from TB soon.' I went cold. I often think of that girl and how she thrilled me in that restaurant in Lima." (ibid)

In 1980, Yma performed at the El Palmero nightclub in Lima. She also performed in Buenos Aires, Mexico City and Caracas. In 1981, she appeared on the Mexico City television show, "Sempre Domingo." After this, however, public appearances were few.

As far as American readers knew, Yma had disappeared entirely. For years not a mention of her name could be found in American newspapers, magazines, or journals. Roland Barril, the Spanish television interviewer, contacted Yma around this time and was told that she now worked in a woman's boutique, occasionally singing on weekends. When I mentioned this to Bob Covais, his response was, "Oh yeah, but you know to Yma, Woolworth's is a woman's boutique."

During 1981, Cholita died after a long illness in Los Angeles.

It had been a number of years and Americans had heard nothing about the Peruvian singer. It was during this time that Yma had traveled back to Peru. Within a few years, however, she would be persuaded to return to America. Alan Eichler explained:

> I met Yma first in '75 when she played Town Hall in New York. I just went to see her as a fan; I didn't know her. They were giving out posters, and I went backstage after the concert and asked her to sign it for me. There was a market for her obviously. I moved to Los Angles in '81, and that still was in the back of my head, that something should be done with her. Her records were being played, and I saw cas-

settes being reissued in the stores, and I knew there was a younger market, and I just felt that something should be done with her, and I kept writing to her. First I had this number in Beverly Hills, and then somebody was able to get me an address for her in Peru and I wrote to her.

I finally tracked her down in Peru, and she finally answered me. We just started corresponding and she finally agreed to come. (Interview with Gino Falzerano, *DIS-Coveries* 2/90)

Despite Yma's lack of exposure in the American press at this time, people were still "discovering" her. Once such person was Kansas City-born Joe Westmoreland. In 1983 he was a twenty-seven-year-old student in a film class at the San Francisco City College. For an assignment he was to produce a sound film in super 8. The idea was to provide him the opportunity to work with different film mediums. Enlisting the help of two of his friends, Arturo Galster and Lina Fellini Joe decided to make a film called *At Home with the Stars featuring Patsy Cline and Yma Sumac.* Arturo (who specialized in Patsy Cline impersonations) would play Patsy Cline, Lina would play Yma and Joe would direct. He told the two actors what he wanted in general, but basically they improvised the rest.

What resulted was an amusing twelve-minute sketch. A tongue-in-cheek tribute to Yma, The film took one day to shoot but editing was not completed until Spring of 1984.

It was submitted and debuted at the 1984 San Francisco Gay and Lesbian Film Festival and was also shown in other US cities including Atlanta and the New York Gay and Lesbian Film Festival (1990) and in Brussels. Played at parties for fun, it has become a cult favorite.

Now a professional freelance writer, Westmoreland has had short stories published in such anthologies as 1996 Best American Gay Fiction (Little & Brown) and Queer 13— Lesbian and Gay Writers recall 7th Grade" (1998, Rob Weisbach Books at William Morrow). In 2001, his most recent book was published by Painted Leaf Press, *Tramps Like Us* an autobiographical coming of age novel. After a number of stops on his book signing tour, he did one for a capacity crowd at the Barnes & Noble on 23rd and Sixth Avenue in New York City on July 22, 2001. In the fall of that year, his book was nominated for an American Library Association award.

In 1984, at the instigation of Alan Eichler Yma came out of retirement and began to resume singing. Eichler specialized in the resuscitation of female former celebrities— Mamie Van Doren was one—and taking on the Sumac career was consistent with his particular specialization.

During the 1980s, Yma's recordings showed up in unusual places. Songs from her "Mambo" disk were interspersed between more trendy music in some of the hard-core nightclubs by adventurous deejays, and a bit of "Sauma" (*Legend of the Jivaro*) was used for an Indian-based skit with Bill Murray (who, like another comedian, Lily Tomlin, is one of Yma's fans) in a 1981 segment of Saturday Night Live. Yma's most famous recordings (LP format) were even offered by Publisher's Clearing House for $4.98 and $5.98, Yma's voice being described as "One of the most extraordinary voices in the history of recorded sound . . . "

Having wangled Yma's address in Peru from Norma Foster, the one person in the United States who had it (and who had been sworn to secrecy by Yma) Alan began to write to Yma, asking her if she would be willing to return to performing. At first she resisted, but eventually relented. By 1984, Alan was in charge of publicity for a well-known club in Los Angeles called the Vine Street Bar and Grill. Alan invited Yma to perform there. He admitted later that the place was scarcely appropriate for her. The Vine

Street seats about 50 at tables and can probably squeeze in 50 more at the bar. "It was a jazz club, and there was no stage. You stood in front of the tables and sang. It wasn't theatrical in any kind of way. The owner had never heard of her, and I had to convince him to book her and she wanted a high guarantee. We had to charge twenty dollars a person, which was a lot of money at that time for a cover charge." (Interview with Gino Falzarano, *DISCoveries* 2/90)

Located at 1610 North Vine Street, in Hollywood, the Vine Street Bar and Grill is a restaurant that offers some of the finest names in jazz and cabaret singers for entertainment. Interestingly, the restaurant is about four blocks east of Yma's star on Hollywood Boulevard.

On Thursday, March 29th, 1984, through Sunday, April 1, Yma came out of her semi-retirement to perform two shows nightly. Matt Groening, then a music critic for the Los Angeles free weekly *Reader* (later far more famous as the creator of "The Simpsons"), interviewed Yma before her first performances. Prefacing his article, Groening noted that Yma had been popular thirty years earlier; then, millions of listeners "sat transfixed in front of their hi-fis, listening to the Voice while staring longingly at one of her classic album covers." (3/30/84)

Gracious and relatively articulate in Groening's account of their interview, Yma explained that "On my mother's side I have royal Inca blood, so I am a princess. But I don't like to be called a princess, not here, not over there, nowhere in the world—I am only Yma." (ibid.) She also remembered that in her youth her singing voice was "very thin and high." When asked whether Xtabay was a real word, she replied, "That's no Peruvian name. I don't know why Capitol Records chose that, maybe for exotic name, you know. That comes from Mexico, I think, meaning princess from the Azteca civilization." Yma also spoke about her own compositions, boasting that she had composed more than 2,000 songs. Her method of composition was to tape-record her explorations of ideas, and then choose "the best ones for the mentality—the psychology—of the American people." (ibid) She also expressed a love for Henry Mancini's music.

Perhaps the most important comments Yma made were those that she let slip while talking about other things. Especially about her youth: "Well, I was born in Cajamarca—a big state, like the state of California—in one of the little villages full of farms. In my childhood I was always with my family. My own teacher would come to the house—I was never in public school—and I had my own nana, which is my servant, and I used to play outside with my animals, the dogs and cats, which I adore…" (ibid)

Alan Eichler was nervous but excited about Yma's agreeing to appear at the Vine Street Bar and Grill. Much to his surprise and pleasure, lines for Yma's appearances in the tiny restaurant stretched around the block, and indeed people were turned away from every show. Yma, too, had approached the Vine Street job with some trepidation. In May of 1985, she told Todd Everett of the *Los Angeles Herald,* "I was used to playing the biggest nightclubs and concerts with orchestras. When I asked how many musicians the Vine Street had, they told me, 'None.' And I replied, 'Then what do you want me to do?'"

Yma made at least four appearances during the next few years. Nick Grant, a friend of Yma's in Los Angeles, told me that when she appeared there she sang for two sets a night, for four nights each week,with a guaranteed $2,000 each night.) The shows were sold out before each night. The two sets,which lasted about 40 minutes each, contained no "Incan" material. Although it was expected that some Incan songs would be offered, in fact she offered only folk songs and original compositions. Her accompaniment was provided by a trio of musicians comprising a synthesizer (an electronic instrument that can mimic the sounds of other instruments—like violins, woodwinds and even voices), keyboard and conga.

When questioned about Yma in 1985, Alan Eichler told me, "Everyone I talk to who has worked with Yma refuses to work with her again, but I have always found her very accessible. It's true she gives nothing on stage—she just stands there like a stone and sings, but I feel she shouldn't really be in a nightclub atmosphere. It is too intimate. In her own way, she is still exotic and should not be approachable. Yma should be in a theater or making recordings. I think there is a place for her and she is marketable, but she should have a big production surrounding her."

By 1990, Eichler had had second thoughts. There had been some problems with Yma's appearances at the Vine Street club. Eichler remembers a few outraged customers who found the cover charge exorbitant and the Sumac show inadequate and demanded their money back. "Unfortunately, most of those people had expected a freak show," Alan explained, "and Yma doesn't do that anymore."

Reviewing Yma's April 17, 1985 performance, *Variety* found that Yma "more than lived up to her legendary reputation, tossing off operatic, jazzy, gypsy-like runs and counterpointing ultra-high flakes of sound with samba-tinged incantations and growls." (Enry, 5/1/85) The two pieces that were considered the highlights of the program were "Montana," and a lullaby-like number called "Eyes of Aleli." Few flaws were found with Yma but her back-up musicians were found to be uninspired and often were rebuked "with a corrective glare from the star." (ibid.) *Variety* concluded that "Visually as well as vocally, Sumac came across as larger than life, a kind of south-of-the-border Mae West—haughty, friendly, ironic and sexy."

Todd Everett had an experience with the Peruvian diva that provides insight into her curious and individualistic behavior. For an interview with Yma, he visited the club on the second night of her appearance in May of 1985. The first night had gone rather well, but the second night Yma said she was not feeling well and did not want to sing. The management was not amused and refused to be the ones to tell the audience that she would not be performing. Hoping that they might persuade her to change her mind, they told Yma that if she did not intend to sing, she would have to tell the audience herself.

To their shock and horror, she proceeded to do just that. Todd Everett remembers that Yma was very apologetic in her explanation to the audience. She then told the audience that instead of singing her songs, she would describe the songs she would have sung, while her back-up trio played them. And that is what she did, while the audience sat staring, stupefied. Mr. Everett's comment seems if anything understated: "It really was very weird."

Nonetheless, Yma enjoyed performing again and within a few years she would undertake a comeback that would seriously test her powers as a performer and possibly provide the impetus for her to continue her career as a viable performing artist.

The Vine Street Bar and Grill job also served to reunite Yma with one of her on-and-off friends, Nick Grant. He had originally met Yma in the late sixties, had been a fan of hers for years and attended many of her concerts. Born in 1920 in Albuquerque, New Mexico of Greek parents, Nick was raised in Fairfield, Illinois and attended Military School. His major in Spanish was to play an important part years later when he met Yma. With a varied work background, he worked for an independent oil operator and a steel company in Fairfield and then was drafted in 1942. He worked for American Airlines, TWA, the Stadler Hotel chain, and, for two years (1968–1970) in the casting department of Columbia Pictures.

In the late 1960s, he met Yma during an interview held by the President of the Hollywood Foreign Correspondents. Nick and Yma hit it off and discovering they lived in the same neighborhood, exchanged home telephone numbers. "I told her if she needed anything she should just call me. She did; she asked him to help her move. Nick was thrilled to be able to help and this rather odd, off-and-on friendship began.

When Yma came out of semi-retirement in 1984 to sing at the Vine Street Bar & Grill, Nick hadn't seen or spoken with her for about 6 years. He and a mutual friend of theirs, Zita Zaleske, once in Hungarian cinema, went to hear Yma. Sending his card backstage, Nick was not sure if she would remember him. "We were invited to come backstage and we had a very nice reunion. Yma was very gracious." Since he was retired, and had the free time, Nick often traveled when Yma was making a local appearance, and often even further—to New York or Boston, just to be there and to provide support. He was also present at each of her shows at the Los Angeles Roosevelt Hotel.

Commenting on his odd relationship with Yma, Nick said "She is a study in contradictions. She rarely calls and only if she wants something. And we always speak in Spanish. Lately I seem to be her newspaper man. She has this dog and is always needing newspaper to clean up after it. So the other day she calls me and said she needed me to bring over papers.I have done that before for her but I hadn't heard from her in a while. So I went over and left them there for her." (Private conversation with the author, 1999)

I asked Nick what they talked about when he took over the papers since they hadn't seen each other in such a long time. He said, "Oh she wasn't there. I just left them there." When asked if she had called to thank him for bringing them over he answered, "No." The 79-year-old wryly remembered, "In the old days when I had a party I often would invite her. She would always come—even though she knew that she was to be the centerpiece. Even so, I never really felt that she did it because she wanted to do it but rather because she felt she owed it to me for all the things I did for her. But I have always considered myself more than a fan. I really care for her.

"When we were together—especially in public I could never call her Yma. 'Oh no! don't say Yma!' I was to call her Perita or sometimes I called her Rosita. She was suspicious of everyone, and doesn't want anyone to know who she is. When she goes out all dressed up (as Yma) it is never from her own apartment. She would come over to my place, change her clothes and leave from there. She can be very eccentric. I have known her to use a flashlight rather than turn on the lights, and turn off the hot water to save money. I think she has become obsessed with money—although the rumor is that she has lots of money in various banks throughout the world. When she sang in a country she would put the money in a bank there—like Mexico. I hear she has a lot of money down in a Mexico bank. But that could just be rumor too.

"She knows everything and often seems to make up fantasies to suit her at the particular moment. Once I remember her telling an interviewer at the Ballroom 'You ask Nick, he knows all about me for many years.' I was so pleased and very proud to hear her say that. And yet another time she told someone that she didn't know me. One time she told someone that I was no good, another time that I was very wealthy (which I am not)."

Asked whether Yma ever spoke of her family, Nick mentioned that he thought it odd that she never spoke of her son, Charley. "I mean, usually a mother will talk about her son and all but with her, never a word. During all the time I have spent with her not once has she even mentioned him."

Gale and Nick Limansky with Hernán Braña

Chapter 10

"Tumpa!" (Earthquake!)
1987

After an absence of twelve years, Yma returned to New York City at the beginning of 1987. The reason was a highly desirable three-week engagement at The Ballroom, a popular cabaret in Manhattan (it is now defunct). The Ballroom originally opened in SoHo by Greg Dawson about ten years earlier. After a few years it moved to West 28th Street, in Chelsea. Considered one of the best ethnic restaurants in Manhattan, it specialized in the fascinating assortment of Spanish foods called tapas, and in topnotch cabaret entertainment. Alan Eichler, who had helped secure Yma for the Vine Street Bar and Grill in 1984, had, by 1987, metamorphosed into her manager and arranged for Yma's return to New York.

The Ballroom was a logical choice for Yma's comeback. Aside from the fact that the restaurant-cabaret had an intimate atmosphere suited to Yma's current vocal capabilities and individualistic stage demeanor, one of the owners was also a famous Peruvian chef, Filipe Rojas-Lombardi, and a long-time admirer of Yma's. Because of Filipe, the management of the club bent over backward to accommodate Yma—even when she became difficult or temperamental. During such times, Felipe was one of the few people who could get through to Yma and they were often heard frantically conversing in Quechua.

When Yma was initially engaged, the club's management was skeptical that she could fill a house for three weeks. The longest she had sold out during her Vine Street appearances had been five days. Although Alan assured them of her continued audience appeal, the management refused to guarantee her a salary. Instead, she was to receive a percentage of the moneys received at the door each night. From this Yma was to pay her own expenses, including hotel accommodations, transportation, and the fees of her back-up musicians. The Ballroom management never expected, and was not prepared for, the "earthquake" that shook the cabaret when Yma came to town.

Originally, Yma was contracted for a three-week engagement from February 17th to March 7th, one show a night at 9:00 PM, Tuesdays through Saturdays. Before the first show, however, it became obvious that this was not going to be nearly enough to accommodate the reservations that were pouring into the club. Public response was so overwhelming that an additional show was added each night at 11:00 PM. Even with this, hundreds of people had to be turned away at the doors.

To accommodate the overflow, two shows were added on an extra day, (March 8). By this time, the next act, the slightly scandalous but wonderfully skilled and widely popular transvestite "La Gran Scena Opera Company" was scheduled to open. The demand for Yma was of such unexpected proportions, however, it was decided to squeeze in two more weeks of shows. This was done by offering late shows Tuesdays through Thursdays at 11:00 PM and two shows each Sunday. With patrons paying a cover charge of $15.00 and a two-drink ($25.00) minimum, it became a very lucrative engagement for Yma. As it turned out, she had the biggest audiences in the history of The Ballroom.

Yma's show was short but not skimpy—compact might be the word for it. It was about forty-five minutes long and, for the most part, was the same material offered to audiences in Los Angeles. (Because the set was so short, the wait staff was often frantic, barely able to serve the required second drink before Yma was finished.)

The show opened with an instrumental adaptation of Yma's famous *Voice of the Xtabay* cut, "Tumpa!" (Earthquake), which Stephen Gaboury, the musical director of the New York band of free-lance musicians, had adapted from Yma's 1950 recording.

After this introduction, Yma entered and sang ten songs, which she introduced herself. Four of them she had once recorded, five were original compositions and one had figured prominently in her 1975 Town Hall concerts. The Ballroom show was similar to those given in Los Angeles, except that Alan Eichler and Ron Bernstein scored a major triumph when they managed to convince Yma to open with "Ataypura" (High Andes). Yma had not planned to sing the number because in Los Angeles she didn't get the proper support from her accompanying trio. When Yma heard the creative New York-based band, however, and realized they could simulate the sound of orchestral strings with their synthesizer, she relented and agreed to sing the piece. Originally, Yma had wanted to begin with one of her own, English songs. She thought it important to use popular, souped-up arrangements of current popular songs because she felt it made her singing more accessible to the audience. Alan, however, had noticed that she lost the attention of her Los Angeles audiences when she sang in English.

Playing very heavily into her misconception was, clearly, her vanity; she wished not to be thought of as an ethnic performer. It was important to Yma that she be thought of as an *international* singing star. Although Alan and Ron begged her not to sing in English, Yma told them, "My public loves me because I speak to them in their own language." Despite Yma's conviction, everyone else agreed that she sounded horrible. Generally, it was felt that Yma's awkward handling of the English language just underlined the vocal problems that were emerging as she aged. (Freeman Gunter, who helped care for Yma at this time, reported that while they were selling records at The Ballroom, at least one person in five would ask him if Yma sang in English on the recordings. Before they bought records they wanted to be assured that she did not. "And Yma was sitting there, right next to me," Freeman said.)

During the first week of shows, eleven songs were originally listed in the printed program supplied by The Ballroom. "Eyes of Aleli," a pseudo-lullaby, was quickly dropped. Also, throughout most of the engagement, no encore was offered, though later that lack was corrected. Yma sang more than forty shows in the five-week period.

The program was:
Vivanco: "Tumpa!" (Earthquake)—instrumental
Vivanco: "Ataypura" (High Andes)
Sumac: "Don't Let Me Die Without Love"
Sumac: "My Real Tru Love" (sic)
Zalderrama-Stubbs: "La Pampa y la Puna" (The Plains and the Mountains)
Freire: "Ay, Ay, Ay"
Sumac: "Especially For You"
Vivanco: "Montana"
Sumac: "Didn't You Know I Loved You?"
Sumac: "Huayno"
Ballesteros: "La Molina" (The Mill Song)

Encore used beginning March 7th:
May/Vivanco: "Jungla" (Mambo)
The back-up musicians were:
Stephen Gaboury—Musical Director and pianist
Peter Valentine—synthesizers and trumpet
Jeff Golub—guitar
Lincoln Goines—bass
Kim Plainfield—drums
Roger Squitero—percussion

The musicians were individually excellent and, as a group, they provided Yma with solid support, playing the colorful arrangements with verve and élan. Shows were a little ragged at first, but gained polish as the engagement went on, and altogether, the quality of Yma's back-up had much to do with the success of her set. The band needed a few performances to become familiar with Yma's improvisational flights; she would often change music and rhythmic patterns on what seemed at first to be whims. The musicians loved Yma and worked well with her even though she was sometimes curt with them during performance, criticizing them to cover her own mistakes or inadequacies.

The Ballroom appearances were also the first time Yma had ever worked with a body microphone, which she enjoyed very much since it freed her hands. It was clipped onto her gown with a battery-pack that was attached to the waistband at the back of the skirt. Freeman Gunter, who was present for most shows, remembered one evening when the mic failed to kick-in. "It was at the beginning of the show, during 'High Andes.' I was standing at the back of the club, which is a very long, narrow, deep room. You know the kind of sound amplified rock bands can make. Well, she began to really sing-out and I realized that what I was hearing was the real voice. It was a thrill to hear the power she was capable of—it carried easily over the band and back to where I was. After a while, the mic kicked in. After the show, I went backstage and asked Yma if she had known what had happened. 'Oh yes', she said, 'I knew right away. So I sang out.'"

Tapes of shows given on February 17, 19, and 27, March 7, and 8, show that, overall, Yma's singing improved as the run progressed. By March the show had tightened into a smooth-running unit. There were still some mishaps, however. On March 7th, Yma announced that she would like to offer the "Jungla" Mambo as her encore—confessing, however, that she had not sung it "in a thousand years" and might have trouble remembering the melody. Because of this, she explained, she would follow the band. Melodically, "Jungla" is a very chromatic, complicated song for the singer. Aside from a few high notes that she attempted but did not reach, she sang the piece exactly as she had recorded it over thirty years earlier. The botched high notes mattered little to the audience who cheered each attempt. The next night, Yma decided to sing only nine numbers, and gave the audience an opportunity to choose between "La Molina" (The Mill Song)—which was listed as part of the show—or the "Jungla" Mambo. The audience chose "Jungla." After the same speech about not remembering the song, she launched into the piece, only to become hopelessly lost. Even though the musical director pounded out the notes on the piano as inconspicuously as possible, Yma never found her way back into the melody.

Aside from the occasional misstep, Yma was consistent in the delivery of her music and the acrobatics she chose to insert. As the run progressed, however, and after she grew more comfortable, Yma was more daring and abandoned in her attack of notes above high A and more adventurous in her ornamental improvisations. By March 7th, when these moments had been completely integrated into the music and strongly supported by the band, it was obvious that Yma was enjoying herself and, in a few isolated moments, even matched her brilliance of three decades earlier. If the run had not been extended, it would have been only one week's listeners who would have seen at first hand the reasons for Yma's fame in the 1950s.

Each night at the Ballroom, Yma managed to span at least three octaves, from the baritone D to the coloratura soprano D. As if a clouded mirror were being held up to the audience, she offered listeners a misty reflection of the Yma Sumac of 1950. At such moments, Yma would stand poised, waiting, and then launch into whatever acrobatics and high notes would come out of her throat that night. Oddly, missed notes or garbled, cracked staccati rarely detracted from the overall delivery of the songs. Whatever came out Yma cleverly integrated into the expressivity of the melodic line. High notes shy of the pitch were turned into "coos." High staccati of questionable pitch or direction, or choked, were turned into strong rhythmical accents.

One of the reasons for the success of Yma's Ballroom set was the choice of material which, fortunately, brought back some of her earlier Incan repertoire. It included five songs from her albums: "Ataypura" (High Andes) from *Voice of the Xtabay*, "Montana" from *Legend of the Sun Virgin*, "La Pampa Y La Puna" (The Plains and the Mountains) from *Fuego Del Ande*, and (later) "Jungla" from *Mambo!* These selections satisfied the many fans of her recordings.

Although short, the Sumac show was obviously carefully planned and for the most part offered good, solid entertainment. The only reservations concerned the star herself. Depending on what one was expecting, Yma's voice had, or had not, survived the ravages of time. Certainly anyone who expected to hear the Xtabay voice of 1950 was disappointed.

Another problem was the costume Yma insisted on wearing. Yma had been adamant about wearing one of her 1950s nightclub outfits, now let-out for her fuller figure, which she felt *looked* like an Yma Sumac costume. Unfortunately, the diaphanous outfit had been designed for Yma when she had the figure to display a bare midriff. During the first shows Yma left the outer robe open. She was finally convinced by Alan Eichler to keep it pinned shut. Although that helped, the lavender material was see-through and Yma's unfortunate midriff seemed to draw the eye irresistibly. Nonetheless, dressed in a skirt and top, sheathed in a diaphanous violet outer robe trimmed in silver with batwing sleeves, and with platform heels, eyes a-glitter, beauty marks penciled in, brilliant dangle earrings and inch-long fake fingernails, Yma arrived feeling ready to re-conquer New York audiences—and she did.

Audiences were confronted with definite changes in the Sumac voice since her last appearances in New York, in 1975. Her chest register was now quite raspy, although the upper-middle voice was clean and well focused as was the high register for the most part. When ascending to a sustained high D, however, now Yma's tendency was to drop all diaphragm support, thin-out the tone to an almost inaudible hum or a sinusoidal wail, as in "My Real True Love."

There was also no muscular ability left to decrescendo a note smoothly from loud to soft. This was now done with bumpy, even startling, gradations. The once strong and reliable diaphragm muscles would occasionally not connect, resulting in a thin, wavery or unsupported hummed tone. Because of the nature of these tiny, thin notes, Yma, cleverly convinced her audiences that they were outrageously high or inhuman. The famous Sumac "growl," in any event, remained clear and impressive for its height and intensity. High staccati, when sung with her throat relaxed and open, were just as pure and pointed as always.

Oddly, in a song such as "Didn't You Know I Loved You?" and "Huayno," Yma's diaphragm support seemed quite solid as she would take off in difficult, high, growling phrases and intricate flights of staccati up to at least high C and C-sharp. She also would often ornament the melody line by rapidly flipping the voice in clean triplet figures. Nonetheless, it was obvious to those familiar with the Sumac voice that it could no longer move with the exhilaratingly easy, nonchalant facility of before, and that the core of the voice had decreased in range and quality.

Unfortunately, by 1987, Yma's singing centered on muscular manipulation. (As the years progressed, it became apparent that much of Yma's singing relied on a manipulation of certain throat muscles. This was especially evident on the television appearance made during the Ballroom engagement, where one could see Yma physically manipulating throat muscles in order to sing some of the highest notes and effects.)

It was in the middle area of the voice that Yma had most of her problems. Registers were more pronounced. In particular the notes of E, F, G, A, and B-flat in the middle register were very weak and could only take a certain amount of pressure. Above that area—to the G at the top of the staff, however, Yma could still pro-

Yma at the Ballroom 1987
(photo by Joel Kudler)

duce a certain amount of power. After G, however, the rest of the top range was perilously delicate, and her use of it tenuous. Sustained high phrases in this area had to be carefully manipulated. Most failed high notes were due to Yma (often audibly) choking them off by the exertion of auxiliary throat muscles. Despite occasional support problems, which underlined Yma's register changes, not once did she sing out of tune. Even in tiring, sustained and lyrical songs, such as "Montana," the pitch was always true. Her ear remained as acute as it was when she began her career.

Even more importantly, three of the up-beat songs written for the show, "My Real True Love," "Didn't You Know I Loved You?" and "Huayno," were good showpieces. Catchy and dance-like, they had good structure, rhythm and arrangements—if not lyrics. Yma was not the only one to shine in these three numbers. The supportive band delivered aggressive, foot-stomping accompaniment, giving Yma ample opportunity to show her current battery of vocal exotica and tricks. These included the famous "growl," high staccati flights, pecked-at top notes, coos, slides, wails, emphatic register breaks, hums, and quarter-tone shadings—all presented in new, novel, and non-Incan settings. During performances of "Huayno," Yma introduced a new effect of "fluttering" up a scale to a high note. This was a new sound in the Sumac repertoire of effects and is similar to, but is not, gargling.

Because of the audience's unfamiliarity with these pieces and because they had never been recorded, depending on how she felt, Yma could and did often simplify them as needed, without the listeners being any the wiser.

"La Molina" (The Mill Song) had occasional, faded bursts of early Sumac brilliance—especially in flights of improvisatory staccati, while "Montana" had changed little over 37 years—except in the ease with which it was sung. Unfortunately, the simple Chilean song, "Ay, Ay, Ay" was ill-advisedly turned into a hybrid, pseudo-dramatic, operatic soliloquy. This mad scene-like interpretation emerged as only self-serving. (This song was originally made famous by the 1923 recording by the Spanish operatic tenor Miguel Fleta, the creator of the "Calaf" in Puccini's opera *Turandot*). Fleta's disk sold 100,000 copies, a sensational figure for that time.) Basically, the song is simple and is meant to be sung that way.

"Ataypura" (High Andes) made the listener long, wistfully, for the abandon and audacity of the 1950 recording. Nonetheless, one was grateful for its inclusion in the program. Always considered Yma's signature tune, it was all that was left from the original, imaginative and colorfully evocative Incan repertoire. Welcome too, was the attempt at the bravura "Jungla" mambo, representative of one of Yma's finest albums.

One of the best-received numbers was "Huyano." With great charm, and in a dusky contralto speaking voice, Yma would quietly explain that the Huayno was the national dance of Peru and listeners were invited to "dance as they feel."

Having attended some of those Ballroom performances, and having listened to tapes of all the others, it is apparent to me that Yma gauged her singing to the response of the audience. It was the cheering and obvious enjoyment of the audience that drove Yma to try and outdo herself in fanciful flights of coloratura (even as she remained formal and aloof; though elegant in her graciousness in thanking audiences).

When Yma reached her improvisatory sections it was also obvious that they were her favorite moments. Because of this "trading" with audiences, Yma often provided her listeners with some excellent performances. On March 7th, a particularly good night for Yma, she sang a rendition of "La Molina" (The Mill Song) that seriously rivaled the one she recorded in 1959, twenty-eight years earlier.

It was interesting to watch Yma's relationship with audiences at The Ballroom. She was always formal in her remarks describing the songs and coolly gracious in thanking patrons for their applause. It became evident as the set progressed, however, that the degree of reaction from the audience powerfully influenced the quality of Yma's offerings to them. One night, as Yma reached an improvisatory spot in "My Real True Love," a fan who had obviously seen the show before and knew what was coming, screamed out "Go Girl!" Far from disturbing Yma or disrupting her presentation, this impelled Yma to further ornament her usual improvisation. This odd relationship of formality on Yma's part and informality on the audience's part provides some hints as to some of the reasons for the wild, almost ecstatic responses of the crowds that went to see Yma.

Yma's reserve is never more obvious than when on stage. But, therein lies one of Yma's secrets. She reserves all overt stage movement for improvisatory scat sections. The sudden combination of vocal fireworks and subtle physical movement prompted by the music is stunning for its understatement and for its ability to drive audiences wild. And for all the impromptu feeling of such movements, they are extremely well calculated.

This stage demeanor was not a new development; rather, a continuation of Yma's distinctive practice of economizing stage movement, as she established it in her famous 1950s shows. *People* magazine called this type of movement "prowling around the stage striking exaggerated poses." (3/16/87)

As in the 1950s, at the Ballroom in 1987, graceful, subtle hand and arm gestures dominated stage action. Any overt movement was well calculated to highlight scat and coloratura flights in her music. At such moments Yma would scoop her chiffon outer-robe up and over her arm in a graceful sweeping gesture. Always with the music prompting her, Yma would position her arms, hands, and even fingers in ritualistic-looking positions as she rhythmically swayed back and forth. Combined with the driving music of scat sections, the visual effect is mesmerizing. At moments like these Yma appeared to be in a kind of trance-like rapture. An audience soon learned that overt movement signaled the beginning of fireworks so they were quickly primed for their arrival. Reinforcing this training of the audience is the consistency of the reserve and feminine elegance, which dominated Yma's physical movement on stage.

During the five weeks Yma was in New York, few days went by without some mention of her in a newspaper or a magazine. Not since the 1950s had she received such publicity coverage in a major American music capitol. Yma experienced a renaissance.

"A proto-new wave avant-garde diva" famous in the 1950s for her "free-floating incantatory flights accompanied by kitsch orchestral arrangements." (Stephen Holden, *New York Times* 2/20/87). "(Although) . . . her Peruvian yodeling now sounds like mainstream New Wave, Yma remains a mysterious relic from another world." (David Hutchings, *People* 3/16/87). *The Village Voice* called Yma "Mambo Queen, Inca Princess…the invention of a different age." (2/24/87).

Newspapers and magazines nationwide proclaimed the event and, a real coup for Yma, *Time* magazine (3/2/87) honored her with a current, color photograph and a short column on their "People" page. *Time* noted that, despite the continuing controversy about her Incan heritage, "no one ever disputed the fact that Yma Sumac's voice was one of the world's sonic wonders."

Of all the voluminous publicity in New York during this time, *Time* was the only publication to correctly note that during her prime, Yma's vocal range was four octaves. All other releases, articles, reviews and interviews, stressed the mythic five-octave range. Readers were expected to believe that Yma still had such a vocal range after 45 years of professional performing. The fact that Yma, herself, continued to encourage this belief only served to undermine the seriousness of her artistic intentions and value before she even opened her mouth to sing.

The articles that sprang into newspapers at this time repeated old legends, offered fact twined with fiction, and occasionally provided rare glimpses of insight. Most of the information and misinformation was provided by Yma at her February 12th press conference. With impressive insouciance she wove her semi-articulate chatter into a tapestry of muddled information. For instance, it now appeared that the Metropolitan Opera *had* been interested in Yma. "The Met offered me $5,000, but I was already making $25,000 in Vegas."

As had been true the entirety of Yma's career, if one had the patience to weed through and separate the facts from the myths, her genuine concern for aesthetics in her music, life, and the image she chose to promote became evident. So did the amazingly complex character traits that made up the Sumac persona.

"You must always have dignity as (an) artist . . . ." (*Village Voice* 2/24/87)

"On stage, I am the artist. I command the people to be quiet. I don't say one word. No, no, no. My manner tells them to be quiet. But when I am not performing, I am so shy. I do not want anyone to look at me. We all have two personalities, you know . . . "(*Washington Post* 3/2/87)

"'All the big stars have come to see Yma.' she says proudly. 'Virginia Mayo, Aldo Ray.' . . . And when told that Cyndi Lauper adores her music, she shrugs and asks, 'Who's he?'" (*People* 3/16/87)

"I haven't heard most of the people I am supposed to have influenced. In the 1950s the singer I admired the most was Doris Day, and today it is Barbara Streisand. She sings with so much feeling." (*New York Times* 2/28/87)

Occasionally, there was an odd, personal revelation, or an unguarded example of ego and attitude.

"If you keep clean your intestines, and don't drink or smoke, it reflects in your face. I do my fastings with water or apples four times a year and have regular colonics. I also keep my mind clean . . . by reading good books.

"Offstage, I may choose some hats to wear for interviews. But Yma would never wear a hat on stage. Yma wears only a crown." (*New York Native* 3/9/87)

"There are many beautiful singers, but there is only one Yma." (*Time* 3/2/87)

"But don't ask her if being a mere farm girl she was intimidated by Hollywood (in the early 1950s). 'I was a farm girl with culture' she explains. 'No hillbilly. I was well educated in a convent—not as a nun, but to learn obedience, how to sew, to be a good wife in the future.' (ibid)

"As I leave, (Yma's) downing squid and telling me, for some reason, that the two songs that make her cry are 'To Each His Own' and "Try to Remember'. I now know the secret of the Incas—behave exquisitely and you are a Peruvian princess." (*Village Voice* 2/24/87)

Writing for the gay publication *New York Native*, Joe Dolce addressed the problem of getting to know Yma in his 3/9/87 article. "Modesty has never been her forte. Mystery is . . . her life is still steeped in more fiction than fact. Even now . . . Sumac is apologizing for her raspy voice during last night's show. She has a cold, she says, but hasn't once blown her nose, coughed, sneezed, or sniffled. Fact or fiction? Who knows? . . . In her day, Sumac was a beauty and a bitch, an exotic blend of Delores Del Rio, Barbara Streisand and Louis Armstrong . . . Today, Sumac is still the high priestess of panache . . . Interviewing Sumac is about as revealing as the liner notes on her albums—rarely does she veer from the official rattle. Though she charmed me with grand-motherly warmth and pulled me down next to her on the couch to chat, she fields questions as deftly as Ronald Reagan at a press conference. Even Eichler, her manager, confesses that, after two years, 'I still don't know what really goes on in her mind.'"

During interviews Yma would often talk about her new compositions. "I've been singing since about nine and have composed about 5,000 songs. I record melodies as they come into my head on a cassette recorder and later I write the lyrics and work with an arranger. My music has always blended the feel of the Peruvian Andes with contemporary musical arrangements." (*New York Times*, 2/20/87)

People magazine printed an article with photographs (one of Yma cooing at a bird perched on her outstretched finger). Huge posters and placards appeared all over Manhattan, heralding Yma's impending return. These sported a wonderful, carefully retouched photo of Yma, reminiscent of those taken at the height of her fame in 1951. Refreshingly, no mention was made of Peru or the Incas on these advertisements, only her name and information about The Ballroom engagement. Previous poster backgrounds of Incan gods, ruins and erupting volcanoes were replaced by Hollywood spotlights and meandering crowds of people. Exotic and immediately riveting, Yma's photo was a clever, atmospheric bust-shot of the singer looking up towards the left-hand corner of the poster. Turbaned, bejeweled and with her "come and get me" look, this sensuality was contrasted by the supplicating positioning of her uplifted hands, ritualistically held near her chin—as if in prayer to the Sun God for a good box office.

While they lasted, large posters were given free to patrons at The Ballroom which Yma would then autograph after performances. Although most people thought the photo originated from 1950s archives, actually it was a current photograph taken by W.G. Harris in Hollywood and masterfully retouched. It was used for the cover drawing of The Ballroom program as well as for most reviews and articles. As such it served its purpose well, perfectly suggesting Yma's inherent mystery and allure.

Reviews of the Ballroom appearances were generally warm. There were a few however, that questioned the necessity of an Yma Sumac comeback.

Writing for *Variety* (2/25/87), Jose found Yma's set "highly palatable" but noted that the cheering section made more noise than the Peruvian diva. He also felt that the show surrounding Yma was more exotic than the singer herself. "Sumac brings in an entirely different look to her Ballroom recital. There are a couple of oversized Incan figures on each side of the stage. Rear slide projections of her native Andes, plus rarely heard song selections, giving her turn an unusual facade.

"Having a so greatly publicized vocal range makes it mandatory that Sumac use as much of it as possible, although her only number warranting that outsized span is her opening Peruvian paean. The rest of her tunes are love songs in English and Spanish. The natural base of her voice seems to be in the mezzo range, which seems particularly suited to the laments of some self-written tunes in the latter part of her act."

Jose found the band excellent, commenting that they "give the act a lot of drive and added interest."

Stephen Holden of the *New York Times* (2/19/87) remembered the original 1950s Sumac show as a "campy, sexy, 'south of the border' stylization of grand opera, in which she portrayed a primitive diva mystically in tune with the forces of nature." Although the current Ballroom performances were less extravagant, they were still "highly theatrical" as was Yma's stage presence. "Time has severely diminished Ms. Sumac's once-leonine lower register while leaving her high coloratura functional though weakened. Imperious and at moments more than a trifle silly, Ms. Sumac delivered a performance that evoked the showmanship of Liberace and the stubborn glamour of a fading diva."

Don Nelson, writing for the *New York Daily News* (2/24/87), judged Yma "a unique musical experience. (She) sings words but they are really of secondary importance. It is her vocal gymnastics that are the main attraction. However, this inaugural evening the octaves diminished....Those she did manage were quite mellow, especially in the upper register. Sumac explained from the stage that she was laboring under the effects of a cold. There was also a suggestion of limited rehearsal time. Though she graciously praised her musicians, she said 'Tomorrow they are going to be much better.' But even this could not still the crowd's ardor. When her set ended, they shouted 'More! More! More! as if possessed by the gods—and the goddess on stage.

"One cannot tell whether these conditions will prevail for every night of Sumac's three-week stay at the Ballroom but let us hope. Such audience abandon is a show in itself."

The *Village Voice* (3/3/87) found Yma "a riveting, if bizarre, stage presence with her midriff hanging out."

Along the same line, *The Native* printed a harshly critical review. Under the March 23rd headline, "Incan Ruins," Martin Schaeffer wrote that the February 19th show found him "somewhat bemused. I wasn't bored, but by all the gods of the Incas, I certainly wasn't royally entertained.

"Sumac's vocal range is now perhaps a mere two-and-one-half octaves, despite the excuse of a cold with which she excused her performance. One couldn't even fudge and say she still has the vestige of secure lower chest tones. The middle and top are in better shape, but the clarity and precision which marked Sumac's voice in her hey day are definitely gone.

"Which brings one to a serious question. Did Sumac approach this comeback seriously, or is she trading on her camp value? When you appear in a diaphanous mauve sari through which your potbelly can clearly be seen, you're tempting fate. And when you flank yourself with two enormous ersatz Incan gods in buff styrofoam, the question of whether you're presenting camp or art is obviously answered. Of course, grand posturing and attitude to spare can add a touch of humor (or is it insult) to the evening."

Contrasting this was the review that appeared in the *New York Post* (2/20/87). Under the heading, "Yma Can Still Scale The Heights," Bob Harrington wrote: "Few legends can stand the scrutiny of time and on that score alone, Yma Sumac holds her own. . . . Time has tattered both ends of her famed . . . range . . . but the unique Sumac can still amaze fans and strangers alike with her avian vocalizations.

"Framed by massive pre-Columbian sculptures, standing against a backdrop of slides of Machu Picchu, Sumac remains an imposing figure. She possesses an electric presence, even without the huge orchestras and stage effects that were once automatic components in her shows. And however lessened by time, the voice still marvels . . .

"Throughout, there's a high camp patina and deep humor to Sumac's performances that is undeniably captivating. She is at once a vocal wonder and an extraordinary entertainer who palms an audience the way Houdini palmed coins."

Time magazine (3/2/87) succinctly noted that after a period of semi-retirement, Yma was back " . . . wowing audiences again with her guttural growls and birdlike trills . . . "

Combined with her idiosyncratic way of singing, which David Hutchings of *People* magazine (3/16/87) colorfully described as "a weird mixture of chirps, wails, moans, scat noises and coos . . . in a hybrid dialect of no known derivation . . . " Yma's stage conduct provided an unusual cabaret act of formal elegance, as unique now as it was when she first appeared on American shores over forty years ago.

In the midst of the 1987 Ballroom engagement, on March 18th, Yma made an appearance on David Letterman's late-night television show singing "Ataypura" (High Andes). This was the 12:30 AM Letterman show, following Johnny Carson's Tonight Show on NBC. Yma had not sung her "Incan" music on American television since her Hollywood Palace appearance in 1964, twenty-three years earlier, after her return from Russia. (Her brief appearance on the 1972 Fol de Rol does not count as "Incan" because of the diluted, almost unrecognizable version of "Taita Inty" [Hymn to the Sun] used that evening.)

Letterman set an ironic, comedic tone for Yma's segment early in his show, when announcing his guests for that evening; reaching Yma's name, he turned to his musical director-cum-sidekick and asked, with ostentatious puzzlement, "Who is this woman?"

Her performance on the show has her in good voice for that time and shows her as an enigmatic, anachronistic presence. Her performance of "Ataypura" (High Andes) for that studio audience was some of the best singing Yma offered to New Yorkers during this five-week stay. The second section of the song boasted the staccati high D's Yma was famous for, and her conclusion differed from that used at the Ballroom in being more grand and operatic.

Yma is charming during a miniscule interview with Letterman, who finds Yma highly amusing. Asked about her famous five-octave range, she explained, "I have five octaves because I was born in the high Andes, and in the high Andes the air makes you expand your lungs." When Letterman asked Yma to demonstrate the high and low ends of her five octaves, Yma looked confused and replied, "But, I did."

Letterman presses. "Let me hear the lowest part again. Can you do that?" Giggling a bit uncomfortably, Yma confesses apologetically, "I don't know if I can. At this time, is very difficult to sing." At which point she loudly cleared her throat. "Oh, that was good," Letterman said. "Now let me hear the high." Yma and the studio audience broke into laughter. Letterman's banter did not suit the seriousness with which Yma typically approached herself and her music, yet she managed to accept it in good spirit, and even though she was on for only about five minutes, and late in the show at that, her appearance was surely a sort of success. The studio audience evidently enjoyed her novelty and cheered her singing.

As far as audiences were concerned, all was hunky-dory with Yma's Ballroom appearances. Behind the scenes, however, there were some rough patches. They arose because Yma's manager, Alan Eichler, who had come to New York to be with Yma, had to return to the West Coast soon after Yma opened. Alan would not be able to return for a number of weeks. Realizing that someone would need to manage Yma, he enlisted the help of a friend, Freeman Gunter, a free-lance writer and former editor-in-chief of *Mandate* magazine. Fortunately, Freeman had time on his hands and been a long-time fan of Yma's. His story of the weeks during the 1987 Ballroom engagement is full of humor, candor, affection and occasionally anger and frustration. I interviewed Freeman in New York City in 1988.

Freeman had originally met Yma in the early 1970s when he was writing an article on the *Miracles* album for *Michael's Thing* (at the time one of the small, upscale publications that dealt with the New York club scene). He met her again at a press conference she gave on February 12th, the Thursday before her opening at The Ballroom for this engagement. Freeman has vivid memories of the press conference.

"It was fascinating. Most of the time she told the same disjointed story—and she is not a good storyteller. But now she was saying that she had written some 5,000 songs—which makes Cole Porter like some kind of amateur!"

Alan re-introduced Yma to Freeman after Freeman agreed to take care of Yma. Freeman remembered Yma as "charming."

Alan explained to Freeman what his duties would be. It had been decided that Yma would autograph copies of her recordings and sell them to patrons after her shows at The Ballroom. Originally, the management of the club told Yma that she couldn't sell her records and tapes at the club. "She pitched a fit!" Freeman laughed, "She was screaming at me—'You go tell them I sell the records!' and I had to act as a mediator between the two. Filipe liked Yma, and he said, let her sell. So we did. Yma was happy because she got her way."

It was decided, however, that no records would be sold after the first show each night, or after the last show on Saturdays because it over crowded the dining room and the waiters had difficulty setting-up and taking-down the tables. Also, Saturday diners at the last show, who had paid top dollar for the food, would complain when they were mobbed at their tables by ardent Yma fans.

Freeman was to hang on to any moneys received from the selling of records. He was to count the money and enter it into a little notebook that he had made up for that purpose. Alan told Freeman not to give Yma any money unless she specifically asked for it because he preferred to have it all accounted for rather than having Yma spend it all shopping. This last stipulation also had to do with the fact that Yma owed Alan money, since he had advanced her the cash to buy crates of her recordings and tapes from Capitol Records, on the assumption that they would be allowed to sell her recordings at the club.

To help Freeman adjust to his new temporary job and as part of the training period, Alan took him to the final rehearsal Yma was to have with the band on the Sunday before her Tuesday opening. Although technically it would have been considered a "dress rehearsal," Yma does not usually have a real dress rehearsal. (A dress rehearsal is when a program is run straight-through as if for an audience. This gives the artists an idea of the pacing needed to keep energy levels up and how the program runs in general. Opening night was usually Yma's dress rehearsal.)

Freeman was understandably excited about going to the rehearsal and saw at once that the band was going to work very well with Yma. Yma was excited too, although not for the same reason. She was excited because she was wearing a pair of chino pants she had bought for $10.00 on 14th Street and was very pleased that she had found such a bargain.

"I learned very quickly that she loves little bargains, and buying little tchotchkes," commented Freeman, "like a little clock that looked like a teapot that she had in her apartment. When I first went there she showed it to me and said, 'Isn't it wonderful?' It was the ugliest thing I had ever seen. But, she loved it."

Dressed casually for the rehearsal with a hat pulled down to cover her hair, Yma put the band through their paces. "She didn't really sing, but every once in a while she would do a phrase here or there to show how something was to go, or for tempo changes. When she did sing out she sounded stupendous. I was very excited. I thought she sounded better than she did when she gave her Town Hall concerts in 1975. She seemed to work well with the musicians; there was no 'star' stuff. She'd correct them if necessary but if she liked something they did, she would say, 'Oh! That's wonderful, do that!' She was just one of the boys when she rehearsed with them."

Opening night, however, found Freeman disappointed. "I felt the show was sloppy and obviously not tightly rehearsed. There were many pauses when Yma couldn't remember what she was singing next. And she sounded odd—not what I had expected after hearing the bits I had heard in rehearsal. But now it seems that Yma sings better when she doesn't have the pressure of a performance. The bottom voice was OK, but the middle was all blown out. The top was OK too, when she went up there."

The second show of the first night was added at the last minute because the first had sold-out. Because of the haste with which it was added and the lack of advance announcement, the room was only about half-full.

"But, I can remember" said Freeman, "sitting there and thinking, 'Well, here we are in this half-empty club—and she sounds awful.' Then the next night, it took off. The reviews, by some miracle, were good. I mean, I had seen the same show as the critics, and I thought it was pretty grim—even if she did do cute things like pointing up in the air—to make you think she was singing really high—it was still pretty bad."

At first, the Ballroom waiters hated Yma's show. They had never seen her before opening night and a couple of them were heard to comment, "Oh God! We have to put up with that for three weeks?" "But," counters Freeman, "that was before anyone realized she was going to be such fabulous business. Later the waiters became big fans. They worshipped her. When Yma and I would be selling and signing records, they would bring us free drinks—fresh orange juice for Yma and Scotch for me. They were really wonderful."

Near the end of the first week Alan left, and Freeman was on full duty, alone.

There was a definite routine for the evenings when Freeman accompanied Yma to the club. First, Yma insisted that he call her at her hotel, which was several minutes away in Greenwich Village, to let Yma know he was on his way.

"I *always* had to call first, I couldn't just arrive at a pre-designated time. When I would get there she would already have her makeup and her sunglasses on. She put her face on in the apartment—a little studio with a Murphy bed."

The apartment belonged to a girlfriend of one of the managers of The Ballroom, who had been persuaded to sub-let it to Yma. Freeman would then collect Yma, her coat, and a series of bags which contained things she took with her to the club, and go outside to catch a taxi.

"I'll never forget the first night," said Freeman. "We had this Cuban cab driver who recognized Yma immediately. This didn't seem to surprise her at all. She really acts as if the whole world should know her because she is such an enormous star. Yet we all know that she lives anonymously in a little court apartment in Los Angeles. Her neighbors just think of her as Mrs. Vivanco, a divorcee. They don't even know she was a singer. 'Perita' is what her friends call her. That's her real nickname. It's short for Emperatriz. That is what I was to call her in public when she didn't want to be recognized. If she's not being Yma Sumac, she doesn't want to be recognized as Yma Sumac because that takes too much energy.

"Anyway, after the driver recognized her they began to talk to each other in Spanish and I was able to follow most of the conversation. He was saying things like, 'You're a great star and I'm just a cab driver' and she was saying things like 'You must be the best you can be, no one is unimportant.' Yma was in a good mood and she was really very sweet with him. While they were talking, I noticed there was a Spanish newspaper on the driver's seat next to him opened to an article of Yma with a beautiful 1950s picture of her. It was a wonderful send-off for Yma that night.

"When we arrived at the stage door of The Ballroom, I saw that that there was a group of people waiting for Yma. Every night before the show, at least ten people would be waiting outside the club hoping that Yma would sign autographs before the show. She was unfailingly sweet to fans wanting autographs."

(Joel Kudler, who took photographs from side-stage of The Ballroom while Yma was performing, was amazed at Yma's willingness to stay and sign autograph after autograph. "She talked with each person," he said, "and listened to what they said. And she looked them straight in the eye. I can't tell you the number of people that wanted their picture taken with her. And all the fans wanted to touch her. That didn't seem to bother her at all. She could be very physical with fans. Once, when she and I were just standing and waiting, she took my hand and squeezed it. It is very unusual for artists to do things like that.")

"I really think she loved them as much as they loved her, and she appreciated their devotion," Freeman continued. "Anyway, we got out of the cab and Yma was standing in the street talking to the driver through the side window in the front. Finally, she said (rather dramatically) to him, 'Would you like to see what Yma Sumac looks like today?' The driver excitedly nodded and said, 'Oh yes!' So she whipped off her sunglasses and stuck her face in the window. The cab driver dropped his jaw in shock, crossed himself and said 'Madre de Dios!' It was just fabulous!"

Yma usually got to the club around 7:15 or 7:30. At that time, Blossom Dearie, a much-admired cabaret singer, very popular with Ballroom audiences, was finishing her show and so Yma and Freeman would tiptoe up the back stairs to the dressing room—which was only inches from the stage area. "Blossom is very temperamental" Freeman explained, "and she demands absolute silence during her act." At first Yma was irritated at having to sneak around and asked sarcastically, "Who is this woman? She puts me to sleep." But, after hearing Blossom a few nights, Yma changed her tune and commented quietly to Freeman, "Her voice is very pure," and she became fascinated with what Blossom was doing on stage.

When settled in the dressing room, Yma would usually have some soup. At first, she had decided the soup at the club was too fatty and creamy. Actually, it was nothing more than pureed vegetables and the club management was finally able to convince Yma of this. If, however, Yma decided that she did not want the club's soup, Freeman would go out and buy some Chinese won ton soup. Yma would eat the won tons, but leave the broth, which she felt was too salty. "She is very health conscious," Freeman explained, "and always talks about things like fasting, roughage, bowel movements, and cleaning out your system."

After her soup, there usually was a period of time when Yma had nothing to do but to change into her costume. Rosemary, the assistant to the Peruvian chef, Filipe, and a lovely, charming woman, volunteered to be Yma's dresser. Freeman had no idea why she volunteered. "I don't know whether she just loved Yma, or had a stake in the club and wanted to make sure things ran smoothly, or what. But it was a very nice thing for her to do. I mean, this was normally the time she would be going home. Her day was over. But, she stayed. Not only that, she stayed until Yma was put in a taxi after the last show. Rosemary also helped Yma off stage. There are steps and you tend to be blinded by the lights when you first come off the stage. She also guarded the dressing room while Yma was performing."

Usually Freeman would leave the dressing room just before the show, when Rosemary came and Yma dressed. But one night, near the end of the run, Rosemary had to leave early because of a prior engagement that could not be changed, and Freeman took over. Yma was being very nice and so Freeman said he would watch the dressing room while she was on stage. The band had begun to play the introductory "Tumpa!" (Earthquake) and Freeman helped Yma put on the body mic. At this point the mic was still off. "The man in the sound booth never turned it on until her entrance," Freeman explained, "If he had, it would have picked up any conversation in the dressing room and broadcast it through the house." As if he wasn't there, Yma began to prepare to go on stage. "She went into what almost seemed like a trance for a minute or two," Freeman said. "Then she began to warm up her voice. It was fabulous to watch her get the mechanism ready. She was like a racehorse, or an athlete, or a machine. She would clear her throat violently several times and then while pacing the room, she would bark these yelpy high notes to get the top of the voice open. Then she abruptly stopped went out and did the show. It was fascinating to see her churn up that energy and blast that top open with those violent, barking noises."

In the beginning of the engagement, after the second show and while Yma was changing, Freeman would go out front and set up a table where Yma's LPs and cassette tapes would be sold. Yma would then come out dressed in a little Chinese wrapper with colorful dragons embroidered on the back and doused with Joy, the perfume she preferred at the time. She would sit with Freeman and sip orange juice, signing autographs while he sold the records and tapes. The records and tapes (at $11.00) sold like hot-cakes. "We had crates of them downstairs," Freeman recalled, "Yma had gotten them from Capitol Records with an artist discount, for about $.33 a piece. It is a common practice for artists to sell their records in clubs for more than it cost them, so that they can make a little money."

By March, however, Yma had sold so many records that they were running out so the signing table had to be stopped. Instead, Yma pre-signed all the copies that were left and an advertisement was put into the Ballroom programs telling patrons that if they wanted to buy one of Yma's pre-signed recordings they should speak to their waiter.

During the signing, Yma was charming to each person and it was evident that she enjoyed meeting them. Still flattered by requests for her autograph, she would sign people's arms, old Playbills of "Flahooley," original 78 pressings of her 1950s albums, and studio photos that fans would bring with them. Yma even autographed the back of a woman's expensive white leather coat. Often Yma would sit for over an hour signing.

Occasionally, however, there was an odd lack of communication between Alan Eichler and Yma. One night, near the end of the run, after the show a group of fans had been told by Alan to wait outside the stage door and that Yma would come out to sign autographs. After waiting for almost an hour in the cold, one of them happened to notice that Yma was inside, eating. After a confrontation with the Maitre'd, he was finally persuaded to tell Yma that a group of people had been waiting for her outside, for over an hour. Yma rose from the table and flashed a look of anger at Alan, who had forgotten to tell her that anyone was waiting. She left the table, went to the group, who had been brought inside, spoke to each, and autographed whatever items they had brought with them. Only after the last person did she return to her dinner.

Sometimes she tired of it. "She would shoot me a look," remembers Freeman, "out of the corner of those eyes, a look that said 'Are we done? Is this the end? Can I go home now?' But she sure enjoyed selling those records—mainly because it was her pocket money. I got $1.00 commission for each record sold. That's why they cost $11.00. That was Alan's idea. It was good he came up with that idea because it was the only money I got during that time—aside from $100 that was supposed to cover cabs, meals and stuff. It was my understanding that I was to receive a small salary for doing the job, but I never did."

After Yma and Freeman were done selling and signing, Yma would change into street clothes and Freeman would take her back to the hotel in a taxi. Sometimes, if Yma wanted, they would go to a neighborhood diner for something to eat. "On those nights I'd get home around 3:00 in the morning. Being used to a 9–5 schedule, my inner-clock was all confused. Once or twice when we did that, Yma would relax and be herself. But even then, there really is no such thing as socializing with Yma Sumac. She is always La Sumac, and you are always the audience. That gets boring after a while."

Everything was running smoothly until the Saturday night of the first week, Freeman's first solo night without Alan's assistance. The musicians' contract stipulated that they were to be paid at the end of each week—after the second show on Saturday. Yma's contract, however, stated she was to be paid a percentage of the receipts two times, once midway through the engagement and again at the end of the run. Had Yma not been successful at The Ballroom, the situation could have been disastrous since she was to pay the musicians out of her money and they each received $1,550 a week.

The management brought the musicians' check for Yma to sign after the first show that Saturday night. It was to be immediately cashed and given as cash to the band.

"This was no surprise to Yma," Freeman told me, "she knew what the deal was and exactly what was in her contract. But all of a sudden she started screaming, 'All this money! And for what?! No money for the STAR and I work like a mule!' she was yelling so loud you'd have thought she was being mugged. Then she said that her contract was shown to her at the last minute, and that all this was a surprise to her. Then she threatened to call her lawyer—she was going to sue. She loves to threaten to sue and all that lawyer crap. By this time the second show was about to start and I couldn't get her out of the dressing room. Then she went into (what I later realized was) her "standard" fit. That's when she says, 'I'm no creature from the cave! I'm no hillbilly! I'm a sophisticated, educated woman! I've studied Philosophy, I've studied Psychology! I will not be treated this way! I'm a wife, a mother! My son respects me! I'm a respectable woman!'"

The scene that night in the club was horrible and Freeman, caught in the middle, was at a loss as to how to remedy the situation. Finally, to quiet Yma, the management offered to open the club safe and give her some money. Yma, however, realized she had gone too far. She did not want any money. Yma signed the check. In the taxi on the way home however, Yma kept complaining to Freeman that she had no money in her pockets; that she couldn't go shopping.

When Freeman and Yma got to her hotel that night Yma decided that she wanted to count the money they had taken in for the record sales. Freeman had the "record book," with him—a little 5X8 spiral notebook that he had bought for that purpose, and that he always carried when he went to the club. He had dressed up the cover by pasting a photo of Yma on it. Yma liked that. The notebook listed the number of records and tapes sold each night, how much money was received, and where any expenditures went. At first he was also asked to keep a tally of the "house" take and enter that into the book as well. This was to verify Yma's percentage against the house figure, in case they tried to cheat her. "That sort of thing sometimes happens," Freeman explained, "though not usually when a house is sold-out. Since the reservations were done by computer, however, it was decided to forget that."

Everything was noted in Freeman's little notebook. For instance, opening night, February 17th, night Alan gave two cassettes to the man who styled Yma's hair. That was written down. Another night, Alan had to pay the club $135 for renting the slide projector used to flash the Peruvian scenes behind Yma. That, too, was entered. On that particular night Yma received $65 pocket money, but on hearing about the sum paid for the slide projector, Yma's reaction was "Give me the money! Who needs a slide projector? They don't come to see pictures! They come to hear Yma!" Freeman commented, "She got cheap all of a sudden. She didn't want any money spent on extra things. She didn't seem to understand that she was being very well presented, and to be frank, considering the way she looked and sounded, she should have been glad for the distractions that helped put the show over."

Below is a portion of the contents of Freeman's record book.

Tuesday, February 17 16 records (+2 cassettess Alan gave to hair dresser) $160.00
Thursday, February 19 33 (15 LPs, 18 cassettes) $330.00
Friday, February 20 45 $450.00
Saturday, February 21 12 $120.00
Tuesday, February 24 22 $220.00
Wednesday, February 25 23 $230.00
Friday, February 27 35 $350.00
Tuesday, March 3 (presigned) 43 $430.00
Wednesday, March 4 24 $240.00

During the nine days I have included here, 253 recordings were sold netting over $2,500, not including the monies received by Freeman.

That first Saturday night Freeman did not get his commission. Yma wanted all the money from his pockets. Luckily, he had set aside the $74 he kept in reserve as a "till" from which he could make change when selling the LPs and cassettes. Despite the late hour that Saturday night Yma wanted to count the money. So they sat on the Murphy bed in the tiny studio and Yma counted the money.

"But I've never seen anything like this," Freeman said. "She was like a harridan. Her makeup was beginning to come off and she looked a mess. At first I was detached enough to find her and the situation funny, but she kept counting and re-counting the money. It was getting late, I was tired and I wanted to go home. But she wanted to keep counting that money. The woman was nickel and dime-ing me—she's making $30,000 and she wants to squeeze out $42.50, counting it over and over in little stacks. Then she made marks in the little book, additions, numbering each page and making me initial each entry before I signed my full name. Then she'd sign her name. Even my commissions each night were signed over to me. At the end, the totals were divided into 'first' and 'second show' columns. The whole thing became ridiculously involved. I was not used to being treated that way. At first I was humiliated. Then I got angry."

The average taken in for recordings per night was about $200, with 20 records sold. Friday, February 20, however, saw 45 records sold, while the next night, there were only 12. By March 3rd records were pre-signed by Yma.

Freeman Gunter; right: cover of Freeman's record tally book; below: pages from tally book

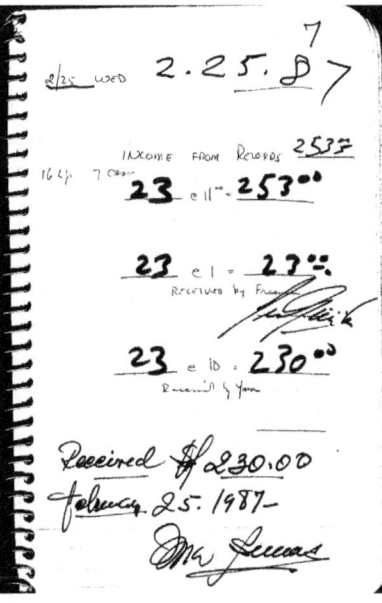

That Saturday evening set an unhappy precedent. Each night Freeman was expected to accompany Yma to her room and help count the money. He had wanted to take it home and count it there without the distractions of the club and all the people. But Yma insisted it was either the club or her apartment. "And if she had any grievances she would use me as a sounding board. But it was always the same speech: 'My son respects me. I'm a star. I'm no hillbilly.' I heard it over and over in the next few weeks."

When Yma had these tantrums, she would always qualify them so that Freeman would know that they were not directed at him. "I'm not mad at you," she would say, and later would apologize for her behavior. "Yma knew what she was doing, and afterwards it often made her feel remorseful for her conduct."

"I remember one time in particular that was rather touching," Freeman said. "Because Saturday was my first night alone without Alan's help, I had taken my friend David along to help me with the record table. Yma liked David and they got along great. Then she had her tantrum.

Soon after that, David got sick and so he never went back to the club. At first Yma didn't say anything, but she must have thought her tantrums had driven him away because in the middle of the next week she asked me, 'Where is your nice friend, David?' I explained that he was very sick. She then asked, 'Are you sure it wasn't because of the way I acted?' and apologized again, very sincerely, for her behavior. She really was very sweet and was obviously sorry for her temper."

It was the impossible situation, rather than Yma's ranting and raving, that bothered Freeman. Yma felt deserted because Alan had gone to the West Coast, as if she was not important enough for him to stay. Because of this, Yma took her frustrations and anger out on others. "It was as if she had looked up and saw that he was gone," Freeman remembers. "She'd say, 'I'm a Star! I'm packing in the people, they love me! Where is he?'"

After that first Saturday night, the glow was gone for Freeman.

The next morning, Sunday, Freeman was to call Alan and let him know how things had gone. Yma knowing this, however, had whispered to him the night before that he was not to tell Alan what had happened. Later she told him that if he called Alan, Freeman was not to mention her name. "The operators will be listening, and I'm a big Star!" she said. Yma told Freeman that he should refer to her as Mrs. Vivanco, or Perita.

Freeman called Alan. Honoring Yma's odd request, he opened the conversation by saying "It's about Mrs. Vivanco . . . " and told him everything that had happened. Alan begged Freeman to just try and keep Yma together until he was able to get back to New York. Later in the day, Alan called Freeman back when Yma was with him and asked to speak to her. By this time, however, Yma had decided she would not speak to Alan, preferring to make him suffer.

Meanwhile, every night the customers came to The Ballroom and Yma sold out almost every night except for a couple of performances during the hold-over, when people did not know she was still in New York. Freeman, who has been to a number of nightclubs and knows a number of famous cabaret personalities, was amazed at the constant turnout for Yma. At one point, The Ballroom even had to add chairs to accommodate the overflowing crowds. None of this surprised Yma, of course. Alan Eichler once said to her, "I've never gotten this kind of publicity for anyone coming into New York." Yma said, simply, "Ah, but I am Yma Sumac."

Every night the customers came, and every night Yma would excuse her singing because of a cold.

"There was no cold," said Freeman. "I was with her every day for hours and I never saw her sniffle, cough or blow her nose. I never even saw a box of Kleenex. And yet every night she made a point of telling the audience that she had a cold. She was just paranoid, scared. But you have to understand—it was very hard for her. She was trying to do something that was really technical. I mean, Peggy Lee could be in bad voice and whisper her way through a piece but if she can put over the song she's a success. She's not judged, like Yma is on the notes she hits and how far apart the top and bottom ones are every time she opens her mouth. Yma was publicized as a vocal paragon so naturally it's harder to live up to that night after night. That's a whole different kind of nightly pressure. Now, add her age to that. I think her paranoia was understandable. The "cold" was just a protection in case anything went wrong. It also got sympathy from the audience, who would say, 'That's OK', 'We love you.'"

When Alan returned to Manhattan, Freeman's job was done. Although he could have gone some of the last nights, by that time he was tired of the act, and of Yma. "Most of the time I didn't think she sounded very good—although one or two shows she was wonderful and I remember one night she made me cry with her singing of 'Montana.' But I was tired of hearing the show over and over. Besides, Alan was back, and he is a very high-pressure person to be around. So I thought, 'Who needs it?'"

When asked who the real Yma Sumac was, Freeman confessed that it was complicated. "I'll be honest with you. With Yma Sumac, the mystery is more intriguing than the truth. She seems to be many things at the same time. She is a great lady, a charming, elegant woman, a giggly little girl. But, she can also be a vicious, petty, little old Peruvian lady plagued with delusions of grandeur. Considering the scope of her career in the 1950s, it must be hard for her now. Unfortunately she's never made the adjustment. My relationship with her during those five weeks was basically wonderful—despite the tantrums. She had a kind of conspiratorial way of approaching me that was rather refreshing and fun.

"I took her to The Tunnel (a club) one night because they were having a party for her. They put her on this dais and all the punk-rockers came up and paid homage. It was very camp, and Yma loved it. But then, that kind of worship-thing fit in perfectly with her perception of her image. I was the one who pulled back in the relationship because I was annoyed at the way she made me jump through hoops about money. I was not used to being treated that way and I resented it. But, I hope I handled the situation with some sportsmanship. Even though she always apologized for her fits, I got tired of them. Yma is very demanding of your time and attention and is very self-involved. That's often part of the territory with famous performers. They can take a lot out of you. If they give it back on some level, it's an even trade.

"In personal relationships, Yma never really gives back what she takes from you. She never really lets you in. I did see, though, that she has a little girl inside her—a playful, joking, and sometimes cruel, little girl. It is all part of a duality with her that is unsettling. At any moment she might demand to be called Ms. Sumac, even if you'd spent days with her—even if you'd seen her without her bra—and I had. A few times she was real and informal. But, there wasn't enough of that. Mainly you had to agree with her and whatever she wanted. And that got boring."

After the shows at The Ballroom, Yma traveled to San Francisco, for appearances at the Theatre on the Square. Because of the success of the New York shows, Yma's set was expanded in preparation for her appearances. This engagement was to stretch from August 12th to 23rd.

Bill Corderre, reporter for the arts section of San Francisco publication, *The Tech* went to the August 12 show. He described the occasion:

"The Theatre on the Square (Union Square) is a relatively small (several hundred seat) house, with only 20 rows on the main floor and another five on the balcony. The tiny stage was dwarfed by twin 40-foot-tall reproductions of Incan carved stone gods. Slides showed pictures of Yma in her wildest costumes, while 'Quiet Village' played in the background. All it needed was a few torches and some fake fog. The six-man combo (two keyboards, bass, guitar and two percussion) crowded onto the stage and played one of Yma's mambos as an entr'acte. The sound was good, played at a moderate level. Then the lady herself stepped out.

"Time has changed Yma. She is older, less energetic, a little heavier than 30 years ago. But once she opened her mouth, it was clear that the voice was still there."

Two weeks later Yma was scheduled to re-enter a recording studio for the first time in 17 years. This was to record "I Wonder" from the cartoon movie, *Sleeping Beauty* for A&M Records. The recording company was planning to release a rather innovative CD of the music of Walt Disney films as interpreted by various artists. Yma was to be in good company: James Taylor, Ringo Starr, Randy Newman and others. Originally, in 1986 Hal Wilner, who produced the album, and Van Dyke Parks, who was one of the album's arrangers, went to hear Yma sing at the Cine Grill in the Hollywood Roosevelt Hotel. They spoke with Alan Eichler about the possibility of using Yma on the album and eventually an agreement was reached. Yma recorded her selection in Burbank, CA, the same night as Ringo Starr.

Chapter 11

"La Molina" (The Mill Song) The Ballroom
1989

Yma's return to Manhattan's Ballroom in February of 1989 had less advance publicity than her previous appearance at that cabaret. By January, small advertisements of the Ballroom's schedule began to appear in the *New York Times*, noting the singer's return. It wasn't until the day of her first show, however, that a few articles began to appear in local newspapers. Most notices were limited to a few sentences about the duration of her engagement. One interview with Blake Green for *New York Newsday* (2/21/89) found Yma making a typical Sumacian statement.

"I am a very simple person. Sometimes I forget I am a descendant of an Incan king. I am a human being—like you."

Generally, however, articles merely regurgitated the usual Capitol biography.

The best publicity for the Peruvian singer wasn't the few notices that appeared, but rather the availability of two of Yma's best selling albums, *Voice of the Xtabay* and *Legend of the Sun Virgin,* on CD. Copies seen in Tower Records on Monday were gone by Thursday.

The Ballroom engagement began Tuesday, February 21, and was to extend through Saturday, March 11. As before, it was arranged that Yma would perform two shows nightly, Tuesday through Saturday. This was the official extent of the run. Because of her tremendous popularity with audiences two years earlier, however, the management of The Ballroom expected, and was prepared, to extend the engagement.

The 1989 booking was promoted as Yma's New York Farewell before retiring. Ironically enough, that would turn out to be truthful.

Yma arrived in New York about a week before the show was to open to prepare for opening night. She was in good spirits and fully anticipated a repeat of the success she experienced in 1987. The management and Yma agreed that, for this visit, she would stay with Filipe, the chef of the Ballroom. Not only was he an ardent fan, but also conveniently, his Chelsea apartment was just around the corner from The Ballroom.

Freeman Gunter stayed far away from The Ballroom and the Peruvian diva. He did agree, however, to attend Yma's opening night show with my wife Gale and me. Freeman enjoyed the show but preferred not to go backstage to see Yma. Although he confessed that Yma's singing could still cast its spell over him, his experience of two years earlier was still too vivid to be dismissed.

The back-up musicians hired were completely different from those used in 1987, but with time proved to be just as excellent.

Ken Werner—director/pianist
Celso Mendez—guitar
Nilson Matta—bass

Tom Rainey—drums
Cafe—percussion
Rick Martinez—synthesizer

It was decided to use the same program as that of 1987. Two additions had been planned—"Moscow Nights" and "Malambo #1." Both songs were quickly dropped, however, and Yma concentrated on just the 1987 material. Although the intervening years saw little change in the presentation of the music, occasionally there was a discernible deterioration in Yma's delivery.

Opening night, February 21, was a shambles, resembling a poorly organized first rehearsal rather than a polished performance. Paying $25.00 a head, patrons were subjected to Yma rambling through her music, suddenly hissing "shhh," and giving other restrictive orders to the band. A few people in the audience enjoyed Yma's unprofessional public spectacle. Others did not.

In his column "La Dolce Musto" for the *Village Voice*, (3/7/89), Michael Musto found the experience exhilarating—and amusing.

"The most dramatic aspect of the show, as always, was her annoyance at the band to which she continually barked, 'Keep a beat,' 'Faster' and other succinct orders. We all felt privileged, as if at a dress rehearsal. Whenever Yma's voice gave out she just looked mad at the pianist—a brilliant move."

Looked at from a professional standpoint, Yma's behavior was neither exciting nor entertaining. It was embarrassing. Behavior such as this should be in private, not in front of paying patrons.

The opening show had serious (but typical) organizational problems. Despite rehearsals and an obvious familiarity with the music, Yma sang cautiously, was as musically confused as her backup musicians, and refused to be a part of an ensemble effort to pull the show together. The musicians seemed ill at ease not only with the music but also with Yma, who belligerently played diva while everything around her began to fall apart.

Yma's show was, however, a full one—a good forty-forty five minutes of music, including an instrumental opener, ten songs and one encore. Four of her famous Capitol albums were represented by as many songs. Although the program listed thirteen songs from which Yma would choose throughout the engagement, her selections centered on the following:

"Ataypura" (High Andes)—Instrumental
"Don't Let Me Die Without Your Love"
"Especially For You"
"Montana"
"My Real True Love"
"Ay, Ay, Ay"
"Didn't You Know I Loved You?"
"La Molina" (The Mill Song)—*also used as an encore*
"Huayno"—*used as an encore*
"Jungla Mambo"—*used as an encore*

Yma's singing was inconsistent at best during the course of the 1989 shows. As in 1987, the "Jungla" mambo was used as an occasional encore and, as before, Yma had trouble remembering the music. As if on cue, in each performance Yma would beg the audience's indulgence because of a cold.

For all the problems and shortcomings of the opening night show, Yma managed to provide listeners with a few unexpected treats—even if by accident. The most startling occurred during "My Real True Love" when Yma lunged higher into the stratosphere than New Yorkers had heard her do in over two decades. While singing an ascending scale passage in the improvisational section of that song, Yma misjudged her beginning note and sang the scale a third higher, landing on a thin, mewled-out high F. Other treats were the occasional volley of high staccati that would ping-out into the audience with the authority of a true virtuoso. Yma's famous growl remained impressive and was still liberally used throughout the show.

Reviews in New York newspapers were mixed. Stephen Holden of the *New York Times* (2/26/89) commented: "Yma Sumac, the Peruvian vocal phenomenon, has always fearlessly straddled the line between the sublime and the ridiculous...today...(she) remains an iconoclast, apparently oblivious to the possibility that her mystique involves more than a little hokum. Long ago her voice lost the quality of seeming to emanate spontaneously from a non-human sphere. Yet she is still adept at making nearly supersonic humming sounds and at producing rhythmically startling woofs and barks from her middle range.

"What the singer failed to do on Wednesday was to make herself intelligible when singing English lyrics. And her poor communication with her mediocre pop-rock band turned the relationship between singer and musicians into an uneasy contest of wills."

The best summation of the 1989 Sumac experience, however, came from Bob Harrington of the *New York Post* (2/23/89): "She's been bamboozling people for years about her range by disguising clever, effective changes in vocal timbre for changes in vocal pitch. If she's got three octaves, she's got one more than most singers, including opera stars. But the effect of her vocal pyrotechnics can nevertheless be stunning. Sumac has achieved what jazz singers strive for—she's turned her voice into an instrument divorced from the emotive power of a lyric. In the haunting 'Montana,' her intonations create the mood and carry the feeling without resort to verbal communication. Running from a low growl to an ethereal chirp in 'High Andes,' she evokes the feral quality of soaring mountains and boundless jungles.

" . . . There is no middle ground for an act like this: you'll either love it or wonder what in the world all the fuss is about. But she is a remarkable performer, and there's a magic to her shows that has to be experienced to be understood."

Despite all the supportive screaming and cheering of audiences at the shows, there were still patrons who felt the show was not worth the price of the ticket. As if mirroring this, the management of The Ballroom found that there was much less business this time around. Advance ticket sales were not as promising as had been expected and shows were not sold-out.

Originally there were to have been thirty shows—two shows a night over fifteen days within a three-week period. By the 23rd of February, the third night into the run, the second show was cut from all evenings except weekends.

By February 27th, in a lame attempt to bolster Yma's popularity within the gay community, newspaper advertisements began to appear heralding an Yma Sumac look-a-like contest. The contest, called "Look Like an Incan Princess?" was to be held at The Ballroom with Yma as one of the judges. Held on Wednesday, March 1, at 1:00 p.m., free tickets to the Sumac show were awarded to all contestants and winner of the contest would be featured during that night's show.

Michael Musto, who assisted Yma and Margaret Whiting in the judging, reported in the *Village Voice* (3/14/89):

"As the diverse contestants bravely took the stage, Yma would ask Whiting, 'Is that a man or a girl?' and Whiting would try and figure out and tell her . . . The winner, inevitably, was Perfida, who's only been rehearsing his entire life for this. Yes, Yma, he's a man."

That night, Yma's show was whittled down to a short thirty minutes, had little singer-audience communication, a "get down to business" atmosphere, and sported terrible singing.

Despite all the hoopla associated with the contest, it did little to further Yma or her shows and failed to increase audience numbers. Because of the obvious decline in attendees, her run was not extended past March 11th.

It is ironic that on the next to last night of the run, March 10th, at her 9:00 show, Yma gave her audience a rare glimpse into the past and the secrets of her power and magic over audiences. More than any of the other shows of the run, this particular one demonstrated who Yma Sumac was and why she had held such a fascination for audiences through the many decades of her career.

By March 10th, the show was a tight unit. After so many run-throughs the musicians were familiar with Yma. Knowing what to expect, they were better able to support and help her through the show. They and Yma seemed in sync with each other with more understanding of each other's roles in the production of the show. A full, fifty-minute show was offered to patrons—eight songs plus what amounted to two and a-half encores of "La Molina" (The Mill Song) as well as the infamous "Jungla" mambo. From the moment Yma slinked on stage, she presented an amazingly understated authority and a vocal ease that seemed to strip away the years before the watchers' eyes.

Rhythmically, she was outstanding for her precise, subtle alterations and inventive use of variants. Although the middle voice was worn and raspy, the top register was in excellent shape—especially staccati in the area of high C and D. During the course of "La Molina" she repeated an intricate staccato variant (that darted repeatedly between high B and D) at least four times. At the other extreme, she displayed a solid low E and D.

Only two of the four pieces in English, written by Yma, were successful. These were "My Real True Love" and "Didn't You Know I Loved You?" where the raspy, almost desperate quality of her middle voice contributed to the plaintive quality of the song. Both featured well-articulated and inventive improvisatory sections that allowed Yma to display her considerable staccato technique. The other two English songs lay too much in the middle and low registers and were far too wordy to be successful.

"High Andes," first sung thirty-nine years earlier had, unfortunately, been corrupted beyond recovery. It was now a watered down piece of fluff and no longer the effective piece it once was. Although everything possible had been done to provide as exotic a flavor as possible, Yma's cautious manner in the high register (it was obviously used as a warm-up song) negated any efforts.

The best performances were those of "La Molina" (The Mill Song), a staple of Yma's repertoire since 1959. It was here that she seemed to finally relax and just sing, letting the voice ring out freely. Listeners sat with mouths open as Yma nonchalantly pecked at her stratospheric staccato ornaments.

Complementing the overall quality of singing that evening was the addition of the novel rhythmical clicks, pops and miscellaneous noises Yma was once famous for interpolating into the fabric of her music during the 1950s. These sounds were amplified by a series of fascinating balletic, posed movements that obviously reached far back into the Sumac career giving that night's audience a taste of the unusual and individual quality of her performances during her hey day.

Fascinating to watch, Yma moved like a serpent through poses and graceful movements that obviously originated thirty years earlier when many of her pieces had been choreographed with subtle movements and secret hand signals whose meanings could only be interpreted by Moisés, Hernán, David Revera, and a very few others. Perfectly matched to musical phrases, there was a rightness to their placement and execution that precluded any thought of artifice.

Coupled with her singing that night, these things gave to those fortunate enough to be present a vivid glimpse of the Yma Sumac of 1954, Carnegie Hall and the many world tours. Although some people in the audience did not realize what they were witnessing, there were others I noticed who did. They sat watching the old, now heavy, singer with their mouths hanging open; stunned by the realization that, for a few moments, they were being given a rare gift from the singer—an opportunity to see into the past.

According to a visitor to the Sunvirgin.com web page, Yma performed in Boston in 1989. Only about 15 people were in the audience and only one or two showed up at her dressing room afterwards. No programs were supplied for the show.

Chapter 12

"La Pampa Y La Puna"
(The Plains and the Mountains)
1989–1993

After returning to Los Angeles, Yma prepared for her next important engagement. Yma was slated to appear at the Hollywood Roosevelt Cinegrill July 26 through 30 and then August 2 through 5. The appearances were jointly billed as her farewell concert—though Yma continued to perform, if sporadically, throughout most of the next decade.

Sunday, August 6th found Yma performing at the Second Annual South American Festival at the Old World Festival Hall in Old World Village, Orange County. The 7:00 pm concert was her first appearance in Orange County. Amateur film clips of part of that concert show Yma giving a rousing rendition of "La Molina"—energetic and imaginative in her singing and balletic in her movement. Obviously on a performing high, Yma gave the audience a taste of her special magic.

In February of 1990, the magazine *DISCoveries* published an excellent and surprisingly comprehensive interview/article on Yma Sumac written by Gino Falzarano. Here as in other interviews, Yma explained her creative method in song composition: "Sometime, in the house I am doing . . . whatever I am doing in the house. Suddenly is coming the melody. You know what I do? I record it immediately. The idea. Any idea who come into the head. Music, or writing or anything. I record it immediately. Then I listen after a few days—not really—two days. I listen. In my mind is already the pattern of notes. Then in a few minutes, I compose the whole music. Every idea, any idea is coming here, see [pressing her hand to her bosom]. In your heart. In music, you have to use your imagination and your heart also."

March 1–18, 1990, found Yma breaking new artistic ground for herself by appearing in the role of Heidi, the aging opera diva of Stephen Sondheim's musical, *Follies* at the Terrace Theatre in Long Beach California. At the beginning of the show, each of the fading stars was introduced (in character). When Yma came on she got a lot more applause than most of the other performers. She also got considerable applause after her song, which comes near the end of the show. Typically, Yma did not wear the usual costume that goes with the show but wore one of her own baggy, flowing gowns and trademark tiara.

Although *Voice of the Xtabay* and *Legend of the Sun Virgin* had both appeared on CD, because of a lawsuit Yma brought against Capitol Records in 1990 for unpaid royalties, the CDs were withdrawn from circulation. They would not return until 1996. Yma also made concert and television appearances in Brussels and Paris in the course of 1990. The French audiences, especially, seemed to enjoy Yma's presentation and approached it respectfully.

October of 1991 found her making a return trip to Germany. This time to Berlin where she gave concerts in predominantly gay nightclubs to amazed, youthful patrons. Some of the concerts and interviews were taped for television. The trip was not all pleasant, however. Some of the photographs taken during the concerts are party stuff. They

show an almost beautiful Yma beaming at her audience and then a frumpy diva scowling at her raggle-taggle band.

1991 also saw the genesis of a fascinating painting by Colorado artist, Tyler Alpern based on Yma and her Incan Legends. (The painting graces the cover of this book. The original oil on canvas measures 48" by 56".) Tyler is a modest, charming man who was very gracious in taking the time to explain not only about his painting but also his creative process.

Tyler's work is unusual in that it is considered narrative painting with a contemporary slant. He was educated at Occidental College in LA, at two different schools in Rome, Italy, and earned his MFA from the University of Colorado where he occasionally teaches. His work has been sold to collectors living on both coasts, in between and in Australia. His work is currently on display at Cliffside on Nantucket, and at Front Range Community College. His website has some wonderful images and some fascinating information: www.tyleralpern.com. In addition to his painting and teaching, Tyler is an accomplished nude figure model who works with numerous artists and photographers in the United States. His sensitive work embraces not only classical but also avant-garde poses. One of the highlights of his figure-modeling career was to pose for the painter, Don Bachardy.

Of his creative process, Tyler commented: "I strive to make exquisite paintings, but am also interested in the whole story that an image can tell. Most importantly, there exists a beautiful work of art; but upon closer inspection, the imagery often reveals a surprising and occasionally candid or frank message in the guise of something far more tame.

"I am very concerned with the actual quality of the painted image. The surface of the work is rich because of the many layers of paint applied over months to achieve the fullness and complexity of color and value that makes the paintings glow. I paint, repaint and repaint until I am satisfied with every element.

"I consider myself a colorist and remain an inventive painter. Just because I have painted something before, such as sky, water or flesh, I do not know how I will paint those same subjects the next time. I have no formulas or routines. I have to discover how to paint a subject

Tyler Alpern (photo courtesy of Chris Reynolds

in each and every new painting. There is very little repetition. I have to reinvent the wheel every time. Because of this I am not a particularly prolific painter. Almost all of my work takes at least a year to complete, yet I do work on multiple pieces at a time. I also do not work in series, I have to find a new subject and story for each work. This keeps me very interested in my own work, slows down my output, but ensures the uniqueness and freshness of each painting. I am not a production painter, there are no shortcuts and I value each individual painting."

Although admitting that the creative process for his painting of Yma Sumac was arduous, Tyler is especially fond of the painting:

"I was still in grad school (I graduated in 1990). My older studio mate had introduced me to Yma but there were none of her old records in Boulder stores. At the time I did not know whether she was alive or dead and no news of the recent popularity had come to me in Boulder. I had to go to the university music library to hear her and see album covers. I was charmed by her singing and found her unnatural gimmicky look and the over the top album notes ripe for artistic reinterpretation. I found the Yma/Amy legend too good to pass up. I knew what I wanted to say in my painting but did not know how to fit the narrative and the reflection of the name into a visual image, but I kept working on the idea in the back of my mind. Translating what I loved about Yma and her legend into one image that explained everything was very tricky. Early sketches tell the story but are awkward and inconsistent. Inspiration struck when I cast the scene in the bathroom and all the real elements could morph in the mirror to become the Yma myth and look. It took two years of playing with the painting to get it right. It got into a juried show at the University of Colorado in 1993 and I know it was wet in places on the wall."

"I moved into my house in 1991, and later that year remodeled the bathroom. The faucet and sink you see in the painting are the ones I installed. The painting is mostly in pinks and salmons. The bathroom wall paper is a print of a vine and bird motif that in the mirror is repeated and expanded to become full on jungle and tropical birds. The toothbrush becomes the comb of a bird, the pink background becomes the Inca Tiki used on the Capitol records. A little girl cast as the young Amy transforms into the mature Yma in the mirror, her pajamas becoming the peasant dress from the Fuego de Ande cover, her name on the wall accurately reflects backwards from Amy to Yma and the ribbon becomes Yma's exotic earrings. Her hair was inspired by Legend of the Sun Virgin. I named the painting Through the Looking Glass because the mirror was a gateway into the fictional world of Yma Sumac, and proved to be a metaphor of how we can all live our lives."

As to the narrative of the work, Tyler explained:

Through the Looking Glass compares the career of singer Yma Sumac to the story of Alice in Wonderland in order to illustrate the power we have to create our own destiny. Claiming to be a descendant of Inca Kings and having learned to sing by imitating birds while wandering Peruvian jungles as a girl, Miss Sumac gained fame exploiting her colorful heritage in a full four octave range. However, rumors persisted that she was born in Brooklyn purely of European descent with the name Amy Camus, which spelled backwards becomes Yma Sumac. My painting depicts the rumored young Amy gazing at her reflection as the mature Yma in her bathroom mirror. Elements of the bathroom are transformed into the Peruvian jungle in the mirror and even her name Amy is reflected backwards as Yma demonstrating since we can create our own reality thus we create too our own reflection. So unlike Alice, we do not have to go through the looking glass to find another world, all we must do is invent it. Therefore anyone can be an Inca Princess, or anything else that they strive to be.

During the early fall months of 1991, a German filmmaker, Günter Czernetsky, came to New York to film various people and places for his television documentary, *Yma Sumac—Hollywoods Inkaprinzessin*. A personable man, he and his staff filmed Perry Street in Greenwich Village, where Yma and Moisés lived during some of their leanest years in New York, as well as interviewed various people for the film. He and his crew also traveled to Peru and talked extensively to not only noted authorities on Peru and its music but also to local natives—many of whom had absolutely no idea who Yma Sumac was. Among those interviewed in Spain was Rosita Vivanco, Moisés' sister—the original soloist for the Compañia Peruanna. Now a mature, elegant well-spoken woman, Rosita spoke of the early days of the Compania. Interestingly during Czernetsky's film there was often an interesting, subtle undercurrent that some people interviewed did not want to talk about Yma. Others overly praised Yma with sycophant-like comments.

One of the most honest of the interviews was that of the Peruvian soprano, Esmila Zevallos. (Sometimes her name was spelled Zeballos.) During her segment she said that she originally met Yma and Moisés when she was young, during one of their return trips to Peru. "The public asked her to sing 'La Pampa y la Puna' and 'Virgenes del Sol' but ... she was not prepared to sing them. So when it was our time to sing, Las Hermanitas Cevallos—that was the name of our group, my father told me to go up there and sing (those songs). So I went on the stage and sang them. After I sang (Yma and Moisés) came up to the stage and thanked me for the nice gesture. Later they decided they wanted to help improve my career. My voice was almost the same as hers. Moisés asked my parents if they could take me to the United States. I had never in my life seen an airplane. We went to live in Beverly Hills. The first couple of years I struggled very much because I didn't speak English. I remembered Moisés and Yma used to fight a lot. She was a very temperamental person. Yma was a horrible figure when she was mad; she was nothing like the 'star' that we all knew. Their fights were violent and I hated to see them fighting. I have bad memories of those times. Also Moisés had affairs with Yma's secretary and other people but I had to remain quiet. I didn't feel comfortable living with them. So one day we were doing a show and I told them I wanted to go back to my country." (*Yma Sumac—Hollywood's Inkaprinzessin*, translated by Gianncarlo Cifuentes)

Later, during the divorce melee, Esmila was summoned back to the United States to testify about the extent of Moisés' extramarital affairs. "So I went back to the United States to testify. In any case I admired Yma Sumac for her wonderful voice and for all

The author (left) and Günter Czernetsky at filming of documentary

those years that she treated me nice. Wherever she is now, I want to ask God to grant her good health and I want her to know that I will always respect her." (ibid)

Since the filming of his documentary took place while I was working on this book, Günter Czernetsky interviewed me as well. My interview was filmed during a lovely summer afternoon, in the home of the stage director Liviu Ciulei. At the time I was working as a receptionist for an interior design firm, Cioppa Rosen, here in New York City, and I remember taking off early from work so that I could rush uptown to the apartment where it was being filmed. I got there out of breath and a bit frantic. I needn't have worried, Günter and his crew were not only kind and accommodating but also helpful as well. For two hours, he asked me a number of questions including aspects about her voice, recordings and range but one of the main ones they wanted me to address was why Yma had such a large, devoted gay following.

In thanks for my help, Günter kindly allowed me the use of any of the information that they gathered during the making of their documentary. In return I lent him many private photographs given to me by Hernán Braña for use in their documentary. Unfortunately, by this time, I had lost touch with Hernán, who by 1990 had been suffering from ill health so he was not interviewed for the film.

The film was a daring venture since neither Yma nor Moisés nor their son Charlie took part. It was, however, remarkably successful in presenting the most honest portrait of the enigmatic performer to date. Drawing on many different types of people who worked with Yma throughout the years the documentary provided a fascinating, yet believable picture of the singer. Although there were criticisms, it was the first time a biography of Yma had been attempted and it did much to dispel many myths associated with the singer.

The documentary was directed by Günter Czernetsky, and produced by Rubicon Film GbR. It was released the following summer and although it was made for German television, it premiered in the United States at the Roxie Cinema on June 24, 1992, as part of the annual San Francisco Lesbian/Gay International Film Festival.

Because it was not released commercially on video either in Europe or America, the 90-minute film is now a serious cult collector's favorite.

The August 10, 1992 issue of *Variety* reviewed the film and gave it a mixed reception, noting: "Best bets for this okay, but far-from-definitive docu lie in targeting cult audiences less interested in musicology than in another era's kitschy glamor."

The reviewer, Dennis Harvey, concluded "Item's entertaining, but maybe another film-maker will be able to persuade Sumac to be an on-camera commentator for a more complete view of her unique career."

The review that appeared in *The Ultimate Guide to Lesbian & Gay Film and Video* stated:

"Gunther Czernetsky's well-researched bio . . . tackles all the myths, and gets at some even stranger truths. . . . Along the way there's a lot of rare footage, including Yma's famous encounter with David Letterman."

In May, 1992, Yma traveled to France and performed at the Grand Theatre de Bourges. Amazed at the length of her career, critics found her performances "merveilleusement bien."

Following the French engagements, Yma traveled back to Germany, spending about eight weeks canvassing the German gay club circuit. Her new audiences went crazy for the Peruvian diva and made her into a new cult heroine. One interesting repertoire choice occurred during this German branch of the tour. On May 15, 1992, Yma dusted off one of her old Incan songs from *Legend of the Sun Virgin* and performed "Suray

Surita." A private recording made during that performance is revelatory. Sung only to piano accompaniment, it finds Yma singing out in a way that she had not in decades. Singing in a healthy mezza forte Yma sang with power and authority, even to a finely supported sustained high B and B flat. Aside from some very minor simplifications, Yma sang the song as she recorded it for Capitol records over 40 years earlier—including some excellent high C staccati. The recording also shows that the German band was much more inventive in their additions to the orchestrations than the New York bands in 1989—in many cases providing some superb background for Yma's warblings. More than any other concert from this time caught on tape, this one shows Yma singing out a number of times—recalling singing of decades earlier. This included a use of the growl all the way to a forceful high G and an ascent to touch a top E. There is also a dynamic "La Molina" with excellent staccati high Cs and Ds. (It is also encored) Her audience responds in kind.

Around this time, the Dutch magazine, Vrij Nederland (11/14/92) published an article/interview with Yma by Rudie Kagle. After having contacted Alan Eichler (who set up the interview) Kagel was told that Yma would not be willing to meet him at her home. The interview would have to be held at a local hotel.

"We shall meet her in Beverly Hills, where she will wait on a street corner. Then we drive to Hollywood where, in a hotel room, the interview can be held." Kagel was warned:

"In the car her manager hastily gives advice to let the conversation be as easy as possible. . . . don't ask about her age. . . . See her only as the big star she was back in the fifties; she dislikes it that her triumphs should only belong to the past. And no word about Amy Camus, Moisés Vivanco and her son. When you ask her about these things, she immediately knocks off the conversation."

"The first thing she says to me, when she takes a seat next to me in the back, is: 'I know about life. I could write a book that should totter a lot of reputations,' she says. 'I have an unusual life behind me with lots of happiness and sorrow, with poverty and wealth.'

"(She) tells me that she leads a sort of retreated life. Many days she sees no other than her own little dog. 'Show business is a tough job,' she says. 'It's always hatred and envy. Not to forget jealousness.'"

When Mr. Kagel asked her about all the hype she received back in the 1950s, she commented, "Capitol Records exaggerated this all too much. . . . They thought of me as an exotic artist. I told the publicity staff a couple of things about myself, but their fantasy really went completely out of proportions. It's true I'm a descendant of the last Inca Emperor."

Yma also inadvertently let slip that she came "from a beautiful region called Cajamarca, which has a richness of minerals." (Translation by Ruud Verkerk)

In October of 1993 Yma was invited by the Miami-Dade Community College in Florida to lecture and perform. Performances on October 7 and 8 at 9 p.m. were well attended with tickets going for $25–$30.00. It had been 33 years since she had last performed in Miami.

Chapter 13

"Especially For You"
1996–2007

A key word of the career of Yma Sumac is "longevity". On March 5, 1996 a division of Capitol Records called The Right Stuff re-released all six of Yma's Capitol recordings on CD with original album art and liner notes and budget priced (about $12.00 a disc). By late March there was also a super-budget-priced sampler that featured one track from each album. The impetus for these new re-releases was the fact that Capitol had finally settled the lawsuit Yma brought against them for unpaid royalties. Thanks to the hard work and persistence of Alan Eichler, Yma was now getting accurate royalties for her recordings, including retroactive ones that dated years back. The suit took six years to work itself out.

Not surprisingly, a new generation of Capitol employees had discovered the mysterious allure of Yma. Tieing it in with the then burgeoning return and popularity of "lounge music," they released the CDs with much fanfare. Part of this fanfare included a celebrity signing which Capitol arranged for Yma at Tower Records in Los Angeles. Yma's signing broke all records at that Tower for the biggest turnout and longest lines of people. Thousands lined up for hours to see and have Yma sign their disks.

Many of them were amazed to find out that the singer who originally recorded *Voice of the Xtabay* some 46 years earlier was still singing. She stayed all day to sign. Celebrating Capitol's decision to re-release the Sumac legacy, a number of West Coast newspapers and magazines printed articles that helped introduce Yma to an entirely new audience.

While praising the re-release of Yma's disks, Curtis Ross of the *Tampa Tribune* described the impact of the initial, 1950, release of *Voice of the Xtabay* with bemusement and irony: "It stunned and titillated listeners with its pagan passion. It was the first musical flowering of postwar America's infatuation with all things 'exotic' and 'Voice of the Xtabay' was de rigueur for suburban stereos as faux-African art deco pieces were for the walls and coffee tables. These passions were, of course, tempered for the benefit of tender, civilized ears. For every native rhythm and jungle grunt in the grooves, there was a tonic of silky strings, plucked harps and Sumac's airy soprano. This was the Sumac/Vivanco team's master stroke. They made the exotic accessible. Serving the foreign on a bed of the familiar gave the music appeal beyond the anthropological. And Sumac's regal bearing gave the Incan princess affair an air of authenticity." Ross summarized Yma's newfound appeal by noting: "The beauty of Yma's re-emergence is its broad appeal. The world's music crowd can savor Sumac's sound-stage interpretations of Peruvian melodies. New-agers can bask in the drowsy mist of her more ethereal material. And the lounge movement should recognize her as its high priestess. What could better complement a space-age bachelor pad more than a dose of Sumac's tribalisms? And now a whole new generation gets its chance to bow before the Sun Virgin." (Friday, May 3, 1996)

Although most writers reiterated the usual Capitol fantasy biography created over forty years earlier, occasionally an interview was intertwined. And within those interviews one occasionally got a glimpse of "the real Yma." In an article called "Bird of Paradise," Yma was asked about her reputation for being difficult. "I never let people get fresh with me. I'm not a cheap woman. They know Yma, they say she has two personalities. If you have more than two personalities, you are sick. My mother was very strict, and I am like my mother. She had one terrible look (does the stern look) then she was tender. Once I did that look to my son when he did something bad. He said, 'Mommy, I prefer that you spank me because when you get mad, your eyes become all green and your whites become with blood and then your veins are swollen. You scare me!'" (*LA Weekly*, May 10–16, 1996)

Libby Molyneaux, in the *LA Weekly* issue quoted from above, found it hard to believe that Yma was once branded as haughty and temperamental "She's warm and vibrant, and though her favorite subject may be 'Yma,' not only is she happy to talk about her extraordinary life and even give out skin-care tips (spend several weeks in the Andean heights of Machu Picchu), she doesn't bristle when that darned Amy Camus subject is brought up." (ibid.)

New and old readers alike learned that when Yma was not working she liked to embroider, read philosophy and psychology, and that her favorite singers were Doris Day and Neil Diamond. When asked when she first began singing she told an interesting story that had an obvious kernel of truth. "I first noticed my voice when I was about 9. My voice was very thin. . . . My inspiration was the nature. The farms in the north are very beautiful. It's cold, but a dry cold, and you hear sounds from the big mountain covered by forest. In the mountains you have very strange sounds that inspire you. I heard the birds, all kinds of birds. I remember in the afternoon, there were two birds singing ready to go to sleep. One sang to the other one; to me is sounded like 'Quien? Quien?' meaning 'Who? Who?' The other answered, 'Yo. Yo.' meaning 'I. I'. I said 'I wish to sing like that.'" (ibid.)

"Mister Lucky," on his Internet review page (www.mrlucky.com) was pleased with The Right Stuff's releases: "(They have) done a wonderful thing in releasing five great Capitol titles. There are no bonus tracks or additional liner notes but the albums are complete and the sound is fine. Who could ask for more?

"Yma Sumac is not for everyone but if you like her, you'll really want to get all five volumes on The Right Stuff. If you're dubious, there's a sampler CD available. The next release to watch out for is her early '70s title with Les Baxter, Miracles . . . .it's beyond description except to say that it tries to cash in on the acid rock trend and Yma somehow manages to sound musical."

More succinctly, The Loud Bassoon Record Guide on the World Wide Web (www.polyholiday.com) proclaimed: "The Right Stuff's 1996 reissue series of five Yma Sumac albums remains one of the best things to come out of the lounge music craze of the mid-90s."

Coinciding with the resurgence of interest in her work by record buyers, Yma received an eloquent tribute from the Award-winning French author and poet, Albert Russo. That year he published a series of poems in a book called *Painting the Tower of Babel*. One of the poems is called "Peruvian Goddess."

Born in Zaire, Russo is extremely versatile, writing fiction, poetry and essays in English and French. He is fluent in Spanish, Italian and German and has a working knowledge of Swahili, Portuguese and Dutch. Residing in Paris, he is a member of the jury of the Prix Europe as well as the prestigious Neustadt International Prize for Literature. Racial, cultural and social conflict, form the substance of much of his work. James Baldwin has said of Russo: "I like your writing . . . it has a very gentle surface and a savage undertow. You're a dangerous man."

Among the poems to be found in *Painting the Tower of Babel* is this remarkable paean to Yma, given here in its entirety by the kind permission of the poet:

THE PERUVIAN GODDESS
when he replays the cassette
and hears his own voice
he winces
feeling the blood rush to his temple
slightly high-pitched
a bit tremulous
with a touch of hysteria
it's not what others would think
rather the way he perceives himself
it's not either that he wishes
he were someone else
no, it is at once simple
and terribly ambitious
like the swish of grass blades
in a simmering July afternoon
where he can't tell whether
it is a sound at all
or the foreshadowing of danger
the senses are so exacerbated
and suddenly, to his delight
he re-enacts a scene
that took place decades ago
bending over his parent's gramophone
a little boy sits mesmerized
the voice coming out
of the scratched 78 rpm record
is that of Yma Sumac
if there is a creator
then she must be a goddess
with her notes scaling the rainbow
from the whispers of genesis
to the explosions of the heart
he can't put a face to this voice
in spite of the cover photograph
even consciously blurs its features
the jungle spills out of those grooves
drawing him into its magic
and the scratch seems to be
that which binds him to the miracle
so frail and yet so timeless

With the emergence of the World Wide Web as an important communication tool Yma Sumac was brought into the 21st Century.

In 1994 Don Pierson, a devoted Sumac fan, opened the first Yma Sumac web page: (www.sunvirgin.com). It soon became the main meeting place for all Sumacians. Since that time a number of other Sumac fan sites have sprung up as well.

On May 29, 1996, with the blessings of Alan Eichler, who was representing Yma at the time, it became the *Official Authorized Yma Sumac Homepage*. While refining the page

Don Pierson, Bob Covais and Patrick Henry. January 1998

over the years, Don came in contact with Sara Cloudwalker (aka Sara Cunningham Carter), who was Yma's personal assistant after Maureen Shea in the 1950s. At Sara's suggestion, the *Official Authorized Yma Sumac Homepage* became the *Yma Sumac Homepage and Archive* so that Yma, not really knowing what the Internet was and having no understanding of the benefits or having her own Web page, might more readily accept it.

During the week after the autographing session at Virgin Records Megastore, Don got a special autographed greeting from Yma specifically for the web page. (The message read: "To all my fans, with all my gratitude and love—Yma Sumac"). A few years later, on October 31, 1998, another special greeting was given by Yma for the web page, this time obtained by Steve Willis, who was unofficially handling her bookings at the time, which said, "To Internet with all my affection and best wishes to my Web page and love to my fans all over the world!! Yma Sumac Los Angeles"

Originally, Don Pierson had grown up hearing the name Yma Sumac. Finally, in the 1960s, when he was 16, he bought one of her LPs and became hooked on her voice. Over the years, he has become an authority on the many international pressings and repressing of her recordings. The *Yma Sumac Homepage* was originally created because of a story about Yma that appeared in a record collector's magazine around 1991. Don wanted to write to the author but first compiled a list of the records in his Yma Sumac collection to include with the letter. The inventory of his collection, which was a computer text-file, became the beginnings of the discography on which the early editions of the Homepage were based and which today is a prime feature of the site. Indeed, it was Don who prepared the discography for this book. Between him and Patrick Henry, a big Yma Sumac fan and a consultant on the issue of the CD *Yma Rocks!* (formerly *Miracles*), they have all eighteen of Yma's 1943 Argentinean selections—in most cases the original 78-rpm disks.

More than 11,000 people visit his site annually and over the years that it has been in existence the web site has proven to be a veritable treasure trove of information on the petite Peruvian. Over the years, the site has become a repository for Sumac memorabilia, including countless photos, and information on other artists and their relation to Yma as well as the remarkable database that chronicles all the various international releases of the Sumac albums.

Don, an enterprising and fascinating man, also collects theremins (and has built several himself), classic Polaroid cameras, and vintage luxury automobiles.

In addition to the creation of the Sumac Web page, articles and informative sites began to spring up that dealt more peripherally with Yma. Coinciding with this surge of Internet visibility for Yma was the growing interest in 1950s "lounge music," especially exotica. Because of this, Web writers now began to re-evaluate Yma and her impact within that movement.

One of the more interesting articles to appear around this time was an article/interview for the on-line magazine, *Goblin* (www.sonic.net/~goblin/yma.htm). In issue number seven, Jon Randall wrote a tribute called "Adoring Yma Sumac."

The beginning of Randall's article evokes the wonder many young men and women felt after hearing the Sumac voice: "Madame Sumac was my very first muse. Whenever there was a gathering at our house I would insist on putting her 'Voice of the Xtabay' on the Victrola. Next step—arrange our collection of bird-nosed 'pre-Columbian' statuettes symmetrically on the fireplace mantel. And then a series of gravely executed Ancient Inca dance 'rituals' (very symmetrical too, of course). Being five years old, I was convinced the sun would fizzle completely without the regular supplications of the Mighty Sun Virgin Yma Sumac and my humble little self." The article was unusual in that it included an interview Jon Randall held with the singer during which she makes a number of interesting comments. When asked about the breakup with Moisés, she replied, "He is cuckoo. All men is cuckoo." (ibid)

She also mentioned a love of opera. "I sing Lakme. To sing that you need a very high coloratura. Then I sang Magic Flute. I have wonderful critics all over the world that say if I wanted to be an opera singer I would be the best, but I don't do it so much because there are thousands of opera singers and I am only one. Other opera singers have tremendous admiration for me because even in my own music which is semi-classical, that I use a coloratura, which is classic. Even Mr. Pavarotti knows Yma Sumac could be the best. But my listeners no like that. They give me sentence. 'You have to sing this music until you die.' So you have to do what they say because they are who make the artist, they are who buy the records. What can I do but obey?" (ibid)

When asked about her current gay following, Yma replied: "They love me, yes. Wherever I go they follow me." (ibid)

Randall summed up the Sumac experience by saying: "There are so few genuinely great icons of the 50s awaiting rediscovery—it's really hard to keep from falling head over heels for this one." (ibid)

After an absence of nine years Yma returned to the Bay Area to sing at San Francisco's Great American Music Hall in June 1996, performing with a six-piece band. As John Blanco insightfully stated in an article in the *Bay Area Reporter* prefacing her performances, "Sumac's true history has never been fully uncovered, but it hardly matters. A certain spuriousness is part of her appeal." (6/6/96)

In an interview with Wayne Saroyan, Yma showed how, over the years, her attitudes and thoughts had changed concerning the old Amy Camus controversy. "If this had happened to me today, I would sue him. But at the time, I said, 'Who cares?' I was more young, and innocent. But I met the man who write this several years later, at a party in Los Angeles. And he run away." (*Contra Costa Times*, 5/31/96) (She may have been recalling an encounter with Walter Winchell, discussed in Chapter 3.)

The 1996 California shows united Yma with one of the most talented of the new generation of jazz guitarists, Skip Heller. Born in Philadelphia, in 1965, Skip played the Philadelphia bar-band circuit during his youth and while making a detour from his music playing in music journalism, he published interviews with a number of prominent musicians including Les Baxter. He and Les got along so well, that by March of

1995, Skip was acting as Baxter's score librarian and publicist. It was Skip who was responsible for the locating and preparing for commercial release the CD, Les Baxter: The Lost Episode in September 1995.

In February 1996, Pulse magazine sent Skip to interview Yma. A few days later he auditioned for her touring band and was hired as her guitarist. After the tour he was so "burned out on lounge and exotica" that he decided to return to playing the music that he truly loved and was soon working with rockabilly legend Ray Campi. But, in 1997, Skip agreed to perform with Yma once more when she sang at the Montreal Jazz Festival. In an interview with Canadian radio Skip commented on both Baxter and Sumac.

"(Baxter) was a pretty blunt talker, but he was a very sweet, generous man. If you took a sincere interest in him and his music, he couldn't do enough for you. He was very good to me." Concerning Yma, Heller wryly observed, "It's been really insane. She cancels a lot of shows, so it really hasn't been a real 'band' experience. We just get the call, do a rehearsal, and make the gig. I hate to be this way, but it's just a job." (ibid.) Heller explained that Yma rarely spoke of Baxter since it was "not a very friendly subject" and allowed that that aside from having lunch with her once in a while they did not spend a lot of time together. "She's not big on hanging out."

When asked what she was like to work with, Heller commented: "She's rough, because she makes vague demands that she can't articulate in musical terms. It's hard to know what she means." (ibid.)

Coinciding with Yma's shows was a record signing at the local Virgin Records "megastore." In his column for the *San Francisco Chronicle*, Herb Caen commented: "Yma Sumac, literally a voice from the past, made no new friends at the Virgin Megastore last Wed., reports Robert Gonzales, who was there. The Inca mummy demanded $5 for autographed photos and $5 to pose for a photo. 'I bought 10 of the Virgin CD samplers to send to my enemies next Christmas,' says Robert. 'The packages will have Nixon stamps on them.'"

In early September of 1996, notices began to appear in New York newspapers that Yma would return to that city for two performances at The Supper Club on West 47th Street. Despite a slew of tickets sold before the show, it was canceled at the last minute. Yma never returned to New York.

Another Yma Sumac concert, to have taken place in Santa Cruz, California, was also canceled at the last minute. By this time the relationship between Yma and Alan Eich-

With Alan Eichler at a signing

ler had become strained to the point of breaking.

Ironically, Yma's cancellation of the Santa Cruz concert signaled the start of an event that during the next few years would more than cover itself with glory. This was the Santa Cruz YmaRama—the brain-child of Curt Keyer and his partner, Maurice Carrillo.

I spoke with Curt on the phone the day after Thanksgiving in 2000. He is a candid and very funny man. He explained that it all started because of Yma's tendency to cancel engagements. Her failure to appear for a concert in Santa Cruz in June, 1996, and her subsequent cancellation of a rescheduled show, left her Santa Cruz fans frustrated. Curt, especially, felt he needed an Yma "fix." A great fan, he has always felt a strong commitment to spreading the word about Yma and her singing. And so he and Maurice decided to take matters into their own hands and remedy the situation by hosting an Yma-themed dinner party. At one point during the evening Curt excused himself from his guests and returned, metamorphosed in drag as Yma. His performance: lip-synching to Yma's 1952 recording of "Wimoweh" (which had recently been released in Capitol's Lounge Series of CDs) proved to be a big hit. It also was the inception of something that would grow well beyond Curt's or Maurice's expectations.

The "Yma" dinner party was such a success that it was decided to have another such gathering the next year. Curt and Maurice realized, though, that there were a number of people they knew who would be willing to present their own interpretation of Yma and her music. And so an expanded version of the original evening was planned, and it was this grander occasion that seemed to demand a name. And so it came to be *The Santa Cruz YmaRama*. Labor day weekend was selected as the right time to hold the new event. For the first official YmaRama (1997) about seven men performed in four acts in Curt and Maurice's back yard to an enthusiastic audience of about 30.

The next YmaRama had six acts and had at least 80 people in attendance. Although originally intended to be a light, basically private entertainment, the YmaRama began to metamorphose into a much more important venue than just a specialized drag show.

Invitations were cleverly created for the event. In 1997, the personal invitations said:

"Let your passions soar into ecstasy!
Pay tribute to the Jewel of the Andes, "Yma Sumac"
See local Artistes sync lips around her golden throat in unimaginable acts of devotion.
Dress for drama—Bring your Act and an edible offering to share."

The one from 1999 was even more clever, boldly announcing:

"Yma Sumac
Old Legends Never Die
See for yourself on Stage
Live Lypsync, Lypsunk and Synking
All Male cast of Hot! Hot! Hot! Homodorables
Dress for Drama (Please) Bring edible offerings to share.
Feasting Begins 3:00 PM in the Temple Garden
Worship and Performances at 5:00 Prompt
Friendship rituals follow 'til all are exhausted."

There were now about a dozen acts that performed for about 200 people—all crammed into Curt and Maurice's backyard. Creative and campy, the acts began to evolve as well. Performers from one year often returned with newer and more outrageous acts. One featured a dramatic reading of Thomas Meehan's comic essay *Yma Dream*. Other acts included not only dramatically interpreted lip-synching to Yma's songs, but also dance interpretations. A former artist of the great drag ballet travesty

YmaRama 2000. (top left) Entrance of "Yma"; (top right) stage; (bottom right) Maurice Carillo and Curt Keyeser.

company Ballets Trockaderos de Monte Carlo offered interpretive dance sequences. Professional puppeteers performed. One skit, built around Yma being kidnapped by aliens, cleverly expanded upon its premise at each succeeding annual YmaRama.

Because of YmaRama's rapid growth in popularity, Curt and Maurice came to devote the entire month of August to its preparations. It became the most important social event for gay men in the city of Santa Cruz; by 1999, they had decided that the event should be exploited for a larger good, and it was decided to undertake serious fundraising. That year they raised several thousands of dollars; in 2000 they raised $6,600 for the Santa Cruz AIDS Project.

That year the invitations were just as inventive and tongue in cheek.

Heralding that the event would begin at 2 PM on September 3, with performances beginning at 3:45 PM, invitees were told that it all would take place at "Yma's Garden Temple at the Palace de Peru." The invitation continued: "Join us for the final YmaRama. Don't miss your last chance to celebrate the Legend of Yma Sumac with the Diva's Disciples and Devotees. Perform for the masses and bear witness to the passion of artists from near and far. . . . Tea dance will follow immediately—an orgy of flesh and frivolitic music by Eric Sassaman. Bring edible offerings to share and dress for drama."

During the YmaRamas, Curt primarily played Mistress of Ceremonies as "Yma" but occasionally he was persuaded to perform. As Mistress of Ceremonies his quick wit and bantering with the audience during YmaRamas were some of the funniest moments of the show. For his entrance in the final, 2000 YmaRama, Curt as Yma was carried in on a litter in full Incan regalia. And for the final act of the evening he created a new, dramatic "play" around "Najala's Lament" from *Flahooley*, where, after having run away with a suitor, he sacrificed himself by jumping into a smoking volcano. Although Maurice also performed during YmaRamas, he was usually content to play the rejected suitors of Curt's fantasies. He was also responsible for getting the large set built. In honor of the event they named their home "Pacheco Palace de Peru."

Their guests were just as creative.

"Our guests have created some clever Yma-inspired foods to share with her adoring public. Knowing how popular Guinea pigs are as a protein source in traditional Peruvian cuisine, one culinary time-saver developed a Guinea Pig Helper especially for YmaRama. Another guest brought YmaRama Llama Balls. He finds these are best served chaffed. Lastly, to honor Miss Sumac's descendency from the Peruvian royalty, a magnificent many-tiered replica of an Incan temple was created out of pink Rice Krispies and marshmallows. It brought back the greatness of a culture long gone." (Private email, 12/4/2001)

Don Pierson and his partner, Richard Nichols went to the final YmaRama.

"As a benefit for the Santa Cruz AIDS Project, it was a show with skits to Yma Sumac songs and most (actually all) were drag. In fact, there were no women there at all. The set was a great stage that looked like an Incan temple with a photo of Yma's face on each side and a smoking volcano on the left. The acts themselves were hilarious! To see Yma doing a bondage S&M version of "Sejollo" (The Whip Dance from *Legend of the Jivaro*) was enough to cause hysterics. It was held in a huge backyard with a grand Inca entrance made for the event. There were about 150 people in attendance." (Private email, 9/5/2000)

On Tuesday, July 16, 1996, Yma began a multi-week engagement at Dan Ackroyd's House of Blues. Dan Heckman, reporting in the Los Angeles Times on July 19, 1996, commented: "Is Yma Sumac a diva? Consider this: At one moment in her performance . . . the crowd started to get a bit rambunctious. The 68-year-old singer drew herself up imperiously and raised one regal hand for silence. The noise was stilled in an instant."

"Dressed in a flowing high-priestess gown and sporting an enormous, flamboyant necklace, Sumac strode the stage with the clear feeling that she was in total control of the room. Visual impact aside, her voice is one of the most remarkable instruments in pop music. In the course of her hour-long set, she tossed in bird calls, soaring operatic bel-canto, scary-sounding shamanistic growls and small intimate whispers.

"If the presentation was occasionally reminiscent of a '50s exotic lounge act, Sumac's divadom was nonetheless guaranteed, not only by her commanding presence and powerful sense of self but by her still-impressive musicality."

One writer felt that "besides her beautiful singing, the highlight of the evening was when she actually turned and yelled at the keyboard player, 'Play professional . . . PLEASE!' (Mr. Damon, 8/7/96 *4-Front*)

Mr. Damon doubted, however, that Yma would return to the House of Blues after her inappropriate treatment by the establishment. "There was no make-up man to powder her face when she needed it. There was nothing for her to drink. Not to mention that this elderly artist simply had no point-of-reference for the Madonna-Blonde-Ambition-Tour head-set microphone they hooked up to her." (ibid.)

Reporting for *Lounge* website (http://www.val.net/Lounge/tikidiv.html) Patrick Tierney found the entire Sumac experience ludicrous. He opened his review with a riddle: "When is a 'house' not a house, 'the blues' not the blues, and a 'Peruvian singer from the Andes' not a Peruvian singer from the Andes?" A. When Yma Sumac appears at the House of Blues. It was the West Hollywood demographic—Yma's adoring cult—who supplied the evening's most fervent applause and appreciation. Not for anything musical, mind you. They flapped like seals for Ms. Sumac's arthritic toreador moves with her

Yma and Steve Willis, 2006 (Courtesy of Steve Willis)

flowing chiffon gown which at one point—in mid twirl—revealed the ancient, macabre mysteries of her own private peaks . . . The whole scene forced memories of the spectacles in the early seventies by Yma's contemporary, the late operatic soprano Eleanor Steber and the clammy command performances she put on in New York City bath houses." He noted that saxman Jay Work had "likened Yma's [singing] to sounds elicited from a Teacup Chihuahua being forcibly administered an ice water enema." (ibid)

It was at about this time that Steve Willis became associated with the Peruvian singer. Dividing his time between New York City and Los Angeles, Steve lives at the famous Chelsea Hotel when in New York. Steve first discovered Yma Sumac in 1987, while living in Los Angeles.

"I was working in a clothing store and one of the nightmare tasks of the job was to listen to really awful music all day. I have always been a huge music fan. I was just beginning to explore old Spanish music like Las Panchos singing with Eydie Gorme. I was also getting into opera. I've always had a healthy appreciation for kitsch—so much so, that I can't really tell anymore what is good taste and what is bad." A friend of his who knew he was a fan of the high coloratura soprano voice brought a cassette of Yma's *Mambo!* to him and Steve was hooked. He began collecting Yma's recordings and since he knew nothing about her except what was on the records, did some research.

As the years went by what began as a strong interest slowly grew into an obsession and Steve decided that he wanted to make a documentary film about Yma. Much of this had to do with the fact that Yma was making a comeback and was performing at the Hotel Roosevelt in Los Angeles. Each show was a combination of pure excitement and incredible stress. "She wore these very low cut dresses that showed too much of her cleavage." Steve learned that by a striking coincidence a friend of his, Terry Valazza, made Yma's dresses at the time. "I told Terry that the dresses were too low cut and problematic. She said she agreed but Yma insisted on them being like that."

Terry also knew where Yma lived. "Before I even knew Yma," Steve says, "I knew where she lived. It was a small bungalow apartment in West Hollywood. I would always try and find my way past her house when I was driving. I would see her walking her lit-

Yma and Alan Eichler at a 2006 signing.

tle dog and I knew that it was her even though she was in a disguise—sort of."

Terry arranged for Steve to meet Yma when she came to Terry's for a fitting. Yma and Steve had an immediate rapport and decided to go out to dinner. Yma had severed her relationship with Alan Eichler and was looking for new management. Although Terry had tried to explain what Steve did, Yma got it into her head that he was an important agent. Steve, thinking there might be possibilities there, agreed to take on that job. "I thought I would give it a try. It seemed easy to find her a few gigs and make some money on the side." They went to dinner at the Hotel Roosevelt and Steve listened as Yma regaled him with stories. "I could hardly understand her with her thick Peruvian accent and a lot of chicken in her mouth." Because he was introduced to her by someone she trusted, Yma felt comfortable enough with him to exchange telephone numbers. At that time he didn't mention his idea of making a documentary to her.

"Yma and Alan Eichler had had a falling-out because of various things." Steve commented, "She felt Alan was speaking too much on her behalf and doing things without informing her of what he was doing."

According to Nick Grant, Yma's breakup with Eichler had many facets but one was her objection to being given a contract at the last minute—often with stipulations that she did not like. "You should see her when she talks about Eichler or Moisés, all the veins in her throat come out."

Although new to the concept of being an artist's representative, Steve had considerable experience with popular music and musicians. He had produced documentaries on such artists as Bon Jovi, Vanessa Williams and Mother Love Bone. He had also directed or produced music videos of such singers as Patti Labelle, Maxi Priest, Jason Nevins, Mary J. Blige, Chante Moore, Mariah Carey, Cyndi Lauper and Julio Iglesias. So he felt that the situation might work. He decided to give Yma and her career all he could—even though he also had a career of his own. He decided that probably the best way to get involved and to get a feel for what was necessary was to contact Capitol Records and their publicist on her behalf. Usually when contacting Capitol Records, Yma would go to the offices in person.

When there, Willis accessed her file and was surprised how unprofessional and disorganized it was. "There were articles, press clippings and contracts in there as well as letters from her husband about the new releases. He had hand scratched his name in as composer after each song. I photocopied as much press stuff as I could. There was also a letter from Moisés with his detailed instructions for the packaging and the artistic crediting he wanted for the re-releasing of Yma's CDs.

"As I made contact with people who were dealing with her, I started hearing that people were surprised that I would take on such a job. They warned me how difficult Yma was. I tried to contact venues for concerts. So many people had never heard of her and weren't interested. I called the places she had worked before. People didn't want to work with her again. I was too nervous to call Yma. How can you tell someone this?"

"I have to confess that, as her manager, I was not very successful. It's a tough business and I have another career that keeps me busy and I found I couldn't take on another whole career and then try to juggle both of them. In order to get her performances I would have had to invest too much time. She made it even more difficult because she wants a lot of money and the places to be very large. And a lot of places don't feel that she can draw in those numbers even though every concert is sold out. "

While trying to act as her manager, however, Steve wasn't idle. He was also attempting to arrange for her return to a recording studio. "To me, I am still amazed at the talent and that she can still perform. She has thousands and thousands of songs that are unrecorded that she has put on her own tape player or in a studio. They are very rough but they are amazing. We had a lot of meetings with record producers but no one seemed to be willing to go through with the project. She is very angry and won't talk with Capitol."

"We were talking with independents because that was the way she wanted to go. People that do rock or jazz, or dance music. The reactions were all the same. They were interested but busy, they just weren't sure. They would say 'Yes, yes I want to' but then they never called. Months and months I pursued these different avenues."

During this period Hernán Braña, in his mid-80s, was in failing health; he died on May 10, 1997.

On July 1 and 2, 1997, Yma made her last important concert appearance. It was for the Montreal Jazz Festival. Although originally secured for Yma by Alan Eichler, it was Steve Willis who accompanied Yma to Canada. By that time Steve had phased himself out from working as Yma's booking agent. Nonetheless, Yma asked him to go with her.

"I was thrilled! I couldn't believe it. We met at the airport. I came from New York City (where I was at the time) and she came from Los Angeles with her little lap-dog, Cholita."

Although he was at the Festival as Yma's friend, Steve agreed to act as her contact with the Festival staff. He also transported her around (Yma has never driven), made sure her dresses were cleaned, helped her on and off the stage and other things. They were there three nights—Yma performing two nights. On the first night she called Cholita on stage.

"The weather was very hot. I suggested that a fan be put on stage to cool her down but it kind of dried her out." Accompanied by a five-piece band (including Skip Heller on guitar), Yma came and took the Jazz Festival by storm. Dressed in a flowing green chiffon gown with her now trade-mark diamond tiara, long dangling earrings and an odd, almost alien-looking head-set, Yma strode on the stage with energy and confidence despite the hot weather. Among the numbers she offered to the audience were old favorites "Ataypura" (High Andes), "Montana," "La Pampa y la Puna," (The Plains and the Mountains) and "La Molina" (The Mill Song) all from her Capitol albums which she modestly admitted she had "recorded 2,000 years ago for Capitol Records." Also included were some of her own compositions and the ever-present Chilean "Ay, Ay, Ay."

This last was obviously a special favorite of Yma's. Unfortunately the simple song from Chile was given the grand opera treatment, overburdened with tempi changes, dynamic switching back and forth, and tiny Sumacian humming-bird noises. Accompanied only by piano, Yma stood formally in the crook of the piano and let loose with an obviously heartfelt, but completely inappropriate rendition of the music.

"Ataypura" (High Andes) the only remaining song from the 1950 *Voice of the Xtabay* exotica, was still impressive for Yma's ability to hit staccato high Ds and for the use of her famous "Chu-Wah!" at the end. The audience loved it. For "Montana" Yma sat down in a straight-back chair that Steve had brought on stage and positioned her arms as if holding a baby and began humming the melody. Almost eerie, the picture of the grandmother Yma crooning to an imaginary infant was heightened by her still beautiful and graceful hand and arm gestures.

But it was her last piece, "La Molina" (The Mill Song), that proved to be the high point of the evening. The audience, thrilled with her high, ornamental staccato flights often erupted into applause mid-phrase. By this time it was Yma's practice to leave the stage—only to return for another go at the bravura phrases. When she re-entered she would just begin singing, often leaving out or skipping entire pages of music, which forced the accompanying musicians to scramble to find their places.

Obviously enjoying herself immensely, Yma gaily danced during musical interludes and proudly displayed the "growl," pin-pointed high Cs and Ds and superb rhythmical facility. Although the top of the voice was thin, it was there. Unfortunately the middle and much of the bottom register were practically inaudible.

During the concert Steve remained side-stage ready to help Yma on and off making sure she got a secure footing. By the second night the show was relatively smooth, although Yma and the pianist had occasional disagreements as to which song should come next. Also typically divatic, and extremely unprofessional, Yma often tried to conduct the musicians with abrupt hand gestures or loud *"shh"*s that were more disruptive and offensive than the loudness of the musicians.

All during this time Steve never forgot his desire to make a documentary. "On many occasions I have seen her approached for various projects and yet she always refuses. She is pleased with the mystique that surrounds her image and is careful never to compromise her status as a legend. I have asked her to let me tell her story and have the great honor of her approval for my project." At the time of this writing (2007), Steve has begun filming his documentary (working title: *Discovering Yma Sumac*). He has already captured some wonderful footage of Yma singing. He admits that these past years he has found it difficult, however to juggle his own life and his making of the documentary. "There was so much to take care of from getting Yma to agree to take part in the documentary to finding financial backers."

The promotional brochure for the documentary (superbly designed by Steve's sister) says: "*Discovering Yma* will follow Yma as she records her new CD, over 50 years after her biggest hit album. There will also be interviews with some of the many famous musical acts that consider Yma a great inspiration to their work. The grand finale will be live concert footage where Yma performs her old favorites and new classics to an audience of old and new fans.

"Archival footage, current interviews and anecdotal segments from friends, family and business associates will all combine to show the complex twists and turns that have conspired to create this truly unique woman."

Steve's relationship with Yma has metamorphosed into one of friendship. Some things about the singer still amaze him. "She has a big poster of Jesus, which is confusing because her beliefs don't seem to be traditionally Christian. She always talks about nature and the universe. She has a karmic reaction to things and sounds totally new-age most of the time."

"She recommends eating a lot of fruit and water. She only eats chicken and fruit. She feeds her dog chicken as well. She's always trying to tell me how to do everything—including enemas. She's gone into great detail actually. She recommends locking my bedroom door every time I leave the house—against my roommates. She locks up everything. She has a special key for her front door that is Chinese. It is smooth on one side. I have no idea how she got it installed but it means she has other people helping her that I'm not aware of."

Almost simultaneous with Yma's success at the 1997 Montreal Jazz Festival, James Branciforti (Miracles producer) succumbed to cancer after a long battle. Bob Covais, his partner of 38 years, became so despondent after Jim's death that on the 28th of February,1998 he took his own life. Don Pierson wrote a tribute to the two on the Yma Sumac Home page: 'They were both wonderful, caring, thoughtful and generous people who contributed greatly, not only to this site but also to us by their love and support."

A memorial service for Bob was held in Virginia on the 21st of March, 1999. A private event celebrating Bob's life was held on the West Coast as well.

After the Montreal Jazz Festival, the friendship between Yma and Steve became governed by Yma's moods and whims and Steve's willingness to abide by her rules of the friendship. "There is an interesting dynamic to our relationship now and that is that I experience her a lot as a teacher—spiritually; some one who has experienced a lot and is very wise. She takes on the role of a teacher, she likes that, and she lectures and then gives advice. She has a lot to say on subjects and has a very modern philosophy. And I am always amazed how caught up on current events she is. She loves animals and she loves her little dog, Cholita, who was a gift from Alan Eichler."

When asked what he and Yma did when they spent time together, Steve said, "Grocery shopping. She buys a lot of bird seed to feed the birds, we hang out at her house sometimes. She eats a lot of fruit and apples, vegetables, chicken but not much beef—hardly ever. She is very health conscious. And talks about it all the time. She does love Pollo Loco (a fast food chain in Los Angeles) and often if I am going over to her house I will take over some for us to have for dinner.

"What I really loved, though, was when she would come over to my house and we would listen to her records and she would sing. Like a lot of singers she does not listen to her own recordings so I would have to instigate these listening sessions. I also liked it when we would be driving in the car and she would sing and drum on the dashboard. A lot of times she would sing some of her own songs and ask me what I thought of. Sometimes she would talk about what she wanted to do—you know, ideas for upcoming jobs and stuff—and sometimes she would talk about the past. But not too often.

"She feeds all the cats in her backyard. And when she moves—she is thinking of moving, hopefully into Hollywood—she wants to take them with her. Although she has mentioned Las Vegas, that would not be convenient for her, and living in the desert would not be good for her. She hates the hot weather and prefers cold weather. She told me she was very happy singing in Russia, and one of the reasons was because it was cold.

"She is very much into her privacy and not being Yma Sumac and I think 99% of her life is about that. When she goes out from her house she doesn't want to be recognized. If she wants to go out as Yma Sumac she comes over to my house and changes her clothes and comes out of my house as Yma Sumac. There is a dichotomy though. She wants her privacy but she also wants to be recognized. But she wants to be recognized on her own terms. She loves her peace and I think that is what makes her happy."

"One of my most cherished memories of her is when she and I went in September of 1997 to a tribute to her that was put on by the Peruvian Women's Association in Los Angeles at the Wilshire Ebel. They honored her with an award and a production with Peruvian dancers and clips from her films. We were sitting on the side of the stage and the dancers were dancing to her music and she got a little misty-eyed. She was remembering when her parents first heard her music and how they didn't want her to do that and I think the song that was playing was actually the one that her parents had heard. And she was remembering the moment of acceptance on their part and I think that was what was touching for her."

Steve summed it up: "I've found it best for both of us to keep a certain, safe distance. Eventually everyone fails Yma."

September 1998, saw a brief revival of the musical Flahooley in New York. The show opened off-Broadway on September 10. Although the revival received excellent reviews, as if cursed, it failed to attract an audience. It was performed at St. Clement's Church, at 423 West 46th Street with a modest ticket price of $20.00. Singled out for praise was Carol Tammen as the exotic Najala. It was closed by September 26.

On September 19, 1998, Moisés Vivanco died of a heart attack in Madrid. His health had been poor for quite a while and Charlie, their son, had gone to care for him. It seems that Moisés never remarried (neither did Yma, of course) and although in letters to me he proclaimed his great love for America, he never returned. After he returned to Spain decades earlier, Moisés "dedicated [himself] to writing Military Marches and Religious musical works, most of which are still available for recording or film if requested." (private letter, 6/23/93)

I corresponded with Moisés for about a year and although I never spoke to him in person, in letters I found him to be charming, if formal, a bit paranoid about what exactly this book was to entail; still trying, in his way, to grasp control of whatever was happening around him.

I heard very little about Charlie, and all attempts to contact him failed. Of them all perhaps, Charlie remains the biggest mystery. While young he was considered a fine swimmer and later he went to University and studied engineering. A private man, he seems to have had a number of talents. Moisés wrote me that Charlie "was a great rhythm player. He has a lovely melodious voice." Possibly as part of the natural fall out of being the son of two international performers, Charlie decided to go into a career that was more sedate. Moisés was very explicit in his letters to me that Charlie "does not wish his actual personal life to be mentioned." (private letter from Moisés 6/23/93)

I did, however, hear one interesting story. The home where Charlie had his childhood, in Cheviot Hills, had a brightly tiled pool. The inside of the house was usually kept dark with heavy drapes. There were a lot of parties with famous Hollywood stars while he was growing up. It seems that, many years later, while visiting California, Charlie went to see the house where he grew up and introduced himself to the current owners. He was surprised and very pleased at the house's remodeling and told them he would like his mother to come and see it, but Yma never did. At the time that he visited, he was told that mail would sometimes still come to that address for Yma from all over the world.

Yma learned of Moisés' death from Steve Willis. Apparently because of her performing schedule, she had taken her phone off the hook and so did not speak with Charlie, who supposedly called once a week. She did not learn of Moisés' death for a number of days. Even after hearing about Moisés' death and having it confirmed by various members of the family, it seems that for years Yma refused to believe it.

Ironically, almost coinciding with Moisés' death was Don Pierson's release of *Yma Rocks!* a digital re-mastering of the 1971 *Miracles* album. Technically, this was not a reissue or re-release since it was mastered from a slightly different mix, had updated liner notes written by Bob Covais and new cover art by the noted Carmel, California artist, Raymond Bennett. Thanks to Bob Covais, who produced the recording, the two unreleased tracks were also included: "Savage Rock" and "Parade" (the one on which he and Jim Branciforti sang chorus.) The disk was released by ShamLys Productions. Pierson explained: "ShamLys represents, of course, the Shamrock as a tribute to James who was Irish and the Fleur de Lys since Robert was French."

Unfortunately, Bob Covais did not get to see the final product as he had died the previous February. The disk is a remarkable tribute in a number of ways. Despite his love-hate relationship with Yma, the *Yma Rocks!* project proved how enduring Bob Covais' devotion to Yma's art was—but it was also a loving tribute to his partner, James.

During the 1980s, while doing initial research for this book, I was steered in the direction of Bob Covais and Jim Branciforti by Les Baxter. I spent months visiting and talking with them; having them tell me their story and educate me in Peruvian music, culture and traditions. As in many relationships, one of the personalities is stronger. In this case, the stronger personality (the more outgoing) was Bob whose energy and enthusiasm were infectious. James was the quieter, more thoughtful of the two. It always seemed to me that, although he too admired Yma, Jim's enthusiasm and interest in Bob's "Sumac projects" were his way of supporting Robert and showing his deep love for his partner.

During the last weeks of November 1998, Don Pierson began formulating plans to release a new Sumac CD. It was to be called *Especially For You* after one of Yma's own compositions. His original concept was to produce a small number of disks—perhaps a hundred—which would be sold at a premium price with the entire proceeds going back to cover costs of production.

Assuming Yma agreed to all of this, she could then review the CD and make any changes she wanted in the production. The next pressing would be where Yma would receive her royalty—whatever was decided upon. Don confided to me that he feared Yma expected the CD to be a big money maker. He was concerned that she understand that the main purposes of the CD were, first, to keep the rare material from being lost forever, and second, to contribute to the maintenance of the Web site, which cost several thousand dollars a year that Don paid out of his own pocket.

Don asked for my help in selecting the tracks of the CD's program. So, after reviewing all the live tapes I had of Yma in my personal library, I jotted down information about performances that I felt were suitable and sent it off for Don to review. After conversing back and forth, I sent the original tapes to him so that he could go from the masters. On February 1, 1999, Don emailed me the preliminary proposal for the new CD, which was also sent to Steve Willis, who was (once again) loosely representing Yma. It was a very rough draft meant to explain what Don was trying to accomplish with the CD. Steve was supposed to give Don some tips and suggestions for the language. Instead, on February 4, Steve took the proposal to Yma; by February 25, Don had emailed me: "I finally heard from Steve with the go-ahead to proceed on the new CD. This was not an agreement to actually make it— just permission to proceed. The next step is to take a couple of samples to the studio to find if the material can be repaired and enhanced. Then, if it can, I'll get the hardware and begin transferring each tape onto its own CD where I can easily transfer the choices to another CD to take to the studio for re-mastering."

At the end of February, still during the preparatory stages of the new CD, Yma told Steve Willis that she wanted to meet with Don Pierson. Pierson responded to Steve, explaining that he had been advised not to do any business with Yma directly concerning the *Especially For You* CD.

Steve was now in an awkward position. Yma decided that Steve was handling things behind her back, and their relationship became strained despite Steve's best attempts to explain the situation.

By coincidence, in March a name from Yma's past began surfacing again. A posting to the Yma Sumac Forum /BBS was made on March 25, 1999. Bernard Stollman wrote to Sumac via the web page: "It has been a long time since we talked. My record company, ESP-disk has survived and is now flourishing, with international distribution . . . (You remember that you were briefly under contract to me, but I released you from it so that you could make the London rock record.) Please ask your son to contact me. I hope that you are well, and that we shall meet again soon."

In April Pierson left the tapes that had been selected for the new CD with the studio technicians so that the material could be archived onto CD, one per show. After that he would select the tracks he wanted to use for the CD and have those re-mastered onto a separate CD.

During May and June, Don Pierson continued preparations begun earlier in the year to move the Homepage to a larger server and to register it with a new domain name: www.sunvirgin.com. The new site features a Members area, where information not available to the general public can be viewed, such as the Archives of Clippings, a History of Shows and Tours, and features such as a Classified Ads page, along with many other similar research items.

By mid June, Steve Willis had again fallen out of favor with Yma. On June 14, Yma finally contacted Don Pierson, asking him to visit her. Originally the plan was that he was to make the 450 mile trip during the weekend of June 25–27. Then it was moved slightly later. Oddly, Yma seemed more interested in having Don prove to her that she had a business relationship with Alan Eichler. She requested written proof.

Bewilderingly to me at the time, Don asked me to fax some articles and programs from the 1980s that showed that Eichler worked with Yma. I faxed him the material on June 15, 1999. He wrote back to explain: "When Yma wrote the first time, she asked who 'authorized' the Homepage. I replied that it was done by Alan Eichler, who was representing her at the time, though I also said that I 'came to understand later that she denied any business association with him.' She wants me to bring proof of such an association in print. Last night I found it is even printed in a black box in her Ballroom program that he is her exclusive representative, and I found a quote directly from her that he is the one who brought her out of semi-retirement in Peru! Between the things you sent and those I already have, I have plenty to show her. Apparently what's common knowledge for everyone else is not for her" (Private email, 6/15/99)

On Thursday, July 8, I received an email from Don: "I haven't heard from Yma yet about our meeting that was supposed to be this Saturday so I am permanently canceling it. I don't think she has even checked her P.O. Box so doesn't know about it. She has driven away her young friend so there's no other way I can contact her. It's just too much hassle for nothing, especially since she mainly wanted to talk about the Homepage anyway." (private email)

When I originally got Don's note I thought he was referring to Steve Willis, and so asked him.

"No, I don't mean Steve. She had another guy (Damon Devine) who sought her out and befriended her. She has been a real terror to him in nearly every way possible! Some of the stories he has told me would turn your blood cold. . . . He really thinks she is los-

With Damon Devine, 2006. (Courtesy of Yma-Sumac.com)

ing/has lost her mind and I'm inclined to agree. She doesn't know that I have contact with him and would kill if she found out.

"I already knew that the main reason she wanted me to come down was because she wanted to discuss the Homepage rather than to discuss the new CD. She is under the impression that I should be paying her for the Homepage when it should be the other way around. I tried to explain to her, in my last letter, how the Internet works but I doubt she has even checked her P.O. Box so hasn't read it. I wasn't going all the way down there without confirmation and, without her 'young friend' she has no way to get to the post office. She doesn't want to have Alan Eichler take her because he charges her for it— good for him!)" (private email 7/9/99)

(The projected CD *Especially For You* remains in limbo. Negotiations with Yma fruitless, Don Pierson found the project completely stymied.)

By the end of July, during a return visit to New York, Steve Willis called Yma for the first time in a long time, thinking to mend the relationship. When I asked him (later) what had caused the rift, he replied. "It was just a lot of things. But mainly when you become a friend of Yma's you have to be willing to do a lot for her. And most of the time I am more than willing. But there were a few times when we had agreed that I wouldn't do something for her because I had other commitments. She would end up demanding more. I had reached a point of no return."

Probably one of the most interesting relationships Yma had during the late 1990s (and continuing to the time of this writing, in 2007) is that with Damon Devine. At the time they met Damon was a college student without family who was studying the art of theatrical make up. (He is now a professional freelance makeup artist who does independent film and print work.)

Damon was first introduced to Yma's singing by a friend who played him her recordings. He was not much taken with her singing, as it happens, although he recalls that he found "Taita Inty" fascinating. But while at a record show in Buena Park in 1995, he heard that Yma was there and so decided to meet her. He found himself captivated by her charm. "She was so little and cute."

Two weeks later he saw her again at a Tower Records store, when Yma was there for a record signing signaling the re-release of her Capitol recordings on the Right Stuff label. This time he came prepared with photos for her to sign, a camera, and flowers.

He next saw her at the Wilshire Ebel at a life achievement ceremony in Yma's honor sponsored by the Peruvian community. Again, she was pleased to see him. Because they got along so well, Damon decided to send Yma a fan letter. Although he was warned by Alan Eichler of the trouble to be found in a relationship with Yma, when she did not respond Damon decided to find out where she lived and take flowers to her. Armed with flowers and photograph of Yma and himself taken at Tower Records, Damon went to her neighborhood and showed the photo to people to see if anyone would recognize her. One neighbor, recognizing the woman in the photo, was stunned to learned that indeed her neighbor was Yma Sumac. He was able to point out Yma's house. "I walked over to it, very nervous. I remember that a big black plastic sheet covered the front door—which I thought was odd, but knocked on the door anyway."

Yma opened the door and after Damon re-introduced himself snapped at him "How you get this address?" Damon explained why he was there, offered the flowers to Yma and smiled nervously at her. Yma smiled back.

"She then disappeared behind the plastic curtain and after about ten minutes came out dressed in street clothes. Before I knew it we were arm in arm and going shopping for groceries. It was completely unreal. While we walked, I showed Yma the photos that I had brought along and she said "Look at those beautiful hands" pointing to her own hands in the pictures."

Over the next two years (1997–1999) Damon visited with Yma many times—as many, he estimates, as 60 or 80, often spending an entire day with her. "But I never called her Yma, I always called her Perita. That was what she preferred."

Generally very mistrustful, Yma grew to trust Damon. "That first day—when I met her at her home—I never went in to her apartment. She came out to me. It wasn't till much later that she let me in. And then I found that it was cluttered with trunks and all sorts of things—as if she never threw anything away—and it was always very dark."

"The reason she had the black plastic over the front door" Damon explained, "was that she was sure that the landlord 'had it in for her.' She loved animals, though, especially her little, white dog. She loved his quiet loyalty. She would also get teary-eyed when she talked about the plight of the cats and birds in the neighborhood. But people . . . no."

Yma's trust of Damon grew and they became closer. "I remember one wonderful day when it was raining. We were both talking seriously about family, loss and stuff and she hugged me affectionately. That was one of the nice moments."

About halfway through their relationship, she changed their shopping scenario. Usually Damon would go to the store while Yma waited at home. Eventually, though, instead of having Damon go to the store Yma would go and he would remain "to watch the place" while she was gone. "Actually, I preferred to go myself because she could take hours looking at things in the store, although she always came back with some explanation—saying it was very crowded or the lines were very long. I admit that I was often tempted to look around while she was gone but I never did because I was afraid. To be honest, by that time I was never sure if she might not have set a little trap for me to find out if I was snooping.

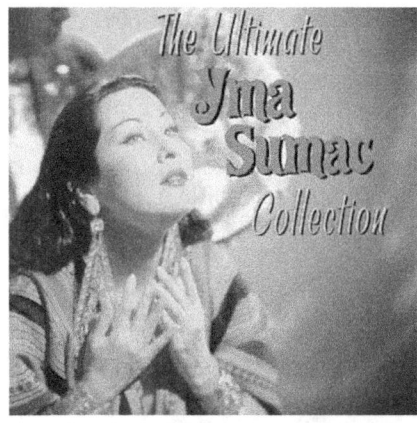

She knew that I was fascinated with her career and that I wanted to see her old photos and stuff.

"One afternoon I took over her recording of "Babalu" that had been recently re-released and played it for her. At first she listened distractedly but then her eyes glistened and she got this pleased smile on her face as if she were thinking: 'God! I really was good wasn't I?' At least that is how I interpreted her expression."

Later that same day Yma and Damon walked down her street to go to GNC to choose some vitamins for Yma. She brought her little dog with her. "When we were in the store," Damon said, "a young Hispanic man came over to us and said the dog was not allowed in the store. Yma heard him but ignored his request and instead kept talking to me." "Excuse me" he said again, "the dog has to go."

"So!" she said "Its alright for a robber to come in and go 'bang bang I keel you' but its not alright for a little dog!" The young man, it turned out was from Venezuela—which impressed Yma. So they started to speak in Spanish. He had no idea who she was, but even so, within minutes, he was completely captivated.

"When we left the store" Damon remembers, "he called out: 'Next time you come I'll give a 10 per cent discount.' Yma turned back toward him, stared fixedly at him, raised one eyebrow and said '20 per cent!'"

In January of 2000, The Right Stuff (distributed by EMI) released *The Ultimate Yma Sumac Collection*, a compilation of some of Yma's finest Capitol recordings, including a few of the unreleased tracks previously only available on the extremely difficult to locate English released RevOla issues. The entire project was the love child of Alan Eichler who selected all the tracks for the disk.

The street date for the release was January 11, 2000. Tower Records' magazine, *Pulse*, noted that Sumac was "set to mesmerize another generation of musical adventurers with her new compilation . . . a smoldering 21-song set that features three previously unreleased tracks . . . ." Tom Laskin, who wrote the article, reported that her vocal range was 5 1/2 octaves(!) and spoke with guitarist Skip Heller concerning the possibility that Yma could tour in support of the new release.

"[H]e figures her latest comeback will be just as fantastical as the last one. Sure, touring with the lapdog-toting diva in the late '90s nearly drove him crazy, but Heller says that Sumac's astonishing creative aura never failed to impress him. 'When we played the Montreal Jazz Festival there were two reviews . . . The English language newspaper rightly tore us a collective asshole. And then there was the French language newspaper, which put its review on the front page with this headline: Yma Sumac Exists! It said that she may not sing as well as she used to, it may not be the Capitol years, but it was incredible to be in the same room with this presence. Which is true. She really is just this incredibly mysterious figure.'

"As for the well-circulated rumor that the 70-something Sumac is actually house-frau Amy Camus, Heller says there's absolutely no truth to it. 'When we were touring, sometimes I'd hold the passports,' he explains. 'And I peeked.'"

The Ultimate Yma Sumac Collection is a good, solid contribution to the Sumac discography—its only weakness being that it does not include any of the 1943 recordings. It does, however, include such classic, but hard to find, recordings as "Babalu," "Inca Waltz," and a *Flahooley* selection.

The CD was well received and continues to sell well to this day. At the time of its release, it was purported that Yma would be undergoing an extensive tour "in support of the album." (Robert Mancini, MTV News Gallery, 12/21/99)

Dan Epstein, writing for *Spectator* online wrote: "Though this stuff is much-loved by the lounge revivalists, it's hardly 'easy listening' in the conventional sense; exotica-tinged songs . . . are informed by Yma's arsenal of bizarre clucks, spine-chilling trills and glass-shattering high notes, all of which seem to imply that the natives are indeed becoming restless. Taken in toto, these 21 tracks are guaranteed to send your roommate (and maybe yourself, as well) screaming into the night."

Doug Balding, reporting for *The American Reporter* (7/4/2000) noted: "(It) is a thorough examination of the singer's years with Capitol (1950–1959). In fact, it's probably all the Sumac that anyone, save a rabid fan, will ever need. The main attraction, of course, is Sumac's voice. She moans, shrieks, warbles and just plain sings, and that's just the first song. Sumac is one of the most original and distinctive singers ever, and this CD demonstrates her voice at its best . . . These 21 tunes . . . complemented by excellent liner notes and photos, is a fitting tribute to this remarkable singer."

Java's Bachelor Pad Hi-Fi Archive online wrote: "Some may argue that Martin Denny or Les Baxter were the heart and soul behind the exotica craze of the 1950's but when you look at it, no one can compare to Yma Sumac . . . Her first album, 'Voice of the Xtabay' . . . became required listening on hi-fi's the world over. Even today, you have not earned your hipster stripes unless you have that original 10 inch as well as the 12 inch record which combines 'Voice of the Xtabay' with . . . Inca Taqui—Chants of the Incans. Sumac's talents have won praise with classical and popular music fans alike . . . She was able to give exotica the credibility it sorely needed . . . (This new release) gathers up 21 tracks spanning the vast range of styles she performed during her career. From folk song to pop song, you can't help but get caught up in the mystery and exotic-ness of her multi-octave voice."

Stephen Grimstead the editor of the web site, www.memphisflyer.com, noted his bewilderment when listening to the album: "What the hell is *this*? That was my initial impression after listening to the first track from *The Ultimate Yma Sumac Collection* titled "Taita Inty" (Virgin of the Sun God). A female voice singing at an incredibly high pitch . . . led me to wonder whether I was reviewing an opera CD by mistake.

"Then that uncanny voice kicked into high gear . . . and I thought I was listening to an electronic theremin trill instead of a human being . . . But really, *what* the hell is this? For a lack of a better term, I'd describe Yma Sumac as a folk singer, but one with a voice and delivery that borders on the otherworldly, at times . . . The power and finesse of Yma Sumac cannot be denied, and that's the enduring truth behind the myth."

In 2001 a slim volume (138 pages) dedicated to Yma Sumac appeared as part of the German "apropos" series of female celebrity profiles. Only in German, the book contained selected reviews and essays, the largest being by the German journalist, Anna-Bianca Krause, who also interviewed the Peruvian singer. Published by Verlag Neue Kritik KG Frankfurt am Main, it was the first book to appear about the singer.

By 2001, Yma's recordings had sold remarkably well, especially considering that they were originally released so many years earlier. The promotional brochure for Steve Willis' projected documentary, *Discovering Yma*, contained some interesting 1990s sales numbers in relation to Yma's Capitol albums. Between the years 1991 and 2001, sales also demonstrated interesting consumer preferences:

Voice of the Xtabay—14,000
Legend of the Sun Virgin—8,500

Mambo!—17,000
Fuego del Ande—6,500
The Ultimate Yma Sumac Collection (released in 2000)—6,500

By January of 2002, Yma had moved from her West Hollywood bungalow into an apartment seemingly without a phone. Her former agent, Alan Eichler, expressed dismay that even he was not able to get in touch with the now oddly reclusive diva. Don Pierson and Sara Cloudwalker contacted Alan and urged him to get back in touch with Yma and mend their falling-out. Writing in 2007, Alan reported:

"I [had] had another falling out with [Yma] . . . when she cancelled dates that were set up to promote the CD release of "Ultimate Yma Sumac" and she was just so difficult and abusive. Then a few years ago a piano player she worked with told me she had died and after some investigation I found that she was alive but living in an Alzheimer's nursing home in Alta Dena. I went there, saw she was actually mentally OK and had her moved to a facility in Hollywood, where my mother lives, which is assisted living and she has her own apartment (bedroom, living room, kitchen and full bath) plus all her meals . . . so now she's living in the same building as my mother and they've become good friends. It's also where [the great jazz singer] Anita O'Day and [the noted boogie-woogie pianist and jazz singer] Hadda Brooks were living. . . . How she got in this situation is too long to write here, but I straightened out as much of the mess as I could." (Private email, 1/17/07)

In 2003, a German writer and avant garde artist, Daniel Emerson Aldridge, wrote a fascinating article called *Why a Princess of the Incas Might be an Icon for German Gays—Musings on Yma Sumac* for Radio Knackpunkt, a gay and lesbian radio program broadcast on the Open Channel in Berlin. As he explained, "[it was part] of a series on icons like Yma Sumac, Klaus Nomi, Freddie Mercury, David Bowie, Madonna, Asta Nielsen or German singer Hildegard Neff (as she might still be known in the US)." Full of complex and ironic humor, the article recounts how Daniel, as a gay man, came to discover Yma as an Icon. During the course of the article Daniel candidly describes her 1990s German concerts in Berlin:

Berlin was the first station of her world tour. Only she herself undertook that journey, along with two costumes and three Inca statuettes. Still, she appeared on the stage with six German musicians with whom she had rehearsed only for a short time, and they would have looked and felt better in a jazz hall (though the famous piano player Kai Rautenberg who also accompanied Hildegarde Neff was heading this band) . . . Three fourths of the audience consisted of the so-called "men with earrings" or the "little boys" as Yma likes to call her present-day main group of fans. . . .

This concert in the "Theater des Westens" turned out to be one of the most iconistic events of this decade as the following happened: An emotion stirred me deeply, I felt touched and moved in a cosmic sense—I saw her (and it was different at that moment already from your usual soft core iconism). She was alive, she was a living person who really sang like on those records. It was no longer an unbelievable dream. It was three octaves, definitely, at that night. Occasionally, there was the effort of the fledging voice to reach four and a half, not entirely successful. (http://www.friedrichshainerschule.de/yma2.htm) [During the concert Yma sang "Ataypura" (High Andes), "Moscow Nights" "Montana," "La Molina", (The Mill Song) and later even resurrected, the lovely "Suray Surita."]

In terms of her voice, she was much more determined and giving during this second part of the concert. She did a lot with her deep "Baoo-aoo-aooa-ooa-ah-ah" roll, still trying for the fourth octave. She knew that she was beyond her highest times, but she was still trying to get as high as possible. For the first time in my life, I felt struck by the real sensation of tragedy. Aside from that, she was just as good as on her old records, according to the statement of an elderly gentleman in the lobby whom we had met during the intermission, a fan of hers ever since her great days. The sensation of time intersections was amazing to me and my neighbors and roommates who were all here with me at this concert. We were all there together.

In the second part, the beautiful operatic aria "TU'CA NUN CHIAGNE!" and the smashing tune "CELEBRATE LIFE" were totally convincing. During the latter, she had to stop at the beginning to show the orchestra how they should do the rhythm (this was unprofessional behaviour, but more on her part than on the part of the musicians). It was all becoming rather strange.

The end came suddenly with many people booing. So far, they had been patient. Yma told the audience that she wanted to sing some songs of the "MAMBO" record, but either she could not get started or the musicians had not made themselves familiar enough with these tunes. And all that Jazz. She broke off the concert unexpectedly although, in her heart, she wanted to continue. . . . She told us about the terrible car accident during which she had broken her arms and leg. That it was still painful. And that the terrible weather in Germany had affected her voice. And that this was the reason why she and the musicians had not had enough time to rehearse. That the musicians had already left. . . . She promised to repeat her concert on Monday (or rather to carry it out in actuality), and that then, everything would be perfect. Afterwards, the director of the "Theater des Westens" decided to cancel this concert. His explanation was he wanted to prevent an almost pre-programmed scandal.

After the concert, she remained in Germany and appeared in two television programs. During the dubious "Schmidt Show" (not to be confused with the "Harald Schmidt Show" but a rather illustrious "gay" TV program from Hamburg's famous Schmidt theatre), she broke off her performance—a stunning sight once again for the television viewer. This time, she was in anger, because somebody in the audience had dared to laugh about her. The other TV program "Boulevard bei Bio" went without any catastrophies. It was during this interview that she told German talkmaster Alfred Biolek (another gay celebrity in the community) her voice ranges through five octaves. Afterwards, she sang "MONTANA," a very slow, accentuated and operatic performance, still touching.

But after this smaller debacle, Yma Sumac suddenly and unexpectedly came back for me on the 22nd of May 1992 into the concert hall "Meistersingerhalle" in Nuremberg. One of her final concerts in Germany. On this evening, she sang for an audience of 120 people in the smaller second hall of this location. Despite another heavy cold which was very real (every listener had to notice), she was almost able to reach the vocal height of former times. Other listeners around me complained between songs that . . . "that she was sleep-drugged, she was tremolating , her voice was very heavy and that she had forgotten some lyrics and that she was croaking false notes . . . I could not continue to listen to these slanderous and calumnious voices . . . They were too painful. On the stage, I saw a human being, a real woman, and in her voice, the sensitive listeners in the audience sensed the echo of the experience and of the emotion of a whole lifetime. One could feel a whole life here within this voice, and it seemed only natural that she sounded different than in former times. Yma had more depth, more authenticity than ever. (http://www.friedrichshainerschule.de/yma2.htm)

In 2004, Damon Devine heard through friends that Yma had moved and actually was living near him. He decided on her birthday to go and see if that was true and found her sitting in her yard. After talking with Yma they both decided that he would become more involved with her as a personal assistant and help take care of her makeup and clothes for appearances.

In February of 2005, Yma took part in a record signing at a big, celebrity convention; 16 hours of signing in two days. It rained and Damon remembers being very nervous about the condition of her makeup. Shortly after that, Norah Krug noted in *The New York Times* (October 14, 2005) that Yma would be appearing at the Hollywood Forever Cemetery, formerly named the Hollywood Memorial Park, in a Latino Day of the Dead festival from 3 to 11 PM.. "Perhaps the most unusual—and wildest—celebration will be at the Hollywood Forever Cemetery in Los Angeles, the 35-acre final resting place of Cecil B. DeMille and stars like Jayne Mansfield and Rudolph Valentino. On Oct. 29, the cemetery will take on a decidedly festive atmosphere, with a crowd dancing and singing on the graves and among the headstones. Scheduled performers include the vocalist Yma Sumac as well as Viola Trigo, a Mexican folk singer, who will perform on the lawn in front of Douglas Fairbanks's grave. The cemetery, which will be closed to burials that day, will also be lined with homemade altars (last year someone built one out of popcorn) dedicated to the builders' relatives or favorite stars.

"This annual event, now in its sixth year, has grown from about 1,000 participants at first to more than 10,000 last year. 'It's out of control,' said Alberto Hernández, the cemetery superintendent and the festival's organizer. 'This is a city with so many cultures: Indian people, Russian people and others come and do it their own way.'" (10/17/05)

Yma was pressured into making this free appearance by the Vivanco family. Although it was intimated that she would perform, she did not. Damon did her makeup again and although awkward because of the presence of some of Moisés' family, he felt she acquitted herself well. "It had something to do with a statue/shrine that his family had erected and they wanted pictures of Yma standing next to it. She wasn't amused. To our great shock, the Vivancos had printed up over 100 copies of laser prints of a page in an old Yma Sumac program and had her sit down and sign, FOR FREE, for any looky-loo that happened to walk in. It was disgraceful. It was set up right next to the giant Vivanco shrine, which Sumac hadn't the slightest interest in and completely ignored. This was all planned behind the backs of both me and Alan, but we "wriggled our way" in to look after her. Sumac posed for HUNDREDS of photos, the press was wild and she signed until even me and Alan had to go home, me sick at the thought of leaving her behind to face more and more signing at her age and leaving the Vivancos in charge. But she was determined to endure all of this, to show the Vivancos she was still loved and well survived without Vivanco. So she did everything requested of her. I was ALARMED at the Vivancos' lack of concern for her age and how exhausted she had become. Indeed, there were MANY true Sumac fans, but soon, any half-interested 'mourner' passing by, walked in to get a freebie autograph, which is not how she, or I, believe in doing things. Today, being more familiar with her on a professional level, I would have stopped everything instantly, at a certain hour. At the time I was new to such spectacles and a bit bewildered. She did not sing. At this point she can only remember tunes, but no lyrics. As always, and what is normal for someone so elderly, she mostly wanted LUNCH. Every important thing we have ever done, she has said 'When is this finished? I'm HUNGRY!'" (Private email, 1/19/07)

May of 2006 brought Yma to a sort of apotheosis of her career. This was a two-week return to Peru to receive a whole array of honors. The trip was actually the result of the work of Hernándo Valderrama Valentin, a great fan of Yma's in Peru. Around October of 2005, feeling that she should be honored by her place of birth Hernándo approached the

Alan Eichler, Hernando Valderrama Valentin, Damon Devine, Miguel Molinari

consul in Peru who eventually contacted the Peruvian consulate in the United States and the two-week celebration began to take shape. Once in Peru there was to be a four-day train tour to Machu Picchu and then a return to Lima, where she would be presented with awards. The trip was promotionally paid for by the hotel chain Orient Express and Peru's Channel 4. Channel 4 filmed her visit, including the trip on the Orient Express train and her visit to Machu Picchu (where she sang a bit for the group) and presented a 15-minute report on Peruvian television called *Diva Sumac*. Reported by Katia Duharte and sensitively filmed by Miguel Piedra, the minidocumentary caught a Sumac who, at times, appeared tiny and frail—needing help to walk. This was contrasted by animated conversations by the energized, excited Yma. At most locations she was greeted by orchestras playing her music and crowds cheering, "Yma, Yma." Often she could be heard humming along with the bands during the film as she tearfully greeted her admirers. Next to her most of the time is Alan Eichler. During the train trip she was entertained by musical groups, and often she joined in. "It was like a Princess coming home," Damon Devine commented, "On May 3rd, 2006, when Yma arrived at the Lima airport at 1:30 AM, there were crowds of people as well as a gold sign which was held up welcoming Yma to Peru. Fans and press were waiting for her as well. It was a great success," Damon said.

During the two weeks cameras were everywhere; the press waited outside of elevators, at airports, the hotel, radio and TV stations, and all public functions. Yma did about 30 more interviews than were planned, some on TV and some on radio, and although Yma does not drink, there was a massive cocktail party in her honor at the beautiful hotel in Lima. It was the first time she had been reunited with three of her sisters in nineteen years. During the festivities in Lima on Friday, May 5, Yma received a series of cultural decorations including Peru's highest honor, *El Orden Del Sol,* in the degree of Commander. The Order of the Sun is a decoration that the government of Peru gives to its citizens and to foreigners who are outstanding in their contributions to the fields of arts, letters, culture, policy and other services to Peru. It was presented to her by Dr. Manuel Burga Diaz. It has only been awarded to selected presidents and royalty in the past. The award was created in October of 1821 by General Jose de San Martin. There are differing degrees of the prestigious award: Great Cruz, Great Official, Commander, Official

Courtesy of Alan Eichler

Yma wearing the Order of the Sun medal, Peru, 2006 (Courtesy yma-sumac.com)

and Horseman. Another great tribute to Yma, though one that was not widely mentioned in the press, was the presence of some of Yma's musical colleagues—other important "flute specialists," including Wara-Wara, Sihuar Ckente and Nusta Nativa. Esmila Zevallos was not there but her ex-husband, Pepe Torres attended. After she received the award, a photograph was taken of Yma with the men who made the whole historical event possible: Alan Eichler, Hernándo Valderrama Valentin, Damon Devine and Miguel Molinari, who arranged every event in Peru with uncommon smoothness. Other awards that she received that day included *The Artistic Palms* from the Ministry of Education, The *Medal of Honor of the Peruvian Culture* by the National Institute of Culture and the *Medal of the City* from the mayor of Lima. On May 6th, in all white, rose and gold, a radiant and obviously moved Yma Sumac entered South America's oldest university (Greater National University of San Marcos) to receive the *Jorge Basadre* award in honor of her career as a Peruvian musician. Although thrilled by the two weeks, they were not easy for Yma. "She still feels the obligation to give people what they want," Damon told me on the phone in January of 2007. "When she is making a public appearance like the one in Peru last May, she still wants to wear these 6" metal high heels." With the accolades from the country of her birth, Yma's career finally came full circle. Proud of her accomplishments, it gave her great satisfaction to receive the recognition from her homeland that she felt she had deserved for so many years.

Part II

The Voice

YMA SUMAC: THE VOICE

Yma Sumac's voice was unique in a number of ways. First there was its natural range of four octaves. Then there was its classic tonal beauty and expert technical facility, as well as her considerable imitative talents and her innate love of improvisation.

From the Capitol recordings and the few tapes of her in live performance, the actual extent of Yma Sumac's range during her prime, was just over four octaves: from low B to the C (or C-sharp) above high C:

Range extensions of about fifty of her recorded songs are illustrated in the supplemental materials CD available fromt he publisher.

Beyond ascribing this to a freak occurrence of nature, the experts cannot confidently explain the causes for such unusual range extensions. Some authorities have said that they believe this type of voice used to appear more often:

Dr. Hollace E. Arment, head of the music department of Auburn University, has ventured the theory that Yma's voice may be a throwback to a more primitive era. Before our present written music scale came into being (around the twelfth century), voices of much greater range than is common today were taken for granted. Dr. Arment also thinks he has detected similarities between Yma's music and early Yemenite, Babylonian and Balinese music. This has so intrigued him that he has suggested that Yma's voice may be a "peephole into the past." (James Poling, "Most Exciting Voice in the World" *Collier's Magazine* 4/14/51)

In the early 1950s, the National University of Buenos Aires studied Yma's throat, taking more than three hundred photographs of its structure. The results left researchers baffled. According to their reports, the only peculiarity evident was that Yma's vocal cords were just slightly farther apart than what is traditionally considered "normal."

Otherwise, there were no abnormalities and very little discernible difference between Yma's vocal cords and those of any other singer.

Although the emphasis publicists and agents placed on Yma's unusual range extensions was meant to spark audience interest, the constant inconsistencies of those claims only served to set off suspicion concerning Yma's authenticity in general. During the course of her career Yma's range was said to cover everything from three to *six and-one-half*-octaves. As publicity stunts can't help but do, this constant emphasis on her range only fostered skepticism and did more harm than good to Yma's standing as an artist of consequence. She may have seen herself as a serious artist but most listeners and readers of her resumé—friendly or unfriendly—did not.

Occasionally, an astute critic would comment on the range Yma used during a concert. On the one hand this was welcome, in that it demonstrated that the critic had been prepared for an accurate analysis and took Yma's work seriously enough to validate it. On the other hand, such close examination inevitably exposed conflicts between Yma's advertised range and what she actually used in performance.

During the early part of her career, when Yma was questioned about the extent of her range she would quietly take a small piece of paper from her purse and read a prepared statement. Although charmingly ingenuous, it bespoke an unfortunate dependence on others to provide her with truthful answers. At that time range was of little importance to Yma. Some days she sang higher, some days lower, depending on the music and her mood.

When Yma was a folk artist in South America, nothing was ever said of her range extensions. She was simply billed as a "Peruvian soprano." It was only after she arrived on North American shores that a vulgar emphasis was placed on Yma Sumac's vocal boundaries by publicists and others who saw the commercial possibilities of "bigger is better." Unfortunately, before long, Yma became caught up in this as well. Soon, vocal range became Yma's main claim to fame and ill advice was given to her, for she began to boast that her range covered five full octaves. As she described it: "Two octaves below middle C, and three above."

The fact is that the Capitol recording studios found Yma more relaxed than on stage and so caught her at her best, both imaginatively and in the use of her extreme range. When performing live, Yma tended to use a range that centered in an area of three octaves, with just an occasional, carefully calculated foray beyond.

Yma Sumac's legacy differs from such other singers as the operatic Maria Callas or the popular Judy Garland, in that her best work was done in the recording studio rather than in front of audiences. Studio recordings by singers like Callas and Garland do not fully capture the magic of what they were able to do in front of an audience. To get the most accurate picture of their work you must hear their live performances—where, in fact, you hear them come alive. The studio did not provide them with the excitement—the burst of adrenaline, perhaps it was—that is created in them by an audience.

Other singers—and Yma was one, clearly—find the studio more relaxing. Because of this she was better able to provide accurate examples of what she could do without the pressure of a critical audience. This is by no means to minimize the importance of their live performances in developing a full appreciation and understanding of their work.

One thing that lent credulity to the idea that Yma's range was limitless was her use of split-second jumps from one register to another. Although the distance between the two notes might have been ordinary (within two octaves), to listeners it might sound enormous because of the different timbres Yma would use to emphasize her contrasting registers. This created the impression that a vast distance was being covered. Helping create this illusion was the fact that Yma was able to execute this feat without preparation and with a cleanness of delivery that often startled by its rapidity and clarity.

As if by instinct, Yma used her entire range only rarely during concerts, reserving its extremes for special impact. In concert she rarely ventured above high F. By doing so she was able to maintain a consistently high level of performance over a long career, retaining most of her range boundaries. Although the highest notes began to disappear as a matter of natural course, she was able to produce a thin, high F as late as 1992, some 50 years after her public debut)

Only one recorded example exists of Yma using her complete range. This is the famous "Chuncho!" (Forest Creatures) recorded in 1953 and found on her third North American album, (or fourth if *Flahooley* is included), *Inca Taqui*. This is Yma at her imitative best. Nothing in the annals of recorded history equals the sounds Yma creates during the course of this three-minute piece.

Another way in which of Yma's voice was unmatched was its uncommonly beautiful timbre and the fact that despite its excessive range, her voice was a homogeneously gorgeous instrument. It was warm, round, and full in the lower reaches, honey sweet in the upper. Yma's lowest tones occasionally took on a misty or husky quality that was often useful in effects. This led into a creamy smooth contralto register of great warmth and color. The middle of the voice was also warm, but subtly lightened as the voice ascended. Around C or D in the staff the voice took on the focus and penetration of a lyric soprano. In classical music this is the "edge" or "buzz" inherent in higher voices, necessary for projecting over (or through) accompanying instruments. It is also the sign of a healthy, well placed voice—even on the early Odeon recordings it is obvious that Yma's voice was perfectly placed by nature. (This is not so rare. Often when singers begin serious study they find that their voices are already well placed and they only need to concentrate on perfecting their breath control and technique.) Yma could carry this clean focus to the high B or C—where there was an area of transition; from that note to the top of her range she deployed a pure, floated head voice.

This head voice was Yma's true glory; feather-like soft, delicate, and rich with upper harmonics, it was as pure as a flute. It was similar to the high registers of such classical singers as Amelita Galli-Curci (1882–1963), Maria Ivogün (1891–1987), Erna Sack (1898–1972), and Rita Streich (1920–1987), but Yma's high notes were even more delicate.

Yma's voice had a natural beauty rather than one acquired through careful and intensive training. Yma insists she never studied voice, and a study of her recordings supports this boast. I seriously doubt she had much legitimate (or traditional) training since one of the results of that training would have been a certain caution or inhibition—especially concerning some of her most famous vocal effects. I believe, however, that she had a lot of *coaching*. The difference between working with a teacher and working with a coach is that a teacher concentrates on technical issues while a coach concentrates on interpretive issues.

Because of the intense concentration necessary for vocal study while working closely with a teacher, a singer learns about the acceptable and the unacceptable ways of producing sound. Guided by the teacher, a singer develops a reflexive tendency to protect the voice from unnecessary pressure or strain, and can become preoccupied with the production of that sound. Yma's singing reveals none of that sense at all, and without it she was free to experiment with her resonance cavities for colorations and effects. There was just never anyone to tell her that she should *not* do something.

By the same token, Yma Sumac also learned to use her naturally large range, finding the best way to integrate both her range and resonances into her everyday technique. A classically-based vocal instructor would never have allowed Yma to experiment with the growl through multi-octaves or let her play with some of her other, more percussive effects. Serious vocal study would have inhibited Yma.

Sylvia Fischer, a famous Australian soprano who was contemporary with Yma and whose career spanned the decades from 1950 to 1970, supports this view. For the article, "The Legendary Sumac" that Maurice Leonard wrote for *Records and Recording* (11/79) she commented:

> The mind is an incredible thing. You can make all sorts of sounds by imagining them. It cannot be done just technically, but the brain can imitate. If you have the quality of imagination there is no limit to what can be done.
>
> For instance, some time ago I was listening to the radio and heard a violin playing a cadenza, incredibly high, something like C above top C, and I suddenly thought, I can do that. I could hear it reverberating in my mind and I sang it, exactly like the violin. Yet if you asked me to reproduce that note technically it would have been impossible. Sometimes there is too much emphasis on the cerebral part of singing today, it can hamper a natural gift.

Although by operatic (or classical) standards Yma Sumac's voice was not large, it was healthy, resilient, sensibly used and capable of considerable projection. Today's operagoers generally accept the fact that voices tend to "burn-out" or become dilapidated after about ten years—especially if the voice is misused or if the technique was faulty or not fully mastered to begin with.

Yet some operatic singers, like Mirella Freni (1935–), Joan Sutherland (1926–), Placido Domingo (1941–), Leonie Rysanek (1926–1998), and Alfredo Kraus (1927–1999) all retained the sheen of their instruments, remaining in repertoire that suited them, refusing to force or over-stretch their voices. By doing so they retained their voices an unusually long time. More recently, Edita Gruberova (1946–) and Mariella Devia (1951–) have shown the merits of being selective in repertoire, and both continue to be exemplary technicians and imposing artistic figures in the operatic world. Both have retained much of the high registers that they were famous for.

Even though Yma's voice was strong and healthy, she rarely sang without a microphone. Only two instances have been documented: performances of the role of Najala in *Flahooley* on Broadway in 1951 (about 40 performances), and a concert given in the ruins of Machu-Picchu, in Peru, in the Spring of 1953. Otherwise, all her known performances were sung with a microphone. Actually, this is not that surprising. Many of Yma's most startling vocal effects were subtle and depended on a microphone for their projection. Without such an aid, her most interesting and inventive work would have been lost to most of the audience. This is especially true of "Chuncho!" (Forest Creatures) which, despite the acrobatics exploited was always intimately performed.

Judged by any standards, Yma's microphone technique was masterly. Viewing it as a valid mode of expression, an extension of her own instrument, she learned exactly how to use it to her best advantage. As the Capitol recordings prove, Yma's use of the microphone was so clever, becoming so advanced and innovative, that it enabled her to sing comfortably, without straining or worrying about vocal projection in large concert halls, arenas, amphitheaters and stadiums. There is never an instance on recordings where she is trying to produce more sound than was comfortably hers by nature. Because she never forced her voice, she was able to preserve its freshness and unusual range boundaries for an inordinate length of time. She was able to sing even her most demanding "Incan" repertoire for at least 15 years.

Although by 1989 and her final appearances in New York at The Ballroom, the technical control of her voice had seriously diminished, Yma was still able to call on at least three full octaves in performance. This is more range than most popular and classical singers can offer during their prime, much less after more than forty years of singing.

Over time, however, Yma became overly dependent on the microphone—even when it was not necessary. Those present at rehearsals for the 1975 Town Hall concerts in New York remember hearing Yma vocalize with a full, ringing voice, strong throughout its compass. Yet when in front of the microphone, she grew cautious, pulled the voice back, and used only half of it—as though afraid of losing control. As the years passed this reticence grew to almost phobic proportions.

In the early 1950s, the president of the German recording company, Telefunken, gave Yma a recording microphone as a gift. Although a highly sophisticated instrument, it was large and bulky—not a detriment in an instrument specifically designed for recording. Inexplicably, Yma would often use it for nightclub engagements, despite the fact that its bulkiness obscured her face when she moved close to it. It went everywhere with her, housed in its solid black box. This caused a number of problems, beginning with the fact that the thing was simply not compatible with most nightclubs' sound systems. The final crisis came in 1968, during an appearance at the Chateau Madrid in New York, when the microphone broke from its stand and crashed to the stage.

An important feature of Yma's technique that has been often overlooked was her remarkable breath control, which enabled her to make perfected gradations of *crescendo* and *diminuendo* (loud and soft), and sustain her highest tones effortlessly. Chiefly responsible for this control was an inherent trait found in Peruvian singers originating from the highland or Altiplano areas. Acclimatization in the Andes develops unusually large lung capacity, which frees these people from anazemia (shortness of breath) so that the high altitude does not render them anoxic. If you never saw Yma perform, you can get an idea of her tremendous lung capacity from her scenes in the 1954 movie *Secret of the Incas*. Although lip-synching her songs, the huge breaths Yma takes are real. Within an instant there is a tremendous lung expansion that seems to change her entire chest structure. This ability to draw in breath quickly, and immediately govern its control, was invaluable to Yma's art.

Another important feature of Yma's success was imitation, a major factor in her art and one that enabled her to achieve such vocal heights and colorations. Since her youth, and the earliest days with Moisés and the Compañia Peruana de Arte, Yma had been a prodigious imitator of the sounds of instruments around her. As she matured, so did this ability. She was an assimilator, not only of the sounds around her, but also of vocal concepts perceived in listening to recordings of other singers. The result of all this assimilation was a voice with a classically based (if not trained) sound and technique, coupled with the probing mind of an imitator.

Like all voices, Yma's had the typical register breaks—places where the voice shifts from one area into another. Because of the extent of her natural range, however, Yma had additional areas of transition in her voice. There was one around high E flat and another around the A above high C. Cleverly, she learned to oscillate both of these areas to imitate trills, as in the famous "double-voiced" trill at the end of "Chuncho!"(Forest Creatures). This is actually a trill consisting of an interval of a minor third beginning on the A above high C, which Yma rapidly oscillates back and forth over the register break. Although clever of Yma, it is not an unprecedented feat—many operatic sopranos learned this trick and became quite proficient in its use. The first to record such a feat was the operatic soprano, *Ellen Beach Yaw* (1869–1947). Yaw could not only trill in thirds but also in fourths–technically fascinating but bizarre to hear.

Other sopranos who were able to utilize transitional areas for trilling purposes include *Selma Kurz* (1874–1933), famous for her trilling ability during the first years of the 20th century, *Adele Kern* (1901–1980), active in Germany in the 1930s was adept at this "trick," as was her contemporary, the English soprano *Gwen Catley* (1906–1996). Nearer our time, *Ruth Welting* (1948–1999) who was active in the 1970s and *Beverly Hoch* (1951–) in the 1980s have demonstrated this ability. When done correctly, the sound is bird-like and impressive for its clean, rapid, rolling sound. Welting and Hoch were both able to use this trick as high as E flat and E natural. Yma took it a fourth higher still. It is true, however, that Yma confessed that sometimes the "double-voiced trill" did not work. Nor did she always take it as high as she did on the *Inca Taqui* album. In her two recorded live performances of "Chuncho!" she does the trill on high F sharp (1953 Lewisohn Stadium) and high E (1961 Romanian concert)

Yma relied on many instincts when singing. The one she followed most closely was, coincidentally, a primary rule of vocal production. This is to let the vocal cords make their own adjustments as you sing, rather than trying to manipulate them into certain areas (low, middle, high). Students usually learn this after years of training and familiarity with the singing muscles. When mastered, the singer is able to prevent muscles from interfering with the singing process. Contrary to what most people believe, when you learn how to sing, you don't learn how to *make* things work so much as you learn how to *leave them alone* to do the work they're capable of—allowing the larynx to make its own adjustments. Without this freedom there is only vocal manipulation. This relaxed freedom from manipulation, coupled with correct support of the breath from the diaphragm, is what produces the smooth legato lines of a singer in all registers.

Under manipulation the voice becomes ridden with tension and pressure. This is physically evident with singers who can be seen with a wobbling jaw or head, a flapping tongue, or neck tension (where the tendons stand out prominently).

We will see that, eventually, Yma did succumb to a serious form of manipulation, but during her most important initial studies this does not seem to have been the case.

Singing is a complex art. The singer is dealing with something that cannot be seen or touched. They can only go by sensation. Because of this, much of voice teaching is done in descriptive terms that instructors use to help students visualize what they should be feeling. And each teacher has their own characteristic ways of describing sensations.

Singers are taught never to listen to their own voice, but rather to concentrate only on sensations. The old adage, if it feels good it's right, if it hurts it's wrong, is a truism of correct singing. The reason singers are not to listen to their own voices is simple: like all of us, a singer can't hear their own voice. Because of internal resonances, they hear a different sound from that heard by the listener, who receives the sound through the air in the space between them. If a singer is singing correctly, they do not really hear their voice since the sound is traveling *out* into the audience and away from them. On the other hand, if a singer does hear a lot of his or her sound then their voice is not carrying the way it should. This is one of the reasons why a teacher is so important. The teacher serves as a pair of ears that listen for faulty tone production or technique. They also watch for unusual or unnecessary facial tics or muscular intervention. And if they are a good teacher, they will be able to help the student correct whatever problems are noticed.

Problems with manipulation occur when a singer tries to dictate to the vocal cords. For example, when singing a rising scale, a singer may try to help the ascent by clenching—auxiliary throat muscles surrounding the larynx. The bad result of this "helping" has happened to most every singer—the voice cracks in two from the pressure or tension. Although there is no pain, it is definitely uncomfortable and the sound is embarrassing. There are many reasons for "cracking." Sometimes the singer makes the mistake of visualizing an upward scale. That can make one's throat go tight as they ascend.

This can be combated, interestingly, by using the reverse pictures in their minds. That is, when singing an ascending scale they will visualize a descending scale. This easy trick can help keep the larynx in a relaxed, lowered position, rather than raised and tight, so that the cords can make their own adjustments. Most singers study for years to learn how to master interfering throat muscles. To do this they must develop muscles to control muscles. This is why operatic singers often have large necks, especially the huge-voiced dramatic sopranos and tenors, whose necks are often thick and muscular. The development of these muscles is such that it allows the singer to move muscles away when they reach for high notes. You can see this "moving" by watching the subtle expansion of their necks at these moments.

Simplistically, when singers study and build their techniques, their main goal is to perfect technical resources to the point that they never have to think about any of this unless they find themselves having vocal difficulties.

Yma Sumac possessed good instincts when it came to singing—although, from interviews and comments she has made, it is doubtful she ever thought of such technical things. One has to remember that her manner of singing was extremely lax in stylistic priorities. If she came to a break in registers, she just rode over it as best she could without trying to fix it into the rest of the voice. Occasionally, as in the rising line (up to high E flat) in "Llulla Mak'ta" (*Inca Taqui*) one can hear Yma almost "feeling" her way through the *passagio* area; treating it gently and obviously being cautious and monitoring what is happening and how it is feeling. Because of this she rarely put unnecessary strain on her voice. (It also explains why the top of Yma's voice always remained delicate.)

On her recordings one can occasionally hear top D's and E flats waver slightly, or change in their vibrato fluctuation. This is because these high notes were always sung in head voice and kept light. This has its good and its bad points. The downside is that these notes were never completely integrated into the other registers so that they could be swelled or diminished at will. On the other hand, because no additional pressure was placed on these notes, Yma's voice remained lambent and youthful and retained its vast range for a long time. (Not surprisingly, other singers mentioned—*Maria Ivogün, Amelita Galli-Curci* and *Erna Sack*—all had flute-like, soft top registers and had similar problems integrating their highest tones with the rest of the voice.)

Because of her singular repertoire, however, if Yma's voice cracked, she could just use it as an effect. She often used intentional register breaks in such songs as: "Najala's Lament" (*Flahooley*), "Ataypura" (High Andes), "Chuncho!" (Forest Creatures), "Tumpa!" (Earthquake!), and "Panarima." This gave the illusion of vast distances between her top and bottom registers, made her voice seem endless and inhuman, and lent a certain, primal earthiness to her singing.

To native Peruvians, it was not her high register that was the most startling thing about Yma's voice. It was her unusual low register, the natural beauty of her voice and her smooth, elegant delivery. These are features not commonly associated with singers originating from the Andes. Yma's voice never had the astringent tonal quality often found in Peruvian sopranos.

Voices indigenous to Peru show an interesting phenomenon in that both male and female singers generally have high voices. Even untrained singers from the high, Altiplano regions and who sing in an unrefined, piercing style of chest voice, use an uncommonly high tessitura. Although Peruvian folk music is generally not vocally demanding, the use of a high tessitura makes it all but unsingable by folk singers originating in North America.

The Effects

By the time Yma arrived in America as part of the newly formed Inca Taqui Trio, her technique had been perfected. Gone were the occasional flaws that one can hear on the 1943 recordings. Before her North American arrival, Yma's singing consisted mostly of straight folk music. It was only once in a while that she would incorporate stratospheric (or subterranean) excursions for melodic emphasis in the tradition of flute-singers. European-like scale work or trills were never used, but grace notes, gentle turns, rhythmically pointed staccato, and high-octave legato singing were—as in "Amor Indio" (Indian Love), where the melody was sung in one octave and then repeated in another.

By 1950, however, Yma's vocal priorities had changed as new effects began to be integrated into her style of singing. The range of these new sounds was astonishing for their diversity and innovativeness within a song's framework. They included an ability to alter the frequency of vibrato, as well as the introduction of clicks, pops, growls, hums, etc. all of which were woven into the fabric of Yma's music.

One of Yma's most famous effects was the "growl." It is not clear when this concept was first used by Yma, but it was after 1943, and before February of 1950 (when *Voice of the Xtabay* was recorded) since it first appears on that album, in Tumpa! (Earthquake). Most probably she developed it around 1948, after her arrival in North America. In 1956, in an interview to publicize her *Mambo!* album, Yma gave a hint. "I first loved Louis Armstrong many years ago in South America. I feel close to it. Because you see I don't follow so much the music, just the way I feel. And I felt that Louis had a new sound: like from his heart." (*Metronome Magazine* 4/56)

According to the same interview, after Yma had arrived in America, she often sang with jazz groups in Manhattan, including Armstrong's. Reputedly, in one club a tape was made of Yma singing "St. Louis Blues," a tape that has been unsuccessfully sought by collectors for decades.

Undoubtedly, the novelty of the "growl" appealed to Yma's imagination and imitative instincts and she obviously patiently played with the effect, imitating what she heard until she found an easy (and safe) way to do it without harming her voice. There is no getting around it, this is a tricky process. If not produced correctly, this guttural vocal effect can cause permanent vocal damage because of the harsh, unrelenting grating on the vocal cords. Yma's success with the effect was phenomenal. By the time she recorded *Voice of the Xtabay* in February of 1950, the growl had been startlingly perfected and securely integrated into her mode of expression. It was this part of her technique that horrified many singers and musicians, including the famous operatic basso Ezio Pinza (1892–1957). Pinza was outraged at Yma's juxtaposition of this effect with her traditional, almost operatic singing, and prophesied that she would ruin her voice if she continued to sing in that manner. Pinza, however, was notorious for his opinion of the high soprano voice, which he detested. Rumor has it he once told a friend that he would rather strangle his daughter to death than have her be a coloratura soprano. Pinza was not alone, however, in his fears for Yma's voice. Many voice teachers were horrified at Yma's liberal use of the growl and the heights to which she would take this particular effect (often up to high A and B). Nonetheless, as time has proven, even if only governed by instinct, Yma knew her voice and its capabilities inside and out. The unusual thing about Yma's use of the growl was that it was not limited to one register. She perfected its emission to the degree that she could call on the effect anywhere within three octaves.

How was she able to do this without harming her voice? This has always been a point of contention among critics and teachers. Since Yma is completely inarticulate about her singing technique, she cannot provide the answer. The answer, however, may be simpler than one first imagines.

One of the most important aspects of Yma's singing, and especially her success with this particular feat, was the absence of any vocal tension. Yma was a natural singer in that all her creative instincts and physical development pointed to this kind of vocation. Gifted with imaginative creativity and an ability to mimic sounds around her, and not being inhibited by complex training, Yma just sang, always governing the production and use of her voice by her strong and accurate instincts. When she wanted a certain coloring to match what she was feeling, she drew upon her imagination and experimented until she found exactly what she was looking for. And as we have said, in the case of the growl, Yma sang it a number of different ways. The growl used in "Tumpa!" (Earthquake) and "Choladas" (Dance of the Moon Festival), both on the *Voice of the Xtabay*, is quite different from that used in the "Five Bottle Mambo" (*Mambo!*) and "Remember." (*Miracles*)

Lorraine Nubar, a leading classical voice teacher in New York City, and the protégé of the famous operatic mezzo, Jennie Tourel, told me: "From listening to her recordings, I have the feeling that she is partially vibrating the tissues in her throat, while at the same time, she is vibrating her vocal cords. Her use of '*AWH*' helps keep the throat open and the larynx in a relaxed, lowered position. This keeps unnecessary pressure off the larynx and the throat. She must have a lot of space in the throat, too."

Ms. Nubar remarked that, at times, it was difficult to tell whether Yma was gargling on pitch, or using a form of modal register. She stressed, however, that using the growl in the area of high A (as in "Chuncho!") was very dangerous and had to be handled with utmost care to prevent damage to the vocal cords.

Yma's use of the "AWH" placement rather than the usual, brighter "AH" always played an important part in her singing. As early as the 1943 Argentinean disks, she instinctively used "awh" to cover her tones. Although to the reader, this might seem insignificant, it is one of the main reasons why Yma was able to sing for more than forty years.

"Covering" the voice is a term for the physical placement of the voice that gives a rounder tonal beauty to the voice, and greater freedom in the transitional areas. It is done by placing the voice in the area of the soft palate. "Awh" lowers the jaw naturally, provides more space in the mouth and throat for resonance, and keeps the throat open and naturally relaxed. Not surprisingly, many of Yma's texts or "words" were comprised of vowels that she was able to manipulate and control thus maintaining her "Awh" placement.

Singers and voice teachers call this use of "Awh" the "dome." Pictorially, the "dome" describes the formation in the mouth and back of the throat as well as the physical sensation. Graphically, it looks like the dome of a cathedral due to the height of the soft palate (which is lifted)—as when one yawns.

The reader can experience this lifting sensation and the space it creates by first saying "Ah" brightly or while smiling, and then saying "Awh". Immediately apparent is the dual action of the soft palette lifting in the back of the throat, and the lowering of the larynx.

Yma's control over the vowels she sang had much to do with the success of her work. Although she could sing a text cleanly and rapidly if she wanted to, it was more to her advantage to concentrate on a form of vocalise.

As one can imagine, this made her job much less complicated than that of more classically based operatic artist like Beverly Sills. Sills not only had to cope with the stylistic proprieties of the operas she sang, but also their texts (for which correct vowel modifications had to be carefully worked out in the upper register) and pre-designated coloratura passages and traditional interpolations—high notes and cadenzas—which also had to be selected, or written, and worked into the voice. Most of the time Yma just did what she wanted, incorporating vowel-consonant combinations like ba-na-ba, or waba-ba-ba, when necessary, to help negotiate more difficult configurations in lower regions. Without exception, these combinations originated from "Awh." She also used a chant-like "Mwah-wah-wah" to help her into the upper extremes.

This last sound was similar to another aid Yma used. This was a preparatory "N" or "Nyah" for her approach to high notes. These sounds were used as releasing actions for the jaw and to help secure vocal freedom. This was a very important feature of Yma's work. Based on a version of the hum, these two sounds helped Yma securely place her high notes in the head register. Head resonance is imperative in all singing and provides the height and color for the top register of any singer. Without its use there is no high register.

Instinctively and child-like, Yma played with all her resonance cavities—chest, head, mouth, throat and nose to achieve a palette of tonal variety. Yma herself admits that the entire process of exploring her mind for sounds was more of a spiritual than physical process. "It is as if my spirit was exploring my brain and body to discover the right resonance for what I wish to express through my voice and singing."

Once Yma had discovered the placement of the sound she wanted, she used her resonating cavities to create the same effect as a megaphone. One has only to have watched her in performance to notice that her mouth often took a vertical position rather than lateral. This position kept space in the mouth cavity for resonant projection of tone.

As for improvisation, Yma's selection of what she chose to interpolate was based not only on Andean tradition, but also on classical concepts and technique. Drawing on her knowledge of the technical display of operatic, jazz, blues and popular singers, Yma peppered her music with a hodgepodge of vocalism. Rather than relying on a popular music "belt" voice, for her most brilliant effects Yma used her upper octaves, staccati, wide leaps, and coloratura-like arabesques of sound.

Moisés Vivanco told me in private correspondence: "I can say that it is very difficult to write notes for this special range of voice, and I personally had to teach Yma the positions of the mouth and sing to her myself, until we obtained the results we wanted, based on the written musical notes."

The way a singer positions the mouth has a lot to do with the kind of sound the audience hears. This is because of the amount of space the mouth position allows. A singer who tends to sing with a lateral mouth position will often have a thin, pale-sounding voice because of the mouth position. This is often mistakenly called the "smiling" technique. Although it is true that the cheeks should be lifted as they are in a smile, this is actually more of a lifting of the cheekbones, which again, creates space in the mouth. A singer's mouth position should remain vertical. In this way, the lifting of the cheeks help provide more space in the head for resonance, while the position of the mouth contributes a more rounded quality. By fixing the mouth into a more lateral, smiling position, the singer negates the whole purpose of the lifting of the cheeks.

Yma's technical control was prodigious. She had the mastery of an operatic coloratura soprano, including all the necessary classically-based technical feats, but without the training. New sounds, however, began to make their appearance to accent rhythm or to provide color: nonsense syllables like "Chu-Wah!" (resembling the sound of something being dropped in water from a great height), lip-popping (like bubbles breaking in the water), whisperings (wind rustling leaves), tongue-clicking, chromatic wails, chirps, coos, high and line-thin hums.

Another addition to the Sumac voice after the 1943 recordings was an increase in vocal range. Whereas on the early disks, Yma could touch the top F sharp and had approximately three octaves at her command, by 1950, she had increased this by at least a full octave.

In addition to the "growl" and the other sounds already mentioned, which could be called upon at will, Yma developed all sorts of novel and subtle colorings which quickly became her trademarks as the queen of vocal exotica. Not only was she able to produce myriad tonal shadings and weights, she was able to alter her vibrato, increasing its oscillations to promote intense, hushed weeping, and mysterious effects. This ability, and the occasional overdubbing used on her recordings, is probably responsible for the false rumors during the 1950s that there were two women taking turns at the recording microphone.

One of her most clever and innovative devices was to use voice-less consonants like "sh" and "ch." Rounding out her battery of exotica was her ability to change her tonal placement at will (as in "Chuncho!") to imitate animal sounds. Because her pitch was uncannily acute, she was also able to make use of quartertones for color and emphasis.

During the 1950s, when many technological advances were being made and gradually developed and exploited by recording companies, Yma's brand of vocalism had a tremendous impact. As Maurice Leonard astutely wrote in his article "The Legendary Sumac" for *Records and Recording* (11/79):

> It was the gramophone record that really brought Sumac international recognition. The 1950s was a crucial period in the development of the recording industry. The LP was beginning to make its presence felt on the market, and collecting records, LPs in particular, became the vogue. Sumac's voice recorded impeccably, and she had mastered microphone technique to an unprecedented degree. Quick to spot the possibilities of this instrument . . . she used devices which had not been previously exploited, vocal clicks, whispers, glottal stops, parlandos, hairline pianissimi, accentuated consonants, and frequently, glissandi of three or more octaves, thus taking advantage of the full dynamic range.
>
> Her producers were equally astute, cannily mixing the tracks in a way that only a decade later came into common usage with the advent of such groups as the Rolling Stones and now about every pop record released.

And then there is the "hum." Yma's high note humming technique was crucial in maintaining the longevity of her voice. Generally, this particular technique is only available to the lighter, high-voiced sopranos. It is a sure way of correctly placing and producing high notes so that they are floated and projected without pressure.

Yma is not the only singer who has used this unusual technique. Nor was she the first to record it. The first soprano to have used such a technique on recordings was *Emma Calvé* (1858–1942), the French operatic mezzo-soprano (*cum* soprano) who was famous for her performances of such diverse roles as Bizet's Carmen and Thomas' Ophelia in *Hamlet*. Calvé learned her technique of humming from Domenico Mustapha, one of the last castrato singers who sang at the Sistine Chapel in Rome. Around 1891, after having heard of his remarkable "fourth-voice," Calvé approached Mustapha and asked him if he would accept her as a pupil so that she could learn how to acquire this upper extension. Mustapha told her to practice two hours a day with her mouth closed. At the end of ten years, he said, she might be able to do something with the tones she had built. Calvé mastered the technique within three years. While practicing, she overheard a colleague say the technique was just a trick. When Calvé told Mustapha this, he replied, "Our friends call our achievement trickery when they cannot do the same thing themselves. As soon as they have learned the art, they call it talent."

This specialized manner of singing is not possible for all voices. As Calvé remarked in her autobiography, *My Life* (1922) "These special notes, which I have used since then with great success, are rarely found in the ordinary run of voices. I have tried repeatedly to develop them in my pupils; but in spite of hard work and close application, I have never found one pupil who has been able to imitate them."

One of Calvé's most famous recordings is the coloratura soprano aria "Charmant Oiseau" from David's *La perle du Bresil*, with its flute/voice duet imitating birds. She recorded the aria one half tone lower than the original key of G, and more than once. The 1907 version, however, displays her "fourth-voice" and high D flat to their best advantage, demonstrating the sexless, unearthly high notes perfectly. A century later, this remains a remarkable recording.

The other main exponent of the humming technique was another French soprano, *Lily Pons* (1898–1976). Pons' coloratura voice was of extreme delicacy and height. During her prime she reaped tremendous success in America with an operatic repertoire of about 12 roles. Indeed, for twenty-seven years, from 1931 to 1958, she was the leading exponent of *Lucia di Lammermoor* at the Metropolitan Opera. Although Pons could be rather slovenly in her florid singing, she was noted for having a superlative staccato technique, was capable of lovely lyricism, and was fond of spinning out high Fs of great vibrancy and beauty. Interestingly, beginning around the 1940s, whenever she had to sing in the area of high E flat, E natural, or F, Pons would begin to subtly close her mouth, as if to contain the sounds. Listeners at the time have said that her highest notes sounded as if they were coming from somewhere behind her. As time went on, Pons relied on the hum for all her extreme high notes. Countless examples of her using this technique can be heard on her Columbia recordings made in the 1940s. Pons continued to sing, if sporadically, until 1973. (Her career, which began in 1928, thus spanned 45 years.)

Other singers have used this humming technique, or some variant of it, to some degree: *Ellen Beach Yaw* (1869–1947) often "mewled" her highest tones of F, G and A flat, as is heard on her recordings. *Margarethe Siems* (1897–1952), the German soprano who created the roles of Strauss' Zerbinetta in the original 1912 version of *Ariadne*, the Marschallin in *Der Rosenkavalier*, and Chrysothemis in *Elektra*, occasionally resorted to this technique for her high notes. During the early years of her career, (c.1943) the French soprano *Mado Robin* used to stun audiences with her ability to hum up to a sustained G above high C.

Most probably, Yma learned her version of the hum from listening to recordings of Lily Pons. When Yma was young, Pons was one of her favorite singers. And she has mentioned in interviews that she was familiar with her recordings. Being a natural imitator, it is probable that she also adopted Pons' way of singing staccato since Yma's work boasted a similar pinpoint exactness. Without realizing it, she managed to assimilate some very important techniques. Yma's use of the hum helped preserve her voice and high range decades past what is considered normal.

The hum was completely integrated into all of Yma's singing by 1950, and as she grew older it became increasingly important for her success in high coloratura flights. But Yma used this technique (as an integrated part of her singing) as early as 1943, as one can hear on her recordings of "Amor Indio" (Indian Love) and "Virgenes del Sol" (Virgins of the Sun), where she prefaces her high E flats with "*Nyah.*" By the time she recorded *Voice of the Xtabay*, Yma reserved this technique for particular effects, such as in the opening phrases of "Taita Inty" (Virgin of the Sun God), where the hum is used to create a mysterious, ritualistic, incantatory atmosphere. In other instances, such as "Choladas" (Dance of the Moon Festival), it is used to make an easy descent from high E flat. By 1971, and the recording of *Miracles,* however, the hum was the primary method Yma used to sing notes above high B. Although small in volume and rather transparent, these tones were pure and unforced.

The sound Yma produces at such moments is difficult to analyze. The physical manipulation involved is best shown to the reader by having them sing the word "hung" on a tone—sustaining the "ng" with the mouth open. You will feel the sound trapped far back in the throat yet resonating in the area of the forehead and bridge of the nose. This is caused by the raising of the back of the tongue, which touches the soft palette and traps the sound in the back of the throat. Trapped, the tone is resonated by the head cavities. Technically, this sound does not have the capability of traveling well in large spaces. Of all the singers mentioned, Yma's version of the hum was the most radical. When she used it, Yma would keep her mouth open to help project the head resonances. By 1987, and her Ballroom appearances in New York, most notes above A at the top of the staff were sung this way. Visually this created a paradox, for although Yma's mouth was wide open, the sound coming out was minuscule and seemed to come from a distance. Because Yma used such an extreme version of the hum technique, it was crucial that she use a microphone so that such soft, tiny sounds could be heard.

The main problem with this technique has to do with the maintaining of support and diaphragmatic control. This type of singing demands absolute control to ensure steadiness of tone and pitch. Lily Pons, whose diaphragmatic support was prodigious, was able to use her hum for at least two decades of public performing. It enabled her to project and sustain a high F for final performances of *Lucia di Lammermoor* in Dallas, in 1962, when she was 64 years old (and without a microphone).

Problems arise, however, if diaphragmatic support is not rigidly enforced. At Yma's 1987 and 1989 Ballroom appearances in New York, it was apparent that either her muscular control had considerably lessened, or she had gotten into a habit of dropping her support whenever sustaining high notes. This made these tones excessively thin and wavery of vibrato. Even though heavily miced, at times they were almost inaudible. (Oddly, this lack of support was not apparent in Yma's flights of rising high staccati.) Because of the inability to put pressure on such hummed high notes, (they are pure head tones) they can be maintained for a longer period of time than full, sung-out notes. At the same time, if not carefully worked into the rest of the instrument, they remain a separate portion of the voice, can sound disconnected, and must be carefully deployed.

In Yma's case, there were good and bad physiological points with her radical use of this vocal production. Since no pressure can be put on these tones, they can only be sung softly, and safely. And, because of this, Yma's high notes were never strained by attempts to push or over-sing, and therefore were never abused. These notes, however, can only have one volume level and it is rarely possible to increase that volume. That is very limiting.

Yma took this humming technique to the extreme. Because of the inevitable results of aging, high notes are usually the first notes of a singer to disappear. Combined with lack of support, and the trapping of the sound in the back of the throat, this makes for some very worn-sounding notes. Nonetheless, Yma's hum seems to have been her way of coping with the results of natural aging. High notes that might have spread or wobbled under pressure, could be controlled or guided—at least to her satisfaction. Unfortunately, any manipulation like this puts the singer at a disadvantage.

Yma also applied mouth resonance to these notes to give them a fuller sound. This mouth resonance is an individual sound and peculiar to Yma Sumac. During her sets at the Ballroom in 1987 and 1989 it was especially evident in "Ataypura" (High Andes), where her nonsense syllables of "Wa-wa-wa-Wah!" while negotiating up to high D gave high notes a certain roundness, but also an odd, muffled quality, as though she were singing the notes with a mouth full of mashed potatoes—the sound was almost masticated.

The Repertoire

"[Down] from the towering Andes comes the exotic music of an ancient civilization, sung by a fabulous Princess of its people. The lovely singer is Yma Sumac and her music is INCA TAQUI, Chants of the Incans.

"For three thousand years music has played a vital role in every activity of Inca life, and musicians have been the most honored members of the Inca community. Yma brings to the outside world the fullness and beauty of her people's spirit, singing traditional chants in a voice of magnificent range and emotional power. The language of the chants is K'eshwa, still spoken today by twenty million South Americans.

"Moisés Vivanco is an eminent authority on ancient music; he has drawn carefully upon native Incan melodies and rhythms in composing and directing the selections for this unique album." (Introductory notes for *Inca Taqui*, 1953)

Many contrasting influences can be found in Yma Sumac's singing, sometimes causing an outrageous, clashing diversity of styles. Like her homeland, Yma's singing reflects her assimilation of all the musical influences that surrounded or were introduced to her during her artistic growth. For example, here is a charting of the effects that can be found in "Tumpa!" recorded on *Voice of the Xtabay* in 1950:

Exotic Elements	Popular Elements	Classical Elements
Title	Rhythmic Structure	Vocal timbre
Lyrics (or lack of them)	Lush Orchestration (typical of the 1950s)	Range of three octaves
Use of the "Growl"	Use of open chest-voice (belting)	Vocal polish and poise
Vocal colorations	Improvisation	Ornamentation (Operatic influence)
Rhythmic accentuation		
Afro-Cuban influence		

On paper at least, there are definite clashes. When listening, however, many of these differences mesh together, lose much of their individual importance and combine to create a new, novel form or style. Part of this is due to Yma's authoritative, no-nonsense delivery and her absolute belief in what she is doing, which transcends many of the theoretical problems. Also, because much of Yma's singing is improvisatory, there is a unique aura of spontaneity on her recordings of these conglomerations that propels the material into an entirely different level. I have often simplistically described her conglomerations as Folk/Popular music/rhythm, set in an exotic framework, classically sung.

It is a fascinating, if unorthodox, combination. Understandably, this mixing of styles and musical forms does not appeal to all listeners. Ernest Borneman wrote an article on Yma in the British magazine *Melody Maker* (5/1/54), in which he stated: "Here are Russian and Italian tunes intermingled and set to a Latin beat. Here you find Hawaiian music perverted with Spanish guitar rhythms. Here are snatches of Hebrew songs gummed to bits of Peruvian folklore—the whole held together precariously by lush fiddle choirs, juicily scored woodwinds, and the deliberate shock tactics of a woman's voice jumping from bass to castrati range."

But it's interesting that Mr. Borneman also disliked Yma's earlier, ethnically pure Argentinean recordings. Although granting the authenticity of the material, he felt the "juxtaposition of (Yma's) highly theatrical voice with Mr. Vivanco's rudimentary material (set) up a teeth-grating clash of styles."

Most of Yma's songs fall into the popular/exotic framework, except for those that are pure program music such as "Tumpa!" (Earthquake), "Chuncho!"(Forest Creatures), "Lament," "Panarima" and "Cumbe Maita" (Calls of the Andes). For those selections colorful and inventive program notes were created to enhance atmosphere and audiences' receptivity.

As a matter of fact, most of Yma's songs fall into three distinct categories, often crossing over each other. During the course of Yma's career, many of her exotic songs were re-arranged or altered in an effort to keep them current or to increase their popularity with audiences.

Traditional (Andean)	**Popular or Dance**	**Program, or Specialty Music**
Virgenes del Sol (Virgins of the Sun)	Babalu	Taita Inty (Virgin of the Sun God) (V.O.X.)
La Benita	Wimoweh	Ataypura (High Andes) (V.O.X)
Que Lindos Ojos	Choladas (V.O.X)	Accla Taqui (V.O.X.)
Un Amor	Wayra (V.O.X.)	Tumpa! (Earthquake) (V.O.X)
Cholitas Punenas	Zana (L.S.V.)	Xtabay (V.O.X)
Picaflor	Ripui (I.T.)	Kuyaway (Inca Love Song) (L.S.V.)
Ccori Canastitay (L.S.V.)	Karibe Taqui (L.S.V)	Kon Tiki (L.S.V.)
Monos (V.O.X)	Mambo!	Incacho (Royal Anthem) (I.T.)
Llulla Mak'ta (I.T.)	Most of *Fuego Del Ande* album	Chuncho! (Forest Creatures) (I.T.)
Chollo Traicionero	*Miracles* album	Most of *Legend of the Jivaro*
La Pampa y la Puna		
Waraka Tusuy		
Montana		
Aullay (Jivaro disk)		
Malaya		
El Condor Pasa		

V.O.X. = *Voice of the Xtabay*
I.T. = *Inca Taqui*
L.S.V. = *Legend of the Sun Virgin*

Even more simplistically, the albums themselves can be divided:

Traditional or Folk Oriented	**Specialty Music**	**Dance**
Early Argentinean Disks	*Voice of the Xtabay*	*Mambo!*
Inca Taqui	*Legend of the Sun Virgin*	*Miracles*
Fuego Del Ande	*Flahooley* (Broadway Show)	
	Legend of the Jivaro	

Yma and Opera

Although Yma occasionally sang operatic arias on concert programs, she was inconsistent in their programming and never recorded any of them commercially. During the 1950s Capitol Records was known as a middle-of-the-road recording firm since they released both classical and popular albums. Because Yma was considered a popular artist and associated with that branch of the firm, it was felt that a crossover recording of Yma singing opera arias would have little selling power.

The timbre of Yma Sumac's voice would have suited many operatic heroines: Donizetti's Marie in *Fille du Regiment*, Delibes' *Lakmè*, Strauss' Zerbinetta in *Ariadne auf Naxos*, and Bellini's Amina in *La sonnambula*, for instance. Because of her early vocal coaching and development under Moisés, however, with its emphasis on Peruvian folk music, imitation and improvisation, it is doubtful Yma could have settled down into an operatic career. It is also doubtful that she would have relished taking the time to undergo the intensive studies necessary for a specialization in opera. These studies would have had to include learning how to read music, a complete re-working and strengthening of her voice for the rigorous demands of singing in large halls without the aid of amplification, the mastering of languages such as French, Italian, and German as well as extensive coaching in the various styles of expression for traditional operatic style. Besides, Yma was already an internationally famous singer. If she wanted to sing opera she could schedule arias into her programs. She would simply sing them in the "Yma Sumac style."

Yma had an intrinsic love of music in all its forms and a compulsion to explore its many facets. The fact that requisite stylistic proprieties were disregarded seemed of little importance. Amazingly, Yma would simply conform the unfamiliar style to fit her own, eccentric style. Similar to what her ancestors did with the captured peoples of Peru, Yma simply made the music fit her own concept of it—whether correct or not.

The situation between Yma and opera was actually rather unfortunate since, despite her occasional digs at it, she had a true love for the art form and a vocal timbre that was perfectly suited to its beauty of expression. Nonetheless, important subtleties eluded the singer, which prevented her operatic selections from being successful. Instead, she had to content herself with introducing its strong influence into her singing.

Realistically, had Yma concentrated on classical music or opera, parts of her voice would not have been fully utilized (or exercised) since there are no written operatic roles that require the unusual range Yma had by nature. Even with traditional coloratura interpolations, operatic roles generally do not exceed two-and-a-half octaves. Eventually, the tones not used would have atrophied and disappeared from lack of use. Yma had little choice but to perform music arranged or tailor-made expressly for her voice in order to best use her instrument and, subsequently, retain its natural, vast extensions; music which allowed her the freedom to wander through her range at will. Since Yma originated from the Andes, it was a logical choice to compose or arrange music that stemmed from her heritage. There was, however, a price to be paid. Although it is true that Yma's "Incan chants" freed her from musical restrictions and comparisons, later this music imposed severe limitations on her ability to remain a contemporary popular performing artist.

Even though from all reports, it seems that Yma loved singing arias, it is doubtful she relished the idea of having her performances analyzed or compared with the then currently available recordings of such artists as Lily Pons, Roberta Peters or Maria Callas. At least in her own music no comparisons could be made.

According to program notes and the memory of Hernán Braña, Yma's operatic repertoire included the following arias.

Delibes: "Bell Song" (*Lakmé*)—very rarely, and only in South America

Verdi: "Ah fors'e lui . . . Sempre libera" (*La Traviata*)—rarely, only in South America.

Donizetti: "Chacun le sait" (*La fille du regiment*)

Mozart: "Der Hölle Rache" (Queen of the Night's Vengeance aria) from *Die Zauberflöte*
Puccini: "O mio babbino caro" (*Gianni Schicchi*)—most frequently programmed
Puccini: "Vissi d'Arte" (*Tosca*)
Puccini: "Un bel di" (*Madama Butterfly*)

I have been told that Yma also sang arias by Rossini and Wagner, but have found no proof. Allegedly, she also sang arias from Puccini's *La boheme*, although, again, I have seen no documentation, nor do I know whether she sang the music of Mimi or of Musetta.

Yma also programmed songs by Bizet, spirituals, Italian folk songs and a lyrical vocalise arrangement of Debussy's "Clair de Lune." Indisputably, Yma's most famous opera selection was her version of the Queen of the Night aria from Mozart's *Die Zauberflöte*. It was a common practice for Yma to sing the aria twice—once relatively close to Mozart's composition and the second as a type of "Queen of the Night Mambo." As to the closeness to Mozart's original, Yma has commented "I don't bother with the words . . . only the rhythm." Of her own, mambo version, "The notes have to be exactly the same, but the phrasing is different." This aria stayed in her repertoire for over a decade and was probably last performed at the Hollywood Bowl in 1965. Unfortunately, it was never recorded.

Puccini was Yma's favorite operatic composer and she frequently used Lauretta's aria from *Gianni Schicchi* in concerts. Of all the arias she learned, it was the simplest and the least demanding. The reaction of critics, however, was not favorable.

Such critical reaction was inevitable, but unfortunate, since Yma had wanted to sing operatic music since the beginning of her career. Opera was certainly not unknown to her since she herself reported in interviews that when she was young her two favorite singers were Lily Pons and Miliza Korjus (1909–1980). Despite what seemed insurmountable cultural differences, Yma studiously prepared her operatic ventures with her Peruvian compatriot, Alejandro Granda. Yma also learned arias from recordings. Hernán told me, for instance, that Yma learned the arias from *Lakmé* and *Die Zauberflöte*, from 78 rpm records made by Lily Pons.

Although one might think that Yma's voice would be a good match for operatic music, in fact it was not. It was not so much a matter of her vocal material but the mind behind that material. The deficiencies of Yma's operatic singing lay in inaccurate concepts of breathing and phrasing in relation to standard operatic practice. These were concepts that even coaching from Granda could not eradicate. Other serious problems originated from stylistic differences between the smooth, clean line necessary in operatic singing and the bumpy, Peruvian folk tradition of linking lines, and even vocal entrances, with grace-notes. The juxtaposition of this Peruvian style with operatic music gave Yma's singing a choppy feeling that clashed with the requisite style. Yma's free-form vocalization, carefully nurtured and perfected over the years, also contradicted the restricting confines of operatic proprieties and tradition. It is ironic that Yma's recordings of "Taita Inty" (Virgin of the Sun God), "Lament," "Suray Surita," "Incacho" (Royal Anthem), and "Kon Tiki" were more correct in operatic style than her "real" operatic numbers. In many of her "Incan chants" Yma tackled vocal hurdles similar to those found in music by Donizetti and Richard Strauss.

Even though Yma's music definitely limited her in certain respects, by the same token it allowed her to fully explore her own special gifts, without the inhibiting restrictions of pre-existing artistic forms, standards, or recordings. She created a unique style all her own.

This brings us to the crucial question—is there a single, correct way to present such a voice and individual talent? To which the only answer must be that there is no one way that has proven completely successful. The talent is, by definition, individual, to the extent that it must be characterized as unique.

Generally speaking, Yma's performing repertoire was quite extensive, even though Moisés tended to concentrate on programming pieces that had proven to be most popular with audiences. Some songs that she sang in public were never recorded and some that were recorded were never performed before audiences. The songs Yma was most famous for were also the most pyrotechnical. They are what I call the "Sumac Quintet:"

Taita Inty (Virgin of the Sun God, Hymn to the Sun)
Ataypura! (High Andes)
Tumpa! (Earthquake)
Chuncho! (Forest Creatures)
Kuyaway (Inca Love Song)

Following these five in popularity were "Montana," "Lament," "Suray Surita," and "Mamallay." Yma's particular favorites are the quintet, and her favorite album remains *Voice of the Xtabay*.

It is interesting that the range needed for Yma's songs (sung publicly or in the studio) differed greatly. For example:

Song	Public or Recorded	Range (Basic)
Amor Indio	recorded	3 octaves
Ataypura	both	3 octaves
La Benita	recorded	3 3/8 octaves
Chicken Talk	recorded	2 1/2 octaves
Cholados	recorded	2 1/2 octaves
Cholo Traicionero	both	2 octaves
Chuncho!	both	4 1/8 octaves
Cumbe Maita	recorded	3 octaves
Gopher Mambo	recorded	3 octaves
Incacho	recorded	3 1/4 octaves
Jungla	both	3 octaves
Karibe Taki	recorded	3 1/4 octaves
Lament	recorded	3 octaves
Llulla Mak'ta	recorded	2 octaves
Montana	both	1 1/2 octaves
Nina	recorded	2 7/8 octaves
Sansa	recorded	2 1/2 octaves
Suama (Magic)	recorded	3 1/2 octaves
Taita Inty	both	3 1/2 octaves
Wanka	Recorded	1 octave

Yma's public performances can be listed in two categories: concerts and nightclub engagements. The same songs were often used for both, their set up and the sequence of their distribution were different. For nightclubs Yma sang anywhere from three to ten numbers depending on the nature of the engagement, introducing the selections herself. Often interspersed with the songs were special dance sequences performed by Cholita (or other dancers) and instrumental solos.

For formal concert-hall programs Yma usually sang 15 numbers, which were strategically (and cleverly) distributed in four groups, interspersed between dance and orchestral numbers. Generally, Yma opened the second section of the concert, entering with the music of "Ataypura" (High Andes) and usually concluding with a trio set featuring herself, Moisés on guitar and Hernán Braña (or someone else) on percussion and flute. This last was the most authentic and esoteric segment found on Yma's programs. It was also the most magical and eerie.

French or Italian art songs listed on programs were often replaced with Andean numbers and sometimes other songs were switched as well. This depended on the audience, or Yma's mood at the time. The nature of such switches was most often to replace arias with more traditional, Peruvian fare.

After about 1965, Yma concentrated on international folk music. Gone were specialty pieces such as "Chuncho!" (Forest Creatures), "Taita Inty" (Virgin of the Sun God), and "Tumpa!" (Earthquake!). This change was inevitable and sensible. Only "Ataypura" (High Andes), remained, mainly used as entrance music, to remind listeners that once, it was her signature tune. Although newly arranged and simplified, "Ataypura" (High Andes) still had the ability to be dramatically effective.

Other songs now became typical:
"La Molina" (The Windmill)
"La Pampa y la Puna" (The Plains and the Mountains)
"Sunrise, Sunset" (Fiddler on the Roof)
"Clavelitos" (Carnations)
"Fenesta che Lucive" (Italian folk song)
"Clair de Lune" (Vocalise)—occasionally resuscitated.

As time went on, and against the advice of agents and friends, Yma added more English songs, even composing some, which she naively offered to audiences who were confounded by her eccentric, often unintelligible pronunciation.

Incan Chants

There has always been a serious problem, one that continually turns up in reviews, with Yma Sumac's repertoire of "Incan chants," and that is the question of their *authenticity*. This is a complex situation; like her resumé it consists of fact mixed with half-truth, meshed together with complete (sometimes shameless) fantasy.

Actually the problem does not concern the songs themselves so much as what was said or written about them by the Sumac camp. As discussed elsewhere, it was Moisés' error to blatantly claim that the music written for Yma was authentically Incan. Ironically, even in Moisés' audacious boasting there was a fragment of truth. What made and compounded the problem was the constant, conflicting information—transparently false given its wild inconsistency—supplied to the public about this music. For instance, below are the actual origins of some of Yma's songs.

1. "*Monos*" (Monkeys on *Voice of the Xtabay*) is a reworking (or spruced-up arrangement) of a South American song, "A ti solita te Quiero," which is also known as "El Congorito," and originates from the coastal regions. Yma originally recorded this song in 1943.
2. "*Cholo Traicioniero*" (Song of Youth, or Llulla Mak'ta on *Inca Taqui*) is an authentic Peruvian folk song. Yma's version is an arrangement adapted to her voice.
3. "*K'arawi*" (Planting Song on *Inca Taqui*) contains fragments of an ancient, traditional Peruvian planting chant, but most of the song is pure fantasy arranged to frame Yma's voice.
4. "*Incacho*" (Royal Anthem on *Inca Taqui*) has nothing to do with Incan ceremonials, contrary to what was boasted in programs. It is a reworking of an authentic huayno called "Hatun Tusuy."

5. *"Montana"* on *Legend of the Sun Virgin* is an authentic Peruvian folk song. Confusingly, Yma's version is a mixed-up combination of the original melodia andina "Mamallay" and a waltz called "En tu Dia" (On Your Birthday). (The song called "Mamallay" on *Legend of the Sun Virgin* has nothing to do with the original, authentic song of that title. Yma's "Mamallay" is a fantasy.)
6. *"Sansa"* (Victory Song on *Legend of the Jivaro*) does not derive from the Amazon but rather from the Andes. It has fragments of the song "Mashiringa," a song once recorded by Rosita Vivanco and Moisés' Compania in 1943.
7. *"Aullay"* (Lullaby on *Legend of the Jivaro*) is not from the Jivaro tribe, as stated in the album's liner notes. It is an exquisite Andean lullaby called "Indian Cradle Song." It is sung in the original Quechua by Yma.
8. *"Malaya"* (My Destiny on *Inca Taqui*) is not an Incan chant, but a popular song called "Malhaya" that originates from the coastal areas of Peru and the Black influence.
9. "Cumbe-Maita" (Calls of the Andes; *Inca Taqui*) is a complete fantasy and bears too much resemblance to a flute solo written and performed by Hérnan Braña during Sumac concerts in the 1950s to be coincidental.
10. "Batanga Hailli" (Festival on *Legend of the Jivaro*) is also not from the tribe of Jivaro head-hunters. It was first heard two years earlier by Sumac fans as "Carnavalito Boliviano," on the *Mambo!* Disk.
11. "Nina" (Fire Arrow Dance; *Legend of the Jivaro*) suspiciously resembles an Argentinean song called "Himno al Sol" (Hymn to the Sun).
12. "Zana" (*Legend of the Sun Virgin*) is another song that originated from the coastal areas and the Black influence. For the recording it was re-worked for Yma and turned into an odd, pop-coloratura extravaganza.
13. "Entre Y Mendoza Y San Juan" is not Peruvian. It is a popular cueca dance from Chile.
14. "Que Lindos Ojos" (Beautiful Eyes) a 1943 recording by Yma is a typically confusing piece. Also known as "Suspiros al Aire," it is a popular marinera and has been recorded in differing versions by Sipas Ticka and Sumac Koya.

Complicating problems with the origins of Yma's music are the arrangements that framed her traditional songs. In many of them the pure fragments are overshadowed, almost completely subsumed beneath bombastic commercial presentations.

With songs such as "Lament," "Tumpa!" (Earthquake!), "Accla Taqui" (Chant of the Chosen Maidens), "Ataypura" (High Andes), "Kon Tiki," "Cumbe-Maita" (Calls of the Andes), "Xtabay" (Lure of the Unknown Love) and "Chuncho!" (Forest Creatures) you are dealing with original compositions, not traditional Peruvian melodies.

Obviously a single musical fragment does not make an entire piece an authentic representation, as was claimed. On the other hand, these fragments should not be dismissed as meaningless. They exist side by side with the fantasy. In many instances the fragments are very old. This coexistence of fact and fiction was responsible for most of the problems that Yma and Moisés faced with the promoting of her unique repertoire.

Adding to the public's and critics' confusion and resulting suspicion, many songs sung in public were considerably different from their recorded performances. On recordings, the following pieces were given lush, exotic orchestral accompaniment:

"Taita Inty" (Virgin of the Sun God, Hymn to the Sun)
"Ataypura" (High Andes)
"Suray Surita"

"Ccorri Canastitay" (Golden Basket)
"Waccai" (Cry)
"Llulla Mak'ta" (Andean Don Juan, Chollo Traicioniero)

In public, however, these songs were performed in a more traditional, ethnically accurate manner, some accompanied only by guitar, percussion and flute. The differences between the slick, commercialized versions found on recordings and the occasionally stark performances offered to the public were often dramatic. And, needless to say, nightclub appearances were another matter entirely, because of the instrumental forces available (or financially feasible).

Peruvian Music and Flute Singers of Peru

Peru's folk music and its performers have things in common with those of North America, in that they can be divided into certain groupings. The music of the mountain regions (Altiplano) is similar to the North American Appalachian folk music in that melodies originate from very old, traditional sources, and are often passed down through generations orally. Performers from the Peruvian Altiplano area, like our Appalachian singers, are often untrained singers. The Peruvian folk song from this region is usually rapid, dance-like, and has many verses which are often repeated almost endlessly. The effect can be mesmerizing. Tourists in the high Andes often hear this type of singing during festivals held at Cuzco, where groups of singers will perform endless stanzas of these songs, the female voices traveling very high for such uncomplicated songs of unison singing. One example I heard was a unison duet sung by a soprano and tenor that had eight or nine verses. Both singers, though raw-voiced, sang over 20 high B flats during the course of the simple song.

The coastal areas of Peru show the influence of the Black settlers from the Congo region in Africa, who worked on the coast and in the ports.

The later European influence (both socially and musically) in Peru produced an unusual mixture not heard anywhere else. This is the mestizio, a music that combines all these influences. Peru contains a vast, rich culture of varying musical contributions. Today, the Spanish influence is easily recognizable, as is the Black influence from the coastal areas, and the starkness of the Altiplano contributions. The vals (waltz) remains the central musical form of the large cities. Closely following in popularity, however, is the marinera, which comes from the Black music of the coast, imitating the Spanish colonial influence. The huayno is the national dance of Peru and is the oldest of them all—dating to the time of the Incas. It is a graceful, courtship dance still performed all over the country. On almost all of Yma's concerts, either a huayno or a marinera was prominently featured. In addition to these dance forms, there were many other forms originating from surrounding cultures: lament, danza, and cueca. As in most cultures, when outside musical influences were introduced, Peruvians assimilated them. Since the beginning of the country, and especially during the Incan reign, Peru has been an assimilator of surrounding influences, musical, religious, and political. The Incans were organizers not originators.

Because of its three primary forms, vals, marinera and huayno, most traditional Peruvian folk music has a dance-like structure. Even at its most simplistic, however, this music is more rhythmically complex than even the most advanced American folk music. It should also be noted that the Peruvian vals is very different in tempo, atmosphere and rhythmic structure from the waltz of European extraction. Definitely dance-like, it requires more energy and is more rhythmically frenetic than the smooth, German-based *1* 2 3. Although the Peruvian dance music seems to have little grace when compared to what North Americans recognize, it has a more visceral connection to nature and the earthiness of physical exertion.

Rhythm is of primary importance in all Peruvian music. Since the time of the Incan empire, music governed all social functions and all traditional music stemmed from a dance form. Based on a five-note scale, music was of extreme importance to the Andean people—even though there was no system of notating it in their culture. Since rhythm and its inventive use were very much a part of the background and heritage of Yma Sumac, it comes as no surprise that some of her most inventive singing can be found on disks such as *Mambo!*, where the emphasis is on her ability to clearly outline and subtly alter rhythmic patterns.

The most important musical influence for Yma during her formative years was the pervading vocal traditions of Peruvian music. The foremost instrument of Peru is the quena, an antiquated form of the modern-day flute. The quena was usually made of bone and figured prominently in all forms of Peruvian musical expression. In some ways it resembles a recorder and had a range of about six notes. Today, in the large commercial cities of Peru, the most highly regarded folk singers are the sopranos who can imitate the pure sound and instrumental precision of the ancient quena. In her early years, Yma was one of these specialists. As far as I can ascertain, she was one of the first, if not the first, flute specialist to record such music.

At least six other sopranos of this type can be found on recordings imported from Peru (often with differing spellings). They include *Sipas Ticka, Siwar Q'ente, Sumac Koya, Wara Wara, Intig Ñusta* and *Esmila Zevallos.* Each of these singers is what we in America would call a folk singer. At different times, Sipas Ticka, Siwar Q'ente and Wara Wara all performed with the famous Peruvian group, Conjunto Sol del Peru. This is a still famous musical ensemble created during the 1950s by Luis Durand Rodriguez. They have made many recordings and their work highlights the compositions of prolific Peruvian composers such as Daniel Alomía Robles, Luis Duncker Lavalle, Brave Jorge de Rueda, Benign and Ballón Farfán and others who constitute what is now considered classical Peruvian folk music.

Sumac Koya performed and recorded with the Peruvian harpist Florecio Coronado, and Esmila Zevallos with the Peru Folklorico per Europe. All performed in large cities, such as Lima.

In cities such as Arequipa, Lima and Callao, the music, like the singers, is more refined. This is similar to such popular American folk singers as Odetta, Peter Paul & Mary, and Joan Baez, in that authentic folk music is sung but is being presented in a more accessible, commercial package. The popularity of Sipas Ticka and Sumac Koya is, understandably, restricted to areas where this type of ethnic material is valued and appreciated. Although Wara Wara did venture to North America during the 1970s, because of her particular brand of singing, she was considered a Sumac imitator in this country, rather than a true folk singer of distinction. Much of this may have been due to the influence of Moisés Vivanco, with whom she studied and who introduced a heavy Sumacian influence into her work. As he commented in private correspondence to me, "I taught and worked with Wara Wara on her voice and taught her a lot, also of how to sing my works. I at many times worked with other singers and sometimes had them perform within our performances. There are many singers in Peru, who try to imitate Yma, and also sing my music." (private correspondence)

Peru is not the only country to value this type of singer. Cuba and Argentina also favor the high soprano. In the case of Argentina, this tradition dates back to when the country was part of the very large Incan empire and still susceptible to its musical traditions. The Argentineans of today, however, consider themselves European; anything but "native"; their taste in vocal music (even folk music) veers toward the cultured, classical, or operatic vocalism of the West. This taste is typified in the singing of the very refined, folk/popular artist, *Ginamaria Hidalgo*. Active during the 1970s, her voice was sweet, had a finely-spun vibrato, was obviously well schooled, and showed much elegance in the area of high D and E natural. Without any noticeable effort, Hidalgo could spin out a lovely, delicate high E flat.

Hidalgo, however, reserved the use of her upper register for special moments. Otherwise, she sang in a well-mixed chest and head register. Nowhere in her singing was there ever a sense of strain. She was charming and unfussy.

At variance with this tradition, Ecuador, also once a part of the great Incan empire, does not favor the soprano voice, or even the solo voice, preferring groups of singers or instrumentalists.

The flute singers heard today in Peru continue an old tradition of imitative, instrumental vocalism. It was Yma, the renegade, who broke away from the accepted, specialized singing into more exotic and commercial forms. Due to the inherent aspect of imitation found in all the "flute singers" of Peru, one can see how easily Yma experimented and broadened her palette to encompass other European influences and sounds.

Yma's early 1943 disks are related to all of them—the chief differences being the superb, international quality of Yma's voice and her authoritative, individual singing. None of the other women mentioned above (except possibly Wara Wara) have a vocal quality suitable for an international career, or one based in more classic European repertoire. While they are obviously part of an ensemble, Yma was unmistakably a solo performer and her singing reflected this.

Perhaps because of the emphasis on ensemble rather than solo that predominated their formation as musicians, none of the flute singers mentioned seem to have the type of temperament necessary for a career of wider scope. Bob Covais and Jim Branciforti, who saw a number of these singers perform in Peru during the 1970s, commented that invariably they are lacking in magnetism on stage ("have the stage presence of a plum," is how they actually put it). Although on recordings it is obvious that these women have an intrinsic authority when performing their music, it is much more understated than someone of Yma's temperament. From the beginning, Yma showed a strong individuality in her performing. She always sang like a soloist rather than as part of an ensemble. In her very early Argentinean disks, there is already present a refinement of style, calm authority in delivery, and individualistic musical touches that immediately set her apart from other singers of this type. Moisés, recognizing the extent of Yma's gifts, fought to have control in the development of them, and took a chance to spotlight her talent; setting her apart from the rest of the ensemble. Instead of being integrated into a group, she became a headliner with a back-up ensemble.

Generally, recordings that include flute specialists are not what we in the United States would call solo albums. Rather they are instrumental albums with perhaps three or four vocal selections interspersed between the instrumental compositions. (Analogy might be made with American swing bands of the 1930s and '40s with their singers featured on only some numbers.) Accent is on the ensemble, not the performer.

Vocal priorities on these recordings are interesting for the bizarre contrast of brilliant virtuosity with bland delivery. Imitation of the flute's tone and musical line is seconded only by imitation of the violin's tone and line—a Spanish influence. This imitation has no relation to the European-originated coloratura variations, but rather is solely concerned with reproducing the melody line and the timbre of the ensemble instrument. The only ornaments that make any regular appearance are grace notes—which are used as a type of vocal attack, triplets, and *gruppeti*. Rarely does a cadenza make an appearance. When it does, it is short (usually of European extraction) and usually at the instigation of the flute. In most cases the use of extreme range is due to the singer repeating the melody line up an octave for emphasis or to add color to the ensemble.

These melodic lines, however, can be very intricate. A good example of this is "Warak'a Tusuy," a danza ceremonial, as sung by Sipas Ticka and Wara Wara (and Yma). The singer's line imitates, sometimes simultaneously, flutes and accompanying instruments. One section of vocal staccati is supported by an equally intricate counterpoint of instruments that weave in and out with the voice. Although brilliant, the voice is used purely in an instrumental fashion. This is also true of "Serrana Ingrata," as sung by Siwar Q'ente. Although she rises to G above high C, the sound, manner of execution, and resulting effect are just as they would have been if done by a flute. There is no discernible personality between the notes and the listener. The soprano's use of high notes is a coloristic device meant only to enhance the ensemble's sound.

This is stark music, for the most part. American audiences would find it difficult to sit through much of this music, although coloratura and high note fanciers would find much of interest in the singing and the recordings of these artists. As is typical with the folk music of all countries, there are many arrangements of the same piece, some more interesting or inventive than others depending on the quality of the composer/arranger, the musicians performing, and the area of the country.

A study of the recordings made by these flute singers show a fascinating emphasis on certain vocal effects, all of which are used to underline the main melody. Staccati passages are abundant. This is an obvious favorite manner of singing for these women. In most cases, brilliance of performances is due to the use of this technique. It is apparent, however, that it is only used for rhythmic accentuation of a melody, or for the pointing of a phrase—not for any ornamental reasons. The repetition of a melody in octaves emphasizes the theme and rhythmic structure.

The voices of the flute singers vary.

Sipas Ticka is one of my favorites and was a popular singer with the ensemble Conjunto Sol del Peru. She has a frontal, wiry quality similar to a Slavic operatic high soprano. She can, however, float a soft high D very impressively. Her range extends to about G above high C and the most impressive aspect of her technique is her clean and brilliant staccato technique. Her manner, when singing, seems charming, if a bit on the retiring side. During the 1970s she was one of the most popular of the authentic flute singers and on recordings, it is her "Virgenes del Sol" (Virgins of the Sun) that vies with Yma's in vocal ease and beauty. Other selections with this artist (but spread over various disks) include "Pokra" (a danza guerrera and a brilliant study in staccato singing), "Warak'a Tusuy," and "Paras-Shayan," a lyrical, lullaby-like danza. I did find an album on the Internet called *Sipas Ticka Con El Conjunto Sol del Peru* (SONO RADIO—L.P.L.-1018) where 10 selections are listed—including a few I have already mentioned. But I have not tracked down a copy of the LP to verify that all 10 selections are sung by Ticka.

Both *Siwar Q'ente* and *Sumac Koya* have delicate, flute-like voices that ascend to at least G above high C. Both singers are lovely for the delicacy of their work and are completely without artifice.

Sumac Koya is popular on recordings and capable of great virtuosity. Her recording of "Montana" differs considerably from Yma's lyrical version. Koya's recording boasts an extended cadenza of staccati fireworks capped by a sustained high F. Other selections she has recorded include "El Condor Pasa," "La Benita," "Suspiros al Aire," and "Flor del Altipampa."

Siwar Q'ente (whose name has also been spelled Sihuar Quente and *Sihuar Ckente*) is considered by many to be one of the greatest coloraturas of Peru and the successor to

Yma Sumac. Her real name is Ana Condori Sulca and although mainly famous in the 1960s and 1970s, is still performing. Her name in Quechua means "Sparkling Violet tear." She was only 19 when she began her career touring the United States, Japan, Argentina, Chile, Ecuador and Bolivia. During her career she has worked with many of the great specialists of Andean folklore and has received many awards for her contributions to Peruvian music. She has a sweet and pure top register that is contrasted by a middle voice plagued by a husky wobble that often vitiates her efforts in those areas. Her range was extensive and she often peppered her music with high notes up to sustained F and even the A flat. Like Koya and Ticka, *Q'ente* has a formidable mastery of staccato work. She has recorded at least an hour's worth of music documenting her voice.

Esmila Zevallos has a technique and vocal timbre similar to Sipas Ticka with a wiry top register, but solid breath control and technique. Her recording of "El Condor Pasa" is the classic performance of this piece as interpreted by the Peruvian flute-singer. Typical Andean virtuosity is well blended with folk material and a range to the top F. She has made at least one solo album.

Wara Wara (which means "little star") is a special case. Despite her faults I find her entrancing and I return to her recordings often. She is the only one of the group mentioned above to have a career that even came close to being international. And her career, like Yma's came early. A Brazilian publication, *O Cruzeiro* (7/16/57) printed an article saying that the Lima-born singer had been signed with Vivanco. "Many believe she will replace Yma Sumac following the divorce granted a short time ago."

Wara Wara, whose real name is Judith Acuña, was, according to the article, 20 years old in 1957. Her stage name was given to her by the "Lima-based journalist Guido Monteverde, who also gave her much encouragement when she was starting out." (ibid)

When asked how Moisés learned of her singing, she told the reporter "One of his sisters, Teresa Vivanco, sent him some of my recordings and it seems he liked them." (ibid)

She mentioned that she was looking forward to a two-month tour of Greece at the time. "The only thing I want is to be a success....even if it means sacrificing a lot." (ibid)

"Her initial contract is for $100 per week, plus return flight and all expenses paid." (ibid)

Wara Wara often appeared in shows when Yma was appearing but never at the same time. By 1970, she had performed in the United States, Russia, Greece, Italy, France, Israel and others. Like Yma, it would seem that a highlight of her career was a concert tour of the Soviet Republic between 1969 and 1970. As of this writing, January 2007, Wara Wara is living just north of Lima and works as an art teacher.

Of all the singers mentioned above, Wara Wara is by far the most important. Wara Wara's voice was larger and heavier and had more tonal bite than the other specialists mentioned above. It was also more naturally beautiful. Although she too could perform some remarkable high feats in her songs, they were more cautious and obviously carefully planned. Her top register had more oomph than Yma's, and on some of her recordings she lets loose some stunning, sustained high E flats or E naturals. But she was not, by nature, as high a soprano as her arrangements try to make her. Actually, Wara Wara was more of a lyric-mezzo-soprano who had an unusual, added extension in *altissimo*. The true base of her voice sits much lower than the other singers mentioned. Not surprisingly, therefore, with Wara Wara, a high E can be variable.

Also unlike the other singers discussed in this section, Wara Wara made at least three solo albums. Some of the performances are wonderful, some not quite so good. Her "Virgenes del Sol" (Virgins of the Sun), for example, should never have been commercially released. It did her a grave disservice as a serious musician. Recorded in the same key as Yma's and Sipas Ticka's versions—which is the traditional, high key—nowhere can you find the easy beauty of Yma's singing in the highest phrases. In Wara Wara's performance high E flats are squeezed out in obvious discomfort and a few staccati phrases don't come any where near correct pitches. It is also apparent (at least in this song) that Wara Wara's constant swooping and scooping up to notes is not within the established tradition, but rather, sloppy technique due to vocal exhaustion from having to deal with such a cruelly high tessitura. It becomes obvious very quickly that although Wara Wara could reach high E and F, she could not remain in that area for any length of time.

Labeled a Sumac imitator, Wara Wara sang many of Yma's traditional "Incan chants." And, since she coached with Moisés, it is not surprising that she also uses his arrangement of "Kuyaway" (but reverting back to the original name of the song, "Amor Indio"). (Wara Wara's version is sub-titled an Incan Fox Trot.) It comes complete with growl. unfortunately, Wara Wara did not produce this difficult effect correctly and her florid work is not at all improvisatory. Like Yma, she introduces into "Amor Indio" what is supposed to be an improvisatory vamp, but the limp tempo, her cautious, retarded delivery, and hesitant high register make it anticlimactic.

Despite her inconsistency on high, Wara Wara had a most distinctive and most engaging manner of singing. And her voice was very attractive—especially in its lower regions. Some of her selections are superb, such as "Wiracocha," (cancion), most of which lies in her creamy lower register, "La Pampa y la Puna," (The Plains and the Mountains), "Cuando El Indio Llora (Camel Ikaico)—probably one of her best recordings—the upper register sweet and true, "Vale un Peru," (cancion), and "Malabrigo,"—both hauntingly beautiful. Although the range in these songs may travel into the area of high D and E, the accent is on lyricism in lower regions, rather than instrumental virtuosity in the high. One of my favorites remains the "Vale un Peru" for the sweet caress she gives to the vocal line and the lack of pretension in Wara Wara's singing.

Wara Wara's first album was called simply *Wara Wara* LPL 1015 (Stereo, Industrial Sono Radio S.A.—made in Perú) This record has such traditional pieces as Amor Indio, Virgenes del Sol, India Bella, Ccori Canastitay, and Carnaval Arequipeño.

The second album, *La Voz de Oro de los Incas* (The Golden Voice of the Incas), has traditional Peruvian folk tunes (for the most part) including the aforementioned "Amor Indio," accompanied by native instruments. Although the presentation of the music is stark, a few of the selections are excellent for Wara Wara's contributions. As I've said, this is especially true of "Cuando El Indio Llora" (When the Indian Cries) where her singing is quite engaging. Her voice is unusually lambent and she is able to swoop to a number of excellent high Fs with little effort and great rhythmical exactitude.

The third album, again called *Wara Wara,* is a more commercial effort. Although folk and popular material still predominates, it is now accompanied by a full orchestra. This album includes a second version of "Amor Indio" which is even less attractive than the first. Unfortunately, for the most part the arrangements on this recording are soggy and uninventive.

Like other flute singers, before she made these albums Wara Wara appeared on a number of anthology disks as part of an ensemble. Like Yma, however, Wara Wara had a definite, soloistic quality that set her apart from other, similar performers. Wara Wara's inconsistency had nothing to do with the core of her instrument but rather stemmed from her constantly having to overstretch the natural range of her voice in order to reach the obligatory high notes of her arrangements.

Contemporary with Wara Wara is the Bolivian flute specialist, Luzmila Carpio, a Quechuan native who made her first recordings in 1969 and who continues to perform today. Her recordings can be found on line at CD Baby—http://www.cdbaby.com/found?allsearch=Carpio and include at least three solo albums of authentic folk music.

Her voice is a very youthful, high, sweet soprano that easily reaches into the area of the G and even B above high C. She has made a number of albums and one in particular, *Musica Boliviana* (Accords Croisé ACCD07), recorded in 1999, shows this ability well. Recorded with authentic instruments and stark in the extreme—some of the selections are even sung a capella. Like other flute specialists, Carpio uses her highest register for effect and only to underline the melody. In the song "Quyllur" she travels over high F sharp and the A above high C while reiterating the main theme. Although a bravura effect, the result is much more understated because of its lack of artifice. In "Homage to Maria Sabina" she goes all the way to the B above high C. Again, the effect sought is emphasis of the melody rather than brilliance. Listening to the first half of the song one would not even know that she had such an extension. North American listeners more used to the European vocal placement will find Carpio's light, slightly nasal, squeezed singing hard to take after a few songs. Also, the many strophic verses of pieces can become tiresome. In "The Language of the Birds," however, Carpio imitates the calls of many birds with amazing fidelity. But don't look for the operatic bravura of Yma in this song. These are literally bird imitations, made over a gentle melody hummed by Carpio and overdubbed. There is a haunting beauty to this piece.

Nicknamed "The Voice of the Andes," Carpio represents a more modern concept of the Andean flute singer. But as with the others, the high register is not used in an egotistic manner but solely to highlight the melody of a piece.

Epilogue

Yma Sumac continues to be an influence in America. Over the decades since her first appearance here, a number of singers have been compared to her, or publicized as having Yma's range or exotic appeal.

One of the most famous was Bas Sheva, who was in fact a contemporary of Yma's. Born Beatrice Kurzman, she was from a prominent Philadelphia family. When she decided to go into show business she took Bas Sheva as her stage name, which is the biblical Bathsheba. A contralto of considerable power and dynamic imagination, she began her career around 1950. In 1953 she was hired by the bandleader Hal Mooney as the soloist for *Soul of a People*, a collection of traditional Hebraic chants with an orchestra conducted by Mooney that was released by Capitol (LP 10" L 8287).

But it was in 1954, when Les Baxter chose Bas Sheva to record the controversial role of "The Woman" in his musical suite *The Passions,* that she became a celebrity. *The Passions* (which include Despair, Terror, Lust, Hate, Jealousy, Joy) was released as a 10" LP and although well composed and sung, was too outré for most of the record buying public at the time. Certainly, Bas Sheva's grunting, howling and panting, accompanied by full "violent" orchestra, can be a bit unsettling–but for a taste of uninhibited vocalism, you can't do much better than *The Passions*. Even though that period of American popular music was in a "stretching" mode, Baxter's edgy, complicated and wordless score and Bas Sheva's all too real interpretation of the emotions being portrayed proved to be too much for popular success. The album never quite took off and Bas Sheva never recorded again.

Bas Sheva's career went on for a time—she appeared on the Ed Sullivan Show in 1957—but was tragically cut short. While entertaining on a cruise ship in 1960, she died of diabetic shock at the age of just thirty-four.

Coming on the heels of Bas Sheva was the mysterious Leda Annest. She only made one album—*A Portrait of Leda,* recorded for Columbia in 1959. It is another descriptive suite composed and conducted by the veteran voice coach, Phil Moore. The 12" LP (Columbia WL 114) offers Leda vocalizing through a suite of music that shows both jazz and operatic influences. This is another disk that is considered a collector's curio and avidly sought after. Leda sang quite a bit higher than Bas Sheva, (at least up to high E flat) but her voice—like Bas Sheva's—has an unattractive edge which lessens the overall appeal for repeated listenings.

Then there was "Tiki," the otherwise nameless soprano Les Baxter used in his 1962 Reprise album, *The Primitive and the Passionate*. Like Yma, Tiki had a very sweet upper register which is definitely shown off to advantage on the recording. As far as I know that was her only recording—although she may have made others using a different, "real" name.

Probably the most interesting singer of this group appeared in the 1960s. It was at that time that the record label Mercury put out a record of a singer called Elizabeth Sands. Sands grew up as an orphan in Harlem and at first made a hit in the gospel circuit. The composer Jack Hammer heard her sing and recommended her to the recording company. The result was the album *Untamed!*–twelve selections, most songs performed with only percussion and flute. Hammer wrote the arrangements and Elizabeth warbled her way through some very interesting numbers. The most startling is a peculiar arrangement of "Old Man River" where she spices up the music with high Ds and Fs. In "Ku Ku Ba" she even sings a good, firm staccato high G. The traditional, Gershwin "Summertime" is given a very untraditional performance that few will forget after hearing it. Publicity hailed Sands as "the American Sumac" claiming she had "the range of Yma Sumac and the soul of Mahalia Jackson." If, in reality she did not quite have Yma's range, she nonetheless had a good voice and manner of singing and a very sweet, enjoyable high register that is easy on the ears no matter how high she goes. Unfortunately, *Untamed!* was her only album. It, too, is now a collector's item.

Yma's influence can even be found in the music of a recent exotica recording by Don Tiki. On his second album, *Skinny Dip* (Taboo 8889) he offers an often tongue-in-cheek homage to Yma's voice in the song "Axolotl." Lana Warner, the singer for this vocalize, travels through a long range (from at least low G to the G above high C). The song is an obvious tribute to the Peruvian singer—the music managing to be both fun and menacing.

Yma's name has other resonances (for one thing, it seems likely to live forever in crossword puzzles!). Her singing was referred to, for example, in a 1976 short story by James Wade (1930–1983) called *The Silence of Erika Zann*. This story is from a subgenre of fantasy fiction called the Chthulhu Mythos, centered around concepts and characters created by the fanstasy/horror master H. P. Lovecraft. (The term was coined by a devotee of Lovecraft's work, himself a fantasy author, August Derleth.) Wade's delectable little gem has to do with a rock singer named Erika Zann, who in the story gathers much acclaim for her voice. While describing Erika's voice, Wade writes: "Whether she'd always had it in her or the new gimmicks added something, wailing was no word for it. At the climaxes of those long sets, which left her drained and shaking, she'd take off into wordless stratospheric flights that reminded you of Yma Sumac, the freak Peruvian soprano of a while back." (from *The Disciples of Cthulhu* Second Revised Edition, Chaosium Publications 6011, February 1996)

In April of 2005, Sasha K. created a poll called "Yma Sumac–A Lost Treasure" which (with a couple of errors) presented Web surfers with the opportunity to test their knowledge of the Peruvian singer (*www.misterpoll.com*). Also in 2005, Steve Venright of Toronto, writing liner notes for the CD *Sounds From the Almond Spire: Samuel Andreyev's Songs of Elsewhere*, seemed to create a new Sumacian legend, one I had never heard. While telling stories about singers' rituals when recording, he makes the comment: "Yma Sumac, legend has it, twirled upside-down in a snakeskin harness during her *Voice of the Xtabay* sessions (hence that unearthly tremolo)." (www.torporvigil.com)

In the last decade or so a number of movies have featured Sumac recordings within their soundtracks: *The Big Lebowski* (1998) (Ataypura); *Men with Guns* (1998) (Ataypura); *Aprile* (1998) (Gopher Mambo); *Death to Smoochy* (2000) (Goomba Boomba Mambo); *Confessions of a Dangerous Mind* (2003) (Gopher Mambo); *The In-Laws* (2003) (Gopher Mambo); the French *15 Août* (2001) (Taki Rari Mambo).

And in 2006, a portion of "Bo Mambo" was used for a United States commercial for chocolate Liquor.

Writers continue to find her fascinating and tributes still occasionally appear.

Meanwhile Steve Willis has not been idle. His documentary *Discovering Yma* is still in process. Always a go-getter, Steve has been gathering accolades for other film endeavors. As Mark Bell reported on the website *Film Threat*: "During this time Steve developed a friendship with Rebecca Romijn that ultimately lead to the insanity that is attempting to choreograph a fountain show at the Bellagio in Las Vegas while also documenting the experience. The fruit of such an endeavor, 'Wet Dreams', is currently making its way to the festival circuit." (*www.filmthreat.com*) His work continues on *Discovering Yma* and filming of interviews has begun. His goal? To have Yma perform live in concert with the band Pink Martini. Their Web site describes them: "Somewhere between a 1930s Cuban dance orchestra, a classical chamber music ensemble, a Brasilian marching street band and Japanese film noir is the 12-piece Pink Martini." Yma and Steve have already met with China Forbes of the group.

Compilations of Yma's recordings—many of them bootleg—continue to appear with some regularity. Ironically, coinciding with this was the devastating news for many record buyers that Tower Records filed for bankruptcy on August 20, 2006. The last store was closed on December 22, 2006. This changed the complexion of record buying in America in an indelible way. Only a few record stores are now left where customers can browse in person. Now most record buying is done online through Amazon.com, Barnes and Noble and other smaller, independent Web sites.

Meanwhile the controversy continues. When it comes to Yma Sumac there is always something brewing. In September 2006, I was contacted by Gerald Van Waes from Antwerp, who was preparing a radio show about Yma Sumac with "PVHF," Radio Centraal, in Antwerp. In conjunction with that he created a Web site that promoted the radio show and Yma. After getting my permission, he used some information I had about Yma Sumac on my site, *www.divalegacy.com* . He also included many photos that he culled from various sources.

By December his site had been taken down. In an email, he wrote: "You cannot believe what kind of and how many threats I received from the Yma-Sumac website (Damon Devine, I assume it is Yma herself?). I tried to give arguments, but the more I did the more threats there came. They did NOT [sic] want me to use any picture of Yma on my webpage.

"I was tired of this and removed the whole webpage. I guess I will have to wait until she's dead to pay tribute to her. In your biography you were right I think about the whole story. I think she has become a control freak now with no reasoning *at all*." (Private email, 12/18/2006)

Yma, China Forbes of Pink Martini, and Steve Willlis (Courtesy of Steve Willis)

On his Web page, he posted this message: "The entire Website of Yma Sumac has been removed. I received too much threatening by Yma Sumac's webmaster called 'Damon Devine' in the name of Yma Sumac because I used pictures which I mostly got from a Peruvian fan to illustrate the webpage. Some of them were taken from newspapers. A few came from other Yma Sumac web pages. I never understood why I had to remove ALL pictures but then the lawyers threat came with even more anger as before. ..." (sic)

For a while, on his website, Gerald had a link (*http://psychevanhetfolk.homestead.com/YMA_SUMAC.html*) that led to a collection of emails between him and Damon Devine. They made interesting, if unattractive reading.

Although the original Yma Sumac home page, *Sunvirgin.com*, created by Don Pierson, was created more than a decade ago and had a personal message from Yma to her fans, Damon Devine now claims his own site, www.Yma-Sumac.com, is "the first truly authorized website for Miss Yma Sumac. She is very much a part of the site, and thrilled to welcome you aboard." (Taken from *http://easydreamer.blogspot.com/2005/02/yma-sumac.html*).

Recently, another Sumac site appeared: *http://www.freewebs.com/yma-sumac*, which characterizes itself: "This is an 100% Unofficial FANSITE. Dedicated to the Divine Songstress Yma Sumac." The webmaster, Alexander Steben, is a devoted young Sumac admirer. Completely without pretension he created his site purely as a tribute to a singer who captured his imagination and admiration. It is his way of thanking Yma for the magic.

The Web site *www.lastfm/* a popular music download site, offers a section of Yma Sumac recordings for download. Interestingly, through a charting program on the site you can find out which of her songs have been downloaded the most. I found it fascinating that by January 30, 2007, the most requested download of Yma's songs was "Ataypura" (High Andes) with 899 hits. Close after that was the "Taki Rari" mambo with 526. Yma's famous "Chuncho!" (Forest creatures) got 116 hits and "Taita Inty" (Virgin of the Sun God, Hymn to the Sun) 127 hits.

Even in 2007, some fifty-seven years after her American breakthrough, the mystery and allure surrounding Yma Sumac endures. There was an art behind the legend.

(March, 2007)

Index

Aldridge, Daniel Emerson, 244–45
Alpern, Tyler, 218–19

Ballroom, The (New York), 62, 191–210, 211–215, 252, 261
Bas Sheva (Beatrice Kurzman), 277
Baxter, Les, v, 1, 3–5, 33–35, 39, 41–45, 48–50, 58–60, 147, 156–59, 161–63, 166–71, 224, 227–28, 238, 243
Beatles, The, 147
Braña, Hernán, v, 23, 27–29, 31, 35–36, 45, 52–53, 72, 75, 81–82, 86–89, 93–95, 120, 130, 137, 141–43, 152, 158–59, 164, 175–76, 178, 182, 214, 220, 234
Branciforti, James, v, 86, 159–61, 163, 168–69, 236, 238

Calvè, Emma, 259–60
"Camus, Amy" (urban legend), 53–54, 64–65, 74, 111, 125, 130, 149, 177, 227, 242
Capitol Records, 3, 5, 8, 11, 14, 26–28, 33–37, 39, 41, 49–50, 84, 134, 136, 156–158, 168, 217, 223
Carnegie Hall, 10, 22, 91–92, 98–99, 101, 123, 125–26, 159
Carpio, Luzmila, 274–75
Carrillo, Maurice, 229–31
Chants, Incan, 34, 38, 136, 267–69
Colon, Augie, 3
Compañia Peruana de Arte, 12–13, 16–19, 125, 219
Cotillion Room (Pierre Hotel, New York), 61–62, 77, 130–33
Cook, Barbara, 55–57
Covais, Robert, v, 51, 86, 148, 159–69, 171–72, 176, 180–81, 236, 238, 277
Czernetsky, Günter, 13, 33, 37, 43–44, 219–21

Della Chapelle, Gerard, 175–76, 178–79, 182–83
Denny, Martin, 3–5, 34
Devine, Damon, 239, 240–242, 245–48, 279–80
Devon, Pru, 51

Eicher, Alan, 185–88, 191–92, 201, 206, 221. 224–25, 228, 233–34, 240, 242–44, 247–48
Exotica (popular music genre), 3–6, 34–35

Fiedler, Arthur, 45–46, 50, 104

Fischer, Sylvia, 252
Flahooley (musical comedy), 54–57, 63, 86, 230, 237, 252
Flute singers of Peru, 269–275
Fuego del Ande (recording), 141–42, 156, 159

Godfrey, Arthur, 29
Granda, Alejandro, 50, 78, 81, 85
Grant, Nick, 187–89, 233
Gunter, Freeman, 178, 181, 192, 201–10, 211

Haley, Bill, 130
Head, Edith, 132
Heller, Skip, 227–28, 234, 242
Hoch, Beverly, 254
Hollywood Bowl, 44–45, 149–50, 155
Hollywood's Inkaprinzessin (documentary film), 13, 37, 44–45, 219–221

Inca Taqui (recording), 60, 79–80, 86, 88–89, 91, 108, 129, 136, 159, 243, 262
Inca Taqui Trio, 19–29, 32, 52, 95, 113
Inty Raymi Festival (Peru), 10, 32

Kaye, Danny, 51, 140
Kelley, Tom, 47–48, 60, 89
Keyer, Curt, 229–31
Korjus, Miliza, 265
Koya, Sumac, 272
Kreppel, Robert, 159–60, 163, 165, 169

Lamparski, Richard, 7, 22, 172–73
Legend of the Sun Virgin (recording), 35, 41, 58–61, 67, 78–81, 91, 105, 108, 126, 130, 136, 157–58 211, 217, 221
Legends of the Jivaro (recording), 134–35, 156, 231
Leonard, Maurice, 137, 184–85, 252, 259
Letterman, David, 200–201
Little, Ramon, 27
Livingston, Alan, 33–34, 37, 43–44, 48, 58–59, 73
Loves of Omar Khayyam, The (film), 47, 136, 140
Lyman, Arthur, 4

Machu Picchu, 2, 39, 80–81, 89–90, 108–110, 123, 247

Mambo! (recording), 112–13, 123, 130, 135–36, 158, 232, 245, 256
Meehan, Thomas, 146
Michener, James, 3
Mitchell, William P, 8–9, 74, 86
Miracles (Yma Rocks) (recording), v, 51, 59, 86, 113, 156, 159–174, 177, 238, 224, 226

Nubar, Lorraine, 257

Odeon Records, 18, 36, 74
Opera, Incan, 122
Opera and Yma Sumac, 54, 84–86, 101, 227, 263–65

Pierson, Don, 7, 60, 225–26, 231, 238–40, 244
Poling, James, 20–21, 25, 30–32, 34–35, 37, 40, 51, 54, 107, 249
Pons, Lily, 102, 114, 260, 261, 265

Q'ente, Siwar, 272–73

Ravel, Maurice, 3, 41
Recordings, 37, 41, 45, 47, 51–52, 279
Revel, Harry, 3
Revera, David, 51, 61–62, 68, 70–72, 75, 77, 82, 104, 214
Rivero, Cholita, 19, 23, 26, 27, 78–79, 82–83, 127, 143, 150, 163, 185
Rivers, Walter, 26–27, 35
Rizzo, Marco, 131, 175, 180–181
Rizzo, Vilma, 131–34
Robin, Mado, 39, 260
Rose, John, 32– 33, 46–47, 62–63, 158
Russell, Anna (musical satirist), 121
Russo, Albert, 224–25

Sack, Erna, 39, 102, 215, 255
Sacre du Sauvage (recording) –3, 35
Sands, Elizabeth, 277–78
Secret of the Incas (film), 89–90, 108–110, 136, 253
Shea, Maureen, 68, 70, 89–90, 108–110, 130, 134, 136–38, 253
Stollman, Bernard, 152, 160, 164, 239
Synovec, Yosef, 146, 159, 181–83

Thomson, Virgil, 99–100
Ticka, Sipas, 272
Town Hall (New York), 148, 175–76, 178–81, 253

Valentin, Hernándo Valderrama, 246–248
Vivanco, Carlos "Charlie" (son of Yma Sumac), 22, 54, 72, 78–79, 103, 115, 130, 138, 142, 147, 150, 237
Vivanco, Rosita (Rosa), 12, 15, 137, 219
Vocal Effects, 256–61
Vocal Range, Yma Sumac, 249
Voice of the Xtabay (recording), 3, 7, 11, 34–35, 38, 41– 45, 47–50, 57–58, 67, 73, 79–80, 84, 87, 104, 108, 116–17, 136, 157, 162, 167, 211, 217, 233

Waldo, Elisabeth, 93–95, 114, 127
Wara Wara, 173, 273–74
Welting, Ruth, 254
Westenburg, Richard, 126
Westmoreland, Joe, 186–87
Willis, Steve, 232–37, 240, 238–39, 278–79
Winchell, Walter, 53, 64, 177

Xtabay (legend), 107–08, 187
Yaw, Ellen Beach, 253, 260
YmaRama, 229–31

Zevallos, Esmila, 138, 219, 270, 273

www.ingramcontent.com/pod-product-compliance
Lightning Source LLC
Chambersburg PA
CBHW081210230426
43666CB00015B/2706